Water and The West

Water and The West

The Colorado River Compact
and the Politics of
Water in the American West

NORRIS HUNDLEY, jr.

University of California Press
Berkeley   Los Angeles   London
1975

For Wendy and Jacqueline

University of California Press
Berkeley and Los Angeles, California
University of California Press, Ltd.
London, England
Copyright © 1975 by The Regents of the University of California
ISBN: 0–520–02700–0
Library of Congress Catalog Card Number: 73–93054
Printed in the United States of America

Contents

Contents

8

Preface

Water is today among mankind's greatest concerns—a problem
that has become a crisis of worldwide importance. Scientists,
statesmen, environmental groups, and citizens everywhere recognize that water is a resource no longer to be taken for granted.
Even those areas with plenty of water are struggling with pollution and problems of management that worsen yearly as population grows and industry and agriculture expand.[1]

No area of the world is more aware of the current water crisis
than western America, a vast arid and semiarid region embracing
nearly half the continent of North America. Except for a strip
along the north Pacific coast and isolated areas in the high mountains, the West is a region of sparse rainfall and few rivers. The
implications of these facts of geography have been enormous.
From the time of the first settlers to the present, few westerners
have failed to comprehend that control of the West's water means
control of the West itself—its industry; agriculture; population
distribution; and, withal, the direction of the future. Because the
West has always had a water problem, its experiences provide
valuable insights into the crises faced by other water-shy areas;
and they also offer a preview of the even more serious problems

[1] For a sampling of some of the many books dealing with the "water
crisis," see Jim [James] Wright, *The Coming Water Famine* (New
York, 1966); Frank E. Moss, *The Water Crisis* (New York, 1967);
Donald E. Carr, *Death of the Sweet Waters* (New York, 1966; rev.
ed., 1971); Frank Graham, Jr., *Disaster by Default: Politics and Water
Pollution* (New York, 1966); and Nathaniel Wollman and Gilbert W.
Bonem, *The Outlook for Water: Quality, Quantity, and National
Growth* (Baltimore, 1971).

that must involve the entire nation and the rest of the world as
population grows.

Water rights have, of course, been a concern of society since
earliest times. Scarcity of water, argue some scholars, called forth
responses that led to the development of the first great civiliza-
tions in the valleys of the Nile, the Euphrates, the Indus, and the
Hwang Ho. To cultivate nearby lands on a large scale and to
determine rights to water required planners, *homines fabri,* men
whose success depended on a permanent staff—engineers, scribes,
mathematicians, and astronomers—that could calculate periodic
fluctuations in river flow and work together within a framework
of established authority. Whatever the merits of this argument,
it is clear that the phenomenal growth during the twentieth
century of the arid West's urban centers, with their universities,
museums, art galleries, drive-ins, freeways, and other symbols of
civilization, has been intimately connected with success at obtaining water. So, too, has been the transformation of much of
the West into one of the world's great agricultural areas. This
heavy dependence on water may be difficult to appreciate for
those who arrive in the West by jet plane and then do little
more than turn a tap to get all the water they need. But even for
them the picture becomes clearer when they learn that a city
like Los Angeles possesses a local water supply capable of supporting dependably only about 20 percent of its present population. The comparable figure for the greater Denver metropolitan
area is about 30 percent; for San Diego, 13 percent; and for
nearly all western cities similar statistics could be cited.[2]

Despite the critical importance of water to westerners, historians have largely overlooked the subject. Little has been done
on the water problems of the nineteenth century or even on those
of the twentieth century, the period when western growth and
competition for water have reached peak intensity. To be sure,
valuable books and articles have been produced—most notably
by Walter Prescott Webb, W. Eugene Hollon, Leonard Arring-
ton, Betty Dobkins, Robert Dunbar, Lawrence Lee, and Beverley

---

[2] These percentages are based on census data and on information
provided by Alan J. Williams, general manager of the Colorado River
Association; J. L. Ogilvie, manager, Denver Board of Water Commissioners; and Felix Sparks, director, Colorado Water Conservation
Board.

Moeller—but the list of titles is small when measured against
the scholarly output on such topics as land policy, state-building,
exploration, the Chicano, and the Indian. In part this imbalance
is probably due to the events of the 1960s and early 70s that
understandably—and correctly—prompted many scholars to focus on ethnic minorities and problems of social unrest. Then, too,
many have undoubtedly balked at the forbidding task of clarify-
ing the complicated and often contradictory legal and engineering questions involved in conflicts over water. Until recently,
their efforts would also have been hampered by lack of critical
source materials. The struggle for water, especially during the
last half-century, has caused many nervous officials—both active
and retired—to refuse interviews and to lock up important manuscripts and other primary materials. Fortunately, some of the
decades-old conflicts over water have been resolved, or at least
the issues sufficiently modified, so that many documents are
being made available and some interviews freely given. The
opening of files and loosening of tongues, together with the growing interest in environmental studies, augurs well for the future.

This book is about the greatest conflict over water in the
American West. To be more precise, it is primarily a book about
an alleged peace treaty, the Colorado River Compact. But like
most books about peace, it is really an account of war. No bullets
were fired in this war; yet the life and death of cities and states
in an enormous area were at stake. The Colorado River drains
practically the entire lower left-hand corner of the continental
United States. It is not a particularly heavy-flowing stream (it
ranks only about sixth among the nation's major rivers), but it is
virtually the sole dependable water supply for an area of 244,000
square miles, including parts of seven western states—Wyoming,
Colorado, Utah, New Mexico, Nevada, Arizona, California—and
Mexico. Its influence is also felt far beyond its own watershed,
for its waters have been diverted hundreds of miles and used to
stimulate and sustain the urban, industrial, and agricultural
growth of such other areas as eastern Colorado; western Utah;
and the coastal plain of southern California, a vast megalopolis
of ten million people that stretches from north of Los Angeles
to the Mexican border. Equally to the point, the problems faced
by the Colorado River states are now having serious repercussions for westerners in other river basins.

At the heart of the Colorado River problem is the fact that the river carries enough water for only a handful of cities and industries and farms. Most of the West has been condemned to remain a desert, and this stark reality was the principal reason for the Colorado River Compact of 1922, an interstate treaty involving the seven basin states and the federal government. This book is about the movement for the compact and the complex legal and political battles that spawned it and continue to influence the lives of westerners today. The story begins long before the drafting of that agreement and ends more than half a century after it was negotiated; but the focus is on the shaping of the compact, a treaty that is still the fundamental "law of the river" and a matter of vital concern to millions of people who have never even seen the Colorado.

Though the focus of this book is on the compact, its perspective extends beyond that agreement and even the West. Some two decades ago, Earl Pomeroy sensed the need for a "reorientation" of western history, for a greater awareness of "outside influences" and the continuity between eastern and western development.[3] The findings of this book lend strength to his appeal. Eastern interests are invariably present, most often in the forms of Congress, the Supreme Court, and the Reclamation Service (later the Bureau of Reclamation), but also in the guises of the State Department, eastern farmers, and Wall Street investors, to name only the more important. Indeed, a major topic of this study is federalism: the attempt of the Colorado Basin states to work out their destiny in concert with the government in Washington. The attempt has been dogged almost from the start by conflicting notions of sovereignty, as each side has sought to assert its supremacy in areas jealously coveted by the other.

On another level this study discloses further evidence of the important role played by government—federal, state, and local —in the development of the West. A prominent theme is the western desire to tap the federal largess without incurring federal control. Westerners have long sought a device that would permit them to obtain federal funds for a host of projects—railroads, roads, canals, dams, for example—and at the same time to

[3] Earl Pomeroy, "Toward a Reorientation of Western History: Continuity and Environment," *Mississippi Valley Historical Review* XLI (1955): 579–599.

preserve the integrity of state government. During the nineteenth and early twentieth centuries, some westerners thought they had found a constitutionally satisfactory solution to their reclamation problems in such devices as the "cession" of public lands to the states and the Reclamation Act of 1902. Many later saw the compact as another key to the national treasury, although, like those before them, they wanted the treasure without surrendering any prerogatives. Then, as now, the attempt to get the purse without the purse strings proved an impossible task.

The connection between East and West is underscored by today's concern for water in all parts of the country. The West has always had a water problem, but the East has also been faced with problems over the quantity and, especially in more recent years, the quality of water. Yet according to the East's own experts, the struggles over water in that part of the country have, thus far at least, paled beside those of West. "Water politics in the West," observes an eastern authority, "were more fiercely contested than in the East." [4] This book helps explain why; and in so doing, it lends support to the arguments of such scholars as John Caughey, Howard Lamar, and Gerald Nash, who emphasize the significance of the recent West in American history.[5]

The concern of this study becomes, inevitably, international as well as national: Mexico is present in the Colorado River Basin, and for years many Americans in southern California's Imperial Valley were unable to obtain water for their lands without first securing Mexican cooperation. Then, too, Mexico itself sought a share of the river for lands that were long considered the most

[4] Nelson M. Blake, *Water for the Cities* (Syracuse, N.Y., 1956), p. 287; see also, among others, Roscoe C. Martin, *Water for New York: A Study in State Administration of Water Resources* (Syracuse, N.Y., 1960), p. 1; Charles H. Weidner, *Water for a City: A History of New York City's Problem from the Beginning to the Delaware River System* (New Brunswick, N.J., 1974).

[5] John Caughey, "The Insignificance of the Frontier in American History," *Western Historical Quarterly* V (1974): 5–16; Howard Lamar, "Persistent Frontier: The West in the Twentieth Century," *Western Historical Quarterly* IV (1973): 5–25; Gerald Nash, *The American West in the Twentieth Century: A Short History of An Urban Oasis* (Englewood Cliffs, N.J., 1973).

fertile in that nation. Though denied participation in the compact negotiations, it naturally had a vital interest in their outcome and watched them closely. Another international dimension —though one beyond the scope of this book—emerges from a realization that other countries (most notably Egypt, the Sudan, India, Pakistan, Israel, and Jordan) have looked to the compact for insights into the handling of their own water problems.

Preeminently, however, this is a study of interstate conflict and cooperation within the United States over the Colorado River. It begins with the dream of many people, especially Arthur Powell Davis of the Reclamation Service, to harness the water and hydroelectric power resources of the Colorado River. It describes how Davis's dream took a major step toward reality when he envisaged a high dam at Boulder Canyon and when settlers in the Imperial Valley threw their support to him in exchange for his promise to aid their quest for an aqueduct that would free them from their dependence on Mexico. It then traces the role played by Los Angeles, the West's most notorious water hustler, in cementing this California-Davis accord—an accord which prompted a bitter reaction from the other Colorado River states, particularly those in the upper portion of the basin, where most of the river's water originated.

Scarcity of water was, of course, the major reason for the concern of the upper states, but another factor was the western law of waters, a complex, ever-changing body of doctrine about which the basin states disagreed sharply. Not only did they differ with one another in the legal codes regulating water rights within their own boundaries, they also disagreed over the fundamental principles that should guide their relations with one another and with the federal government. Their fear of Washington was particularly intense because many high-ranking federal officials sought to establish the authority of the United States over the unappropriated waters in the West's streams, a move that promised to void decades-old practices and reduce state control of water resources to a cipher.

The distrust among the basin states and between those states and the federal government blocked for years all schemes of river development and forced water leaders to seek an accommodation with one another. Through the intercession of the League of the Southwest and then through the mediation of a special commission on the Colorado River, they tried to hammer out an agreement, a task made more difficult because of the lack of precise knowledge about the basin's irrigable potential and because of major differences over the production of hydroelectricity, a commodity that was revolutionizing American life and prompting one of the great political debates of the century over Boulder Canyon, as well as over Muscle Shoals, Great Falls, and the St. Lawrence.

Finally, on November 24, 1922, after intense bargaining, basin leaders agreed to a compact dividing the waters of the river between the upper and lower sections of the watershed, a division that would, they hoped, make possible the harnessing of the Colorado. Eventually it did, but its immediate effect was renewed hostility. The Arizona legislature rejected the agreement, claiming that it threatened the state's future development. When the compact was made part of the Boulder Canyon bill, it sparked a battle that reflected not only factionalism within the basin, but also the fears of eastern farmers and the conflicting desires of public and private hydroelectric power interests.

Not until the passage of the Boulder Canyon Act in 1928 did Congress approve the compact, but even then Arizona persisted in its opposition, primarily because it feared that California would get a greater share of the Colorado than it would. Though the pact assured the upper states of a water supply, it did nothing to protect Arizona from its faster-developing lower-basin neighbor, California. The Boulder Canyon Act altered the picture by providing for a six- as well as a seven-state compact and by requiring California to limit itself to a specific volume of water if Arizona did not ratify the pact. This California did when Arizona continued to withhold its approval; but almost at once the two states began quarreling over the meaning of the self-limitation provision and over several key sections of the compact, particularly those dealing with the lower-basin tributaries. The imbroglio between the two states continued for decades, eventually reaching epic proportions and causing the so-called Arizona-California controversy to become one of the legendary conflicts of the West.

While doing research for this book, I discovered a copy of certain missing minutes of the Colorado River Commission, the body that drafted the compact. When read with other material,

those minutes—specifically the minutes of the nineteenth to the
twenty-seventh meetings—shed considerable light on the intentions of the negotiators. As readers will discover, these documents do not fully support the positions adopted by either
Arizona or California in their long quarrel. Moreover, these
materials, together with findings I have presented elsewhere,[6]
provide strong evidence that the Supreme Court in 1963 misread
the historical record when formulating the landmark decision of
Arizona v. *California.*

But this study also suggests more. For one thing, the debate
over hydroelectricity during the 1920s did not involve merely
the question of public versus private power development. Historians have tended to see the conflict in simplistic terms, in
which advocates of cheap public power battled with the monopo-
listic forces of private industry—the "power trust." There was
such a battle; but public agencies—federal, state, local, municipal—also battled among themselves as revealed in the conflicts among such groups as the city of Los Angeles, the state of
Arizona, the Interior Department, and such powerful publicly
chartered agencies as the Imperial Irrigation District and the
Salt River Valley Water Users' Association.

This study confirms the important role traditionally assigned
to Delph Carpenter of Colorado in promoting the compact, but
it also reveals that Herbert Hoover played a key part in breaking
the impasse that developed during the final negotiations at Santa
Fe in November, 1922. Hoover, as Beverley Moeller has pointed
out, probably did not originate the idea to apportion the water
to the two basins rather than to each state, as he later claimed
in his memoirs. Time—nearly thirty years—had dimmed his
memory, but time has also caused many of us to attach too much
significance to the two-basin concept. Contrary to current opinion, the two-basin idea did not "save" the Santa Fe negotiations.
Long before those talks had begun, nearly every basin leader
had concluded that an apportionment to basins, not to states,
was the only reasonable way to approach the problem. The controversy that nearly quashed the negotiations and occupied the
attention of the delegates throughout almost the entire two weeks

[6] Norris Hundley, jr., "Clio Nods: *Arizona* v. *California* and the
Boulder Canyon Act—A Reassessment," *Western Historical Quarterly*
III (1972): 17–51.

in Santa Fe was over the *quantity* to apportion to each basin, an issue complicated by differences over how to handle the lower-basin tributaries. In the resolution of this dispute, Hoover artfully and patiently used his position as chairman to ask probing questions, to keep the delegates talking to one another, and to suggest compromises that helped produce the final settlement.

Hoover—as well as the other negotiators, for that matter—also seems to have been unfairly criticized by some contemporaries for refusing to write the Boulder Canyon Project into the compact. The evidence shows that Hoover favored flood control and power production, but he, like many others, also recognized that the Boulder Canyon Project was essentially a measure to benefit California. To bind the project to the compact would have doubtlessly frustrated plans to get the pact approved by all the state legislatures except those of California and, possibly, Nevada. As it turned out, ratification proved difficult enough to obtain.

Somewhat more understandable is the criticism leveled in recent years at the framers of the compact for the ambiguities they wrote into that document, for their failure to anticipate the controversy between Arizona and California, for their lack of attention to Indians, and for their false assumptions about stream flow. Despite these criticisms, the compact remains the "law of the river" and continues to control the actions of state and federal officials. It made possible Hoover Dam, at the time the world's highest dam and the nation's first major multiple-purpose project. It facilitated the development of many—perhaps too many—other dams and aqueducts that have contributed to pollution as well as to significant urban, industrial, and agricultural growth. It set the stage for sharp differences among the basin states and between the United States and Mexico. It now figures prominently in plans to combat the energy shortage by developing the enormous reserves of oil shale—possibly the world's largest untapped oil supply—in Utah, Colorado, Wyoming, and New Mexico. And it figures just as prominently in schemes being devised to import water into the Colorado River Basin from other river basins as far away as Alaska and Canada. These plans may lead to conflicts that cause earlier water controversies to seem slight by comparison. But regardless of what the future brings, it is patently clear that the compact has been a critically important document, the first and most significant treaty of its kind, and one which has inspired a host of similar pacts, all of which have been less controversial, largely because they have dealt with less complicated problems and smaller geographic areas.

This book is, then, an account of the movement for the Colorado River Compact of 1922 and an analysis of the major controversies over its ratification and meaning. Though the Arizona-California dispute is described in some detail, the upper basin's supplementary agreement of 1948 is only briefly discussed because it did not involve the heated and prolonged controversy over the meaning of the compact that characterized the lower-basin embroilment. Readers should also be aware that this is not primarily a book about dam building, farming practices, Indian water rights, big land developers, acreage-limitation laws, and other related topics that often do make an appearance. All are important and deserve book-length treatments of their own, but to provide such treatment here would require a different kind of book—and one many times larger.

Indeed, one purpose of this study is to suggest how little we know about the West's major rivers—the Colorado, the Columbia, the Missouri, the Rio Grande, the Sacramento–San Joaquin—as well as the numerous smaller but no less important streams. Before we can generalize about the ways westerners have handled the problem of aridity, we need additional studies—studies describing and analyzing the decision-making process from an historical perspective; assessing the economic uses to which water has been put; approaching river development from the point of view of the Indian, whose interests are often at stake and just as often overlooked; measuring the impact of water politics on agricultural development, the urbanization process, and the natural environment. Some specialized work has been done, nearly all of it by lawyers, engineers, political scientists, and economists. But we also need studies by historians who are willing to draw upon these other disciplines and provide the broad historical perspective needed by regional planners in all parts of the country as they grapple with problems of water shortage and ponder the effect of their decisions on the environment. To deal fully with such problems will require a monumental effort, yet monuments need bricks, and I hope that this book, with its emphasis on the political and legal configurations involving the Colorado River Compact, provides a few for future scholars.

There has been, so far, no careful study of Colorado River politics in general or the compact in particular. Nearly half a century ago, Reuel Olson discussed some aspects of the pact in a work dedicated to showing that the agreement had failed and should be abandoned.[7] But his privately printed account, published while the controversy over ratification still raged and before important manuscripts and other materials in many public and private depositories were available, understandably lacked perspective and dealt tangentially or not at all with many important topics.

My account rests primarily on documents in the National Archives, in the archives of the seven basin states, and on materials in more than a score of other public and private depositories. Among the many helpful individuals at the National Archives to whom I am especially indebted are Harold Pinkett, Patrick Garabedian, Mark Eckhoff, and Jane Smith. In Wyoming Gene Gressley of the Western History Research Center at the University of Wyoming and Katherine Halverson of the Wyoming State Archives went far beyond the call of duty in chasing down elusive documents. So, too, did Myra Ellen Jenkins of the New Mexico State Archives; Saundra Taylor of UCLA's Department of Special Collections; Frederick Gale of the Nevada State Archives; Gerald Giefer of the Water Resources Center Archives of the University of California at Berkeley; Merle V. Budd of the Utah State Archives; Blaise Gagliano of the Arizona State Archives; Phyllis Ball of the University of Arizona's Department of Special Collections; and Charles Colley, Sue Abbey, and Doris Dewey of Arizona State University's Department of Special Collections.

Similarly, the generous help and suggestions of Bert Fireman of Arizona State University and William O. Hendricks of the M. H. Sherman Foundation cannot be adequately acknowledged. I am also grateful to César Sepúlveda of the National University of Mexico and to Antonio Carrillo Flores, former Mexican Minister of Foreign Affairs, for helping me gain access to materials in

[7] *The Colorado River Compact* (Los Angeles, 1926).

Mexico's Secretaría de Relaciones Exteriores. Special thanks are due as well to Orville and Corrie Jones for doing some prospecting for me in the newspaper files of the El Centro Public Library. Invaluable assistance was also provided by the staffs of the Herbert Hoover Presidential Library, Bancroft Library, Arizona Historical Society, Phoenix Public Library, Colorado State Archives, California Department of Water Resources Archives, the Colorado River Board of California library and archives, the Department of Special Collections in the Honnold Library of the Claremont Colleges, the Huntington Library, the Hoover Institution, the Imperial Irrigation District archives, and the Los Angeles Department of Water and Power archives. Thanks are also due to the guardians of manuscripts and books in the libraries at Stanford University, the University of New Mexico, Brigham Young University, the University of Nevada at Reno, and the University of Nevada at Las Vegas. As for the UCLA librarians in charge of interlibrary loans, I am indebted to them far more than they can imagine. (On second thought, they know full well my debt to them.)

To Judge Donald Carpenter of Greeley, Colorado, I would like to express my appreciation for his warm hospitality and his permission to examine and make copies of the papers of his father, Delph Carpenter, the man who, if anyone, should be regarded as the "father of the compact." There is also a host of people involved—or formerly involved—in Colorado River matters who provided me with information without which this book could not have been written. Among them are Northcutt Ely of Washington, D.C.; Myron Holburt, Vernon Valantine, and Robert Figueroa of the Colorado River Board of California; Gilbert Lee and Edward York, Jr., of the Los Angeles Department of Water and Power; Wesley Steiner of the Arizona Interstate Stream Commission; William C. Mullendore and Gilbert Nelson of Los Angeles; Charles Corker of the University of Washington; Floyd Bishop, Wyoming State Engineer; S. E. Reynolds, New Mexico State Engineer; William R. Kelly of Greeley, Colorado; J. L. Ogilvie of the Denver Board of Water Commissioners; Alan J. Williams of the Colorado River Association; Ellis Armstrong, Commissioner of the U.S. Bureau of Reclamation; and Raymond Simpson, attorney for the Confederation of Lower Colorado River Indian Tribes.

For financial support of this study, I owe special thanks to the University of California Water Resources Center; to UCLA's Committee on International and Comparative Studies for a Ford Foundation grant; to the Sourriseau Academy of California State University, San Jose; and to the American Philosophical Society. I am also indebted to John Caughey, John Schutz, Robert Dunbar, and Harwood Hinton for helping me to iron out some of the cowlicks in the manuscript, to Norman Thrower for guiding me to the Gemini V photograph of the Imperial Valley, to Noel Diaz for his cartographic skills, and to Gary Dunbar and Tom McKnight for placing their imprimatur on my maps.

Finally, my deepest gratitude goes to the three women in my life—my wife, Carol, and my daughters, Wendy and Jacqueline —for their constant good humor and for putting up with this book.

Norris Hundley, jr.

Pacific Palisades, 1974

Maps

Tables

1

Dreamers and Planners

The date was November 24, 1922. The speaker was Herbert Hoover, secretary of commerce and future president of the United States. "This conference has stood out in my mind as different. . . . It is the only conference of important character where I haven't . . . come to have a complete conviction of dishonesty on the part of somebody." "What is more," added Hoover, "this conference" has dealt with "one of the problems of more extreme complexity than will ever be appreciated by the outside world." [1]

Secretary Hoover was speaking to a small group of haggard men gathered at Bishop's Lodge, a plush resort situated three and a half miles outside of Santa Fe, New Mexico. In the audience were representatives from seven western states, men who had nearly finished drafting the Colorado River Compact, a treaty that divided the waters of the Southwest's most valuable stream and climaxed weeks of intense negotiation and years of bitter struggle.

Hoover was harsh in assessing earlier conferences, but he did not mean to imply that he had not differed with many in the

[1] Colorado River Commission, "Minutes of the Twenty-Seventh Meeting" (November 24, 1922), p. 8, file 032, Colorado River Project, Bureau of Reclamation Papers, Record Group 115, National Archives.

1

audience or that disagreements over the Colorado would not continue. Moreover, his prediction notwithstanding, many in the "outside world" would come to appreciate the complexity of the problems faced by those gathered in Santa Fe. Still, his claim about the importance of the task just completed was modest. Hoover could have used even stronger words to characterize the events of the preceding fifteen days, for those listening to his congratulatory remarks realized fully the significance of what they had achieved.

Hoover's audience knew from experience that in the arid western United States no commodity was more important to society than water. They knew, too, that no body of water had been the subject of more bitter controversy than the Colorado River, the major water supply for 244,000 square miles, an area embracing parts of seven states—Arizona, California, Colorado, Nevada, New Mexico, Utah, Wyoming—as well as some 2,000 square miles in Mexico. Nor did the secretary of commerce have to tell them about the thousands of people who were alert to the regional, national, and international implications of the Santa Fe negotiations and who had followed closely in scores of newspapers the progress of the meeting. The federal government itself had revealed a year earlier the importance of the undertaking by appointing Hoover its representative on the Colorado River Commission, the body charged with drafting the pact and the group to which the secretary now spoke.

Hoover had brought to the venture his expertise as a world-famous engineer, gained from work in the United States and abroad, and his reputation as an international hero, won through his efforts to relieve hunger, first in Belgium and later in all of Europe. As a high-ranking cabinet official and personal adviser to President Warren Harding, he had also brought to the conferees at Santa Fe the expectation of presidential endorsement of their work. That endorsement would be important in winning the congressional approval needed for any agreement among states, and the compact clearly represented a major precedent in interstate diplomacy—the first time that more than two or three states had sought to settle a problem among themselves by treaty.

But the pact would come to signify much more. "Measured by the vastness of the region and the magnitude of the interests regulated," legal experts Felix Frankfurter and James Landis would observe in 1925, "the Colorado Compact represents, thus far, the most ambitious illustration of interstate agreements." [2] For the first time a group of states had apportioned the waters of an interstate stream among themselves for irrigation and other consumptive uses. This agreement on the Colorado, in turn, would spark attempts to achieve similar treaties on other rivers—the Rio Grande, Pecos, La Plata, South Platte, Arkansas, Red, Republican, Belle Fourche, Costilla, and Snake—but none would involve as many states or deal with as large an area or as complex a set of problems.[3]

The compact had still other important implications. The long struggle for its ratification, like the struggle to obtain agreement at Santa Fe, would hone differences among state and federal officials over constitutional interpretation and over the role of the national government in western development. It would aggravate disputes

[2] Felix Frankfurter and James M. Landis, "The Compact Clause of the Constitution—A Study in Interstate Adjustments," *Yale Law Journal* XXXIV (1925): 702. See also Delph Carpenter, "Application of the Reserve Treaty Powers of the States to Interstate Water Controversies," *Colorado Bar Association Report* XXIV (1921): 45–101; Arthur Powell Davis, "Press Release," November 27, 1922, file 1-M/307, Herbert Hoover Papers, Hoover Presidential Library, West Branch, Iowa; Frederick L. Zimmermann and Mitchell Wendell, *The Interstate Compact Since 1925* (Chicago, 1951), pp. 5, 13–15; W. Brooke Graves, *American Intergovernmental Relations: Their Origins, Historical Development, and Current Status* (New York, 1964), pp. 600–601.

[3] Zimmermann and Wendell, *The Interstate Compact*, p. 16. The roots of the compact, of course, run deep into the colonial, as well as the national, period of American history. The first use of the compact clause under the Constitution occurred in 1789, the same year in which the Constitution was ratified. Until the twentieth century, however, the compact clause was only infrequently invoked by the states; and when it was used, it was usually employed to settle a boundary dispute involving no more than two states. For a discussion of the history of the compact clause, see, among others, Frankfurter and Landis, "The Compact Clause of the Constitution," pp. 685–758; Zimmermann and Wendell, *The Interstate Compact;* Vincent Thursby, *Interstate Cooperation: A Study of the Interstate Compact* (Washington, D.C., 1953); and National Water Commission, *Interstate Water Compacts* [PB 202 998], by Jerome C. Muys (Washington, D.C., 1971).

over hydroelectric power that would tax the patience and skill of businessmen as well as officials of government on all levels. It would exacerbate clashes between those advocating public owner-ship of natural resources and those championing private industry's right to develop such resources. It would add another chapter to the story of the decades-old struggle to control the Colorado River's devastating floods—floods that had claimed numerous lives and annually destroyed farms, businesses, and homes. In addition, it would continue to reveal a generation little interested in the Indian or his rights to water, despite the fact that Indians had been the first to cultivate major portions of the Colorado Basin. It would also disclose a public more interested in exploit-ing nature than in preserving wilderness areas for their aesthetic values.

Concerned as they were with the efficient use of the nation's re-sources, those gathered in Santa Fe took special delight in the belief that the compact would prepare the way for taming the Colorado with massive engineering works. For many the greatest triumph would occur six years later, in 1928, when President Calvin Coolidge would sign the Boulder Canyon Project bill, a law authorizing the construction of Hoover Dam, then the world's largest dam and the harbinger of numerous other dams, aqueducts, and hydroelectric power plants that, in turn, would contribute to the phenomenal growth of the twentieth-century West, including the large urban and industrial areas of southern California, north-ern Utah, and eastern Colorado.

Though aware that their action would have important con-sequences, Hoover and his audience could not, of course, have known the precise nature or timing of those later developments. Nor did they know that the compact would take on added sig-nificance as later generations quarreled over its meaning and turned again and again to the United States Supreme Court as a referee. Had they been able to foresee such difficulties, they would have been greatly disappointed, for they considered the pact an alternative to controversy, an escape from the costly and time-consuming litigation that had frustrated the development of scores of western communities.

Their disappointment would have been even greater had they known that congressional approval of the pact was six years in the future and that their calculations of stream flow were grossly overestimated. They would, moreover, have been disillusioned by future judicial decisions that would misconstrue their intentions and create controversies where they had thought none possible. They would also have probably regretted their inability to anticipate certain problems, like those emerging in the mid-twentieth century over water quality; and in time they would have doubtlessly come to lament those instances where their desire to cooperate had caused them to retreat into ambiguities that set the stage for future disagreement. In particular, they would have regretted the frustrated attempts of future water leaders to negotiate the subsidiary pacts made mandatory by their action that day in Santa Fe. They had divided the Colorado's waters between the upper and lower portions of the river basin, an all-important first step, but one which left to future negotiation the apportionment of specific amounts of water to each state. Not until 1948 would the upper states divide their share among themselves. The lower states would never do so, in large part because Arizona and California would be unable to agree on the meaning of key provisions of the compact; and in 1963 the U.S. Supreme Court would settle the matter for them.[4]

But those gathered with Hoover in Santa Fe would have been pleased with what the compact did make possible—the many dams and aqueducts and the enormous increases in agricultural and industrial productivity throughout the Southwest. They would also have been delighted by the compact's durability. Long after all of them were gone, it would remain a vital document, a remarkable achievement in view of the obstacles that had blocked earlier agreements. Though actual negotiations for the pact had taken place over a relatively short period of time, the powerful economic and political forces that at first had prompted, then threatened to scuttle, and finally shaped their actions in Santa Fe had been set in motion decades earlier.

I

No one was more familiar with the earlier struggles than the conference's principal technical adviser, a bespectacled, square-jawed, and solidly built man sitting quietly at the side of the

[4] U.S., *Statutes at Large* LXII: 31; *Arizona v. California et al.*, 373 U.S. 546 (1963).

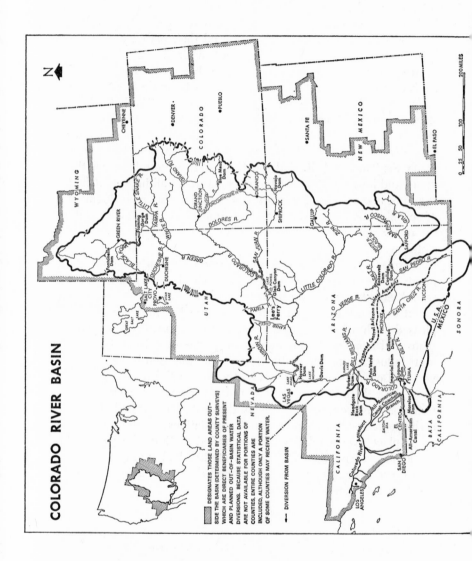

COLORADO RIVER BASIN

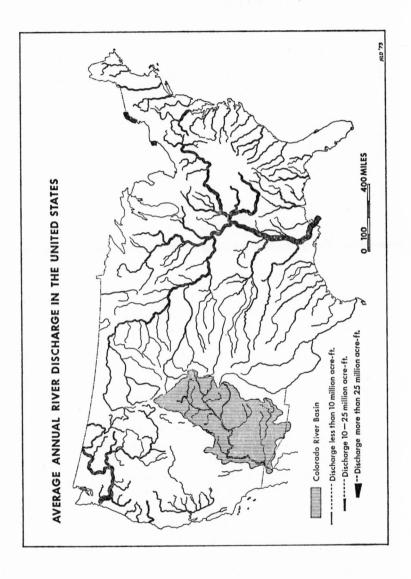

AVERAGE ANNUAL RIVER DISCHARGE IN THE UNITED STATES

Colorado River Basin

----------- Discharge less than 10 million acre-ft.

━━━━━ Discharge 10 — 25 million acre-ft.

◄▬▬ Discharge more than 25 million acre-ft.

0   100   400 MILES

NLD '73

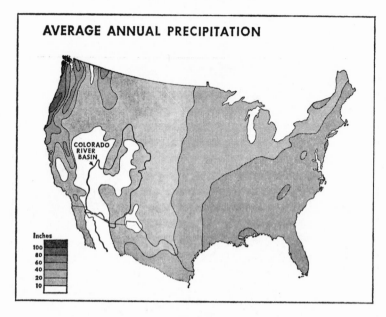

AVERAGE ANNUAL PRECIPITATION

room and listening to Secretary Hoover's congratulatory speech. Arthur Powell Davis, distinguished director of the United States Reclamation Service and still youthful looking despite his gray hair and sixty-one years, knew that the compact represented only a preliminary step toward his lifetime goal; but it was a necessary step, clearly the most important thus far. Davis's dream was nothing less than the comprehensive development of the Colorado River from its headwaters in the Rockies to its mouth on the Gulf of California. By battling for this dream against those with less vision, he had played a leading role in precipitating the conference that had drafted the compact.

Although Davis was not the first to argue for a comprehensive program for the Colorado, he was the most effective. In part, his importance can be attributed to timing. When his uncle, John Wesley Powell, the famous explorer and second director of the U.S. Geological Survey, had urged development of the West's watercourses in the late nineteenth century, he had encountered major obstacles—the need for further scientific surveys, shortage of funds, and differences with congressional leaders over how to proceed. But spurred by his belief that the West's water supply, no matter how carefully managed, could irrigate only a small

portion of the land area, Powell had persuaded the federal government to underwrite the discovery of reservoir sites and the land
most suitable for irrigation. As early as 1878, in his famous "Report on the Lands of the Arid Region of the United States," he
had predicted that reservoirs would some day make it possible
to divert much of the Colorado's surplus water to southern California's fertile valleys. Though he had great vision, Powell apparently did not envisage a high dam in the Boulder Canyon area,
the dam that in his nephew's later plans became essential to the
taming of the Colorado.[5]

Powell's ideas were shared by others, including the popular
western journalist Richard J. Hinton, who urged massive federal
involvement in Colorado River development. "The disposition of
its waters," declared Hinton in 1878, "is a subject over which the
General Government should assume entire control, devising some
wise and comprehensive plan for irrigation works." [6] At that time,
however, most westerners preferred to have reclamation under
state control. But during the next two decades, the inadequacy of
such a policy became apparent to careful observers. The enormous
expense of river development, the interstate character of most
major streams, the federal government's position as the largest

[5] J. W. Powell, "Report on the Lands of the Arid Region of the
United States," *H. Ex. Doc. 73*, 45 Cong., 2 sess. (1878), pp. 23, 85,
149–163; "Geographic and Geological Surveys West of the Mississippi," *H. Rept. 612*, 43 Cong., 1 sess. (1874), pp. 10, 53; "Reservoirs in Arid Regions of the United States," *S. Ex. Doc. 163*, 50 Cong.,
1 sess. (1888), pp. 2–6; "Sundry Civil Appropriation Bill," *S. Rept.
2613*, 50 Cong., 2 sess. (1889), pp. 109–110; Everett W. Sterling,
"The Powell Irrigation Survey, 1888–1893," *Mississippi Valley Historical Review* XXVII (1940): 421–434; Wallace Stegner, *Beyond
the Hundredth Meridian* (Boston, 1954), pp. 202–350. Several writers
claim that Powell selected a reservoir site on the mainstream of the
Colorado in the Boulder Canyon area, but they cite no supporting
evidence; and I have found none. See, for example, William Culp
Darrah, *Powell of the Colorado* (Princeton, 1951), pp. 307, 399;
John Upton Terrell, *The Man Who Rediscovered America: A Biography of John Wesley Powell* (New York, 1969), p. 254. Leonard
Wibberly, *Wes Powell: Conqueror of the Grand Canyon* (New
York, 1958), pp. 206–207, seems to agree with Darrah and Terrell.

[6] Richard J. Hinton, *The Hand-Book to Arizona* (San Francisco,
1878), p. 66.

landowner in the arid West—all pointed to the need for federal
involvement. By the end of the century, many state leaders agreed
with the famed army engineer Hiram M. Chittenden that "a
comprehensive reservoir system in the arid regions of the United
States is absolutely essential" and that "it is not possible to secure
the best development of such a system except through the agency
of the General Government." [7]

As Chittenden was making his appeal, hundreds of others were
agitating for the same goal through their congressmen and through
powerful irrigation lobbies. As their numbers mounted, so did
their pressure, until Congress finally responded with the Reclamation Act of 1902. Ironically, that measure, which embodied many
of Powell's ideas for a more rational approach to western development, became law as the old explorer lay dying. Though the
act was long overdue in the eyes of many, it represented a major
advance by establishing a special agency, the Reclamation Service,
and directing it to construct irrigation projects with the proceeds
from the sale of public lands in the arid states.[8] When Arthur
Powell Davis joined the newly created Reclamation Service, he
found it a ready-made vehicle for pursuing his uncle's—and now
his own—goal.

II

Besides his crusading spirit, Davis brought to his job considerable knowledge about the workings of government. He was

[7] "Preliminary Examination of Reservoir Sites in Wyoming and
Colorado," *H. Doc. 141*, 55 Cong., 2 sess. (1897), p. 58.

[8] Paul W. Gates, *History of Public Land Law Development* (Wash-
ington, D.C., 1968), pp. 419–420; John T. Ganoe, "The Origin of a
National Reclamation Policy," *Mississippi Valley Historical Review*
XVIII (1931): 34–52; see also Lawrence B. Lee, "William Ellsworth
Smythe and the Irrigation Movement: A Reconsideration," *Pacific
Historical Review* XLI (1972): 289–311; Stanley R. Davison, "The
Leadership of the Reclamation Movement, 1875–1902" (Ph.D. diss.,
University of California, Berkeley, 1951); Samuel P. Hays, *Con-
servation and the Gospel of Efficiency* (Cambridge, Mass., 1959);
William Lilley III and Lewis L. Gould, "The Western Irrigation
Movement, 1878–1902: A Reappraisal," in Gene M. Gressley, ed.,
The American West: A Reorientation (Laramie, Wyo., 1966), pp.
57–75.

born in 1861 in Decatur, Illinois; and during his youth, he had learned much about congressional maneuvering from his father, John Davis, a Kansas farmer, newspaperman, and Populist, who had served two terms in the House of Representatives. He had learned even more from his uncle, whom he had accompanied on trips west and whose plans for western development he had faithfully supported. But Davis also brought technical skills gained during his years at Kansas State Normal School and later at Columbian College (now George Washington University), from which he earned a degree in civil engineering in 1888. Even before completing his schooling, he had embarked on a career with the federal government by accepting his uncle's offer in 1882 of a position as assistant topographer with the Geological Survey. This job brought him into contact with the arid mesas and canyon lands of Arizona, New Mexico, and California. It also fed his growing interest in the Colorado, a river that he saw for the first time in the summer of 1883 as he stood on the rim of the Grand Canyon.[9]

An opportunity for Davis to increase still further his knowledge of the river came in 1894, when he assumed responsibility for measuring the flow of streams throughout the West, and in 1896, when he advanced to hydrographer in charge of measuring all rivers canvassed by the Geological Survey.[10] His talents made a

[9] See the various biographical sketches prepared by Davis and others in the Arthur Powell Davis Papers, Western History Research Center, University of Wyoming, Laramie. See also Colorado River Commission, "Hearings" (Phoenix, March 16, 1922), pp. 55–56, file 032, Colorado River Project, Bureau of Reclamation Papers; Charles A. Bissell and Frank E. Weymouth, "Arthur Powell Davis," *Transactions of the American Society of Civil Engineers* C (1935): p. 1582; Sherman M. Woodward, "Arthur Powell Davis," *Dictionary of American Biography* (New York, 1944), XI, supplement one, pp. 224–225; *Who's Who in America, 1934–35* (Chicago, 1934), p. 675; *New York Herald Tribune*, August 8, 1933; U.S. Dept. of the Interior, "Memorandum for the Press," July 10, 1933, Davis Papers; House Committee on Irrigation and Reclamation, *Hearings on Protection and Development of Lower Colorado River Basin*, H.R. 2903, 68 Cong., 1 sess. (1924), pp. 1375–1377.

[10] In 1925 Davis stated that his first attempt "to outline some project for irrigation from the Colorado River" occurred "some 33 years ago"—apparently in 1892. Senate Committee on Irrigation and

deep impression on his superiors, and in 1902 they appointed him assistant chief engineer in the newly created Reclamation Service.

Davis came to his job with more than his technical skills and familiarity with the West. He also arrived as a dedicated advocate of the "gospel of Henry George," whose single-tax scheme revealed conclusively to him "that the rights of the individual and the rights of property are not in conflict." For Davis as well as for George, this conclusion rested on a special understanding of the nature of property—an understanding that suggested a special remedy for human misery. "A slight change in our taxation method is all that is required," he wrote. "Exempt from taxation every article of wealth owing its existence to human effort; retain nature's store for the benefit of all by taxing society created values and land to its full rental value." [11]

Like many other idealists who were drifting into the Progressive movement, Davis abhorred monopoly, romanticized the small farmer, worshipped efficiency, and viewed the federal government as a major instrument for social and political reform. Though he labored in vain for Henry George's program, he never faltered in his belief that land was a major key to understanding and correcting society's ills. To counter the demoralizing effects of land monopoly, the end of the frontier, and the urbanization of American society, he dedicated his professional life to reclaiming the desert wastes so that more farmers could be put on the soil and the nation's moral fiber thereby strengthened. While he was a captive of what historians have called the "agrarian myth" and a firm advocate of local control, he also recognized the necessity of central planning and federal funding if the enormous problems

---

Reclamation, *Hearings on Colorado River Basin*, S. Res. 320, 69 Cong., 1 sess. (1925), p. 173; cf. House Committee on Irrigation and Reclamation, *Hearings on Protection and Development of Lower Colorado River Basin*, H.R. 2903, p. 1378.

[11] A. P. Davis to Gifford Pinchot, May 14, 1912, Davis Papers; Davis, *The Single Tax from the Farmer's Standpoint* (Minneapolis, 1897); *Pacific Builder and Engineer*, July 11, 1914. For an incisive and provocative discussion of Davis, see Gene Gressley, "Arthur Powell Davis, Reclamation, and the West," *Agricultural History* XLII (1968):241–257.

posed by the West's rivers were to be overcome. And no river attracted his attention more than the Colorado. "I . . . considered problems in all of the Western States," he later recalled, "but there [was] . . . none which . . . excited my interest and imagination and ambition so much as the development of the Colorado River basin." [12] Other western rivers, like the Columbia, might possess a larger volume of water, but none, he believed, was accessible to more irrigable acreage—and, hence, more future farms—than the Colorado.

As early as the spring of 1902, shortly before Davis joined the Reclamation Service, he outlined for fellow engineers a general plan for "the gradual comprehensive development of the Colorado River by a series of large storage reservoirs." By the fall he was ready to suggest the location of dam sites. "It is my present idea," he told Joseph B. Lippincott, a noted California engineer and the head of federal reclamation activities in the Southwest, "that the first construction should be a dam at the gorge below the mouth of Bill Williams' Fork, as high as appears practicable from the local conditions." After that, dams should be built at Bulls Head, just above the first reservoir, and in Black Canyon, some twenty miles below Boulder Canyon.[13] Actually neither Davis nor anyone else had accumulated enough technical data to justify immediate construction at the locations he had mentioned. But he knew that the Reclamation Service was preparing to conduct a broad search for dam sites in the West, and he wanted to make sure that no major sites on the lower Colorado were overlooked.

The reconnaissance of the lower Colorado, completed by Lippincott in late 1902, proved most encouraging to Davis and others interested in developing the river. Though much field work remained to be done, the report revealed considerable irrigable acreage near the stream and the existence of numerous reservoir sites from which water could be diverted to surrounding mesas.

[12] League of the Southwest, "Minutes" (Denver, Colo., August 25–27, 1920), p. 34, copy in box 477, Imperial Irrigation District Papers, Imperial, Calif.

[13] Arthur Powell Davis to J. B. Lippincott, October 10, 1902, file 187, Colorado River Project, 1902–1919, Bureau of Reclamation Papers, Record Group 115, National Archives (hereafter cited as Bureau of Reclamation Papers, CRP).

But "the best dam site," noted Lippincott, was in a "narrow box canyon known as Boulder Canyon." [14]

Though the reconnaissance dramatized the federal government's interest in the Boulder Canyon area, others had mixed feelings about the storage potential of northwestern Arizona's deep canyons. In the 1890s Nathan Oakes Murphy, who had served twice as Arizona's territorial governor, was ridiculed by his Democratic opponents for his "great chimerical schemes to dam the Colorado and irrigate every foot of land between the grand Canyon and Phenix and between Phenix and the border line" with Mexico.[15] Ironically, one of those poking fun at Murphy was Anson H. Smith, editor of the Kingman *Mohave County Miner* and eventually a leading proponent of damming the Colorado. By late 1894 he, too, was advocating storage reservoirs on the nearby river and urging his readers "to grasp the good things laying at our very threshold." This storage, he predicted, would provide cheap electricity for the state's numerous mines and irrigation water for the fertile valleys; it would make possible a "veritable Garden of Eden." [16]

While Smith and the others who shared his dream continued to agitate on Arizona's behalf, the federal survey of 1902 significantly altered the picture by arousing Washington to the reclamation value of the Boulder Canyon and Black Canyon areas. The possibility of dams on the lower river proved exciting, but the cost of such an undertaking and the need for additional surveys prevented early action. Even Lippincott dragged his feet, downplaying on one occasion the need for storage and on another arguing that dam construction should be confined to the upper river. "Storage on the Lower Colorado is impossible," he declared in 1904, "because of unsatisfactory bed rock conditions and

[14] U.S. Geological Survey, *First Annual Report of the Reclamation Service, 1902* (Washington, D.C., 1903), pp. 106, 109. Davis eventually selected Black Canyon, about twenty miles below Boulder Canyon, as the site of Hoover Dam.

[15] Kingman *Mohave County Miner*, November 3, 1894.

[16] Ibid., December 1, 1894; January 12, 19, and February 2, 1895; J. Hubert Smith to Norris Hundley, November 24, 1971. I am indebted to Bert Fireman, director of the Arizona Historical Foundation at Arizona State University, for first making me aware of Anson Smith's activities.

the high percentage of silt." In disagreeing, Davis joined with two colleagues and prepared a rebuttal statement, which they sent to Frederick H. Newell, director of the Reclamation Service. If dams were limited to the known sites on the upper river, they argued, then the flood waters of more than a dozen tributaries accounting for half or more of the river's runoff would be lost. They believed good sites were available on the lower river and sought permission from Newell to inaugurate exploratory studies, especially in the Black Canyon area, that would prove them correct.[17]

While Newell was sympathetic, he lacked funds and had to contend with public impatience over long-term projects. Reluctantly he vetoed the request. "I appreciate that we should guard the interests of the future," he explained, but "at the same time we must show to Congress as few of these general expenditures as possible and not have a great number of petty charges made on account of future work." [18]

Despite the setback, Davis's interest in a comprehensive program of development continued and increased markedly in 1907, when President Theodore Roosevelt, alarmed by a major flood on the river, urged Congress "to enter upon a broad, comprehensive scheme of development for all the irrigable land upon [the] Colorado River." [19] Nothing was done, however. Lack of funds, insufficient public pressure, and the passing of the flood threat caused Congress's interest to wane and led to a tapering off of sur-

[17] A. P. Davis to J. B. Lippincott, October 10, 1902, Bureau of Reclamation Papers, CRP; J. B. Lippincott, "Report on the Necessity for the Regulation of the Colorado River . . ." (July 23, 1904), p. 9, Bureau of Reclamation Papers, CRP; A. P. Davis, George Y. Winser, and W. H. Sanders to F. H. Newell, September 26, 1904, Bureau of Reclamation Papers, CRP.

[18] F. H. Newell to A. P. Davis, November 10, 1905, Bureau of Reclamation Papers, CRP.

[19] *Cong. Rec.*, 59 Cong., 2 sess. (1907), p. 1029; A. P. Davis and others to chief engineer, January 7, 1907, Bureau of Reclamation Papers, CRP; House Committee on Irrigation of Arid Lands, *Hearings on All-American Canal in Imperial County, Calif.*, H.R. 6044, 66 Cong., 1 sess. (1919), p. 99; U.S. Dept. of the Interior, *Fourteenth Annual Report of the Reclamation Service, 1914–1915* (Washington, D.C., 1915), p. 323; "Colorado River Development," *S. Doc. 186*, 70 Cong., 2 sess. (1929), pp. 40–41.

veys on the lower river. Still, Davis managed to retain his enthusiasm; and as he advanced in rank within the Reclamation Service, he never lost sight of his goal.

By 1913, when Davis was serving on the Reclamation Commission, a panel then in charge of the Reclamation Service, the development of the Colorado had become almost an obsession with him. His position within the service's hierarchy encouraged him to go to his associates on the commission and ask for authority to initiate "a systematic investigation of the Colorado River." But his colleagues did not think the time was right for such an undertaking, and they rejected his request. He then appealed to the newly appointed secretary of the interior, Franklin Lane, a man who had earlier claimed to be a strong advocate of federal conservation and reclamation programs. Davis decided to test Lane's commitment to western irrigation development, and he was delighted to find that the secretary was as good as his word. In late 1913 Lane released enough funds to inaugurate the long-sought "investigation of the Colorado River basin, with a view to making plans for its full development." [20] That investigation was a lengthy undertaking, often threatened by inadequate funding, but Davis was able to guide its efforts personally after 1914, when he became director of the Reclamation Service. In his new position he was also better able to seek out and stimulate public and private support for his ideas. His warmest advocates turned out to be Californians, especially those living in a southeastern part of the state known as the Imperial Valley. Developments there, though encouraging to Davis, eventually sent shock waves throughout the Colorado River Basin.

[20] A. P. Davis to supervising engineer, November 25, 1913, Bureau of Reclamation Papers, CRP.

2

Imperial Joins the Crusade

Settlers in California's Imperial Valley showed little interest in the comprehensive plans of Arthur Powell Davis. They sought, instead, a special irrigation canal, an "All-American Canal" as they called it, that would give them control over their water supply and assure the growth of their area. Even so, the peculiar nature of their problem and the force of their demands encouraged Davis and in time sparked a reaction on the national level as well as throughout the Colorado River Basin.

I

That Californians in the Imperial Valley were interested in water, and particularly in a special irrigation canal, was inevitable. Their homes and farms were located in a most arid region, bordered on the east by the forbidding Sonora Desert and on the north by the desolate Colorado Desert. Rainfall is virtually nonexistent in the valley, averaging three inches and dropping to as little as a half-inch in some years, and temperatures sometimes soar to more than 120° during the summer months. Located below sea level, the valley forms part of the Salton Sink, a great basin surrounded by mountains on all sides except the southeast

17

and divided by the international border. Running from northwest
to southeast, the basin is about 100 miles long and 35 miles wide,
forming at its narrow northern end California's Coachella Valley
and at its southern end Mexico's Mexicali Valley. Sandwiched
between are the 600,000 acres of the Imperial Valley.[1]

The river is the valley's lifeblood and also the source of the
area's enormously rich soil. During past ages the stream, which
flowed on a ridge above sea level, periodically tore through its
banks and poured into the low-lying valley, creating a large inland
lake of fresh water. Primarily responsible for these diversions was
the silt picked up by the river as it gouged its way through arid
upstream canyons in its passage to the sea. In its natural state
the Colorado was one of the heaviest carriers of silt in the world
—carrying about five times that of the Rio Grande, ten times
that of the Nile, and seventeen times that of the Mississippi. As
the river neared the delta, its speed decreased and it dropped
much of its silt load, thus causing the channel to rise above the
surrounding countryside. In past centuries the channel, or broad
bed, was often unable to contain the heavy spring runoffs or the
flash floods of summer. When this occurred, the river ruptured its
banks and flowed into the nearby basin until silt deposits again
altered its course. By the twentieth century, these periodic
floods (the last major one occurred only shortly before Spanish
discovery in the mid-sixteenth century) had gradually extended
the delta many miles south into the Gulf of California and
north into the United States. The floods had also left behind
enormous quantities of rich alluvial soil that was thousands of
feet deep in places. This soil attracted the attention of the earliest
inhabitants.[2]

[1] "Irrigation in Imperial Valley, California," *S. Doc. 246*, 60 Cong.,
1 sess. (1908), p. 5; Fred B. Kniffen, *The Natural Landscape of the
Colorado Delta* (Berkeley, 1932), p. 150; H. T. Cory, *The Imperial
Valley and the Salton Sink* (San Francisco, 1915), pp. 15, 49; D. T.
MacDougal et al., *The Salton Sea* (Washington, D.C., 1914), p. 17;
U.S. Geological Survey, "Colorado River and Its Utilization," *Water-
Supply Paper 395*, by E. C. LaRue (Washington, D.C., 1916), p. 13.

[2] Munson J. Dowd, *Historic Salton Sea*, 4th printing (n.p., April,
1965), pp. 6–9; Godfrey G. Sykes, *The Colorado Delta* (Washington,
1937), pp. 128–154, passim; Kniffen, *Natural Landscape*, pp. 165–
166; U.S. Dept. of Agriculture, "Silt in the Colorado River and Its

Among the first to appreciate the fertile soil and nearby water
supply were Yuma, Cocopa, and Kamia Indians, who concentrated their efforts on the lands subject to seasonal flooding along
the river's lower reaches. Most numerous were the Cocopa, whose
crops of maize, beans, and pumpkins supported a population of
perhaps 22,000 at the time of white contact. Because of little
initial interaction between whites and delta Indians, the population remained stable until the mid-nineteenth century, when increased contact and the introduction of European diseases deci-
mated the natives. By the turn of the century, only a few hundred
remained, and these were adopting the ways of the white man,
often constructing his irrigation works and serving him as field
hand or cowboy.[3]

II

As the number of Indians tilling the overflow lands of the lower
delta declined, white interest, especially in the nearby Imperial
Valley, increased. First to formulate a feasible way to irrigate the
valley by gravity canal was Dr. Oliver M. Wozencraft, who conceived the idea in 1849 while passing through the area on his way
to the California gold fields. Not until several years later, however,
when William P. Blake, a government geologist who had gone
through the region in search of a railroad route, publicized the
valley's agricultural potential did Wozencraft turn his full energies
to a reclamation scheme. Together with an engineer friend, the
San Diego County surveyor Ebenezer Hadley, he devised a plan

Relation to Irrigation," *Technical Bulletin No. 67*, by Samuel Fortier
and Harry F. Blaney (Washington, D.C., 1928), pp. 61–62.

[3] Edward F. Castetter and Willis H. Bell, *Yuman Indian Agricul-
ture: Primitive Subsistence on the Lower Colorado and Gila Rivers*
(Albuquerque, 1951), pp. 25–65, passim; Fred Kniffen, *The Primitive
Cultural Landscape of the Colorado Delta* (Berkeley, 1931), pp. 51–
57; C. N. Perry to H. T. Cory, December 23, 1911, C. N. Perry
Papers, Water Collection, Honnold Library, Claremont Colleges; David
Henderson, "Agriculture and Livestock Raising in the Evolution of
the Economy and Culture of the State of Baja California, Mexico"
(Ph.D. diss., University of California, Los Angeles, 1964), pp. 166–
197; Jack D. Forbes, "Indian Horticulture West and Northwest
of the Colorado River," *Journal of the West* II (1963): 6–9; Jack
D. Forbes, *Warriors of the Colorado* (Norman, 1965), pp. 5–43.

to irrigate the valley by diverting water through the Alamo, an overflow channel of the Colorado River which went through Mexico and bypassed the large, shifting sand hills that separated the river from the valley on the American side of the border.[4]

Unfortunately for the success of his scheme, Wozencraft felt that he had to own the land to be reclaimed. In 1859 he persuaded the California legislature to support his request for a grant of 1,600 square miles from the public domain, but Congress, preoccupied by the threat of civil war, found little time for the proposal. Finally, when it considered the matter in 1862, it rejected Wozencraft's plea. Some House members considered the cession too large and valuable for one man, while others denounced the scheme as foolish. Undaunted, Wozencraft spent the remaining twenty-five years of his life and his entire personal fortune in a vain attempt to persuade Congress to change its mind.[5]

Wozencraft failed, but his dream was largely realized in the accomplishments of Charles R. Rockwood, who "rediscovered" the Imperial Valley in 1892 while investigating the possibility of irrigating lands in nearby Sonora. Like Wozencraft, Rockwood believed that the valley could be transformed into a garden, but unlike his predecessor, he felt no need to own the land. He realized that the area was virtually worthless without water, and he drew up plans to introduce and control a water supply. To further his aims, he created the California Development Company in 1896 and traveled to American and European financial centers in search of the necessary capital to underwrite his project.[6]

[4] Otis B. Tout, *The First Thirty Years, 1901–1931* (San Diego, [1931]), pp. 25–26; "Reports of the Explorations and Surveys, to Ascertain the Most Practicable and Economical Route for a Railroad from the Mississippi River to the Pacific Ocean," *S. Ex. Doc. 78*, 33 Cong., 2 sess. (1856); Barbara Ann Metcalf, "Oliver M. Wozencraft in California, 1849–1887" (M.A. thesis, University of Southern California, 1963), pp. 81–83.

[5] *Calif. Stats.*, Tenth Session of Legislature (1859), pp. 238–240, 392–393; *Cong. Globe*, 37 Cong., 2 sess. (1862), pp. 2379–2381; Tout, *First Thirty Years*, p. 26; Metcalf, "Oliver M. Wozencraft," pp. 87–96.

[6] Charles R. Rockwood, *Born of the Desert* (Calexico, Calif., 1930), pp. 2–12; W. T. Heffernan, *Personal Recollections* (Calexico, Calif., 1930), pp. 3–10.

Depressed economic conditions and poor management nearly scuttled the undertaking before Rockwood enlisted the support of the famed engineer George Chaffey, now looking for new ventures following the completion of his irrigation projects in Australia and at the southern California communities of Etiwanda and Ontario. Though previously convinced that white men could not live in the harsh climate of the Imperial Valley, Chaffey had changed his mind as a result of his Australian experiences. In 1899 he joined Rockwood, and almost immediately his reputation, expertise, and financial backing attracted national attention to the undertaking. Though monetary difficulties would continue, by 1900 settlers were pouring into the valley in response to the promise of water and the attraction of the area's new name, "Imperial Valley," which Chaffey preferred over New River Country or the more forbidding Colorado Desert or Salton Sink, as the area had been known.[7]

Wasting little time, Chaffey tapped the river just north of the border and, following a plan closely paralleling that devised earlier by Wozencraft, fed the water into the Alamo, which went around the California sand dunes and through Mexico for fifty miles before turning north again to the United States. On June 21, 1901, the first water reached the valley.[8]

The introduction of water touched off a major land boom. Within eight months, 2,000 settlers had arrived, the towns of Imperial and Calexico were laid out, 400 miles of canals and laterals built, and more than 100,000 acres readied for cultivation. Contributing to the phenomenal growth were the mutual water companies created by the settlers to purchase water from the California Development Company and handle distribution to individual farmers. The plan worked well. By 1909 the population had mounted to 15,000; and 160,000 acres were under irrigation.[9]

[7] Rockwood, *Born of the Desert*, pp. 17–21; J. A. Alexander, *The Life of George Chaffey* (Melbourne, 1928), pp. 283–294; M. J. Dowd, "History of Imperial Irrigation District and the Development of Imperial Valley," typescript (El Centro, Calif., 1956), p. 18, copy in library of the Imperial Irrigation District, El Centro, Calif.; Tout, *First Thirty Years*, pp. 29–40, 45–50, 162, passim; Edgar F. Howe and Wilbur J. Hall, *The Story of the First Decade* (Imperial, 1910), pp. 39–65, passim.

[8] Tout, *First Thirty Years*, p. 48.

[9] "Irrigation in Imperial Valley," pp. 14–16; Tout, *First Thirty Years*, pp. 34–35, 48, 190; "Report of the American Section of the

Though the rapid influx of settlers and the ready market that farmers found for their crops pleased valley leaders, other developments began causing concern. Especially vexing was the valley's deteriorating relationship with Mexico, a predicament stemming largely from some special agreements made by Rockwood.

III

To control the diversion route below the border, Rockwood had been compelled to negotiate with Guillermo Andrade, who owned the land through which the route passed. In their agreement Andrade sold 100,000 acres, but for payment he wanted water as well as money; in fact, he demanded "all water necessary . . . for the irrigation of the other lands" below the border in which he retained an interest—more than 600,000 acres.[10] The price was not so steep as it seemed, however, since the water brought through Mexico could also be used to reclaim 85 percent of the land which Rockwood and his associates planned to purchase from Andrade. "While our principal object in purchasing this tract of land was to acquire title to the Alamo Channel," noted Rockwood, ". . . we expected, through the increase in value of the land itself, to more than repay the cost of building the entire system." [11]

International Water Commission, United States and Mexico," *H. Doc.* 359, 71 Cong., 2 sess. (1930), p. 103; Imperial County Board of Supervisors, *Imperial Valley, 1901–1915* (Los Angeles, 1915), pp. 2–5; Imperial Land Company, *Imperial Valley Catechism,* 12th ed. rev. (Los Angeles, March, 1904), pp. 1–5, passim.

[10] Copies of the contracts which Rockwood and his associates negotiated with Andrade can be found in the Colorado River Land Company Papers, M. H. Sherman Foundation, Corona del Mar, California. See, especially, the contract of June 29, 1898. I want to thank William O. Hendricks, director of the Sherman Foundation, for bringing these contracts to my attention. For an excellent discussion of the attempts by Andrade and others to develop lands along the lower Colorado in Mexico, see William O. Hendricks, "Guillermo Andrade and Land Development on the Mexican Colorado River Delta, 1874–1905" (Ph.D. diss., University of Southern California, 1967).

[11] C. R. Rockwood, "Value of Stock of Sociedad Irrigacion y Terrenos de la Baja California," n.d., C. R. Rockwood file, Water Collection, Honnold Library, Claremont Colleges, Claremont, Calif.

Mexican law complicated Rockwood's scheme, however, since foreigners were forbidden to own land within 100 kilometers of the international border. In 1898 he skirted this difficulty by creating a Mexican corporation—Sociedad de Irrigación y Terrenos de la Baja California—and placing the acreage in the company's name.[12]

News of the agreement and subsequent diversion of water angered the Mexican government, which had been unaware of the negotiations between Rockwood and Andrade. In late 1901 the Mexican ambassador lodged a strong protest in Washington, claiming that the diversion might result in "a change in the course or complete exhaustion of the Colorado River," thereby violating his country's navigation rights as guaranteed in the treaties of 1848 and 1853.[13]

The United States, however, was convinced that there was no treaty violation. Since the water had been diverted in American territory, stated investigators, Mexico could not properly claim jurisdiction over U.S. citizens within their own country. To hold otherwise would be to surrender national sovereignty. This position had been taken six years earlier by Attorney General Judson Harmon, when a similar situation had arisen with Mexico over the waters of the Rio Grande.[14]

Though dissatisfied with the American reply, Mexico did not interfere with Rockwood's operations. It had no interest in using the river for navigation, and its officials realized, reluctantly, that by 1901 the settlement of the Imperial Valley was a fait accompli. To interfere with the area's water supply now, they believed, might lead to the loss of Baja California and a "new mutilation"

[12] Rockwood, *Born of the Desert*, p. 13; Heffernan, *Personal Recollections*, p. 8; House Committee on Irrigation of Arid Lands, *Hearings on All-American Canal in Imperial County Calif.*, H.R. 6044, 66 Cong., 1 sess. (1919), pp. 105–106, 213–215; Compañía Mexicana de Terrenos del Río Colorado, S. A., *Colonización del Valle de Mexicali, B. C.* (México, D. F., 1958), p. 78.

[13] M. de Azpíroz to John Hay, November 27, 1901, in "Report of the American Section," p. 254.

[14] David D. Caldwell to Attorney General, July 15, 1902, Dept. of State Papers, file 711.1216M/533, National Archives; Marsden C. Burch to Attorney General, September 28, 1903, Dept. of State Papers, file 711.1216M/533; U.S. Attorneys General, *Official Opinions* XXI: 274–283.

of Mexico "like that . . . which North Americans have euphe-
mistically called the 'Gadsden Purchase.' " [15] Nevertheless, Mexico
was anxious to strengthen its position, and three years later it
found an opportunity to do so.

Ironically, the United States government provided the opportunity when in 1904 it refused to approve Rockwood's diversions
from the river. Even though Rockwood and his associates had
carefully established their claim under California law in 1899,
when they had filed for 10,000 cubic feet of water per second,
they had overlooked the fact that the government of the United
States, as well as that of Mexico, considered the Colorado to be a
navigable stream.[16] Thus, permission to divert water had to be
obtained from the Department of War, but Rockwood had neglected to do so.

As far as most Washington officials were concerned, the river's
value for navigation was slight. Nevertheless, navigation, even if
largely a fiction, represented a powerful weapon in the federal
arsenal, and many believed that it could be used to aid the newly
created Reclamation Service in its piecemeal attempt to develop
the Colorado. Reclamation officials planned to construct four
large reservoirs between Needles and Yuma for reclaiming 90,000
acres along the river, most of them in Arizona's Yuma Valley.
To reduce the cost of the reservoirs, they wished to include the
Imperial Valley in the project. If this were done, however, the
Reclamation Service would have to take over the operations of
Rockwood's California Development Company, a move which
would put Rockwood and his partners out of business. To
strengthen its hand, the Reclamation Service announced that the
company's diversions were illegal and then appealed to the Imperial Valley settlers to join the Yuma project.[17]

[15] Compañía Mexicana, *Colonización del Valle de Mexicali,* p. 79.

[16] A copy of the 1899 water filing can be found in the Colorado
River Land Company Papers. Rockwood and his associates filed for
water as early as 1895. Dowd, "History of Imperial Irrigation District,"
pp. 26–27; California Dept. of Public Works, Division of Engineering and Irrigation, "Irrigation Districts in California," *Bulletin No.
21,* by Frank Adams (Sacramento, 1929), p. 339; Heffernan, *Personal Recollections,* p. 5.

[17] Rockwood, *Born of the Desert,* pp. 27–28; J. B. Lippincott to
F. H. Newell, March 24, 1903, Dept. of State Papers, file 711.1216M/

Panic-stricken, Rockwood pleaded with the War Department for the necessary permission to divert water. The department refused, claiming that it could not approve projects already completed, though it promised not to interfere so long as the company's operations did not affect the river's navigability. This decision offered little comfort to Rockwood and his associates because they could not persuade Congress to declare the river more valuable for irrigation than navigation. Congress declined to come to their rescue, since it wanted to avoid disputes with Mexico over the navigation clauses and with the Reclamation Service over that agency's irrigation plans. It also doubted that the California Development Company was capable of sound management.[18]

Blocked in Washington, Rockwood and his allies soon faced a threat from another quarter. The intake of the Imperial Valley canal had silted up during the winter of 1903–1904, and the settlers were deprived of water for which they had contracted. Bypasses were cut around the headgate, but these, too, silted up; the result was crop losses and the filing of damage suits totaling a half-million dollars.[19] Frustrated now by a combination of obstacles north of the border, the company decided to ask Mexico for permission to divert water below the line.

Mexican officials observed the company's plight with increasing interest. Although they had resented the surreptitious manner in which Rockwood initially brought water into the valley, they saw

---

533; David D. Caldwell to Attorney General, July 15, 1902, Dept. of State Papers, file 711.1216M/533; Cory, *Imperial Valley and Salton Sink*, pp. 1271–1274; Dowd, "History of the Imperial Irrigation District," pp. 50–53; L. M. Holt, *The Unfriendly Attitude of the United States Government Towards the Imperial Valley* (Imperial, Calif., 1907), pp. 36–41; Howe and Hall, *Story of the First Decade*, pp. 127–133; Tout, *First Thirty Years*, pp. 97–98; J. B. Lippincott, "The Lower Colorado River" (1904), in the Joseph B. Lippincott Papers, Water Resources Center Archives, University of California, Berkeley.

[18] *Cong. Rec.*, 58 Cong., 2 sess. (1904), pp. 4963–4978; "Irrigation in Imperial Valley, California," pp. 12–13; Tout, *First Thirty Years*, pp. 97–99; Cory, *Imperial Valley and Salton Sink*, pp. 1274–1275; Rockwood, *Born of the Desert*, pp. 27–28; A. H. Heber, *Address . . . to the Settlers of Imperial Valley* (Los Angeles [1904]), pp. 7–39.

[19] Cory, *Imperial Valley and Salton Sink*, p. 1275.

that his problems gave them an opportunity to improve their own position. In May, 1904, they let him cut an intake in their country, but only in exchange for some important considerations. As Andrade had done, they insisted on water, demanding rights to as much as half the water diverted. In addition, they demanded the authority to set water rates for Mexican lands and to determine where the water would be used. They also forbade Rockwood and his associates to sell the concession to any foreign government or to enter into partnership with another country. Moreover, the entire undertaking was made subject to the Mexican judicial system, and any appeal of grievances to a foreign power would terminate the agreement.[20] While the terms were harsh, company officials believed they had no choice except to agree to them.

At first all seemed to go well. The new heading was constructed, water delivered in time for the 1904–1905 winter crops, and pressure from federal officials lessened. Since the United States could not own the concession in Mexico, the Reclamation Service dropped its attempt to merge the Imperial Valley with the Yuma Project. Encouraging news also came from the secretary of the interior, who recommended that valley settlers be protected in their present water rights.[21] Despite the promise of renewed calm, however, problems arose that in time sent valley residents scurrying for help from the same federal government from which they had earlier sought to escape.

[20] México, Secretaría de Relaciones Exteriores, Oficina de Límites y Aguas Internacionales, *El Tratado de Aguas Internacionales* (México, D. F., 1947), p. 23. A copy of the 1904 contract is in box 497, Imperial Irrigation District Papers, Imperial, California (hereafter IID Papers). A copy can also be found in House Committee on Irrigation of Arid Lands, *Hearings on All-American Canal in Imperial County, Calif.,* H.R. 6044, pp. 209–213. See also Secretario de Fomento to Secretario de Relaciones, November 16, 1905, Papers of the Comisión Internacional de Límites entre México y los Estados Unidos, file 842 (iv), Archives of the Secretaría de Relaciones Exteriores, México, D. F.; Manuel Calero to Secretario de Relaciones Exteriores, August 19, 1912, Papers of the Comisión Internacional, file 803 (i); memo from F. P. Puga, July 26, 1912, Papers of the Comisión Internacional, file 843 (i).

[21] A. H. Heber to H. G. Otis, May 19, 1905, portfolio 9, Colorado River Land Company Papers; "Use of Waters of the Lower Colorado River for Irrigation," *H. Doc. 204,* 58 Cong., 3 sess. (1905), pp. 1–2.

IV

The new difficulties stemmed primarily from the Mexican concession. Valley settlers soon found intolerable the tandem arrangement with Mexico that the concession had fastened on them. Disenchantment began growing shortly after a disastrous flood wreaked havoc in the valley from 1905 to 1907. Just as he must be held liable for so many of the area's problems, Rockwood must take a major share of the responsibility for the flood and the increased strain in relations with Mexico that it caused.

Because high water had seldom been a threat in previous winters and because his company was in financial straits, in 1904 Rockwood had failed to provide his new Mexican intake with an adequate headgate. Unfortunately for him, 1905 proved to be an unusual year. Flood waters began rising in February, gouging away at the banks surrounding the cut faster than he and his men could fill the breach with pilings and sand bags. Five floods eventually hit during the winter and spring until by August, 1905, the entire river was pouring into the intake, now a half-mile wide at its juncture with the Colorado. In a matter of weeks, much of the Salton Sink became the Salton Sea.[22]

The flood destroyed Rockwood's dream of financial fortune and ruined the California Development Company. In the spring of 1905 the firm surrendered its management and much of its stock to the Southern Pacific Railroad in exchange for help. The task challenged even the resources of the Southern Pacific, which labored until February, 1907, before railroad crews finally controlled the river. For two more years the Southern Pacific managed the valley's water affairs, until creditors forced the California Development Company into receivership. At that point relations with Mexico, already strained because Rockwood had failed to obtain Mexican approval of the engineering features of the intake, became even more tense.[23]

Part of the difficulty stemmed from the appointment of two receivers, one American and the other Mexican, to handle the company's assets. This arrangement subjected irrigation opera-

[22] Cory, *Imperial Valley and Salton Sink*, pp. 1276–1291; Tout, *First Thirty Years*, pp. 98–105.

[23] Tout, *First Thirty Years*, pp. 101, 106–110.

tions to the vagaries of two legal systems and led to numerous disagreements between the receivers. One result was that protective work on the lower river came almost to a halt, causing the levee system to deteriorate badly. Only the absence of severe flooding prevented a repetition of the earlier disaster. Compounding the problem and increasing the alarm of valley residents was the fact that the principal canal and most of the company's levees were in Mexico, while the revenue necessary to maintain those works came almost entirely from the United States. American creditors were anxious that as little money as possible be spent on maintenance and canal extensions, preferring instead that revenue be credited to the company's account. "No one seems to think it worthwhile to worry about the condition of the Alamo Channel," complained C. N. Perry, Imperial County surveyor. "Two dredgers lie moored to the bank and no one seems to care." Too many people, he grumbled, are "fighting about how to take care of the water at this end and then ignoring the fact that it has to be brought here first." [24] Not surprisingly, settlers soon began clamoring for redress. To free themselves from the receivers, they demanded public ownership of the water supply system; and to eliminate the problems with Mexico, they demanded a canal wholly in the United States, an All-American Canal.

Since valley residents considered the dual receivership their most immediate difficulty, they concentrated first on achieving public ownership. They took a major step toward their goal in 1911, when they created the Imperial Irrigation District. The leader in that movement was John M. Eshleman, a brilliant lawyer and a former state legislator from northern California, who had come to the valley four years earlier for reasons of health. Eshleman early demonstrated those qualities of leadership that would eventually make him a California lieutenant governor by winning election his first year in the valley to the district attorneyship of El Centro and by backing the town's hard-fought struggle to become the county seat of Imperial County.[25]

[24] C. N. Perry to H. T. Cory, January 31, 1912, Perry Papers, Water Collection, Honnold Library. See also Imperial Irrigation District Board of Directors, "Minutes" (October 24, 1913), I, p. 135, passim (these minutes are in the offices of the Imperial Irrigation District, El Centro, Calif.); *El Centro Progress,* February 17, 1912; Tout, *First Thirty Years,* pp. 110–111, 137.

[25] Tout, *First Thirty Years,* p. 74.

As a community leader, Eshleman realized the importance of safeguarding the valley's water supply. Together with Phil Swing, his young law partner, and Marvin Conkling, a prominent valley settler, he made a study of California's Bridgeford Act, the measure under which numerous irrigation districts had been created and under which many had failed. The three men believed that if the law were properly amended, it would provide a solution to the valley's problems. They took their message first to valley residents, whom they persuaded to approve creation of the Imperial Irrigation District, and then to the legislature, which they and others induced to enact the necessary amendments, the most important of which permitted the district to own property in a foreign country.[26] Under the amended law, the newly created district gave the people a powerful voice in valley affairs. Through the officers they elected to the board of directors, they could issue bonds; levy assessments; condemn property; and, most importantly, purchase and operate the valley's irrigation system.

Following its organization, the district moved immediately to acquire the irrigation system, but legal complications involving the two receivers and damage claims arising out of the 1905 flood delayed action until 1916. In that year the Southern Pacific purchased the assets of the old California Development Company at a receiver's sale and then, except for the company's irrigable land in Mexico (some 70,000 acres of the original 100,000-acre tract remained), turned around and sold everything to the district for $3 million. The railroad, busy with its other operations, had no wish to go into the irrigation business. The district, of course, was delighted with the railroad's decision, but to assure no violation of Mexican law, its board members agreed to place the stock of the Mexican subsidiary—now called the Compañía de Terrenos y Aguas de la Baja California—in their own names rather than in the name of the district.[27] With this move public ownership of

[26] Dowd, "History of the Imperial Irrigation District," p. 91; Tout, *First Thirty Years*, p. 114; Imperial Irrigation District Board of Directors, "Minutes" (January 4, 1912), I, pp. 20–21; Calif. Dept. of Public Works, "Irrigation Districts in California," pp. 17, 32, 334; A. L. Cowell to George L. Melton, January 14, 1913, box 491, IID Papers.

[27] Imperial Irrigation District Board of Directors, "Minutes" (January 4, 1916), II, pp. 110–118; (February 10, 1916), II, p. 127; M. J. Dowd, *The Colorado River Flood-Protection Works of Imperial Irriga-*

the canal and levees was finally achieved; and one problem, solved. But other difficulties with Mexico continued, causing many to increase their clamor for an All-American Canal.

V

Insistence on a water delivery system located wholly in the United States mounted steadily following the creation of the Imperial Irrigation District in 1911. The reasons were readily apparent. Public ownership might give valley residents greater control over their water supply, but as long as the main canal remained in Mexico, their control would be far from complete— or even decisive. This fact was dramatically brought home to them in 1911 and again in 1914, when revolutionary conditions in Mexico threatened to disrupt the supply. At one point in 1914, following the American invasion of Veracruz, about six hundred Mexican soldiers, armed with machine guns, camped just across the border. In response to the valley's frantic calls for help, the California governor sent a battalion of the state militia into the area, and it was quickly joined by a volunteer cavalry troop of local residents. Valley settlers were prepared to invade Mexico to protect their water supply.[28]

Unsettled conditions in Mexico had other disconcerting effects. Dead horses and mules were often found in the canal; so, too, were the bodies of victims of the revolution.[29] Since valley residents took most of their household water from the canal, they were understandably upset. They were also alarmed by Mexico's

---

tion District: History and Cost (n.p., July, 1951), p. 25; Tout, *First Thirty Years*, pp. 114, 121; House Committee on Irrigation of Arid Lands, *Hearings on All-American Canal in Imperial County, Calif., H.R. 6044*, p. 117. The new Mexican company had been organized in 1910 by the Southern Pacific. The Mexican government permitted it to hold the concession of the original company. Dowd, "History of the Imperial Irrigation District," pp. 78–79, 93–94.

[28] Tout, *First Thirty Years*, pp. 192–193, 196; James J. Hudson, "California National Guard and the Mexican Border, 1914–16," *California Historical Society Quarterly* XXXIV (1955): 157–158.

[29] House Committee on Irrigation and Reclamation, *Hearings on Protection and Development of Lower Colorado River Basin, H.R. 2903*, 68 Cong., 1 sess. (1924), p. 270, passim.

refusal to play a decisive role in helping to check the flood threat below the border. Because much of the land on the Mexican side sloped downward to the north, a break in the canal could lead to a duplication of the earlier disaster. The United States Congress had recognized the problem following the 1905 break and had authorized several appropriations for flood-control work, but even its aid was hampered by sensitive Mexican officials. American army engineers were compelled to don civilian clothes and to operate through a Mexican company. They also lost considerable time and encountered great difficulty in importing necessary supplies and equipment. Once the revolution broke out, they had to make special arrangements with General Esteban Cantú and other revolutionary leaders in northern Mexico who imposed requirements of their own. By 1915 Congress had decided to withdraw from the increasingly awkward situation. Believing that it had done its share, Congress refused to expend more money and thus forced valley residents to shoulder the burden of flood control in Mexico.[30]

That burden was assumed reluctantly, not only because of continued Mexican harassment, but also because of the worsening of the flood menace, which caused expenditures to increase sharply. Farmers watched the cost of protective work jump from $100,000 in 1915 to nearly $1,000,000 in 1916. Though the expense declined in 1917, it hovered around $500,000 during each of the next four years.[31] Even so, much water, perhaps 30

[30] Dowd, *Colorado River Flood-Protection Works*, pp. 6–24; "Lower Colorado River," *H. Doc. 972*, 61 Cong., 2 sess. (1910); "Work of the Interior Department," *H. Doc. 504*, 62 Cong., 2 sess. (1912), pp. 129–186; "Protection of Lands and Property in the Imperial Valley, Cal.," *H. Doc. 1476*, 63 Cong., 3 sess. (1915); "Plan for Protection of Imperial Valley, California," *H. Doc. 586*, 64 Cong., 1 sess. (1916); "Irrigation in Imperial Valley, California: Its Problems and Possibilities," *S. Doc. 246*, 60 Cong., 1 sess. (1908); "Flood Waters of the Colorado River," *S. Doc. 846*, 62 Cong., 2 sess. (1912); "Colorado River," *S. Doc. 867*, 62 Cong., 2 sess. (1912); "Imperial Valley, California," *S. Doc. 232*, 64 Cong., 1 sess. (1916); "The Colorado River in Its Relation to the Imperial Valley, California," *S. Doc. 103*, 65 Cong., 1 sess. (1917), pp. 28–31.

[31] Dowd, *Colorado River Flood-Protection Works*, pp. 61–62; see also All-American Canal Board, *Report of the All-American Canal Board* (Washington, D.C., 1920), pp. 14–15.

to 40 percent, was lost through seepage and evaporation in Mexico, where the canal's poorly defined banks merged with nearby sloughs and swampy areas.

But seepage represented a minor hindrance compared with the threat of a major flood, which constantly hung over the valley. As the silt raised the bed of the river, levees had to be strengthened and extended. This work, in turn, required a heavy cash outlay, which the valley raised through tax assessments on land. Those assessments skyrocketed from $.70 for each $100 of assessed valuation in 1915 to $3.25 in 1918, nearly a five-fold increase in three years.[32]

Of course, valley residents made money during these years of rising taxes. By 1918 they had more than 360,000 acres under cultivation and their property exceeded $100 million in value, more than nine times its worth in 1907, the year when the flood had been checked and farming operations normalized.[33] Still, many resented Mexico's refusal to share in the cost of the levees below the border, levees that protected Mexican as well as American land. They resented, too, the duties that they were often forced to pay on equipment, rock, and animals used in protective work south of the line. They denounced the requirement that all plans and specifications for improvements be cleared with officials in Mexico City, a requirement that led to costly delays and saddled them with two masters—California's state engineer and Mexico's Secretarío de Fomento—who often disagreed over how valley engineers should proceed.[34]

[32] House Committee on Irrigation of Arid Lands, *Hearings on All-American Canal in Imperial County, Calif.*, H.R. 6044, pp. 129, 147–148; House Committee on Flood Control, *Hearings on Colorado River Survey, Imperial Valley Project*, H.R. 3475, 66 Cong., 1 sess. (1919), p. 22; Ray S. Carberry to President, Imperial Water Co., January 25, 1915, Imperial Water Company No. 1 file, Water Collection, Honnold Library.

[33] "Report of the American Section," p. 103; House Committee on Irrigation of Arid Lands, *Hearings on All-American Canal in Imperial County, Calif.*, H.R. 6044, pp. 63, 108; Tout, *First Thirty Years*, p. 190.

[34] Arthur M. Nelson to W. R. Snow, December 28, [1919], box 491, IID Papers; House Committee on Irrigation of Arid Lands, *Hearings on All-American Canal in Imperial County Calif.*, H.R. 6044, pp. 116–118, passim; House Committee on Flood Control, *Hearings on Colo-*

But in order to maintain growth, they endured such hardships and did even more to secure Mexico's goodwill. "We were invited at one time," complained an irrigation district official, "to build a road of a certain length in Mexico. We are not in the road-building business, and we are under no obligation to build roads, yet we built the road." [35] Such "favors" only intensified the valley's desire to take its water supply route out of Mexico.

An even greater spur to activity among valley residents was the realization that the land in Mexico protected by their flood-control appropriations belonged to Americans. The largest single landholder on the Mexican delta was the Colorado River Land Company, a syndicate controlled by Los Angeles businessmen, the most prominent of whom was Harry Chandler, publisher of the *Los Angeles Times*. Chandler and his partners owned some 840,000 acres, which they had purchased in 1904–1905 and then leased piecemeal to Mexican; Japanese; and, especially, Chinese farmers.[36]

Chandler's use of Oriental labor intensified the anger of valley farmers who accused the Colorado River Land Company of giving to "Japs and Chinamen" water which properly belonged to "red-blooded, free Americans." The racism in their hostility was

---

rado River in Arizona, 65 Cong., 3 sess. (1919), p. 12; House Committee on Flood Control, *Hearings on Colorado River Survey, Imperial Valley Project*, H.R. 3475, pp. 16–17; Senate Committee on Irrigation and Reclamation, *Hearings on Colorado River Basin*, S. 727, 68 Cong., 2 sess. (1925), pp. 172–175. At times even U.S. immigration officials interfered with the valley's attempt to bring laborers into Mexico to work on the levees. Leroy Hall to Robert Lansing, October 16, 1918, box 488, IID Papers.

[35] House Committee on Irrigation of Arid Lands, *Hearings on All-American Canal in Imperial County, California*, H.R. *6044*, p. 118.

[36] Hendricks, "Guillermo Andrade," pp. 200–208; Aurelio de Vivanco, *Baja California al Día* ([Los Angeles], 1924), pp. 387, 389, 410; "Report of the American Section," pp. 161–162; U.S. Dept. of Commerce, Bureau of Foreign and Domestic Commerce, "Mexican West Coast and Lower California: A Commercial and Industrial Survey," *Special Agents Series No. 220*, by P. L. Bell and H. Bentley MacKenzie (Washington, D.C., 1923), pp. 306–309; House Committee on Irrigation of Arid Lands, *Hearings on All-American Canal in Imperial County, Calif.*, H.R. *6044*, p. 108; Pablo L. Martinez, *A History of Lower California* (México, D. F., 1960), pp. 530–531.

unmistakable, and they used the opportunity to denounce Asiatics
in their own country, who, they claimed, "undermine our social
standards, destroy the efficiency of our schools, and fill our court-
rooms." By aiding such people, they declared, Chandler was be-
traying "the real American home builder" and, in addition, sub-
jecting Americans to unsanitary conditions. "Who wants to drink
from a stream," asked W. H. Brooks, a member of the Imperial
County Board of Supervisors, "when he knows that there are 7,000
Chinamen, Japs, and Mexicans camped on that stream a few miles
above in Mexico?" [37]

As Brooks and others north of the line watched Chandler's
operations expand, however, they became less disturbed about
who was using water in Mexico than by the fact that water was
being used. Their attention came to focus increasingly on the concession of 1904, the agreement permitting farmers below the
border to take up to half the water diverted through Mexico.

When it was first negotiated, the concession seemed to represent no serious danger. The Mexican delta was sparsely populated,
lacked capital, and possessed inadequate means for transporting
goods to market. But the arrival of Chandler and his associates, the
containment of the 1905–1907 flood, and the completion of the
Inter-California Railroad between Mexicali and Yuma in 1909 led
to rapid development of lands below the border. As early as 1908,
about 7,000 acres were under cultivation, and within two years
that figure more than doubled and then doubled again during the
next three years. Although revolutionary conditions worried
settlers in the Imperial Valley, there was little interference with
agriculture in either country. By 1916, the year when the Imperial
Irrigation District purchased the water delivery system from the

[37] House Committee on Irrigation of Arid Lands, *Hearings on All-
American Canal in Imperial County, Calif.*, H.R. 6044, pp. 164, 173,
passim; House Committee on Flood Control, *Hearings on Colorado
River Survey, Imperial Valley Project*, H.R. 3475, pp. 16–17. Cf.
Chandler's testimony concerning the expense of flood protection in
House Committee on Irrigation and Reclamation, *Hearings on Protection and Development of Lower Colorado River Basin*, H.R. 2903,
pp. 1590–1592, 1619, *passim;* see also Epes Randolph to Carl Hayden, September 2, 1919, box 600, folder 6, Carl Hayden Papers, Arizona State University Library, Tempe.

Southern Pacific Railroad, farmers in Mexico were irrigating over 67,000 acres, planted mostly in cotton. Two years later the figure stood at 118,500 acres, and it continued to mount in response to rising cotton prices and improvements in transportation.[38]

These dramatic increases in acreage below the border alarmed settlers in the Imperial Valley. Their alarm intensified during the summer months, especially in 1916, when a marked drop in the river's flow forced the rationing of water.[39] Farmers in the United States became convinced that the limited water supply, Mexico's growth, and the 1904 concession cast a cloud over their future, a cloud which they did not think the American acquisition of Baja California could dissipate. In fact, they believed that such a move would only worsen the situation. "If you took this [Mexican] territory . . . ," announced a valley leader, "you would allow these people down there who have made contracts with the Mexican company . . . the right to go into our courts and enforce them against us and, naturally, that is what the people down there want. It would be a fine thing for them," he declared, "but it would put . . . a bunch of millionaires against a bunch of farmers, and . . . it would be absolutely ruinous to us." [40]

Imperial Valley farmers need not have worried. Mexico, too, opposed such a solution. Still sensitive over its nineteenth-century territorial losses to the United States, its leaders refused even to

[38] "Report of the American Section," p. 103; Vivanco, *Baja California al Día*, pp. 387–391; Tout, *First Thirty Years*, p. 277; U.S. Dept. of Commerce, Bureau of Foreign and Domestic Commerce, "Mexican West Coast and Lower California," pp. 299–309; Henderson, "Agriculture and Livestock Raising," pp. 209–210. Eugene Chamberlin and Pablo Martinez believe that development would have proceeded considerably faster if the Colorado River Land Company had been willing to sell its lands instead of leasing them. See Chamberlin, "Mexican Colonization versus American Interests in Lower California," *Pacific Historical Review* XX (1951): 45; Martinez, *A History of Lower California*, p. 530.

[39] House Committee on Irrigation of Arid Lands, *Hearings on All-American Canal in Imperial County, Calif.*, H.R. 6044, pp. 121, 139, 143; Tout, *First Thirty Years*, p. 121.

[40] House Committee on Irrigation of Arid Lands, *Hearings on All-American Canal in Imperial County, Calif.*, H.R. 6044, pp. 57, 128.

consider the alienation of land.[41] Unable and unwilling to solve their problem by territorial acquisition, valley spokesmen concluded that their only alternative lay in building an All-American Canal.

VI

Talk about such a canal preceded the problems with Mexico. As early as 1876, the Army Corps of Engineers had investigated the possibility only to consider it impractical. Shortly after the turn of the century, the Reclamation Service looked into such a canal as a way of tying the Imperial Valley into its Yuma Project, but the estimated costs were so high that nothing was done.[42] Though the topic attracted occasional interest thereafter, serious consideration did not begin until 1912, when the newly created Imperial Irrigation District began looking for a way to escape the Mexican receiver of the bankrupt California Development Company. On March 23 board members inquired into the possibility of a canal, but the costs—as well as the district's decision to concentrate its attention on acquiring and improving the already

[41] State Dept., memo, May 22, 1911, Dept. of State Papers, file 711.1216M/286; P. C. Knox to John D. Works, February 10, 1912, Dept. of State Papers, file 711.1216M/318. Before development below the border became extensive, the Imperial Irrigation District favored the purchase of the Mexican delta. Imperial Irrigation District to John D. Works, April 15, 1911, Dept. of State Papers, file 711.1216M/286; Imperial Irrigation District to Works, January 26, 1912, Dept. of State Papers, file 711.1216M/318.

[42] "Report of the Secretary of War," *H. Ex. Doc. 1*, 44 Cong., 2 sess. (1876), Part 2, Vol. II, pt. III, p. 337; J. B. Lippincott, "Report on the Lower Colorado River" (1904), pp. 82A–83, copy in Imperial Irrigation District Library; House Committee on Irrigation of Arid Lands, *Hearings on All-American Canal in Imperial and Coachella Valleys, Calif., H.R. 6044 and H.R. 11553*, 66 Cong. (1920), pp. 128, 572. In 1911 Judge F. C. Farr and C. K. Clarke, a construction engineer, argued for a "high line canal" connecting the valley with the river and bringing water "through a steel tunnel through the sand hills." They believed that the canal's cost could be met largely through the sale of hydroelectric energy developed along the aqueduct. *Imperial Enterprise*, September 15, 1911.

existing irrigation system—caused interest to lag.[43] Leadership then passed to Mark Rose, an aggressive, blunt-spoken farmer who was motivated by the growing problems with Mexico and his own desire to make money.

Rose had arrived in the valley in 1901 as a young man of twenty-seven anxious to make his fortune. He had gone to work on the ditch gangs of the California Development Company, saved his money, and in time became a successful farmer with scattered holdings throughout the valley. He was especially attracted by the possibilities of a 200,000-acre tract known as the East Side Mesa. The acreage was at too high an altitude to be watered by the canal through Mexico, but a canal located wholly in the United States could do the job.

To further his scheme, Rose joined with thirty associates to create the Imperial Laguna Water Company and badgered irrigation district officials for support.[44] Though he persuaded them to include the mesa lands within the district's boundaries, he found

---

[43] First reference in the district's minutes to "friction" between the two receivers which threatened to lead to a water shortage appeared on January 24, 1912. (Imperial Irrigation District Board of Directors, "Minutes" [January 24, 1912], I, p. 28). On February 28 the board discussed the possibility of surveying a "permanent supply canal line" (I, p. 33), and on March 12 it asked J. Chester Allison to gather data on reconstructing the Alamo canal, on constructing a "New High Line Canal (the so-called Rockwood Survey)," and on building a canal from Laguna Dam to the intake then being used (I, p. 35). On March 23 the board instructed its secretary to ask Rockwood for any information he had on an "All American line" (I, p. 38). Rockwood said he had no data (April 2, 1912, I, p. 40). For the district's negotiations with the railroad for the irrigation system, see the board's minutes, passim. See also Dowd, "History of the Imperial Irrigation District," pp. 99–110, passim; Tout, *First Thirty Years*, pp. 119, 137.

[44] Phil D. Swing, "The Struggle for Boulder Dam," pp. 60–61, Phil D. Swing Papers, Department of Special Collections University of California, Los Angeles; Imperial Irrigation District Board of Directors, "Minutes" (October 13, 1915), II, pp. 70–73, 80–83; House Committee on Irrigation of Arid Lands, *Hearings on All-American Canal in Imperial and Coachella Valleys, Calif., H. R. 6044 and H.R. 11553*, p. 367; Tout, *First Thirty Years*, pp. 121, 122, 151.

them unwilling to undertake construction of the expensive canal. He then decided to skirt the district's opposition by going to Washington, where in 1917 he negotiated a contract with Secretary of the Interior Franklin Lane that permitted him and his partners to build the canal if it proved feasible.[45]

News of Rose's contract alarmed irrigation district officials. They feared that he might acquire a prior water right and thus put the district in an even more precarious position on the river. They also worried that he would create a serious drainage problem for the valley if he failed to take adequate precautions when he poured water onto the sandy upland areas. To protect themselves against these threats, they quickly took defensive steps. They frustrated Rose by denying him permission to cross land which they owned in the path of his proposed route. They then went on the offensive.

"If an All-American Canal was to be built," the district's chief counsel told the board members, "they should build and operate it." [46] District officials agreed. In November, 1917, they asked the secretary of the interior to make an immediate survey to determine the cost and feasibility of an All-American Canal connecting the Imperial Valley with Laguna Dam, a small diversion facility located just north of Yuma and used since 1909 by the Reclamation Service to supply its Yuma Project.

The tie-in at Laguna Dam represented an important consideration. It offered a special advantage to Imperial Valley farmers and promised to lessen the resentment of some Yuma settlers who felt threatened by Imperial Valley operations. The problem with the Arizonans derived from difficulties experienced by the valley in diverting sufficient water during periods of low flow. At such

[45] Rose obtained authorization to investigate the possibility of constructing the canal entirely within the United States or partly in Mexico. Franklin K. Lane to Mark Rose, July 6, 1917, box 488, IID Papers; see also House Committee on Irrigation of Arid Lands, *Hearings on All-American Canal in Imperial and Coachella Valleys, Calif., H.R. 6044 and H.R. 11553*, pp. 369–374; U.S. Dept. of the Interior, *Seventeenth Annual Report of the Reclamation Service, 1917–1918* (Washington, D.C., 1918), pp. 381–382.

[46] Imperial Irrigation District Board of Directors, "Minutes" (December 19, 1916), II, p. 250; (December 23, 1916), II, p. 252; (November 13, 1917), III, p. 92; Swing, "The Struggle for Boulder Dam," p. 61, Swing Papers; *El Centro Progress*, November 11, 1917.

times an expensive weir, or small dam, was placed in the river near the Imperial Valley heading in order to raise the level high enough to permit diversion. But the weir created a flood danger to Arizona lands upstream. During periods of heavy runoff, it caused the river to back up, inundating valuable farmland and in 1916 even flooding the town of Yuma. Arizonans struck back by obtaining a court injunction forbidding the use of the weir except under carefully controlled conditions. The Imperial Irrigation District was required to post a $500,000 bond and to remove the weir before the high-water season. District officials agreed to the conditions, though reluctantly, since the building and dynamiting of the weir increased their annual operating costs by more than $100,000. In addition, the district expended some $155,000 to protect Arizona lands against erosion caused by the weir.[47] But construction of an All-American Canal with a heading at Laguna Dam promised a permanent settlement of the problem. And such a solution seemed mandatory when worried Arizonans began threatening to force removal of the weir regardless of the steps taken by the valley.

Determined to eliminate the difficulty involving the weir and to escape the threat from Mexico, district officials turned for support to Secretary of the Interior Lane and Reclamation Director Davis. Both men were sympathetic. Now that Rose had been removed from the picture, Lane agreed to a canal survey, but only on condition that the district pay $30,000, or two-thirds of the survey's cost. He also agreed to the connection at Laguna Dam, but he insisted that the district pledge $1,600,000 for the privilege. His conditions received the strong approval of valley residents at a mass meeting in early 1918. In mid-February a contract was signed with the government and a committee of three engineers, a so-called All-American Canal Board, was appointed to make the survey.[48]

[47] House Committee on Irrigation of Arid Lands, *Hearing on All-American Canal in Imperial and Coachella Valleys, Calif., H.R. 6044 and H.R. 11553*, pp. 23, 27, 124–125, passim; Dowd, "History of the Imperial Irrigation District," pp. 111–115, 117. On November 1, 1911, the district decided to approach the Reclamation Service about obtaining water from Laguna Dam. Imperial Irrigation District Board of Directors, "Minutes" (November 1, 1911), I, p. 17.

[48] Imperial Irrigation District Board of Directors, "Minutes" (Janu-

In December the engineers issued their preliminary report. To the delight of valley residents, they recommended construction of the canal, though their estimated cost of $30 million for the sixty-mile aqueduct caused some residents to have second thoughts. Still, enthusiasm remained high—so high, in fact, that in January, 1919, settlers went to the polls and voted by a five-to-two margin to endorse the irrigation district's contract with the Interior Department. Strong opposition came only from residents near Calipatria and Calexico, where Chandler and his partners owned considerable acreage.[49] Since Chandler and his friends possessed even more land in Mexico, they naturally opposed the All-American Canal as a threat to their holdings below the line.

Also unsettling to Chandler was another proposition on the ballot in 1919. It asked voters whether they favored making the Imperial Valley part of a "unified Colorado River project" in which major storage reservoirs as well as the canal would be sought. Responsible for the query were Roy McPherrin and J. S. Nickerson, two irrigation district directors who believed that the valley would never be safe without adequate storage. Their proposition received strong endorsement from the settlers, who approved it by an overwhelming vote of 2,355 to 495.[50]

ary 14, 1918), III, pp. 115–116; (February 5, 1918), III, pp. 124–126; House Committee on Irrigation of Arid Lands, *Hearings on All-American Canal in Imperial and Coachella Valleys, Calif.*, H.R. 6044 and H.R. 11553, pp. 228–229, 541; U.S. Dept. of the Interior, *Seventeenth Annual Report of the Reclamation Service, 1917–1918*, p. 382; Walter B. Kibbey to Edward C. Finney, April 23, 1920, box 488, IID Papers.

[49] The vote was 2535 to 922. Imperial Irrigation District Board of Directors, "Minutes" (January 27, 1919), III, pp. 262–264. See also All-American Canal Board, "Preliminary Report" (December, 1918), box 477, IID Papers; House Committee on Irrigation of Arid Lands, *Hearings on All-American Canal in Imperial and Coachella Valleys, Calif.*, H.R. 6044 and H.R. 11553, pp. 44, 228–234; House Committee on Irrigation and Reclamation, *Hearings on Protection and Development of Lower Colorado River Basin*, H.R. 2903, pp. 1782–1783; Tout, *First Thirty Years*, p. 348.

[50] Imperial Irrigation District Board of Directors, "Minutes" (December 24, 1918), III, p. 249; (January 27, 1919), III, p. 264.

VII

Beneath the surface, however, there was considerable disagreement among valley leaders over the question of storage. Many in favor of flood control nevertheless objected to tying the canal to any larger project. Such a move, they feared, would raise ticklish questions concerning water rights and funding that would delay, perhaps even kill, attempts to obtain the much-sought aqueduct. Their resistance lessened somewhat in March, 1919, when representatives of the West Side Irrigation Company, the Imperial Laguna Water Company, and the newly created All-American Canal Association of Los Angeles attended an irrigation district meeting. These representatives wanted to develop some 400,000 acres, mostly public land, located outside the district's boundaries and at too high an altitude to be watered by the Mexican canal. Also in attendance were officials of the Coachella Valley County Water District, who were anxious for a supplementary water supply for 100,000 acres then under cultivation but dependent primarily on a limited supply from wells. The delegates offered to join in the fight for the All-American Canal as long as they could be assured of water for their lands. After considerable discussion, board members endorsed a resolution urging "congressional action to finance and construct such canal and storage works as may be required for the irrigation of the whole of said arid lands." [51]

Despite the resolution, many valley leaders still advised against asking Congress to provide for both the canal and storage in the same bill. Once the canal was completed and Mexico's stranglehold broken, they believed that it would be a simple matter to obtain enough water for their lands. Strong support for this view came from Phil Swing, the talented chief counsel of the irrigation district and a prominent valley spokesman almost from the day of his arrival in 1907. He had earlier campaigned with Eshleman for the creation of the Imperial Irrigation District and had later served as Imperial County district attorney when Eshle-

[51] Ibid. (March 11, 1919), III, pp. 279–280; House Committee on Irrigation of Arid Lands, *Hearings on All-American Canal in Imperial and Coachella Valleys, Calif., H.R. 6044 and H.R. 11553,* pp. 17, 386.

man resigned to take a position in Governor Hiram Johnson's
administration. In 1911, following his appointment as chief counsel for the district, he supervised the purchase of the water-delivery system from the Southern Pacific and made a study of
water problems which convinced him of the need for federal
help. As early as 1918, he had gone to Washington to push for
"one great irrigation project" for the entire basin, but his experiences persuaded him that the valley would be better served
by concentrating its efforts on an All-American Canal.[52]

Swing's legal background and his knowledge of the river made
him the logical choice to direct the district's lobbying activities
in Washington. Less than two months after the March, 1919,
meeting with land speculators, he was in the capital, handing out
cantaloupes produced in the valley and conferring with William
Kettner, representative from California's 11th District, of which
the Imperial Valley was part. With him were a half-dozen other
valley lobbyists, including Mark Rose, who had decided to join
forces with the irrigation district now that his canal scheme had
been taken over by others. Rose wanted an All-American Canal,
and he did not care who promoted it so long as it was built.
Moreover, both he and Swing opposed complicating their task
with a bill calling for storage as well as a canal. Nevertheless, a
majority of the district's board of directors instructed them to
work not only for the canal but also for the "complete solution"
of the valley's "international relations and flood control" problems.[53]

In Washington the district's lobbyists began quarreling among
themselves over their instructions and the best way to proceed.
Swing and Rose precipitated the controversy by insisting on a
bill directing the Interior Department to build only a canal "of

[52] Tucson *Citizen*, January 22, 1918; Phil D. Swing, "The Struggle
for Boulder Dam," pp. 27, 35–36, 60–61, Swing Papers; Imperial
Irrigation District Board of Directors, "Minutes" (May 6, 1919), III,
pp. 298–301; Tout, *First Thirty Years*, pp. 114, 124, 257. Beverley
Moeller's *Phil Swing and Boulder Dam* (Berkeley and Los Angeles,
1971) contains no discussion of Swing's attitude toward storage during these early years.

[53] Imperial Irrigation District Board of Directors, "Minutes" (May
6, 1919), III, pp. 298–301; "Notes on Meeting of Imperial Irrigation
District, Sept. 16, 1919," box 486, IID Papers.

sufficient size and capacity" to supply the lands of the Imperial Irrigation District "as well as all other lands within the United States susceptible of practical reclamation." The reference to "other lands" represented an appeal to the land speculators and farmers who had attended the irrigation district's March meeting.

The other valley lobbyists cautioned delay and urged "a more mature investigation and canvassing of the attitude of the different Departments before taking action." Some also insisted that the bill be broadened to include flood control and a provision permitting the "Secretary of the Interior in his discretion to be able to deal with Mexico." Swing and Rose reluctantly agreed to a brief canvass, but steadfastly refused to go any further. Angered because they felt the district's instructions were being violated, two members of the lobbying committee resigned.[54]

Even before the resignations, Swing had gone to Kettner with the bill he favored. Kettner listened attentively. He sympathized with the request for the canal, but he also recognized the need for storage and had already introduced bills calling for flood control on the Colorado, as California's Charles H. Randall and Arizona's Carl Hayden had also done.[55]

Also helping to focus the attention of Kettner and others on the need for storage had been the petitions for river control submitted by chambers of commerce and regional booster groups such as the League of the Southwest, an organization claiming to repre-

[54] J. C. Allison and F. S. Lack to Imperial Irrigation District, July 2 and 22, 1919, box 486, IID Papers; see also the minutes kept by the valley's lobbyists in box 486, IID Papers.

[55] For the earlier bills introduced by Kettner, Randall, and Hayden, see *Cong. Rec.*, 65 Cong., 3 sess. (February 3, 1919), p. 2647; (February 7, 1919), p. 2934; (February 18, 1919), p. 3738; 66 Cong., 1 sess. (May 19, 1919), pp. 22, 24; (May 27, 1919), p. 309. Nevadans had also shown an interest in the Colorado, though their concern was with hydroelectricity, not flood control. In 1909 a Tonopah businessman, Henry C. Schmidt, filed an application with Arizona and the federal government to develop power at Boulder Canyon. The undertaking collapsed when the French capital to finance construction became unavailable following the outbreak of the First World War. "The Hoover Dam Documents," *H. Doc. 717*, 80 Cong., 2 sess. (1948), p. 10; Russell R. Elliott, *History of Nevada* (Lincoln, 1973), p. 275 n.

sent scores of businesses and local governments.[56] Strong additional support for reclamation along the Colorado had come from a group billing itself as the "Soldier's, Sailor's and Marine's Land Settlement Congress," which met in Salt Lake City in January, 1919. Attended by leaders from the seven Colorado Basin states, the conference had strongly endorsed an Interior Department proposal to reclaim several million acres "for homes for returned soldiers and sailors" of the First World War as well as for any others desiring "to avail themselves of the opportunity." Hailing the proposal as a way "to recognize and reward . . . the sacrifice made by men who offered their lives for the preservation of freedom," those at the Salt Lake City meeting also praised the recommendation because it would make jobs available—jobs that would help "defeat the flare-up of Bolshevikism evident among men to whom necessity knows no law." [57]

Such pressure had helped generate the flood-control bills of Kettner, Randall, and Hayden, but none of those measures had the support necessary for enactment. Congress was not aware of the seriousness and larger implications of the basin's problems, and this deficiency bothered Kettner. Still, his commitment to storage was not so strong that it made him unsympathetic to the bill brought to him by Swing. He recognized the merit of dealing separately with storage and the canal. And on June 17, 1919, he introduced a bill calling only for the construction of the much-sought aqueduct.[58]

[56] *San Diego Union,* November 17, 1917; Tucson *Arizona Daily Star,* January 20, 1918. See also Rufus B. von KleinSmid, "The League of the Southwest: What It Is and Why," *Arizona, the State Magazine,* XI (May, 1920): 5.

[57] Salt Lake City *Desert Evening News,* January 18, 20, and 21, 1919; *Salt Lake Tribune,* January 18 and 19, 1919.

[58] *Cong. Rec.,* 66 Cong., 1 sess. (1919), p. 1258; House Committee on Irrigation of Arid Lands, *Hearings on All-American Canal in Imperial County, Calif.,* H.R. 6044, p. 8; House Committee on Flood Control, *Hearings on Colorado River Survey, Imperial Valley Project,* H.R. 3475, pp. 17–18; Tout, *First Thirty Years,* p. 124. In his reminiscences, Swing nods when he suggests that all along he favored a bill providing for both storage and the canal. Swing, "The Struggle for Boulder Dam," p. 48, Swing Papers. See also Swing to W. F. McClure, September 20, 1919, Papers of the California State Engineer, Roll M-612, California Dept. of Water Resources Archives, Sacramento.

VIII

Almost immediately the measure came under sharp attack. Among the strongest critics was Arthur Powell Davis, who saw the bill as an opportunity to lobby for storage on the lower river. Davis agreed that the canal would help limit Mexican agricultural expansion, enable valley settlers to compel those below the border to share in flood-control expense, and lessen the threat to the water supply posed by revolutionary conditions. But the canal, he insisted, could offer no real solution to the valley's problems unless it was accompanied by storage. "If 300,000 or 400,000 acres of additional land is put under irrigation without storage," he argued, "it will threaten the water supply of the whole valley." Moreover, construction of the canal alone would not eliminate the flood threat from Mexico. But "if we had complete storage," he emphasized, "the flood menace would be removed." [59]

Davis's views were shared by Arizona's Carl Hayden, who not only worried about the flood threat to lands along the lower river, especially to his own state's valuable Yuma project, but who also believed that more water would have to be made available for the basin's parched lands. "There must be reservoir construction," he emphasized, and the Imperial Valley "should pay some equitable part of the cost of the water storage." [60]

Such a payment was exactly what Rose and Swing wanted to avoid. The valley "will participate in the cost of the canal," stated Rose, "but not in storage, because there is ample water" for Imperial Valley lands. "We believe we can irrigate every acre of the land without any reservoirs," he declared. Rose admitted that protective works below the border would have to be maintained, but he insisted that the canal would enable the United States to force landholders in Mexico to share levee costs. Besides,

[59] House Committee on Irrigation of Arid Lands, *Hearings on All-American Canal in Imperial and Coachella Valleys, Calif.,* H.R. *6044 and* H.R. *11553,* pp. 94, 142, passim. See also Swing, "The Struggle for Boulder Dam," p. 62, Swing Papers; House Committee on Flood Control, *Hearings on Colorado River in Arizona,* pp. 4–5.

[60] House Committee on Irrigation of Arid Lands, *Hearings on All-American Canal for Imperial and Coachella Valleys, Calif.,* H.R. *6044 and* H.R. *11553,* pp. 48–50, 94, 287. Hayden eventually drafted a bill which reflected his desires on these and other points. Ibid., pp. 265–269.

he emphasized, even if the river broke loose, it would first "flood the Mexican land." "And that land does not belong to Mexicans," he reminded Congress. "It belongs to some good, shrewd Americans, and they are not going down there and cut that levee" or allow it to be breached by flood waters.[61]

Swing also argued against storage, particularly on the upper river, claiming that it would menace the valley's water rights. "If we built storage, we would have no way of policing the stream and preventing upstream diverters from taking all they need," he explained. Nor, he added, would storage aid the valley in its attempt to escape from Mexico. In fact, if storage preceded the construction of the canal, Mexico's encroachment on the valley's water supply would be furthered. The 1904 concession, explained Swing, makes no distinction "between the natural flow and stored water." Consequently, reservoirs, by controlling the river, would make it possible for more water to be diverted into the Alamo canal and from there onto Mexican lands. But the All-American Canal was mandatory, argued Swing, for without it Mexico would eventually take all the water. Swing had no evidence to support such a claim, but this lack proved no deterrent. "These Mexican . . . lands menace us like a great sponge," he declared, "which threatens to absorb more and more water, until such time as they will take all of the natural flow of the river." [62]

Rose and Swing had no trouble convincing most of their listeners that a canal was necessary, but few accepted their objections to storage. The two men were unable to counter the claims of Davis and other Interior Department experts who contended that reservoirs were necessary if valley lands were to be assured a year-round water supply. In addition, their fears about the valley's water rights were challenged by Davis's contention that the upper and lower portions of the basin were not in competition. "My position," stated Davis, is that "there is certainly no antagonism between irrigation in the upper valleys and irrigation in the lower valleys, provided . . . that the water is not taken out of the basin [by the upper states] and kept out; and provided, also, that storage reservoirs are not . . . used for

[61] House Committee on Irrigation of Arid Lands, *Hearings on All-American Canal in Imperial County, Calif., H.R. 6044*, pp. 37, 48, 262.
[62] Ibid., pp. 116, 127.

storage during the low-water months." The upper states "should store their water during the high-water months." [63]

Davis's position received strong support in July, 1919, less than two weeks after hearings had begun on the Kettner bill, when the three engineers hired to investigate the feasibility of the All-American Canal issued their long-awaited final report. They strongly endorsed the building of the canal, but they also urged "the early construction of storage reservoirs . . . as part of a comprehensive plan for the betterment of the water-supply conditions throughout the entire basin." [64] Davis was delighted, while Swing accepted the fact that the canal had become inseparably linked with the question of storage and bowed to the Interior Department's wishes. He agreed to a storage amendment permitting the secretary of the interior to assess costs against the lands to be benefitted. In fact, only a few days later in testimony before the House Committee on Flood Control, he reaffirmed his support for storage and even parroted Davis's claim that there would be enough water for everyone if the river were controlled. Swing's conversion seemed complete; and it pleased those irrigation district leaders who felt that he should have supported storage all along.[65]

Swing's decision helped align more closely the goals of the Imperial Valley with those of Davis and the Interior Department, but it did not guarantee congressional approval of the canal or a moratorium on attacks on the bill. Other critics proved as difficult to silence as Davis and Hayden. Secretary of State Robert Lansing objected strongly to the construction of an All-American Canal until the United States and Mexico had negotiated a treaty dividing the river's waters. Though he believed that the United States

[63] Ibid., pp. 7, 142–143, 551.

[64] All-American Canal Board, *Report,* p. 64.

[65] Swing agreed to the storage amendment even before the All-American Canal Board issued its final report. The board's preliminary report, issued in December, 1918, also called for storage. House Committee on Irrigation of Arid Lands, *Hearings on All-American Canal for Imperial and Coachella Valleys, Calif., H.R. 6044 and H.R. 11553,* pp. 8, 162, 234, 282–283; House Committee on Flood Control, *Hearings on Colorado River Survey, Imperial Valley Project, H.R. 3475,* pp. 15, 20, 22; "Notes on Meeting of Imperial Irrigation District, Sept. 16, 1919," box 486, IID Papers.

was not obligated to surrender water, he felt that "considerations of equity and comity" entitled Mexico to some of the river's flow, and he cited as precedent the 1906 treaty on the Rio Grande, which had awarded Mexico 60,000 acre-feet. "I may call to the attention of your committee," he wrote Moses Kinkaid, chairman of the House Committee on Irrigation of Arid Lands, "the apparent inconsistency which would result should the government of the United States, having acted to prevent the monopolization by private parties within the United States of the waters of the Rio Grande, provide in an analogous case for monopolization by the authorities of the United States of the waters of the Colorado River." [66]

Even more outspoken in his criticism of the bill was Secretary of the Treasury Carter Glass, who considered the measure's financial features "wholly untenable." The bill directed the Treasury Department to accept the Imperial Irrigation District's bonds; and then, to avoid the need for a congressional appropriation, it required the department to obtain funds by issuing certificates of indebtedness. In effect, it compelled the government to underwrite the project by guaranteeing the district's bonds and by itself going into debt—a move which Glass refused to countenance. The government should be paying off all national obligations, not adding to them, argued Glass, displaying the economic notions of many of his contemporaries. "If the project is meritorious," he advised, then it should be handled "in the simple old-fashioned way" with "a direct appropriation of a specific amount for the purpose." [67]

Advocates of the measure insisted that the financial arrangement was sound and that Congress lacked the funds for a direct appropriation. They also argued that construction of the canal should not await a treaty. Revolutionary conditions in Mexico would preclude successful diplomatic talks; and besides, negotiations should follow, not precede, the canal's completion so that the United States could bargain from a position of strength. In this instance, Arthur Powell Davis threw his support to those

[66] Robert Lansing to Moses Kinkaid, August 20, 1919, Dept. of State Papers, file 711.1216M/475.

[67] House Committee on Irrigation of Arid Lands, *Hearings on All-American Canal in Imperial and Coachella Valley, Calif.*, H.R. 6044 and H.R. 11553, pp. 9–10, 421.

from the Imperial Valley who argued against giving priority to a treaty. "If we . . . hold . . . that we must not take any action of this kind until we get an agreement with Mexico, it simply announces, 'We are in your hands; do with us as you please.' " [68]

Especially upset by the State Department's recommendation was the Coachella Valley's Thomas Yager, delegate from the water-starved area immediately to the northwest of the Imperial Valley. "The waters of the Colorado River are inherently ours," announced Yager, as he posed as spokesman for all Americans, "and . . . I cannot understand why our State Department suggests that comity requires so much from us." "Wherein . . . does equity and comity compel American citizens to concede rights to Mexico depriving American farmers and American lands of the water of the Colorado River?" he asked. Mark Rose was equally bitter: "It strikes me as queer that the Secretary of State of the United States should be pleading for the interest of some foreign country rather than the interests of . . . the United States." [69]

These protests disturbed many congressmen, especially those already uneasy because of certain provisions in the bill. The vexing provisions were those giving advantages to land speculators like Rose who would profit from the water which would be made available at government expense for the public lands on the East Side Mesa and elsewhere. Even some Imperial Valley leaders, including the irrigation district's board of directors, found this troubling, the more so as they noted the growing opposition to the Kettner bill. Most apprehensive were veterans' groups that joined with Elwood Mead, an internationally known irrigation expert and the chairman of the California Land Settlement Board, in demanding changes in the bill. Government lands made irrigable by construction of the All-American Canal, argued Mead and his supporters, should first be offered as small homesteads to veterans and society's less fortunate members.[70]

[68] Ibid., p. 290.

[69] Ibid., pp. 299, 302, 296, 303; Thomas Yager to Moses Kinkaid, August 26, 1919, Dept. of State Papers, file 711.1216M/478; Mark Rose to Moses Kinkaid, August 28, 1919, Dept. of State Papers, file 711.1216M/478.

[70] Imperial Irrigation District to House Committee on Arid Lands, January 20, 1920, box 491, IID Papers; Elwood Mead to W. F. McClure, September 29, 1919, Papers of the California State Engineer;

Mead and his allies soon received the open support of the Imperial Irrigation District, which realized the appeal to voters of a provision aiding veterans. In September the district urged Congress to amend the bill and give ex-servicemen a prior right to file on the new lands to be watered by the canal. This move bitterly disappointed Rose, but he refused to abandon the project. He owned other lands which he believed would benefit from the canal, and he continued in the fight to remove the valley's water supply from Mexico.[71]

Though Congress was anxious to aid veterans and sensitive to the Imperial Valley's problem, it was impressed by the reservations of Treasury Secretary Glass and Secretary of State Lansing. It refused to bring the Kettner bill to vote. Undaunted, Kettner responded to Imperial Valley pressure and introduced another measure in January, 1920. This bill provided for the canal, for preferential treatment of veterans, and for small homesteads. Developers of new lands could receive water for no "more than 160 acres . . . in any one ownership." In addition, the bill responded to the demands for storage by directing the secretary of the interior "to construct such storage reservoirs and other works as in his judgment are necessary to provide an adequate supply of water for the successful irrigation of such lands." It also proposed a financial arrangement less offensive to the Treasury Department and a provision calculated to soften the opposition of Secretary of State Lansing.[72] To placate Treasury Secretary Glass, it provided for a direct congressional appropriation—to be repaid by those benefitting from the project. To satisfy Lansing, it au-

House Committee on Irrigation of Arid Lands, *Hearings on All-American Canal in Imperial and Coachella Valleys, Calif., H.R. 6044 and H.R. 11553,* pp. 363–364, 438–488, passim. For an excellent discussion of Mead's career, see James R. Kluger, "Elwood Mead: Irrigation Engineer and Social Planner" (Ph.D. diss., University of Arizona, 1970).

[71] Imperial Irrigation District Board of Directors, "Minutes" (September 16, 1919), III, p. 354; F. H. McIver to Moses P. Kinkaid, September 22 and October 14, 1919, box 486, IID Papers.

[72] *Cong. Rec.,* 66 Cong., 2 sess. (1920), p. 1204; House Committee on Irrigation of Arid Lands, *Hearings on All-American Canal in Imperial and Coachella Valleys, Calif., H.R. 6044 and H.R. 11553,* pp. 412–413, 418, 429–430, 468, 488, passim.

thorized the secretary of the interior to supply Mexico with water unneeded in the United States, though with the understanding that such a gesture would establish no precedent. Lansing still favored a treaty, but he believed that the new provision might stimulate negotiations and consequently endorsed this second bill.[73]

In the meantime, Congress was impressed with the need to obtain detailed scientific information, particularly about storage sites, and it was also disturbed by Rose's attempt to obtain compensation for the surveys he had made under his earlier contract with the Interior Department to build a canal. Rose was even more insistent on reimbursement now that veterans were to be given preferential rights to new lands, but he opposed the storage studies because he believed they were unnecessary and would delay construction of the canal. "I don't like the idea of putting into the hands of the allies of the Mexican interests . . . an opportunity to say 'let's wait.' "[74]

But Congress elected to wait, especially after the Imperial Irrigation District repudiated Rose's position and after Arthur Powell Davis strongly underscored the need for further studies. "The most feasible point for storage . . . is in the Boulder Canyon," explained Davis, but investigations were incomplete. "We have made surveys there for a high dam," he noted, "and we were pursuing them until driven out partly by exhaustion of funds and partly by high water, and that survey needs completing."[75] Congress agreed. In May, 1920, it approved the Kinkaid Act, which directed the secretary of the interior to complete the survey and to investigate carefully the Imperial Valley's problems.[76]

By 1920 the All-American Canal had the sympathy of many congressmen. Moreover, the crusade for the canal had lent strong support to Arthur Powell Davis's plans for regulating the Colo-

[73] Robert Lansing to Moses Kinkaid, January 17, 1920, Dept. of State Papers, file 711.1216M/481.

[74] House Committee on Irrigation of Arid Lands, *Hearings on All-American Canal in Imperial and Coachella Valleys, Calif., H.R. 6044 and H.R. 11553*, p. 589.

[75] Ibid., p. 574; Imperial Irrigation District to Charles McNary, April 8, 1920, box 486, IID Papers.

[76] *Cong. Rec.*, 66 Cong., 2 sess. (1920), p. 7360.

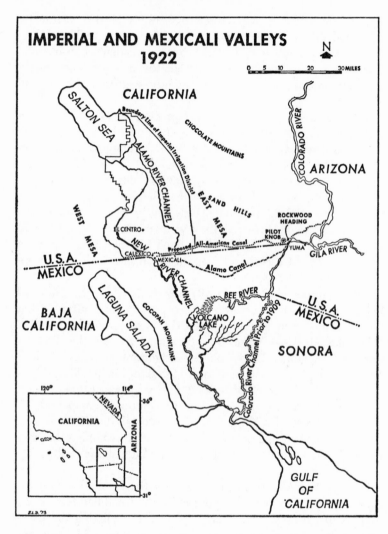

IMPERIAL AND MEXICALI VALLEYS 1922

rado River. In effect, the Reclamation Service's desire for a program of comprehensive development and the valley's demand for an All-American Canal had produced a powerful alliance. Though informal and uneasy, that alliance would alarm and frighten leaders throughout the Colorado River Basin.

3

The League and the Law

The lobbying of California's Imperial Valley settlers and the activities of Arthur Powell Davis combined to arouse water interests far beyond the borders of California. As news of Congress's action filtered into state capitals and small towns throughout the Colorado River Basin, farmers, businessmen, and politicians acknowledged once more their need to guard against threats to their water supply. They considered the future growth of their states to be inextricably tied to the waters of the Colorado, and most states had already established uses to some water flow and registered claims to much more than they were then consuming —in some cases more than they could ever conceivably consume. But once they learned of Congress's interest in a major project to control and reclaim the river's waters, they became more alert than ever.

Interstate rivalry over the waters of the Colorado was nothing new. As early as 1879, when Arizona territorial Governor John Charles Frémont had endorsed a scheme to change the climate of the Imperial Valley area by flooding the Salton Sink with Colorado River water, Arizonans had sharply objected. They did not want to share any of their precious water with California. Californians, too, had always been vigilant about reclamation

activities elsewhere, especially in Mexico, but also in the upper
basin, where most of the river's waters originated. Whenever developments upstream seemed to pose a serious threat, as in 1912,
when Coloradoans planned to take water by tunnel to another
river basin, Californians had made strong protests.[1]

Responsible for the apprehension permeating the basin were
considerations obvious to all observant westerners. One consideration was geography: the Colorado's water supply was limited
(though exactly how limited no one knew for sure), while the
ambitions of those wishing to utilize the river's waters were not.
Equally serious was the western law of waters, a complex, ever-
changing body of doctrine that confused disputants and exacerbated tensions. These two considerations—a limited water supply
and a disconcerting legal system—alarmed water leaders throughout the basin, especially those in more slowly developing areas
who were wary of the influence exercised by Californians in
Washington. The more thoughtful recognized that unless everyone could overcome the legal barriers and agree on a program of
reclamation and flood control, no one stood a chance of obtaining
from a money-conscious Congress the broad help that would
benefit the entire basin.

The situation was, then, characterized by almost paradoxical
sentiments—distrust coupled with the need to trust; fear of those
with whom cooperation was manadatory. That dilemma caused
many water leaders to seek a way to resolve their differences,
particularly their disagreements involving the law. No one could
transform the West from an area of low rainfall and few rivers
into a replica of the humid East, but westerners could do something about the law, a human institution that could be modified
to aid, rather than obstruct, the need for cooperation. Even before William Kettner had introduced his bills, some thought they
had found a possible solution to their problems in an organization known as the League of the Southwest, a pressure group that

[1] Prescott *Weekly Arizona Miner*, June 13, 1879; Tucson *Arizona
Citizen*, June 13, 1879. I am indebted to Bert Fireman of Arizona
State University for the information on Frémont. Imperial Irrigation
District Board of Directors, "Minutes" (November 12, 1912), I, pp.
31–32, copy in the offices of the Imperial Irrigation District, El Cen-
tro, Calif.

forced attention on those legal barriers and played a major role in the movement for the Colorado River Compact.

I

Formed in November, 1917, nearly two years before Kettner introduced his bills, the League of the Southwest only gradually assumed a position of importance in the interstate struggles over the Colorado. It began as a regional booster organization dedicated to trumpeting the beauties of the Southwest and promoting the area's economic growth. These goals clearly reflected the ideas of the league's founders, a group of business and professional men who scheduled the first convention in San Diego, where the highlight of the four-day organizational meeting was a "good-fellowship banquet" held in the Victorian opulence of the city's Hotel Del Coronado. This was an era when "good fellowship" and the promotion of business already ranked high in the scale of social values and would soon rank even higher: the 1920s spawned thousands of civic-betterment clubs, fraternal orders, trade associations, and similar groups.[2]

Like most such booster societies, the league employed patriotic themes, which received special emphasis at this initial meeting because of the reports arriving daily on the progress of the war in Europe. The United States had formally entered World War I only seven months earlier, and league organizers responded to the martial spirit sweeping the country by arranging at nearby Camp Kearny for a parade of 30,000 soldiers, who passed in review "with bands blaring and flags and guidons snapping." An even more extravagant presentation was the "Pageant of Freedom," which featured a cast of hundreds and attracted more than 25,000 spectators to what the press described as "one of the most gorgeous spectacles ever seen west of Chicago."[3]

Such lavish displays and appeals to patriotism served well the

[2] *San Diego Union*, November 14, 1917; *Los Angeles Times*, November 17, 1917; R. B. von KleinSmid, "The League of the Southwest: What It Is and Why," *Arizona, the State Magazine*, XI (May 1920): 5; Preston W. Slosson, *The Great Crusade and After, 1914–1928* (New York, 1930), p. 188.

[3] *San Diego Union*, November 18 and 19, 1917.

serious intentions of the league's organizers. Pageantry assured
news coverage and helped lure delegates—estimated at four hundred—from many parts of the Southwest. Eight states—California, Nevada, Utah, Arizona, New Mexico, Texas, Colorado,
and Oklahoma—sent representatives, and delegates also came
from as far away as England, France, Italy, Japan, China, and
Mexico, all countries keenly interested in strengthening trade ties
with the southwestern states. Guests of honor included three state
governors, a dozen mayors, and a score of university presidents
and other educational leaders. President Woodrow Wilson even
sent a personal representative, who joined with the other delegates in drafting a constitution pledging the league to "foster
closer social and commercial relations and to link the communities of the Southwest in a spirit of brotherhood and the promotion
of the civic, commercial and social interests of the territory." [4]

The need for an organization to lobby for such goals seemed
self-evident to the delegates. "We of the southwest have been
sort of orphans to the great republic of the United States," declared Lyman J. Gage, one of the keynote speakers at the opening
session and former secretary of the treasury under both William
McKinley and Theodore Roosevelt. "The resources of this great
galaxy of states, properly developed, reach beyond the wildest
dreams of avarice." But, he cautioned, "it is not the aim to antagonize" other parts of the country; rather it is "to increase the
mutual strength and to create a mutual interest in all that pertains
to the development of our section of the United States." [5]

That Gage and other San Diegans should take the lead in promoting an organization with such goals came as no surprise to
those familiar with the long struggle to establish a strong economic base in San Diego. The city possessed in microcosm many
of the problems of the Southwest. Despite its beautiful natural
harbor and the determined efforts of city fathers to attract industry, business growth had remained unimpressive. To Gage and
his fellow San Diegans, the league represented a vehicle for

[4] *Los Angeles Times*, November 16 and 17, 1917; *San Diego Union*,
November 14 and 15, 1917. See also Von KleinSmid, "The League
of the Southwest," p. 5; Arnold Kruckman to A. P. Davis, February
28, 1920, file 021.6, League of the Southwest, Bureau of Reclamation Papers, Record Group 115, National Archives.

[5] *San Diego Union*, November 15, 1917.

transforming the city into the long-sought commercial metropolis. "San Diego is the natural . . . port for the southwestern country," he explained, and its failure to achieve its potential "is attributable solely to deficient means of communication and transportation." The league could overcome such difficulties, he believed "by bringing together men of the clearest and widest vision to estimate the ultimate in the development of the resources of this wonderful country." [6] By improving the transportation system and developing the natural resources and latent industries of the Southwest, local leaders could benefit the region as well as the city. Ironically, neither the league nor any other group transformed San Diego into a major industrial center, and in a short time even the league's headquarters would move elsewhere—to Los Angeles, the city that regularly outstripped San Diego in the race for new industry. But those gathered for the meeting in 1917 could not know this. Even if they suspected it, their enthusiasm reflected no lack of confidence in the widely publicized claim that the Southwest was "destined to be the greatest empire on the face of the earth." [7]

Though San Diegans served as midwives for the birth of the league, they emphasized their strong interest in the "Great Southwest" and labored to draw others into the organizational machinery. Featured speakers included Governor Julius Gunter of Colorado, Congressman Scott Ferris of Oklahoma, and Governor Simon Bamberger of Utah. Bamberger also served as chairman of the committee that drafted the organization's constitution, and his committee had representatives from a half-dozen states. Even so, representation was selective. Though American Indians were more numerous in the Southwest than in any other part of the country, none was invited and none came. Mexico's Esteban Cantú, governor of Baja California, accepted an invitation to participate, but Mexicans were ineligible for membership. League cartographers made sure that their "Southwest" carefully observed national boundaries. Moreover, the location of the meeting ensured a prominent place for Californians; not surprisingly, in

[6] Ibid. On San Diego's struggles to establish a strong industrial base, see Richard Pourade, *The Rising Tide* (San Diego, 1967); Robert Fogelson, *The Fragmented Metropolis: Los Angeles, 1850–1930* (Cambridge, Mass., 1967), pp. 43–62.

[7] *San Diego Union*, November 16, 1917.

view of later developments, Imperial Valley delegates were well represented and one of their number, A. L. Richmond of El Centro, won the first election to the vice-presidency.[8]

Despite some imbalances, the constitution and slate of officers produced by this first meeting reflected the attempt of league organizers to obtain broad-based support. Executive authority was vested in a committee consisting of a president (the first was Rufus B. von KleinSmid, president of the University of Arizona), nine vice-presidents (one elected by the convention and eight ex-officio, the governors of the eight member states), and a secretary-treasurer. While the other officers (including the president and the one vice-president elected by the convention) were usually prominent political or social leaders whose principal occupations left them time to do little more than preside at the annual conventions, the secretary-treasurer exerted year-round influence. Although he ordinarily operated behind the scenes, he also called the meetings, established the agenda, scheduled speakers, supervised publicity, handled correspondence, and served as the only real symbol of continuity during the long intervals that usually separated meetings. In a variety of subtle and not so subtle ways, he left his imprint on the organization.

In many respects the league was fortunate to have selected as its secretary-treasurer Arnold Kruckman, a San Diego publicist and aviation enthusiast. Kruckman had sensed the desire of business and political leaders in San Diego and elsewhere in the Southwest for an organization like the league. He conceived the idea, planned the publicity barrage, directed the "Pageant of Freedom," and through his friends in San Diego city government was primarily responsible for the presence of political leaders.[9]

Though Kruckman knew the value of political backing, he and his fellow organizers were determined to keep the league from becoming the tool of any political party and thereby losing its credibility and impact. "This organization," they insisted, "is and shall always remain a non-political alliance." [10] In this boast they

[8] Ibid.; *Los Angeles Times*, November 17, 1917.

[9] *Los Angeles Times*, October 14, 1917; *San Diego Union*, November 15 and 17, 1917; enclosure in Arnold Kruckman to Will R. King, March 17, 1920, file 021.6, League of the Southwest, Bureau of Reclamation Papers.

[10] Von KleinSmid, "The League of the Southwest," p. 5.

were largely successful. In other claims, especially their contention that "the League grinds no axes, backs no particular schemes, represents no special interests or factions," they fell short, a fact later made readily apparent in their deliberations concerning the one topic which eventually dominated their meetings—the Colorado River. Their failure merely reflected the importance attached to the river by the people of the Southwest. More precisely, it also reflected the overriding interests of the kinds of people who chose to associate with the league.

Membership lists reveal that the "substantial" elements of a community—business and political leaders—joined the league, a development no doubt due to the organization's constitution, which invited membership only from "mayors of cities, town trustees, county supervisors and commissioners and members of commercial, civic and social organizations." Even more telling about the league's posture, however, was its decision to deny individuals the right to vote. Individuals could become members, but "only organizations as units" could vote. Eligible organizations included "any civic, cultural, commercial, industrial, county, city, town or state organization in the eight southwest states." "In short," explained Kruckman to a potential applicant, "any organization . . . interested in the up-building of the Southwest is eligible for full membership with vote." Thus, while the franchise was broadly distributed to groups that could afford to pay the price, it was, of course, democracy on a cash basis. Member organizations were assured that for twenty-five dollars they could purchase as many votes—and memberships—"as they see fit," and some saw fit to acquire "as many as ten memberships." [11] Though such a policy eventually created problems, initially it assured the league of sufficient income from dues to manage operations.

II

The common outlook of league members was also reflected in the three major resolutions that they passed, resolutions dealing

[11] *San Diego Union,* November 16, 1917; Arnold Kruckman to Frank C. Emerson, July 2, 1920, Papers of the Wyoming State Engineer, Colorado River Commission file, Wyoming State Archives, Cheyenne. See also enclosure in Kruckman to Will R. King, March 17, 1920, file 021.6, League of the Southwest, Bureau of Reclamation Papers.

with the war and issues affecting "the great southwest." They urged the federal War Industries Board to alter its priorities and approve the "uninterrupted construction of highways" needed to weld the region into an economic unit and to move goods of "definite military value." In a second resolution, they revealed their opinion of revolutionary unrest in Mexico as well as their attitude toward Spanish-speaking citizens north of the border. While acknowledging that "native or Spanish-Americans . . . had enlisted in the service of the nation in great numbers," they believed that "it should be the purpose of league members . . . to stimulate further enlistment both to strengthen the defensive forces of the United States and to warn non-descript factions below the border that they would find no sympathy nor aid in American territory." [12]

Though enlistments, unrest below the border, and highways were high on the league's list of priorities, so too was the Colorado River—the subject of the third major resolution. Governors Bamberger and Gunter set the stage for the league's actions by emphasizing the stream's unusual importance to southwestern development, a point made even more forcefully by Carl E. Grunsky, a noted San Francisco engineer and a former member of the Isthmian Canal Commission. Grunsky had acquired his knowledge about the Colorado while advising Imperial Valley developers on ways to hold the rampaging river in check. He detailed the seriousness of the flood threat and won league endorsement of his resolution calling for congressional aid "in solving the ever-present problem of the refractory" stream and promoting the "reclamation of lands along the river." [13] Those present also agreed to Grunsky's suggestion that the league help "organize the interests along the Colorado to co-operate" with the federal government in any undertaking. Governor Gunter accepted the responsibility of inaugurating the movement. These steps were taken quickly and with little discussion; they seemed altogether reasonable to those at the meeting, many of whom had firsthand knowledge of the river and all of whom recognized its importance

[12] *San Diego Union,* November 17, 1917.

[13] *Los Angeles Times,* November 17, 1917; *San Diego Union,* November 17, 1917. Grunsky's activities in the Imperial Valley are detailed in the Carl E. Grunsky Papers, California State Archives, Sacramento.

to southwestern development. Once the delegates had expressed their approval, they took up no other topics of consequence. Instead, satisfied that they had already accomplished a great deal, they thanked their hosts and moved for adjournment.

This first meeting was naturally full of organizational problems, banquets, parades, and self-congratulatory speeches, but the delegates had taken steps that hindsight would reveal as significant. They had attracted wide attention and established a new organization. More important, they had expressed their strong interest in the Colorado River, though discussion of the stream did not dominate the meeting and one basin state—Wyoming—had yet to join the organization. Nevertheless, they had shown their commitment to reclamation and to promoting cooperation among the basin states and the federal government. Their increasing interest in the problems of the river became readily apparent only two months later, when they gathered in Tucson, Arizona, to discuss new crises of regional concern.

III

Wartime pressures limited to fifty the number of league delegates who attended the January, 1918, meeting in Tucson. But those present were anxious to discuss the serious matters that had brought them together, especially reports of a plan to cut back rail service to the Southwest and a drought that was threatening the livelihood of everyone in the region.

Since most delegates felt that lack of adequate transportation facilities had been a principal reason for the Southwest's slow economic development, they turned immediately to the rail problem. They proceeded carefully, realizing that the difficulty was related to the nation's war effort. As the United States had increased shipments to its European allies, there had developed in railroad operations a traffic snarl that led to delays in overseas delivery of freight. According to widely circulating rumors, Washington planned to eliminate the snarl by curtailing passenger rail service throughout the country. Rumors aside, such a policy had become a possibility when President Woodrow Wilson appointed William Gibbs McAdoo to the newly created post of director general of railways and ordered him to manage the rail lines as if they belonged to the government. Acutely aware of

McAdoo's power, league delegates urged him to avoid rail cuts unless "national needs" made them absolutely mandatory, and they begged him to spell out his intentions "so that prospective tourists will not be deterred from visiting the southwest." [14]

While tourism was vital to the region's economy, far more important was water. League members expressed grave concern about the drought then gripping the Southwest and already responsible for the loss of thousands of acres of grazing land. Little hope of relief was held out by scientists, who predicted no break in the drought until fall. Especially alarmed were the cattle and sheep growers who had foolishly overstocked the public range. Even under the best of conditions, forage and water were in short supply, but now the lack of rainfall had reduced further the carrying capacity of the land. The results had been bitter competition among stockmen and the destruction by overgrazing of the public domain. To prevent the loss of remaining grazing lands and protect the livestock growers, who seemed unable to regulate themselves, league members pressed Washington to intervene. They asked federal authorities to regulate land use more carefully, to open to entry all unappropriated range land, and to formulate a comprehensive plan for the maximum utilization of the unreserved public lands.[15] Their request reflected the West's traditional willingness to turn to the federal government for help, and this tendency became even more apparent when one of them advocated renewed discussion of the Colorado River.

Too little time had elapsed since the San Diego meeting to report progress on the move to organize the Colorado River states, but Carl E. Grunsky, the consulting engineer who had introduced the resolution urging the basin states to join forces, used this opportunity to advance his cause. He counted upon the delegates' turning their full attention to the Colorado, a major source of water for all but two of the states represented at the meeting.

Grunsky elaborated on his reasons for major federal involvement, which he had only briefly sketched in San Diego. Emphasizing the "vital need" for federal assistance in eliminating "the

[14] Santa Fe New Mexican, January 19, 1918; Tucson Arizona Daily Star, January 20, 1918; Tucson Citizen, January 20, 1918.
[15] Tucson Arizona Daily Star, January 20, 1918; Santa Fe New Mexican, January 19, 1918.

annual flood menace," he called for Washington's participation in harnessing the river for hydroelectric power production and irrigation. "The government," he announced, must "aid the work of building reservoirs along the river" because the undertaking is simply "too big for private capital" and "the difficulties of financing" are too great. In addition, he proposed the creation of state boards that could aid in the discovery of feasible irrigation projects, and he called for the centralization of all federal engineering work under a single public works chief.[16]

The delegates shared Grunsky's sentiments and readily endorsed again his appeal for federal help, this time asking Washington to investigate "the entire Colorado drainage basin, with a view to selecting necessary and feasible sites and constructing and operating the works required." Only through such "unified administration and control," they claimed, could "the efficient conservation and utilization of . . . water in agriculture and in power production, and the prevention of damage by floods . . . be accomplished." Nor did the delegates neglect the international problems posed by Mexico's presence on the lower river and the complicated way in which the Imperial Valley received its water supply. They asked the State Department to open negotiations with Mexico "for a revision of the present treaties and agreements in such manner as to allow a just apportionment of water for irrigation purposes and flood control on both sides of the international boundary." [17]

But resolutions did not guarantee results—as the delegates knew. Until the basin states could agree among themselves on the actual use of water and then engage in "concerted and co-operative" lobbying activities, they stood little chance of making real progress. This candid admission was important, but even more so was the recognition that the law represented perhaps the greatest obstacle. The problem lay primarily in the confused nature of the law, especially in the significant variations in water law among the basin states and the lack of a clear-cut interstate law of waters. These formidable problems were complicated further by questions concerning international law and the rights of the federal government. In short, the delegates realized that they faced

[16] Tucson *Arizona Daily Star*, January 20, 1918.
[17] Ibid.

knotty legal issues on several levels, and they wisely asked for an interstate conference charged with "obtaining greater uniformity in the codification of water laws." Only when that was accomplished did they believe that they could find "the solution of the great problems" facing them over the Colorado River.[18]

IV

League delegates had not exaggerated the legal complexities confronting the Colorado River states, but they did not analyze those problems at the Tucson meeting. There was no reason for them to do so, for such matters had become a well-acknowledged part of life in the arid West. Legal institutions have a way of reflecting that which society holds dearest, and this was nowhere more apparent than in the western United States, where the courts had spent more time on water disputes than on anything else.

Responsible in large part for these legal hassles was the federal government. Following the acquisition of the Southwest from Mexico in 1848, Congress had decided to forego any authority that it might possess over the distribution of water rights on the public lands. Had it determined otherwise, it might have imposed a uniform system of water law on the region, though in view of the well-known difficulties that developed over the federal land policy in the area, there is no reason to assume that Congress would have devised an ideal system of water law.[19] In any event, Congress had decided to avoid the complex matter, and in 1866 it had first officially announced that intention in a law dealing with mining practice. This legislation had pledged the federal government to recognize "rights to the use of water" as determined by "local customs, laws, and the decisions of courts." [20]

By the turn of the century, subsequent legislation and Supreme Court decisions had broadened the 1866 statute until the states had been vested with complete control over water distribution. "Each State has the power," announced Clesson S. Kinney in the

18 Ibid.

19 For an excellent discussion of federal land policy, see Paul W. Gates, *History of Public Land Law Development* (Washington, D.C., 1968), passim.

20 U.S., *Statutes at Large*, XIV, p. 253.

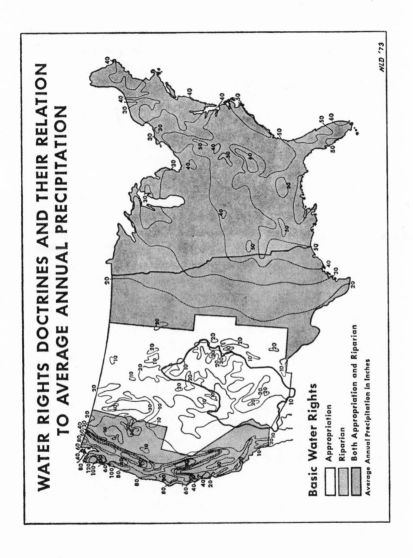

WATER RIGHTS DOCTRINES AND THEIR RELATION
TO AVERAGE ANNUAL PRECIPITATION

Basic Water Rights

Appropriation
Riparian
Both Appropriation and Riparian

Average Annual Precipitation in Inches

NLD '73

1912 edition of his monumental treatise on water law, "either by legislative enactment, or by court decision, to adopt such a rule governing the waters flowing or standing therein, as it sees fit." [21]

The decision by Congress to forego its authority had naturally encouraged the western states to chart individual courses of their own. By the time the Colorado River began attracting the attention of the League of the Southwest, the seven basin states had devised legal systems which, while reflecting agreement on many important points, also revealed significant differences. The most critical difference resulted from developments in California, a state which operated somewhat unclearly and at times contradictorily under two systems of law. Because of California's determined interest in the Colorado and its prominence as the fastest growing state in the basin, its laws were of special concern to water leaders elsewhere.

V

One legal doctrine under which Californians operated was the common law system of riparian rights. Adopted by the first legislature in 1850, the year that California entered the Union, it was the work of newcomers unfamiliar with the area's climate, but impressed with how well the common law had worked in England and in the eastern United States.[22] The riparian doctrine guaranteed to the owner of land bordering a river the full flow of the river, less only a reasonable amount taken by those upstream to satisfy domestic needs and to water livestock. An owner's right was strictly usufructuary—that is, he had a right to use the water, but he did not own the stream itself. Most important, however, he had a right to the full flow, undiminished in either quantity or quality, and he was enjoined from impairing the similar right of other riparians. Use was not necessary to create his right, nor did nonuse terminate it. Location alone was paramount, and the water right simply resided in the ownership of the land.

Californians soon realized, however, that the riparian system failed to meet adequately the needs of everyone in the state, especially the thousands of gold seekers who poured into the

[21] Clesson S. Kinney, *A Treatise on the Law of Irrigation and Water Rights and the Arid Region Doctrine of Appropriation of Waters*, 2nd ed., 4 vols. (San Francisco, 1912), I: 1025.

[22] *Calif. Stats.* (April 13, 1850), p. 219.

area in the wake of John Marshall's discovery in 1848. Taking little note of the finer points of the law, they single-mindedly pursued their search for mineral wealth, a search that relied heavily on the availability of water. Large amounts of water were imperative for working gold-bearing soil, especially the placer deposits, which attracted most newcomers. Since the diggings were often located at great distances from streams, miners unhesitatingly responded in the only way that made sense to them: they diverted the water from the rivers through flumes and ditches to the waiting sluice boxes, stamp mills, and other hydraulic machinery.

Necessity, not the law, sanctioned such actions. This hardly bothered the miners, for at first the law did not even sanction their search for gold. Nearly all the land on which they did their digging and panning belonged to the federal government, which looked on them as trespassers. But the lack of an adequate federal force in the area made it impossible to evict them. Besides, most officials believed that the presence of the miners helped strengthen the American hold on the newly acquired territory and that much of the gold, in the form of taxes, would eventually find its way into the federal treasury. "This is public land," Colonel Richard B. Mason, the military governor, told the miners, "and the gold is the property of the United States; all of you here are trespassers, but as the Government is benefited by your getting out the gold, I do not intend to interfere." [23]

The military's hands-off policy merely dramatized the legal vacuum existing in the camps of the forty-niners. The miners found themselves beyond the reach of established law, and in the American tradition of self-government that goes back to the Mayflower Compact, they responded by devising their own regulations. Acting on the assumption that natural resources like gold and water were free for the taking, they concluded that the person with the best right to them was the person who first appropriated them to his use. "Priority of discovery, location and appropriation" became the basis of all mining rights, and the principles were applied to water as well as to the mining claim to be worked.[24]

[23] Quoted in Samuel C. Wiel, *Water Rights in the Western States,* 3rd ed., 2 vols. (San Francisco, 1911), I: 72.

[24] Ibid., p. 73.

A water right thus went to the first person taking water from a stream so long as he continued to use it beneficially. Other miners might appropriate water from the same source, but priority of right went to the first user, and he did not have to own land abutting the stream. The principle evolved was a simple one—first in time, first in right—and it led to the establishment in the United States of the legal system eventually known as the arid region doctrine of appropriation. Though the practice of prior appropriation was an old one found in mining regions throughout the world,[25] it differed sharply from the riparian system. Unlike riparian law, it allowed a person to diminish the flow of a stream and even to change its course. It also severed water rights from the land, thus making them personal property, which could be sold without selling the land.

California's miners understandably began clamoring that their practices be given legal sanction. Acutely sensitive to the importance of mining in the new state's economy, the legislature responded in 1851 by approving all mining "customs, usages, or regulations." [26] But it did so in a way that planted the seeds of future conflict. It approved mining practices, but only when they were "not in conflict with the Constitution and Laws of this State"—and one state law, which in 1850 had authorized the common law, remained on the statute books. Nevertheless, as long as population remained small and mining the principal industry, no serious collision occurred between the two legal systems. In fact, within a few years the courts broadened the law so that the principle of prior appropriation could be invoked to protect the water rights of others besides miners. By 1857 the state supreme court confidently announced that "the right to

[25] According to legal scholar William Colby, "the doctrine of prior appropriation of water has been almost universally in force in the important mining regions of the world, and . . . even antedates the extant records." By tracing the doctrine to the Middle Ages, Colby challenges the claims of those who, like Clesson Kinney, believe that it originated in the California mines. William E. Colby, "The Freedom of the Miner and Its Influence on Water Law," in Max Radin, ed., *Legal Essays in Tribute to Orrin Kip McMurray* (Berkeley, 1935), pp. 67–84; cf. Kinney, *A Treatise on the Law of Irrigation*, I: 1043–1044.

[26] *Calif. Stats.* (April 29, 1851), p. 149.

appropriate the waters of the streams of this State, for mining and other purposes, has been too long settled to admit of any doubt or discussion at this time." [27]

VI

Within a few years, however, serious doubts arose as agriculture assumed an increasingly important role in the state's economy. Especially affected were those farmers who lived where rainfall was less than twenty inches and ordinary crop-growing techniques were impossible. For them irrigation was mandatory; water had to be diverted from nearby streams and often stored. But such practices denied downstream users the full flow of the river and hence violated riparian law.

The inevitable conflict between riparians and appropriators finally emerged when two groups of land- and water-hungry settlers came face to face in the San Joaquin Valley. Ranged on one side were the legendary land barons Henry Miller and his partner, Charles Lux, who owned thousands of acres in Kern County and were anxious to expand their holdings. Poised against them were two other Kern County land magnates, James Haggin and Lloyd Tevis. Both groups looked to the Kern River for the water necessary to develop their holdings, and neither wished to share the valuable stream with the other.

Haggin and Tevis took the initiative by diverting water from the river onto their fields. The step angered Miller and Lux, whose lands were downstream, and they responded by going to court and claiming that their rights as riparians had been violated. When Haggin and Tevis objected, insisting that their actions were sanctioned by the law of prior appropriation, they forced a showdown between the two great land interests and between rival doctrines of water law.

For eight years the litigants battled one another until the state supreme court in 1886 handed down a landmark decision in *Lux v. Haggin*.[28] It was a complicated as well as monumental opinion, covering more than two hundred pages in the official reports. The court announced that the riparian doctrine was paramount

[27] *Hill* v. *King,* 8 Calif. 336, 338 (1857).
[28] *Lux* v. *Haggin,* 69 Calif. 255 (1886), 4 Pac. 919 (1884), 10 Pac. 674 (1886).

in California. Citing the California legislature's adoption of the
common law in 1850, the court majority insisted that it could
reach no other conclusion. That it might have, however, is indicated by the four-to-three vote of the justices. More important,
it is also revealed in the court's careful avoidance of any statement that could have been construed as rejecting the principle
of prior appropriation. In other words, the justices placed riparian law in the ascendancy, but they did so in a way that denied
the doctrine an unqualified victory. Herein lay a dilemma that
would trouble California and the Southwest for generations.

The court, with the aid of legal legerdemain, saddled California with a dual system of water law. Its motivation was un-
complicated, but the system it produced proved far less so. The
court had faced a ticklish problem: it wanted to uphold riparian
law, yet it also recognized the necessity of accommodating appropriation. Mining custom and the dependence of agriculture
on irrigation underscored the practical wisdom of that system.
Moreover, earlier courts had too often upheld the principle to
permit its being voided out of hand. The court's solution was to
fasten on the state elements of both theories; from that formula-
tion emerged a new system, eventually dubbed the "California
doctrine."

Briefly stated, the California doctrine upheld the supremacy
of riparian law, but it also recognized the legitimacy of appropriation—so long as the appropriation was made *before* an
affected riparian land owner had acquired his property. In other
words, riparian rights were fundamental in California; they inhered in all land as soon as that land passed into private hands;
but they were also subject to appropriations made before the
transfer of title.[29]

In searching for evidence to support its theory, the court went
beyond the California statute of 1850 and grounded its system
in federal authority—or, at least, in what it claimed was federal
authority. In so doing, it emphasized another major feature of
the California doctrine, a feature that came to represent a critical
difference between California water law and the legal systems
that developed in the other Colorado River Basin states. The
court claimed that the United States was the ultimate source
of all water rights acquired on land formerly a part of the public

[29] Wiel, *Water Rights,* I: 135–138, 177–183.

domain—and the public domain embraced most land in California. The court based its contention on a principle known as the right of absolute territorial sovereignty. The United States, reasoned the court, was the original owner of the public lands, and as such it possessed absolute rights to everything on those lands, including the waters. But its water rights were those of a riparian, and this fact meant that as soon as California was acquired by the United States and even before the state legislature acted in 1850, the riparian system obtained in the area. Not only did it obtain in the area, it automatically inhered in all public land acquired from Mexico and passed naturally with the land when title was transferred to private ownership.[30]

This interpretation did not mean, however, that the government could not modify or even abrogate the riparian system. As the sole owner of the public lands and waters, the government could deal with them as it saw fit. Had it wanted, it could have insisted on strict adherence to the common law, or it could have adopted the laws of Mexico and granted concessions to certain individuals for the exclusive use of the waters. Instead, it delegated to the states the authority to control the distribution of water. But, argued the courts, this delegation did not mean that Congress had surrendered its rights to the unappropriated waters or that it could not later revoke its decision and dispose of any unappropriated waters in another fashion. As absolute sovereign, the government was free to take any of these steps.

Thus, the California doctrine rested on federal ownership and authority to control the distribution of unappropriated waters on the public domain. In later years this feature did not go unnoticed by those federal officials who were eager to have a larger role in reclamation than that envisaged in the Reclamation Act. They wanted Congress to build reservoirs trapping flood waters and then to dispose of those waters as it chose. As future developments were to make clear, this theory was rejected by the other Colorado River states and even held suspect by many Californians.[31] Predictably, however, California proved less

[30] *Lux* v. *Haggin*, 69 Calif. 336–340, passim; Kinney, *A Treatise on the Law of Irrigation*, II: 1098–1105.

[31] Californians apparently began worrying early about the extent of the federal authority over water that was implied in their theory of water law. In 1911 the state legislature announced that "all water or

suspicious of federal development of the Colorado than most states.

VII

In sharp contrast to the California doctrine was the system adopted by the other Colorado River states. Here the lead was taken in 1861 by the Colorado territorial legislature. Like California, it adopted the common law, but unlike California, it did so only to the extent that the system was "applicable" to the Colorado situation.[32] To the Colorado territorial supreme court in 1872, this provision meant the repudiation of the riparian doctrine, a view shared by the drafters of the state's constitution, who in 1876 abrogated the system and explicitly approved prior appropriation.[33]

Though California miners had earlier worked out the basic principles of the appropriation doctrine, Colorado was the first state to adopt them without equivocation. In recognition of its pioneering role, the appropriation system became known as the "Colorado doctrine" and spread rapidly to other states in the arid West, including all the Colorado Basin states except, of course, California.

The principles adopted by these states dovetailed in important essentials. Water rights could be acquired only by those who actually appropriated the water and continued to use it beneficially and in reasonable amounts. Priority of right went to users in the order in which they made their appropriations. The right

---

the use of water within the State of California is the property of the people of the State." *Calif. Stats.* (April 8, 1911), p. 821. For a discussion of subsequent developments in California water law, see, among others, Wells A. Hutchins, *The California Law of Water-Rights* (Sacramento, 1956); and Gordon R. Miller, "Shaping California Water Law, 1781 to 1928," *Southern California Quarterly,* LV (1973), 9–42.

[32] *Colo. Stats.* (October 11, 1861), p. 35.

[33] *Yunker* v. *Nichols,* 1 Colo. 551 (1872); *Coffin* v. *Left Hand Ditch Co.,* 6 Colo. 443 (1882); *Schilling* v. *Rominger,* 4 Colo. 100 (1878); *Crisman* v. *Heiderer,* 5 Colo. 589 (1881); *Sieber* v. *Frink,* 7 Colo. 148 (1883); *Fuller* v. *Swan River,* 12 Colo. 12 (1888); *Colorado Constitution,* Art. 16, secs. 5–7 (1876).

to water was usufructuary only, since, as in the riparian system, no one could own the *corpus* of the water itself. There was no restriction on the place where the water could be used, and the state was responsible for the administrative machinery governing the acquisition and determination of water rights.

The Colorado doctrine differed from California's dual system not only in practice; it also differed in its assumptions about the ultimate source of water rights and the power of Congress. Those adhering to the Colorado theory denied the basic premise of the California system: the principle that all water rights derived from the federal government as the original owner of the public lands. They admitted that the United States was the original owner of those lands, but they insisted that the federal government had immediately "left or surrendered" all ownership and control of water to each state or territory as soon as it had acquired the new lands. In other words, an appropriator acquired his title solely from the state or territory where the appropriation occurred. The riparian system never inhered in the land, either before statehood or after, and the United States possessed no water rights except those acquired under state law.[34] Thus, unlike the California doctrine, the Colorado doctrine did not permit the federal government to lay claim to the unappropriated waters on the public domain or attempt to dispose of those waters. This feature not only pointed up a fundamental difference between the two doctrines, it also represented a significant area of potential disagreement with any federal officials who wished to assert Washington's control over waters stored behind federally financed dams. Though the basin states usually resisted such moves, they were hampered by their inability to harmonize their theories of water law.

VIII

An equally serious obstacle to cooperation among the Colorado River states, and one that developed naturally from the differences already noted, was the lack of a clear-cut interstate law of waters. State officials could regulate uses within their own state's borders; but when they were forced to protect their citizens from adverse developments elsewhere, they could invoke

[34] Kinney, *A Treatise on the Law of Irrigation*, II: 1098–1124.

no readily agreed-upon principles. Consequently, the Colorado River states, like states along the West's other major streams, often acted as if they were independent nations, adopting policies calculated to further their individual self-interest.

Such premeditated self-interest brought the states into conflict and into the U.S. Supreme Court, the only tribunal with original jurisdiction in interstate disputes and the only agency then capable of formulating principles to guide the states in their dealings with one another. Unfortunately, by the time that the Colorado Basin states began agitating for development of the river, the Court had spoken too seldom to be of much help. Indeed, in only one instance had the Court dealt squarely with the issue, and the decision in that case had raised more questions than it had answered. Still, that decision, as well as another case pending in the court, troubled leaders in the basin, especially those who were looking to the League of the Southwest as a possible way out of their dilemma.

The earliest and most important decision concerning withdrawal of water from an interstate stream for consumptive use was handed down in 1907 in *Kansas* v. *Colorado*.[35] At issue were the waters of the Arkansas River, a stream rising in the Rocky Mountains and traveling some 280 miles through southeastern Colorado before entering the dry flatlands of western Kansas. The Arkansas was a relatively light-flowing stream, but its waters were vital to irrigation, and farmers in both states watched one another suspiciously. Kansans were the first to protest when they noted that increased activities upstream in Colorado were diminishing the river's flow. Since the stream's entire runoff originated in Colorado, the developments there naturally created consternation among farmers downriver, who pressed Kansas officials to take defensive action before it was too late. Kansas leaders responded by going to the Supreme Court, invoking riparian law, and demanding an end to all diversions in Colorado.

The approach adopted by Kansas was inconsistent, for the state essentially asked the Court to allow its farmers to continue diverting water from the river, while it denied the same privilege to Coloradoans. In part it felt justified in taking such action because its courts had proclaimed the riparian system paramount

---

[35] *Kansas* v. *Colorado*, 206 U.S. 46 (1907).

within the state's borders. This failed to impress critics of the state, however, who pointed out that those same courts had also made allowance for the principles of appropriation, especially when invoked to sanction irrigation in Kansas's drier western counties. In other words, Kansas, like California, operated under two legal systems, but this fact did not deter its officials from invoking only the riparian law and laying claim to the waters of the Arkansas River.

Colorado officials retaliated in kind, though they utilized a special approach of their own to justify their claim to the entire flow of the Arkansas. The riparian system would obviously not serve their purposes, but neither would their own Colorado doctrine, since many appropriations in Kansas preceded those in Colorado. Unable to invoke safely either legal system, they asked the Court to apply principles of "international law." "Colorado . . . occupies toward the State of Kansas the same position that foreign States occupy toward each other," they insisted. Consequently, "the rule of decision" that should apply "is the rule which controls foreign and independent States in their relations to each other." And that rule, they announced, should acknowledge the sovereignty possessed by Colorado "over all things within her territory, including all bodies of water." "As a sovereign and independent State," they declared, "Colorado . . . may absolutely and wholly deprive Kansas and her citizens of any use of or share in the waters of that river." [36]

The Supreme Court rejected the contentions of both Colorado and Kansas as grossly unfair. Though the states could determine for themselves whether riparian law or the appropriation doctrine would prevail within their borders, observed the Court, no state "can legislate for or impose its own policy upon the other." When an interstate dispute arises, the "cardinal rule . . . underlying all . . . relations" should be "equality of right." This rule, explained the justices, would be applied in the case. "Whenever . . . this court is called upon to settle . . . [a] dispute" between two states, they declared, it would do so "in such a way as will recognize the equal rights of both and at the same time establish justice between them. In other words," announced the justices, "through these successive disputes and decisions this court is

[36] *Kansas* v. *Colorado,* 185 U.S. 143 (1902).

practically building up what may not improperly be called interstate common law." [37]

In insisting upon "equal rights" for the disputants rather than adopting a rigid formula, the Court underscored the need to ground its decision on the particular facts—"the conditions"—of each case. In regard to this case, the Court believed that Kansas had no cause for complaint. After carefully examining evidence on the irrigation developments in both states, the justices concluded that diversions in Colorado had "worked little, if any, detriment" to Kansas, and they dismissed the suit.[38]

Though the Court settled—at least temporarily—the dispute between Kansas and Colorado, it did virtually nothing to preclude future controversies over interstate streams. The principle of "equitable apportionment" as laid down by the Court might, as the justices hoped, contribute to a body of interstate common law; but until more such decisions were available to guide future judges and disputants, prospects for settling quarrels out of court were bleak. So long as each controversy had to be settled on its own merits, future litigation seemed inevitable; and a casualty in such disputes, especially those involving several states over the same river, would be major reclamation projects. Neither private industry, the federal government, nor the states would be anxious to invest in projects for which no water might be available.

IX

Another case before the Supreme Court dealt with issues equally serious to westerners. Colorado was again involved, only this time its opponent was Wyoming and the subject of dispute was the Laramie River, a small stream rising in Colorado and flowing northward into Wyoming, where it joins the North Platte River. Wyoming, like Kansas in the earlier controversy, had become alarmed about developments in Colorado, especially the plan of Colorado corporations to divert water from the Laramie into another drainage basin. This plan would have made it impossible for the "return flow"—the diverted water not consumed by vegetation or lost to evaporation which ordinarily finds

[37] *Kansas* v. *Colorado,* 206 U.S. 95–98 (1907).
[38] Ibid., 117.

its way back to the mainstream—from Colorado irrigation projects to reenter the river for use downstream in Wyoming. In an attempt to prevent diversions in Colorado, Wyoming had filed suit in the Supreme Court in 1911.

The battle went on for years. By January, 1918, the month in which the League of the Southwest was meeting in Tucson, the litigants were preparing to argue the case for the second time before the Supreme Court. Over the years they had raised a number of major questions, but two in particular dominated the debates and held the attention of the league and others interested in the Colorado River. The first involved the question of whether a state could legally divert the waters of an interstate stream into another basin. Wyoming understandably objected to such diversions, insisting that "one would search in vain for any doctrine of equitable division" that would justify such action. Colorado disagreed vehemently, claiming that its citizens were legally entitled to make such diversions and noting correctly that Wyoming "generally recognizes and permits such diversions . . . within her own territory." [39]

The other major disagreement in the case was over what principle the Court should apply in dividing the waters of the Laramie. Just as it had done in the earlier dispute with Kansas, Colorado insisted that state sovereignty entitled it to all the waters arising within its boundaries "regardless of any prejudice that this may work to others." [40] Colorado was unwilling, however, to rest its defense only on an appeal to sovereignty, especially since the Court had already found such a position untenable in *Kansas* v. *Colorado.* Instead, the state turned for additional support to the principle of "equitable apportionment" as laid down in that decision and insisted that an examination of the physical evidence would reveal the fairness of its position. "The proof shows," it insisted, "that, not only is there ample water in the stream for use of all Wyoming enterprises, but, as well, that Wyoming needlessly wastes more water than will be withdrawn from the stream by Colorado." [41]

Wyoming emphatically denied these allegations and argued that justice would be done only if the Court applied the prin-

[39] *Wyoming* v. *Colorado,* 259 U.S. 429, 443.
[40] Ibid., 466.   [41] Ibid., 442.

ciple of prior appropriation. Since the appropriation doctrine
was the only system of water law recognized by both Wyoming
and Colorado, explained Wyoming's lawyers, it should be applied
in disputes involving the two states. "The people of both States,
by their constitutions, have declared that doctrine to be the just
and reasonable doctrine . . . and neither State could complain
of its use in settling the controversy here." [42] Thus the bickering
continued.

X

There was still another aspect of *Wyoming* v. *Colorado* that
caused anxiety, and this aspect involved the federal government
—in particular, the executive branch of the federal government.
As Wyoming and Colorado reargued their positions in 1918, they
found themselves confronted by lawyers from the U.S. attorney
general's office. The federal attorneys had persuaded the Court
to allow them to enter the case for the purpose of asserting the
authority of the United States over the unappropriated waters in
the West's unnavigable streams—an assertion that would undermine a basic assumption of the appropriation doctrine. Despite
the claims of Colorado, Wyoming, and the other states adhering
to the Colorado doctrine, the government lawyers insisted that
"the United States is, and always has been, since the cession of
the territories now comprised in those States, the owner of all
the unappropriated and surplus waters." This means, they explained, that "the United States had not surrendered to the States
or parted in any way with its original right to use the surplus
waters . . . of innavigable streams in the Western States." [43]
The implications of these arguments for the Colorado River Basin
were formidable. In short, to the extent that the Colorado was
unnavigable, the federal attorneys claimed that the government
had the right to build reclamation projects collecting the river's
surplus waters and then to distribute those waters as it saw fit,
regardless of the wishes of the individual states.

Those gathered for the league meeting in Tucson would not
learn of the government's claims for several weeks, but the news
would not surprise them. They had listened earlier to federal

[42] Ibid., 424.
[43] Ibid., 443.

lawyers make similar allegations, and they knew that the Supreme Court had thus far refused to take a definite stand on the matter. But this case might be the one in which the Court would finally decide to act, and so most westerners intensified their resistance to the federal claims and followed the legal developments with great interest.

A special reason for the heightened concern derived from the considerable influence that the federal government already exercised in the basin. Ironically, much of this influence rested on the assumption that the Colorado was navigable. In other words, while some Washington officials were attempting to expand control over the Colorado by emphasizing its unnavigability, others were asserting a case for federal authority based on their belief that the stream was navigable. The commerce clause of the Constitution, they argued, gave the United States control over navigable streams; and the War Department had already demonstrated the force of that clause to Imperial Valley developers, who for a time had been compelled to take their water out of the river at a point in Mexico in order to escape harassment. Some federal officials even asserted that if the Colorado were navigable, then the government could exercise complete jurisdiction over the stream. The chief counsel for the Reclamation Service neatly summed up the situation from the government's point of view by announcing: "In so far as the Colorado is navigable, the United States has an unquestioned superior right to control the river under the commerce clause of the Federal Constitution." [44]

Most western leaders resisted this assertion as strongly as they resisted Washington's claims to the waters of non-navigable streams. While admitting the federal government's authority over interstate commerce, they pointed out—and correctly so—that the courts had recognized state ownership of the beds of navigable rivers.[45] They also insisted—and here the courts had

[44] Ottamar Hamele, "Memorandum Concerning the Colorado River," January 20, 1922, file 032, Colorado River Project—Settlement of Water Rights, Bureau of Reclamation Papers.

[45] See, for example, *Pollard's Lessee* v. *Hagan et al.*, 3 Howard 228–229 (1845); *Shiveley* v. *Bowlby*, 152 U.S. 27–28 (1894); *Scott* v. *Lattig*, 227 U.S. 1, 242–243 (1913); *Donnelly* v. *U.S.*, 228 U.S. 260–262 (1913).

yet to speak definitively—that the states possessed jurisdiction over the waters of all streams, whether navigable or non-navigable.

Other considerations only intensified these federal-state differences. The federal government's presence as the largest landowner within the Colorado River Basin irritated sensitive state leaders and served as a visible and constant reminder of Washington's power. Especially disturbing to many was Washington's control over the issuance of licenses for hydroelectric power development on public lands and on navigable rivers. Because the states owned the beds of navigable rivers, they insisted that their permission was as necessary as that of the federal government before power plants could be constructed on navigable streams; indeed, they would have preferred to have sole authority. They also worried about the federal government's far-reaching powers as the guardian for nearly sixty thousand Indians on about thirty reservations in the basin. One of those powers—and one which federal officials had so far not exercised with vigor—derived from the government's obligation to protect the water rights of the Indians and to help them reclaim some of the 26 million acres embraced by their reservations.[46] Despite such authority, little was said about Indians or their water rights in any discussion of the Colorado River, including the deliberations at league meetings. Indians were a forgotten people in the Colorado Basin, as well as in the country at large; and their water needs, when not ignored, were considered negligible.[47]

[46] U.S. Federal Power Commission, *First Annual Report* (Washington, D.C., 1921), p. 10; Colorado River Commission, "Minutes of the Twenty-Second Meeting" (Santa Fe, November 22, 1922), part I, p. 26, in file 032, Colorado River Project, Bureau of Reclamation Papers. The statistics on Indians in the basin have been compiled from data in U.S. Dept. of the Interior, *Annual Report, 1920* (Washington, D.C., 1920), vol. II, *Report of the Commissioner of Indian Affairs*, pp. 64–73, 82–85. See also Paul Jones, "Reclamation and the Indian," *Utah Historical Quarterly* XXVII (1959): 51–56.

[47] See, for example, Colorado River Commission, "Minutes of the Twentieth Meeting" (Santa Fe, November 19, 1922), pp. 39–40; "Minutes of the Twenty-First Meeting" (Santa Fe, November 20, 1922), part I, p. 2; Delph Carpenter, *Report of Delph Carpenter, Commissioner of the State of Colorado, in Re Colorado River Compact* (n.p. [December 15, 1922]), pp. 7–8, copy in file 032, Colorado

Attracting more attention and in time becoming a major issue was the treaty-making power of the federal government. All recognized the problem created by Mexico's presence on the lower river and nearly everyone acknowledged that a treaty guaranteeing Mexico some water would have to be negotiated. The critical question, of course, involved the amount that Mexico would get. Complicating attempts to arrive at agreement was the lack of universally recognized legal standards or an international tribunal with the power of enforcement.

Those at the league meeting in Tucson skirted the Mexican issue by simply advocating that "negotiations be opened" and that Mexico be accorded a "just apportionment." [48] This attitude reflected the general lack of knowledge about developments on the lower river as well as a desire to fix Mexico's share as soon as possible. The latter was a consideration of some importance because of the precedent set in 1906 in a treaty with Mexico covering the waters of the upper Rio Grande. The United States had awarded Mexico its maximum uses prior to negotiations, but American diplomats had insisted that it need not have been so generous, and they cited an opinion handed down in 1895 by Attorney General Judson Harmon to support their contention. According to Harmon, the United States possessed absolute territorial sovereignty over its waters and hence was not obligated to give Mexico any water. Nevertheless, out of a desire "to deal with the question on principles of the highest equity and comity," it agreed to recognize Mexico's maximum uses.[49] It was this precedent that was on the minds of those urging an early treaty with Mexico on the Colorado.

River Project, Bureau of Reclamation Papers; *Proceedings of the Third Convention of the League of the Southwest at the Trinity Auditorium in Los Angeles, California, April 1, 2, 3, 1920* (Los Angeles, 1920), p. 49, copy in the Huntington Library, San Marino, Calif. The league did not pay much attention to the Indian until the organization had ceased to be an important factor in Colorado River matters. *Los Angeles Times,* June 9 and 10, 1923.

[48] Tucson *Arizona Daily Star,* January 20, 1918.

[49] Elihu Root to Joaquín Casasús, December 19, 1905, in "Report of the American Section of the International Water Commission, United States and Mexico," *H. Doc. 359, 71 Cong., 2 sess. (1930),* pp. 402–403.

Obviously those members of the League of the Southwest who had gathered in Tucson had much to ponder. Besides a drought, a rumored cutback in rail transportation, and wartime problems, they had the complicated question of the Colorado River to consider. All recognized the need to develop the river if the region were to prosper, and all were aware that any such undertaking would require a monumental investment in planning, engineering skills, and money. But they also realized that their greatest obstacles were their distrust of one another and the legal complexities that helped feed their fears—fears of one another, of the federal government, and of Mexico. For the present, they contented themselves with urging federal aid in developing the Colorado, a "just" treaty with Mexico, and cooperation in obtaining greater uniformity in state water laws.

Thus, the league fully acknowledged the problems facing the basin states and firmly committed itself to harnessing the Colorado. But it did so deliberately and with no unusual sense of urgency. Only those in the Imperial Valley felt especially threatened, but few elsewhere in the basin were either familiar with developments on the border or convinced that Mexico posed an immediate threat to them. Moreover, no one as yet had aroused congressional interest in a major reclamation scheme on the river. But the Kettner bills would soon question theories of local control and force into the open all the fears and ambitions of the basin states. When this occurred, the league would face its greatest challenge.

4

A Call for Diplomacy

The demands of the First World War and the uncertainties of the immediate postwar period deflected into other channels the energy expended on the interstate level to harness the Colorado River and to resolve the complex legal differences separating the basin states. These critical national and international emergencies made it impossible for the League of the Southwest to schedule a convention during the two years following the Tucson meeting of January, 1918.

Gradually, as the nation settled once more into the routine of peacetime, the old issues reemerged and became more complicated and more angrily debated than before the war. They dominated league deliberations and threatened to destroy all hope of harmony in the Colorado River Basin. But those same disputes also led to the discovery of a seldom-used device in the U.S. Constitution that promised to bring the basin states closer together than ever before.

I

During the postwar period, disagreement among the Colorado River states was slow to arise. State leaders at first maintained a flexible attitude that permitted them to work easily with one another, and at a basin meeting in January, 1919, in Salt Lake City, they achieved important results.

Secretary of the Interior Franklin Lane was responsible for the Salt Lake conference, a gathering attended by representatives from the seven Colorado River states. Lane had invited them to the Utah capital to consider his proposal (not spelled out in any detail) to reclaim some four million acres of public land in the basin for World War I veterans and others desiring homesteads. The convention strongly endorsed his plan and even christened its meeting the "Soldier's, Sailor's and Marine's Land Settlement Congress." [1] Of particular significance for later developments, however, was the introduction of a resolution specifying the method that should be followed in harnessing the river. "The history of irrigation throughout the world and for all time," declared the resolution, "has shown that the greatest duty of water is had by first using it upon the upper reaches of the stream, continuing the use progressively downward. In other words," it emphasized, " 'the water should first be captured and used while it is young,' for it can thus be recaptured as it returns from the performance of its duties and used over and over again." [2]

To those even remotely familiar with irrigation practice, these views seemed to represent common sense, and the delegates responded by endorsing the resolution unanimously. [3] But the

[1] Salt Lake City *Deseret News,* January 18, 19, and 20, 1919; *Salt Lake Tribune,* January 18 and 19, 1919.

[2] Salt Lake City *Deseret News,* January 21, 1919.

[3] Years later Delph Carpenter, a water leader from the state of Colorado, claimed that this resolution engendered a bitter dispute between representatives from the upper and lower sections of the Colorado River Basin. Carpenter, a veteran of many subsequent intra-basin controversies, took special delight in noting that his side won. Delph Carpenter, "The Colorado River Compact," p. 12, file 1-M/366, Herbert Hoover Papers, Hoover Presidential Library, West Branch, Iowa. (A rough draft of this memoir—with different pagination—can be found in the Delph Carpenter Papers, in the possession of Judge Donald Carpenter, Greeley, Colo.) A view similar to Carpenter's made its way into such secondary accounts as Remi Nadeau's *The*

attitudes of the basin's water leaders were far from rigid on
even such an apparently reasonable proposition. Less than fifteen
months later many of them would reverse their position. The
occasion was the first postwar meeting of the League of the
Southwest, which convened in Los Angeles in April, 1920.

II

Arnold Kruckman was ready to reassert the league's leadership
in Colorado River matters now that peace had returned, and he
succeeded in attracting to the conference more than a thousand
delegates, including four state governors and two presidential
candidates, Robert L. Owen and William Jennings Bryan. Also
in attendance were many of the same people who had been in
Salt Lake City.

The meeting was memorable not only because of the strong
turnout (though league officials had hoped for an even larger
audience), but also because of the attention devoted to the
Colorado. Discussion of river problems dominated the meeting
and culminated in a resolution that seemed to be at odds with
the sentiments expressed at Salt Lake City. Except for Wyoming,
which was not to become a league member until summer, the
other Colorado Basin states joined with Texas and Oklahoma in
urging that major development begin on the lower river rather
than on the headwaters. Specifically, they requested the Reclamation Service to complete "with diligence" its investigations so that

---

Water Seekers (New York, 1950), pp. 174–175. I can find no evidence to support this view. Nadeau cites no evidence, and Carpenter
admitted that he was not in attendance at the Salt Lake meeting or
at any intrabasin meeting until August, 1920. Moreover, both men
incorrectly identify the Salt Lake conference as the first meeting of
the League of the Southwest. Since the league was already two
years old, this was obviously not its first meeting. Moreover, as the
newspaper accounts and league correspondence in the National Archives (file 021.6, Bureau of Reclamation Papers) indicate, the Salt
Lake conference was not even a league meeting. Finally, the rather
full newspaper accounts reveal no evidence of friction, but rather
suggest the opposite in their descriptions of the unanimous support
given the resolution described above.

"prompt construction" could be made of "a great dam . . . at or near Boulder Canyon." [4]

This turnabout did not result from a bitter struggle, as some commentators have suggested, nor was it a complete repudiation of the action taken at Salt Lake City.[5] The delegates at the earlier Salt Lake meeting had merely endorsed a time-hallowed and general principle of water use. They had adopted no specific program of river development, and none of them had betrayed any fear that their action jeopardized their rights—real or imagined—to the waters of the Colorado. They had, nevertheless, endorsed a principle that did not quite square with the position taken a year later in Los Angeles.

III

The main reason for the change was simple: much had happened in the short interval between the two meetings. When basin representatives had gathered in Salt Lake City, few had been aware of the possibilities at Boulder Canyon, and no strong effort had yet been mounted for storage along the lower river. Those most concerned, the farmers and landowners in the Imperial Valley, had only begun to plan their assault on Congress; and for many of them their goal was an All-American Canal, not storage.

By April, 1920, however, as basin leaders responded to Kruckman's call and poured into Los Angeles's Trinity Auditorium for the league's third convention, the situation had dramatically changed. Congressman William Kettner and his Imperial Valley allies had learned that their canal proposal was out of the question unless they also made provisions for storage. In January, 1920, only three months before the Los Angeles meeting, they had finally bowed to the storage advocates and introduced their second bill, calling for dams and a canal. The hearings on that

[4] *Proceedings of the Third Convention of the League of the Southwest at the Trinity Auditorium in Los Angeles, California, April 1, 2, 3, 1920* (Los Angeles, 1920), p. 155, copy in the Huntington Library, San Marino, Calif. See also *Los Angeles Times*, April 4, 1920; *Denver Post*, April 4, 1920; Tucson *Arizona Daily Star*, April 4 and 7, 1920; *Salt Lake Tribune*, April 4, 1920.

[5] Cf. Nadeau, *The Water Seekers*, p. 175.

measure had ended in disappointment in March, but the debate over it and the earlier bill had served their cause well. Those discussions had highlighted the Imperial Valley's problems with Mexico, called national attention to the flood threat, and dramatized Arthur Powell Davis's interest in a high dam on the lower river. They had also underscored Davis's need for additional funds to complete important surveys. Pending in Congress at the time of the Los Angeles meeting was the Kinkaid bill, the measure that would authorize the needed surveys.

Most delegates converging on Los Angeles, especially those from areas along the lower Colorado, were aware of what was taking place in Congress. Moreover, they seemed encouraged—encouraged by Congress's receptivity, by the demands of World War I veterans for homesteads, by the growing market for hydroelectricity, and by the Reclamation Service's strong desire to build the massive projects needed to harness the river. Sharing their optimism was Kruckman, who had called the meeting because he felt the moment had finally arrived to formulate a specific plan for reclaiming the river's waters—and to do so with considerable chance of success. "It is the psychological time to present the matter properly," Kruckman had told Davis. "The minds of the people are right; their interest is keen, and . . . decisive action may be taken—in other words . . . the Southwest may determine what it wants and then set out and get it." [6]

But Kruckman's enthusiasm and the activity in Congress were not alone responsible for the league's endorsement of a Boulder Canyon dam at the Los Angeles meeting. There were other important reasons, and among them was the testimony of key government officials.

Pressing commitments elsewhere kept Davis away from Los Angeles, but he sent as his representative Frank E. Weymouth, the chief engineer of the Reclamation Service. Though Weymouth delivered his largely factual remarks in a quiet, low-key manner, the enormous possibilities that he envisaged for the basin left a deep impression on the audience. Some 2,000,000 acres were currently being irrigated, he explained, but with proper storage facilities that area could easily be more than

[6] Arnold Kruckman to A. P. Davis, February 28, 1920, file 021.6, League of the Southwest, Bureau of Reclamation Papers, Record Group 115, National Archives.

doubled to 4,400,000 acres in the United States, with an additional 800,000 acres in Mexico. And feasible dam sites were available, he stated, the most promising on the lower river being in Boulder Canyon. If investigations there proved successful, he noted, then "a dam higher than any yet built could be constructed . . . , possibly 500 or 600 feet high, and it may be possible to store as much as 25,000,000 acre feet"—the greatest annual runoff ever recorded on the Colorado. "A reservoir of that capacity," he assured them, "would largely control the floods . . . and the silt deposits," and thus prevent "any material damage for hundreds of years." In addition, "a large amount of power could be developed to operate several thousand miles of railroad which are within the limits of practical power transmission." [7]

Weymouth's remarks proved exciting, particularly to the Californians in the audience, who constituted over 80 percent of the registered delegates and who immediately sensed the value of a dam nearby rather than upstream. But neither they nor others at the meeting endorsed a Boulder Canyon dam merely because of the possibilities suggested in Weymouth's talk. In fact, he was careful not to discount the likelihood that future studies might demonstrate the wisdom of beginning development on the headwaters. Indeed, other federal engineers at the meeting pointed out that proven sites had already been located in the upper basin on the Green and Grand rivers, the Colorado's heaviest flowing tributaries, which together contributed nearly 80 percent of the river's runoff. The most important of these sites, noted Reclamation Service consulting engineer John T. Whistler, were in Utah, at Ouray on the Green River and at Dewey on the Grand River. Neither reservoir alone could control the river, but together they could harness the flood waters to the point where only minor dams would be needed downstream. Whistler suggested that the only reason for "some limited amount of storage on the lower river" would be "to take care of the little floods . . . and any little inaccuracies resulting from being unable to turn out [sufficient water] from the reservoirs a thousand miles or so above." [8]

[7] *Proceedings of the Third Convention,* pp. 33, 38.
[8] Ibid., pp. 19–20; U.S. Geological Survey, "Colorado River and Its Utilization," *Water-Supply Paper 395* (Washington, D.C., 1916), pp. 206–207.

Though Weymouth was aware of such possibilities, he was far less confident than Whistler about where development should begin. "The Service," he cautioned, "has not had sufficient funds to carry the investigation to the point where it can definitely state which reservoirs or combination of reservoirs should be constructed for the full utilization of the Colorado River." [9] Still, he did not deny the possibility that Whistler might be proven correct, and this admission was enough to encourage some delegates, particularly those from the upper basin, to insist that development should begin on the headwaters.

The strongest statements in behalf of initiating dam building in the upper basin came from spokesmen from Colorado, the state contributing more water to the stream than any other. Victor Keyes, Colorado attorney general, informed the assemblage that his state surrendered 85 percent of its water to the river and was anxious to retain part of that runoff for the development of its own lands. He reminded delegates of the principle endorsed at the Salt Lake City meeting—a principle, he argued, calculated to assure prosperity for "the whole of the great Southwest," not simply for his state. "The irrigation of lands on the headwaters of the Colorado will not interfere with the irrigation of the lands lower down." [10]

Keyes's remarks revealed that the stage was set for a bitter encounter. Such an exchange never materialized, however, largely because Keyes and the other representatives from the upper states, though convinced of the wisdom of the Salt Lake City principle, remained flexible in their approach. They were not yet firmly wedded to any particular course, a fact that became readily apparent when some of them took steps that undermined hopes for initiating major construction on the headwaters.

IV

The most important move was made by Governor Simon Bamberger of Utah. Late in the meeting he spoke out vigorously against a dam at Ouray, claiming that a reservoir there would hamper, not further, the economic development of northeastern Utah and northwestern Colorado. Such a structure, he stated, would flood some 250,000 acres of valuable land, including sev-

[9] *Proceedings of the Third Convention,* p. 37.
[10] Ibid., p. 62.

eral small towns, and also prevent the construction of a much-needed railroad line between Denver and Salt Lake City. Since Bamberger was among the highest-ranking dignitaries at the meeting, he effectively used his position to lobby against the Ouray site and went so far as to ask delegates to approve a resolution urging abandonment of a dam there "unless it shall be shown that such site is absolutely essential to the development of the Colorado River." Since no one at the meeting was prepared to argue for Ouray or for a comparable substitute site on the Green River, the resolution passed unanimously; and with it passed hopes for early development of the upper reaches.[11]

Delegates from both basins now turned their attention to Boulder Canyon and the problems along the lower river. Even representatives from Colorado found themselves impressed by government and private spokesmen who emphasized the need to control the floods that annually did damage in excess of a million dollars to the Palo Verde, Yuma, and Imperial valleys. The Imperial Valley's situation was described as particularly precarious. There the principal line of defense currently consisted of a levee located just north of Volcano Lake, a depression about twenty miles below the border into which the river had been pouring its waters since 1909. So long as the Volcano Lake levee remained secure, the flood waters could be deflected south into the Gulf of California. The problem was that over the years silt deposits had steadily raised the flood plain in the Volcano Lake area and forced defenders to raise the levee to a height that threatened its stability. "These are problems that must receive early consideration," declared C. E. Grunsky as he hammered away at a theme he had emphasized at earlier league meetings. To a round of applause he announced: "The League of the Southwest . . . should . . . secure congressional authorization for early construction work by the United States." [12]

Strong support for federal dam construction also came from Harry Chandler of the *Los Angeles Times*. Chandler was anxious for a regulated water supply for his Mexican holdings, and a year earlier he had even made a promise of financial aid to Secretary

[11] Ibid., pp. 155, 157; F. E. Weymouth to A. P. Davis, April 7, 1920, file 021.6, League of the Southwest, Bureau of Reclamation Papers.

[12] *Proceedings of the Third Convention*, p. 28.

of the Interior Franklin Lane. "If there was any proportion of the burden cast upon the United States by the development of the Colorado River," he told Lane in a private conversation, "the lands south of the line to the extent of two hundred and fifty thousand acres would stand their proportion of the expense." [13]

Though not present at the league meeting in Los Angeles, Chandler used the columns of his *Los Angeles Times* to express his backing of river development and the need for cooperation. "Mighty projects, such as . . . harnessing the Colorado River, can be undertaken and carried through to successful conclusion if all the communities of the Southwest are behind them with unity of purpose. . . . We are heirs to a great future, but let us not fight over the spoils of heirship at the risk of losing it all." [14]

V

Such appeals made sense to league delegates; so, too, did the pleas to eliminate the flood menace. Nevertheless, those appeals did not by themselves quiet concern over the issue uppermost in the minds of everyone at the meeting—the question of water rights. Before that issue could be effectively raised, however, federal engineers sought to diminish its potency by repeating what Arthur Powell Davis had told Congress during the hearings on the Kettner bills: there was plenty of water for everyone. "This is my message," announced Reclamation Service engineer John Whistler, who had spent years studying the river. "With . . . storage . . . , a sufficient irrigation supply" can be "provided for the maximum future irrigation development of all land physically and economically possible to reach." "If I am right about it, and I feel certain I am," he stated, "there should be no further cause for quarrel or disagreement between any of the seven States interested, or between this country and Mexico." Chief Engineer Frank Weymouth was in complete agreement. "Sufficient [storage] sites are believed to exist to so control the flow as to permit the irrigation of all good agricultural land that it is feasible to irrigate." [15]

[13] Franklin K. Lane to A. P. Davis, April 29, 1919, file 187, Colorado River Project, 1902–1919, Bureau of Reclamation Papers.

[14] *Los Angeles Times*, April 4, 1920.

[15] *Proceedings of the Third Convention*, pp. 17, 36.

But such claims were not confined to the government engineers who made them. They were repeated by others at the meeting until they became almost an article of faith for everyone present. Even Victor Keyes, the Colorado attorney general who had urged that development commence on the headwaters, eventually joined the chorus. "The great thing," he told the assemblage, "is that there is enough water in the Colorado River to irrigate all the basin." [16]

The ease with which delegates accepted the Reclamation Service's rosy forecasts of water supply showed merely their strong desire to *believe* that the supply was sufficient. Interstate cooperation—and development of the basin—would obviously be more easily attained if the government experts were correct or, at least, if everyone believed they were correct. And many encouraged such belief by proclaiming vigorously their high regard for the Reclamation Service's integrity and professional expertise. In time, the wisdom of some of its actions would be challenged, but not at this meeting. Instead, past accomplishments won praise as portents of the future. "It seems to me," observed F. A. Seiberling, president of the Goodyear Tire and Rubber Company, a firm with extensive investments in Arizona cotton agriculture, "that the history of the Salt River Valley of Arizona under the Roosevelt Project is indicative of what can be done, on a much greater scale, with the Colorado River." Elwood Mead, chairman of the California Land Settlement Board, was even more direct in his flattery. "Preparation of the engineering plans by the Reclamation Service insures their success," he declared in a statement reflecting the views of other spokesmen. "Nothing in our history is finer than the honesty and capacity of this corps of engineers. . . . We can be confident that if their plans are carried out the water problems will be solved." [17]

If the water supply were adequate, as the Reclamation Service claimed, and if the upper basin could not be readily developed, then the conclusion seemed obvious: the league should concentrate its efforts on Boulder Canyon, where the prospects for a major dam seemed good. This the league members did, and they did so at the urging of upper- as well as lower-basin spokesmen.

[16] *Los Angeles Times,* April 2, 1920.
[17] *Proceedings of the Third Convention,* pp. 53, 73.

"Although we are abundantly aware of our own needs and our own uses of the waters of the . . . Colorado," announced Utah's Governor Bamberger, "we realize what it means to the prosperity and future of the communities on the lower river. . . . We feel there is enough of the vital force of life in this stream so that none of us need be apprehensive concerning the needs of the other." [18]

Such encouragement produced unanimous approval of a resolution that not only recommended "prompt construction" of "a great dam . . . at or near Boulder Canyon," but also urged Congress to appropriate $50,000 so that the Reclamation Service could complete its investigation of the area for the dam site. The delegates also acknowledged that a reservoir at Boulder Canyon would "not in any way interfere with the future development of the River in the upper portions," and they called for a "working program" for the development of the entire basin. To map out the necessary program, they created a special committee, consisting of the state engineers of the seven basin states as well as engineers from the Reclamation Service, and instructed it "to study the basin as a whole and prepare a comprehensive plan for immediate action and early development." The delegates also turned their attention to the problems with Mexico and asked the president of the United States to arrange with that country for the joint control of the waters diverted through Mexican territory so that levees and other protective works below the border could be properly maintained. The need for such vigilance would lessen as soon as the Colorado was controlled, but until then a joint effort seemed the wise course.[19]

The Los Angeles meeting marked the transformation of the league into an organization with only one overriding concern—a concern that was henceforth proudly proclaimed on its official documents: "The League of the Southwest holds as axiomatic that the development of the resources of the Colorado River basin fundamentally underlies all the future progress and prosperity of the Southwest." [20] The change was reflected in membership as

[18] Ibid., p. 152.   [19] Ibid., pp. 155–157.

[20] See, for example, league correspondence in file 021.6, League of the Southwest, Bureau of Reclamation Papers. See also *Proceedings of the Third Convention.*

well as language. During the summer of 1920, Wyoming joined the league, and all other nonbasin states except Texas, which remained a member in name only, withdrew. When the membership roll was finally complete, the League of the Southwest became essentially the League of the Colorado River Basin.

But the most noteworthy feature of the Los Angeles meeting was the amity it revealed among Colorado River interests. At a time when Congress was showing considerable interest in the river, the basin states had demonstrated a remarkable ability to harmonize their interests. That harmony soon proved illusory.

VI

The Los Angeles meeting had no sooner ended than rumbles of discontent began echoing through the Colorado River Basin. At first discord was confined to the lower basin, especially to settlers and speculators in the Imperial and Coachella valleys who protested the league resolution asking for joint international control of the waters of the border region. The speculators, mostly absentee landowners who had invested in thousands of acres of undeveloped nongovernment land, voiced their displeasure through such organizations as the Imperial All American Canal Association and the West Side Imperial Irrigation Company. Both groups had headquarters in Los Angeles, and both had investors whose acreage could be watered only by a highline canal wholly within the United States.

The speculators denounced the league resolution as a "great menace" because they feared it would lead to official American recognition of Mexico's claims to half the water diverted below the border and thus to the surrender of "American rights to Mexican interests." They wanted an All-American Canal and all the water for themselves. "We . . . appeal to you . . . ," wrote officers of the West Side Imperial Irrigation Company to Davis, "to use your good office and your familiarity with this subject" to see to it that a canal is constructed "whereby we can take this American water and put it on the American land." [21]

Davis hardly needed persuasion. He already strongly supported

[21] West Side Imperial Irrigation Co. to A. P. Davis, May 28, 1920, file 021.6, League of the Southwest, Bureau of Reclamation Papers; Henry W. Elliott to John Barton Payne, June 1, 1920, file 021.6, League of the Southwest, Bureau of Reclamation Papers.

the idea of a canal, and he completely sympathized with those anxious to develop more lands north of the border. But he also believed there was plenty of water and that no threat came from either the league resolution or Mexico. Yet even if he had believed otherwise, neither he nor Californians would have had cause to worry, because State Department officials rejected the advice in the league's resolution. They pointed out that control of waters passing through Mexico rested in a corporation that was a subsidiary of the Imperial Irrigation District. "This being so," they explained, "the Department would not consider it appropriate to take action . . . unless requested to do so by the Imperial Valley Irrigation District. Up to the present time, no such request appears to have been received." [22]

Nor was such a request likely to be submitted. Most Imperial Valley leaders, like the speculators, wanted the All-American Canal completed before initiating discussions with Mexico. Besides, they knew that the terms of the concession of 1904 expressly forbade them to appeal their grievances to any government but Mexico. An appeal to Washington might lead to a termination of the concession and loss of the valley's privilege of bringing its water supply through Mexico. If that occurred before valley residents had secured an alternate route—an All-American Canal—their farms and towns would be ruined.

The protest over the resolution dealing with Mexico did more than highlight a problem that would continue to plague attempts to achieve harmony in the basin. It also suggested that not everyone accepted the Reclamation Service's claims about water supply. If storage would guarantee sufficient water, as government spokesmen at the Los Angeles meeting had insisted, then there would be no real reason to fear Mexico or to protest the league's

[22] Alvey A. Adee to Arnold Kruckman, May 4, 1920, file 021.6, League of the Southwest, Bureau of Reclamation Papers. Mexico had sent observers to the league meeting in Los Angeles and, following the conference, had asked the State Department to make sure that its "rights" were "given proper consideration in future conferences or agreements." Department officials merely promised to keep Mexico informed about any Colorado River developments that would affect that country. See memo of October 15, 1921, Papers of the Comisión Internacional de Límites entre México y los Estados Unidos, file 42 (ii), Archives of the Secretaría de Relaciones Exteriores, México, D.F.

request for joint international control of the lower river. Obviously, despite the enthusiastic response that had greeted the government's claims, not everyone was convinced.

But doubts about the sufficiency of the water supply were not limited to land speculators on the lower river. Upper-basin leaders were also uncertain. While they did not challenge the Reclamation Service's claims at this time, they soon took steps that unmistakeably revealed their doubts—doubts that eventually compelled basin leaders to devise a novel approach to their problems.

VII

The clearest public expression of upper-basin anxiety occurred in Denver in August, 1920, only four months after the Los Angeles convention of the League of the Southwest. The occasion was another league meeting. At first it was to be a gathering of only the special engineering committee that had been directed to formulate a comprehensive plan of development. Interest in the river had mounted so greatly, however, that a full-scale league convention was scheduled for August 25–27.

The meeting in Denver was significant because a large number of upper-basin representatives attended. They immediately let it be known that their attitudes had changed sharply since the Los Angeles conference. "It is no time . . . for the Western States holding the headwaters . . . to lose any of their rights for any reason whatever," announced Governor Oliver Shoup of Colorado in welcoming remarks that sounded more like a challenge than a greeting. "It is important for us . . . to make this clear to the country at large, so that our future may not be jeopardized." Former Colorado state engineer John H. Field, who took the floor shortly afterwards, was just as explicit. "We have felt in the past that we were looked upon through the large end of the telescope. . . . We wish now to have the telescope reversed, and . . . our problems and our conditions . . . studied close-up." [23]

[23] "Proceedings of the League of the Southwest, Denver, Colorado, August 25, 26, 27, 1920," typescript (n.p. [1920]), pp. 5, 28 (hereafter cited as "League of the Southwest, Denver Proceedings"). Copies of these proceedings can be found in the Papers of the Utah State Engineer, Utah State Archives, Salt Lake City, and in box 477 of the Imperial Irrigation District Papers, Imperial, Calif.

Field and others took advantage of their captive audience to describe upper-basin projects that they felt had been overlooked at earlier meetings. They admitted that the short growing season and the engineering difficulties posed by the topography of the upper-river area had slowed their development, but they believed they could make great strides in the future with proper safeguards. Indeed, they had already taken key steps, like diverting water from mountainous and less productive areas to more valuable lands outside the basin. Colorado was presently diverting some 20,000 acre-feet from the Grand River to the more arid eastern slope of the Rockies, where it was channeled to the fast-growing Denver area. Utah had embarked on a similar project and was diverting about 100,000 acre-feet from the Green River to the valley of the Great Salt Lake. That numerous lesser projects were either in operation or on the drawing boards suggested the need for caution in developing the river. "All Colorado asks is that it be not dealt with in ignorance," announced Field in a plea echoed by delegates from the other upper-basin states. "Colorado does not fear anything if proper investigation and proper consideration has been had." [24]

Obviously Field and others in the upper basin regretted their earlier endorsement of a high dam on the lower river. None of them gave the major reason for the turnabout, but it was implied in everything they said: the water supply might be inadequate. If they could not predict with precision their own future water needs, as Field admitted, then how could they be sure that the Reclamation Service could do so? Their doubts were reflected in Governor Shoup's insistence that the upper states use the Denver meeting to protect their "rights" and in Field's desire to acquaint everyone with Colorado's "problems and conditions."

But even before the meeting the upper basin's concerns had become evident, especially in the activities of the region's political and business leaders, who had sought to alert one another to the threat posed by developments below. "I am very glad indeed that this conference is to be held in Denver," Fred Lucas, a prominent Colorado businessman and an official of the Western States Reclamation Association, had written to Colorado's acting Governor George Stephan in July, "and trust it will result . . . in arousing

---

[24] "League of the Southwest, Denver Proceedings," pp. 14, 28.

Colorado people to the absolute necessity of utilizing their water resources if they ever intend to use them within the state." Particularly alarmed was A. J. McCune, Colorado state engineer and a member of the delegation that had gone to the Los Angeles meeting and supported the Boulder Canyon resolution. McCune, like so many others, now had second thoughts about what he had done. "Our main fear," he had written to a friend only a week before the Denver convention, "is that Los Angeles and the people of the Imperial Valley will get the Government committed to a policy that will interfere with our development." [25]

McCune had doubted the wisdom of a Boulder Canyon dam even at the Los Angeles meeting, when some of the dam's advocates had tried to overreach themselves. Most disturbing had been the attitude of the Los Angeles Chamber of Commerce, which had submitted a resolution asking the government to quash all development on the upper river until the Boulder Canyon project had been completed. The resolution had met with such stiff opposition that Californians wanted to forget they had ever presented it. "They did not get that resolution through," McCune later announced at the Denver meeting, "but that is what they wanted. That, of course, makes us realize what there is up here." [26]

McCune and others had left Los Angeles with doubts that grew into convictions as they pondered the upper-basin situation with more care and reflected on problems involving other rivers. They agreed that they had failed to take adequately into consideration the lessons taught them elsewhere, especially on the Rio Grande and the North Platte. In 1907 the federal government had constructed Elephant Butte Dam on the Rio Grande. That reservoir's primary purpose was to regulate the river so that the United States could deliver to Mexico some 60,000 acre-feet of water promised in a 1906 treaty. This arrangement had created no problem until the Interior Department had withdrawn from entry the public lands on the river's headwaters in Colorado. The main

[25] Fred L. Lucas to George Stephan, July 20, 1920, Records Center Container (hereafter RCC): 3, Oliver H. Shoup Papers, Colorado State Archives, Denver; A. J. McCune to George G. Anderson, July 22, 1920, RCC:3, Shoup Papers.

[26] "League of the Southwest, Denver Proceedings," p. 240. See also A. J. McCune to George G. Anderson, July 22, 1920, RCC:3, Shoup Papers.

reason for the withdrawal had been to assure sufficient water to satisfy the Mexican treaty obligation. Coloradoans were convinced that there was enough water for Mexico as well as for at least some of their lands, and they had vigorously protested the government's action. Despite the objections, federal officials had refused to modify their policy.[27]

A similar problem had been created on the North Platte River, where the Reclamation Service had constructed Pathfinder Dam in 1904. Though located in southwestern Wyoming, the reservoir had ostensibly been built to regulate water for irrigation downstream in Nebraska. Wyoming settlers had approved of the reservoir until federal authorities had placed a moratorium on future development upstream, claiming that the water was needed to fill the dam so that Nebraska irrigation could continue. This move had incensed the people of Wyoming; but despite bitter protests, they had been no more successful than Colorado in trying to get the federal government to reverse its policy. They went to the Denver meeting determined to prevent a repetition of such incidents on the Colorado River.

"For the past two years," complained Wyoming state engineer Frank C. Emerson, "the United States Government has held up rights-of-way, refused segregation, refused desert entries, because their claim was that the Pathfinder needed the water. . . . That is a thing," he stated, "that Wyoming wishes to see avoided in any land on the Colorado River." Emerson was not alone. Prominent Colorado businessman and league member J. H. Jenkins understandably agreed. He and other Coloradoans urged their friends to attend league meetings and remain on guard against a duplication of the "cursed" Rio Grande problem.[28]

Upper-basin leaders had, of course, been aware of the North Platte and Rio Grande problems long before the summer of 1920, but only then had their awareness turned to fear. In large part, this fear was because a high dam on the lower river had become much more of a possibility following the league meeting in Los Angeles. In May, just six weeks after that conference had adjourned, Congress had finally approved the Kinkaid Act, the

[27] J. H. Jenkins to Arthur J. Dodge, July 19, 1920, RCC:3, Shoup Papers; S. *Doc. 142*, 67 Cong., 2 sess. (1922), pp. 313, 316–319.

[28] "League of the Southwest, Denver Proceedings," p. 251; J. H. Jenkins to Arthur J. Dodge, July 19, 1920, RCC:3, Shoup Papers.

measure authorizing an investigation of the Imperial Valley and
the completion of surveys for lower-river storage sites.[29] Arthur
Powell Davis now had permission to complete his studies of the
Boulder Canyon area; and upper-basin leaders nervously noted
that he wasted no time in dispatching men to the field.

Davis had done even more to upset water leaders in the upper
states during the weeks following the Los Angeles meeting. He
had made two separate trips to southern California to discuss details of his plans with interested lower-basin parties. The first trip
had occurred in July, when at the request of the Los Angeles
Chamber of Commerce, he had met with fifty delegates, mostly
Californians. He had assured those from the Imperial Valley of
his support for an All-American Canal and had told everyone of
his desire to locate "a large reservoir site" on the lower river. His
listeners had promised him their full support, even asking that
the secretary of the interior be vested with "authority to determine the construction, maintenance, operation and distribution of
water" and power.[30]

News of the meeting had bothered sensitive upper-basin leaders not only because of the alliance they saw developing between
the Reclamation Service and lower-river spokesmen, but also because of indignities they had suffered at the gathering. Two
upper-basin states, Colorado and Wyoming, had sent representatives to the affair, only to find the doors barred to all but lower-
river delegates. When they finally had gained admittance, they
had discovered that no one was interested in their views. "It was
plain to me that Colorado and Wyoming had only to look on,"
George Anderson of Colorado had complained. "That was made
more so as the meeting progressed," for "the conference considered, solely, the question of constructing the Boulder Canyon
dam." Even when Davis and others had emphasized the need to
seek cooperation among all the basin states, Anderson had still
felt like an outsider, particularly when Los Angeles officials had
implied that they should have a "preferential right" to the "entire
product of power generated by the Boulder Canyon dam site." [31]

[29] *Cong. Rec.,* 66 Cong., 2 sess. (1920), p. 7360.

[30] *Los Angeles Times,* July 2 and 3, 1920; Arnold Kruckman to
Fred L. Lucas, July 3, 1920, RCC:3, Shoup Papers.

[31] George G. Anderson to Fred L. Lucas, July 3, 1920, RCC:3,
Shoup Papers; Arnold Kruckman to Fred L. Lucas, July 3, 1920,
RCC:3, Shoup Papers.

No more encouraging to the upper basin was Davis's second trip to California during the summer of 1920. The trip had culminated in a gathering in San Diego even larger than the one in Los Angeles. Some two hundred representatives, nearly all from the lower basin, had come primarily to discuss the financing of the surveys authorized by the Kinkaid Act. According to the terms of the legislation, Congress promised to put up part of the estimated cost if local interested groups, especially those in the Imperial Valley, would subscribe the balance.

Davis had received not only pledges of money, but also another strong endorsement of his plans. The *Los Angeles Times* had reflected the enthusiasm: "What was hailed as a new chapter in the epic of the transformation of the Great American Desert, a chapter surpassing in magnitude every previous inroad of modern engineering upon the desert country, is beginning to take definite form." [32]

VIII

The upper basin's change of attitude during the brief period between the league meetings in Los Angeles and Denver was most significant. The generous temper displayed in Los Angeles by upper-river delegates gave way to a defensive and suspicious outlook in Denver. Even the general public was affected. "I am very much surprised," observed Governor Thomas Campbell of Arizona, "to note here in the City . . . just a little air of combat, as though there was a big difference of opinion" over "the utilization of the waters of the Colorado." [33] Though Campbell denied the existence of any real differences, the vigor of his denial only confirmed the estrangement sensed by everyone, including Davis, who went to Denver to describe his plans and to try to ease tensions.

Davis knew better than anyone else the threat to his scheme posed by the factionalism now beginning to surface. He would need complete basin support, particularly if he were to overcome opposition developing in Congress because of disaffection elsewhere. Farm groups in the East and Midwest, for example, had

[32] *Los Angeles Times*, August 4, 1920. See also League of the Southwest, *The Southwest*, I (August, 1920): 8.

[33] "League of the Southwest, Denver Proceedings," p. 27.

earlier in the summer filed protests against Colorado River development. They feared it would only add to the current agricultural surplus and cause farm prices to plummet further. Davis knew, too, that opposition could be counted on from many eastern congressmen who looked on appropriations for reclamation as special-interest legislation that did nothing for their constituents. Moreover, any bill for Colorado River development that cleared Congress would have to do so with the approval of two key committees—the Senate Committee on Irrigation and Reclamation of Arid Lands and the House Committee on Irrigation of Arid Lands. These committees contained strong representation from states in both the upper and lower Colorado River Basins.[34] Unless the members of those committees cooperated, little could be accomplished.

To combat the alienation that he found in Denver, Davis stressed his belief that the basin states had nothing to fear from one another and that there was plenty of water. "The irrigation possibilities of the Colorado River, enormous as they are, are not too great for its water supply." In fact, he argued, the supply was greater than the demand. "The Colorado River, taken as a whole, if properly stored and conserved, will serve all of the lands that can be feasibly reached by it, and will have a surplus to spare." [35]

Storage was the key to the entire undertaking, and Davis justified his plans for dam construction on the lower river. He conceded the existence of "very abundant" storage possibilities in the

[34] As of May 1920, the thirteen-member Senate Committee on Irrigation and Reclamation of Arid Lands contained four representatives from the lower basin (Arizona, Nevada, and two from California) and three representatives from the upper basin (New Mexico, Colorado, and Wyoming). The fifteen-member House Committee on Irrigation of Arid Lands contained three representatives from the lower basin (California, Arizona, Nevada) and three from the upper basin (Colorado, Utah, and New Mexico). The chairmen of both committeees came from states outside the basin. U.S. Congress, *Official Congressional Directory: 66th Congress, 2d Session*, 3rd ed. (Washington, D.C., 1920), pp. 175, 198.

[35] "League of the Southwest, Denver Proceedings," p. 45. The pages containing Davis's talk are missing from the copy of these proceedings that is in the Papers of the Utah State Engineer, Utah State Archives. A complete copy is available in box 477, Imperial Irrigation District Papers.

upper basin, and he admitted that development of those sites
would not deprive lower states of needed water. But he believed
the weight of evidence favored construction on the lower river
first. Necessity was one reason. "The present insistent demand and
necessity for storage . . . is in the Imperial Valley and the other
lower valleys in the Colorado basin," he emphasized. Dams on
the headwaters would be a thousand miles away, and "anyone
who knows anything of irrigation and of the control of a reservoir
in accordance with the needs of irrigation and irrigation requirements knows the importance of that distance." "In other words,"
he stated, "any of the feasible reservoirs on the upper . . . Colorado . . . could not be operated at all in accordance with the
needs" of those living at the lower end of the stream.[36]

Davis cited the flood threat as an even more important reason
for beginning with a major dam on the lower river. He admitted
that most flood water originated in the upper basin and that dams
there would trap "the great majority of the water supply." But,
he insisted, capturing nearly all the runoff "has only an indirect
and not very important bearing upon flood protection." The explanation for this was simple: "The flood problem does not come
from . . . the regular freshets" that can be trapped by up-river
dams, but rather from sudden desert rainstorms further downstream that fall "upon the bare, or almost bare, mountain sides
with deep declivity" and run off "in great volume." A major dam
on the lower river, "an unprecedentedly high dam—700 feet, say
—the highest in the world," and a smaller one on the Gila, a
stream that entered the river well below Boulder Canyon, would
effectively control the downstream floods.[37]

Davis pointedly emphasized that a high dam downstream
would be a decided advantage, not a threat, to the upper states.
If upper-basin reservoirs were constructed to regulate the river,
then power production at those dams would often have to be
curtailed in order to assure sufficient water below. But with major
regulatory works on the lower river, there would be no interference with projects eventually built on the headwaters.

Nor, insisted Davis, was there any reason to fear a duplication
on the Colorado of a problem like that involving Pathfinder Dam
on the North Platte. The situations on the two rivers were entirely

[36] "League of the Southwest, Denver Proceedings," p. 37.
[37] Ibid., pp. 38–39, 41.

different. While the water needs of the lands below Pathfinder
were greater than the annual flow of the North Platte, the irrigation needs below Boulder Canyon would be less than the water
supply made available by a Boulder Canyon dam. "And of
course," stated Davis in drawing attention to a principle basic to
all western water law, "no right could be built up or acquired in
excess of the needs below that point." In short, no one, he argued,
could obtain a right to more water than he could reasonably use.
Therefore, there would remain "a very large surplus for application in the upper basin." [38]

So far as Davis was concerned, the upriver states had absolutely nothing to fear. "I am willing to stake my reputation upon
the belief that it is feasible . . . to store the waters of the Colorado River below the cañons of the Colorado . . . and not interfere in any way with the use of the water in the basin above." [39]

IX

Despite his arguments, Davis failed to allay upper-basin anxieties. Some believed his assertions about water supply, but others
continued to have their doubts. "This great enterprise here Colorado approaches with . . . misgivings," replied Colorado state
engineer A. J. McCune. "The building of that reservoir and the
utilization of that water down there," he insisted, could "give
them the preferential rights over us." Wyoming state engineer
Frank Emerson expressed strong agreement. "The Boulder Cañon
dam and reservoir is the solution of the problems that confront
the territory *below* the reservoir," he said. "It is not a solution or
aid particularly to our development on the upper river. . . . It is
possible that the Boulder Cañon dam might be built, the waters
stored, and afterwards applied to beneficial use on the lower
river, and a priority established." [40]

Nor was Emerson relieved by Davis's remarks about the Pathfinder situation. "I still insist that I have a case in point," he
argued. "The fact is that the Pathfinder has retarded development
on the upper Platte in Wyoming. By the same token, Wyoming
wants . . . some agreement that will insure . . . that this same
thing won't happen on the . . . Colorado River." [41]

[38] Ibid., pp. 51, 255.   [39] Ibid., pp. 53–54.
[40] Ibid., pp. 239, 242, 251 (emphasis added).   [41] Ibid., p. 258.

Though the upper states were anxious to protect themselves, they had no wish to play dog-in-the-manger. "We have fifty-five per cent of the flow of the stream coming from Colorado," stated McCune, but "it would not be right for us to say, 'Let us hold this water until we decide how much we want to use,' because that may take fifty years." But McCune and others in the upper basin did want more protection than Davis's mere promise that they would not be hurt. And they did not think this an unreasonable request. "I believe there should be an absolute contract between the different states that are affected," suggested Emerson, "and a contract that would be concurred in by the United States Reclamation Service." Such an arrangement would not only afford needed protection, it might also help eliminate years of costly litigation that could delay indefinitely all river development. "I trust," said Emerson in a statement echoing the sentiments of everyone, "that the Colorado River problems will not go for years and finally wind up in courts." [42]

X

No one warmed more to the "contract" idea than Delph Carpenter, a brilliant forty-three-year-old Colorado lawyer who was attending his first league meeting as a special advisor to Governor Shoup. Though an attorney and a member of the defense counsel in *Wyoming* v. *Colorado,* still pending before the Supreme Court, Carpenter believed that litigation was no way to handle interstate water disputes. As a youngster growing up in the eastern Colorado town of Greeley, the center of a rich irrigated area, he had learned that water was simply too valuable a commodity to waste while wrangling over fine points of law. The lesson applied with even greater force to controversies among states, where the issues were especially complicated and seldom resolved even after years of courtroom fighting.

As early as 1912, Carpenter had become convinced that a better approach to interstate water disputes lay in Article Six of the U.S. Constitution. This article permitted states, once they had secured the permission of Congress, to negotiate treaties among themselves. No states had yet attempted to apportion the waters

[42] Ibid., pp. 240, 251, 254.

of a stream, but they had satisfactorily settled differences over such matters as fishing rights and boundaries. To Carpenter, their successes, even though small and usually involving only two states and never more than three, seemed most encouraging; and he urged Colorado officials to negotiate with neighboring states over water rights rather than to fight interminable legal battles.[43]

In 1912 Carpenter's ideas had met only with skepticism and even ridicule. His treaty suggestion was considered too novel, especially by those who preferred to gamble on a complete victory in the courts rather than to negotiate a compromise. But Carpenter refused to abandon his scheme. Like Davis, who had waited for the proper moment to push his program for developing the Colorado River, he bided his time, talking over his ideas with intimates and watching for the right opportunity to lobby for his proposal.

XI

By the time of the Denver conference, Carpenter had become more convinced than ever of the correctness of his views. His participation in the lengthy Supreme Court battle with Wyoming as well as in a newer dispute with Nebraska was part of the reason, but so was the federal government's claim that it owned all the unappropriated waters in the West's unnavigable streams. Carpenter had been present in Washington in 1918 when federal attorneys forcefully made this claim during re-arguments in *Wyoming* v. *Colorado*. Since then he had grown fearful that if the states did not put their houses in order, the federal government might do it for them—with or without court permission. A disastrous flood on the lower river, he believed, could create such a "hue and cry" that federal officials might take "control of the Colorado River regardless of the rights of the States," thus causing a "weakening of state autonomy on all rivers." [44] To protect the rights of the western states against federal encroachment and, in particular, to protect his own state against possible claims from

[43] Carpenter, "The Colorado River Compact," pp. 19–20, file 1-M/366, Hoover Papers. For a summary of Carpenter's career, see *Who's Who in America, 1950–1951* (Chicago, 1950), pp. 431–432.

[44] Ibid., p. 21.

faster-developing areas on the lower river, Carpenter decided to lobby for an interstate compact at the Denver meeting.

Carpenter was able to work behind the scenes at the conference because he held no official state position. His knowledge of water law was so great, however, that he was given a room in the capitol building where he could be consulted by the governor and other state officials. Midway through the league meeting, he withdrew to his office and drafted his proposal for a compact. At first he considered proposing a general scheme for dividing the river's waters between the upper and lower basins. Further reflection persuaded him that the wisest course was merely to win approval for the idea of an interstate treaty. To lessen the risk of a floor fight, he decided to try to win the support of the league's resolutions committee. As a first step, he showed his proposal to Leslie W. Gillette, state engineer of New Mexico and a member of that committee.[45]

Gillette's affirmative response convinced Carpenter that his chances for success were good, and he then persuaded the New Mexico official to "father" the proposition before the resolutions committee. With the aid of the committee's chairman, Colorado's Governor Shoup, Gillette won unanimous endorsement of the proposal and also helped beat off an attempt by Californians who wanted a resolution advocating that the entire matter of Colorado River development be turned over to the Reclamation Service to handle as that agency saw fit.[46] This maneuver Carpenter and the other upper-state representatives wished to avoid at all costs, not only because it might lead to the construction of a Boulder Canyon dam with no protection for their future rights, but also because it could strengthen the federal government's attempt to control all unappropriated waters.

As finally reported by the committee, Carpenter's resolution was straightforward in its purpose: "The present and future rights of the several states . . . should be settled and determined by compact" and the seven basin states are "requested to authorize the appointment of commissioners . . . for the pur-

45 Ibid., pp. 17, 21–22; "Hoover Dam Documents," *H. Doc. 717*, 80 Cong., 2 sess. (1948), 18 n.

46 Carpenter, "The Colorado River Compact," pp. 21–23, file 1-M/ 366, Hoover Papers; *Denver Post*, August 27, 1920; *Los Angeles Times*, August 28, 1920.

pose of entering into such compact . . . for subsequent ratification . . . by the Legislature of each of said states and the Congress." But the resolution did more. It also expressed opposition
to any restrictions on upper-basin development and called upon
the league to endorse "the early development of all possible
beneficial uses of the waters of the stream upon the upper
reaches along the lines set forth in the resolutions adopted at
the Salt Lake Conference of January 18–21, 1919." [47]

The reference to the Salt Lake resolution did not represent an
upper-basin attempt to quash construction of a Boulder Canyon
dam. It was a reminder to Congress and others not to forget
about the upper basin's reclamation hopes or the wisdom of
early development on any stream's headwaters. Most importantly,
the resolution as a whole emphasized the need for machinery to
protect the interests of the slower-developing states. "We are in
favor of building Boulder Cañon Dam . . . ," observed Colorado's Fred Lucas, "but this . . . must be agreed to by all the
States in order to see that no selfish advantage will be taken of
the building of Boulder Cañon Dam first." [48]

Once the resolution reached the floor, approval came easily
and with no debate. All realized that the interests of each state
could best be served by cooperation, and a compact seemed to
be a reasonable way of achieving the necessary harmony. Some
lower-basin interests, particularly in California, would have preferred unqualified endorsement of a Boulder Canyon dam, but
they recognized the obvious need for upper-basin support in
Congress. Essentially, the situation called for bartering. The
lower basin wanted a dam, the upper basin wanted protection,
and each concluded that they could probably best reconcile their
interests in a compact. Thus persuaded, they unanimously approved the resolution and set the stage for a pioneering venture
in interstate diplomacy. [49]

Carpenter was understandably delighted. "This is just the beginning of what has been the dream of . . . more than one generation," he told the assemblage. "We wish to treat before war,

[47] "League of the Southwest, Denver Proceedings," pp. 287–288.
[48] Fred Lucas to C. M. Sain, October 22, 1920, RCC:3, Shoup
Papers.
[49] "League of the Southwest, Denver Proceedings," p. 290.

and this is, we hope, the beginning of the treaty." [50] It was. But it was also the beginning of a special kind of war.

In less than two years the League of the Southwest had brought the Colorado River states close to a solution of their mutual problem. To a great extent this success simply reflected their realization that they had never before been faced with such an obvious need to cooperate. It was only in the years immediately following World War I that Arthur Powell Davis's desire for a comprehensive program of river development found sufficiently strong support among those on the lower river, especially in California, to create a sense of crisis in the states along the headwaters. By the summer of 1920 that crisis was clearly mirrored in the league's deliberations. By then, too, it had prompted the fear that Colorado River development would be held up indefinitely as the basin states fought with one another in the courts over their rights. When that fear was acknowledged, the league made its most significant contribution by providing the forum where water leaders agreed to initiate treaty negotiations rather than to fight. But the decision to negotiate represented no end to controversy. At times during the coming months it would actually appear to be a call to arms.

[50] Ibid., p. 299.

5

Power Sets the Stage

Following the meeting of the League of the Southwest in Denver, the movement for the Colorado River compact rolled forward slowly but inexorably. Formal talks could not begin until each basin state had given prior approval to negotiations and had then appointed a representative to the Colorado River Commission, the interstate negotiating body created specifically to draft the pact. Even with those preliminaries out of the way, negotiations had to await congressional consent, required by the Constitution for any treaty among states, and the appointment by the president of a federal representative to protect the interests of the United States at the bargaining table.

All this took time—time that saw the Reclamation Service and lower-basin interests continue to press for a high dam on the lower river, and time that witnessed the emergence of a new controversy in Colorado River politics—a battle over rights to hydroelectric power. This dispute, involving primarily municipal and private interests, held special concern for Arizona and Nevada, the two states in whose territory the proposed dam was to be built. Most ominously, the power controversy, which broke on the eve of crucial negotiations for the compact, dealt a critical blow to the League of the Southwest and complicated further the already formidable question of water rights.

I

Colorado's Delph Carpenter, the principal advocate of the compact idea, continued to exercise leadership in the weeks following the Denver meeting. He advised the other states on the form of the authorizing legislation each would have to enact and also spearheaded the drive for congressional approval. He even found time to lay the groundwork for compact negotiations on other interstate rivers in which Colorado had an interest—the La Plata, the Laramie, and the South Platte.[1]

By late spring of 1921 the basin legislatures had given their assent, and on May 10 the governors met in Denver and formally asked the federal government for its approval. To assure favorable action, most of the governors went in a body to Washington, D.C., where, in a White House interview with Warren G. Harding, they received the promise of administration support. They also dispatched to Capitol Hill Delph Carpenter and Stephen B. Davis, Jr., a New Mexico expert in water law, who took along the draft of a bill that they had prepared for congressional action.[2]

Carpenter and Davis received a warm reception, but they

[1] The La Plata was a Colorado River tributary shared only by New Mexico and Colorado. Oliver H. Shoup to Robert D. Carey, January 27, 1921, Records Center Container (hereafter RCC): 5, Oliver H. Shoup Papers, Colorado State Archives, Denver; Shoup to Samuel R. McKelvie, January 27, 1921, RCC:5, Shoup Papers; Shoup to Merritt C. Mechem, January 27, 1921, RCC:5, Shoup Papers; Delph Carpenter to Shoup, February 17, 1921, RCC:5, Shoup Papers; Delph Carpenter, "The Colorado River Compact," pp. 25–30, file 1-M/366, Herbert Hoover Papers, Hoover Presidential Library, West Branch, Iowa; *Denver Post*, April 3, 1921.

[2] Tucson *Arizona Daily Star*, May 11 and 12, 1921; *Los Angeles Times*, May 12, 1921; Stephen B. Davis, Jr., to Merritt C. Mechem, June 2, 1921, Merritt C. Mechem Papers, New Mexico State Archives, Santa Fe; Carpenter, "Colorado River Compact," pp. 25–31, file 1-M/366, Hoover Papers.

also encountered political infighting that foreshadowed the future problems they and others would face in attempts to harmonize interstate jealousies. The difficulty arose shortly after Senator H. O. Bursum of New Mexico had introduced their bill authorizing compact negotiations. Convinced that approval was a foregone conclusion, Davis left Washington, and Carpenter was preparing to go when he learned that Wyoming's Franklin Mondell intended to oppose the measure. Mondell was House majority leader, and his opposition could delay congressional approval or even kill the bill.[3]

To Carpenter, the reason for Mondell's opposition seemed petty. As the ranking western congressman from the Colorado River Basin, Mondell simply wanted to control the legislation himself. Carpenter realized the importance of protecting the Wyoming congressman's ego, so he went to Bursum, delicately explained the situation, and asked the New Mexico senator to withdraw his bill in favor of Mondell's. Bursum was irritated, but recognized the need to placate the House leader. He bowed to Carpenter's request and threw his support to Mondell's bill, which was drawn up with Carpenter's advice and introduced on June 6, 1921.[4]

The arrangement proved successful. With Bursum's strong backing, the substitute measure moved through the Senate without debate. Only in the House did opposition develop, and it centered merely on a provision of the bill authorizing an appropriation of $10,000 for the salary and expenses of the federal representative on the compact commission. "I do not suppose that there is a man in the House opposing the intent and purpose of this bill . . . ," announced one economy-minded congressman, "but it is getting so that we can not pass hardly a week in Congress without appointing some man to a new high-salaried position. . . . I am going to vote against the bill because of that one fact." [5]

[3] Carpenter, "Colorado River Compact," pp. 32–33, file 1-M/366, Hoover Papers. Bursum introduced his bill on May 20, 1921. *Cong. Rec.*, 67 Cong., 1 sess. (1921), p. 1561.

[4] Carpenter, "Colorado River Compact," pp. 32–35, file 1-M/366, Hoover Papers; *Cong. Rec.*, 67 Cong., 1 sess. (1921), p. 2174.

[5] *Cong. Rec.*, 67 Cong., 1 sess. (1921), p. 2772. See also House Committee on the Judiciary, *Hearings on Granting the Consent of*

The bill's proponents easily overcame such opposition. "Peanut politics," they called it. "We are economizing," admitted one of them, but "we have not quite reached the point where we can not spend a few dollars to take care of the important business of the Government." With the opposition reduced to counting pennies and the proponents in possession of strong backing from President Harding, Secretary of the Interior Albert Fall, and Reclamation Service Director Arthur Powell Davis, the bill passed the House by the overwhelming vote of 237 to 15. On August 19 the president signed the measure into law.[6]

II

As Harding deliberated about whom he would appoint to the Colorado River Commission, he learned of new quarrels among the basin states that caused him to delay his decision. Precipitating the latest clash had been a report issued on July 8 by Arthur Powell Davis. This was the long-awaited report on the lower river that had been called for in the Kinkaid Act. It was a preliminary version, not the final draft, but this in no way lessened its importance in the eyes of basin leaders. They realized that the final document would serve as an important guide in any future congressional action; and they knew that if their several views were not to be overlooked, they would have to act quickly.

In most respects the report contained few surprises. Davis, as expected, advocated construction of the All-American Canal and a high dam in the Boulder Canyon area. The canal was to be paid for by those benefiting from it; and the dam, by the sale

---

Congress to Certain Compacts and Agreements between the States of Arizona, California, Colorado, Nevada, New Mexico, Utah, and Wyoming, H.R. 6821, 67 Cong., 1 sess. (1921).

[6] *Cong. Rec.,* 67 Cong., 1 sess. (1921), pp. 2771, 2773–2774, 5864; U.S., *Statutes at Large,* XLII: 171. The ease with which the bill moved through Congress should not be construed as meaning that basin-state leaders supported it with enthusiasm. Some lower-basin spokesmen, particularly in California, feared that it might delay development of the river in their section. Phil D. Swing to Hiram Johnson, August 2, 1921, Phil D. Swing Papers, Department of Special Collections, University of California, Los Angeles.

of hydroelectric power. It was this last provision concerning the financing of the dam that prompted sharp discussion and, eventually, controversy.

Davis believed that hydroelectric power sales could finance the reservoir in one of two ways, and he recommended both to Congress. One approach called for Congress to appropriate the necessary construction funds for the dam and then to recoup most of its expenditure by "leasing the power privileges" at the reservoir site. If Congress refused to approve an appropriation, however, then Davis believed that the government should "contract with any agency or agencies"—public or private—that would build the dam themselves "for the power to be developed." [7]

Actually Davis preferred that the federal government build and own the dam. He did not recommend this policy, however, because he believed that Congress would refuse to go along with such a move, largely because of the expense. Nevertheless, he was confident that the returns from power sales would pay for the undertaking, and he urged that power consumers be made responsible for 85 percent of the cost, while those benefiting from flood control and using impounded waters should contribute the remainder of the expense. He also recommended that state and local government agencies be invited to contribute funds in exchange for "a proportionate share of power at cost." [8]

III

Davis's report had a mixed reception. Some greeted it with enthusiasm, but others, like the Coachella Valley County Water District, protested fiercely. Coachella Valley developers, who were early and vigorous supporters of both a Boulder Canyon dam and the All-American Canal, wanted the government to construct the project and power consumers to shoulder the entire cost of the reservoir. Even sharper objections came from those who claimed to see in Davis's proposals a conspiracy between the federal government and lower-basin advocates of a Boulder Canyon dam. "It is very evident to me," wrote Delph Carpenter

[7] "Problems of Imperial Valley and Vicinity," *S. Doc.* 142, 67 Cong., 2 sess. (1922), pp. 242–243.

[8] Ibid., pp. 242, 247.

to Nevada state engineer J. G. Scrugham, "that the Reclamation Service is making stupendous efforts and doubtless constantly working through secret channels to the objective of planting and firmly fixing their Boulder Cañon Reservoir before the states may act upon the compact." [9]

Carpenter was convinced that Davis was "working through secret channels" by a rumor that the city of Los Angeles was negotiating with the Reclamation Service for rights to the power to be produced in Boulder Canyon. His speculation seemed to be confirmed by the fact that in his report Davis mentioned only Los Angeles when he described the tentative allotment of power. He had done so simply because Los Angeles was the only city then willing to commit itself to purchasing electricity, but even when Carpenter learned Davis's reasons, the news did little to quiet his fears. More alarming to the Coloradoan were reports that Los Angeles intended to build the dam and power plant itself if the federal government for some reason failed to do so.

Carpenter and other upper-basin leaders had a special fear of Los Angeles. They were aware of the unusually aggressive manner in which the city had previously met its water needs. Water had been a crucial concern in Los Angeles from the days of earliest settlement, but it had become almost an obsession after a real estate boom in the 1880s had touched off a phenomenal growth in population. From 50,000 in 1890 the city had grown to 319,000 by 1910 and to 577,000 by 1920. The spiraling growth pattern showed no signs of diminishing, and neither did the city's constant search for the water that sustained it. [10]

At first city fathers had concentrated on winning exclusive rights to the Los Angeles River. By the end of the nineteenth century, when that battle seemed won, they had looked elsewhere for a supplementary supply and had settled on the Owens River, located about three hundred miles away on the western

[9] Delph Carpenter to J. G. Scrugham, July 23, 1921, J. G. Scrugham Papers, Nevada Historical Society, Reno (hereafter cited as Scrugham Papers, NHS); "Problems of the Imperial Valley and Vicinity," pp. 92, 242, 259–261.

[10] U.S. Bureau of the Census, *Fourteenth Census of the United States* (Washington, D.C., 1921), I: 78; Vincent Ostrom, *Water & Politics* (Los Angeles, 1953).

slope of the Sierra Nevada. By 1913 they had completed an aqueduct. Undisturbed by claims that they had "raped" the Owens Valley of its water, they had continued their search, only now they concentrated primarily on finding ways to meet the city's growing need for electricity. This search had soon focused their attention on the Colorado River.

Los Angeles was well aware of the value of the Colorado. As early as 1912, the city had sent to the river an investigator, Joseph B. Lippincott, who had reported on the stream's capacity to support "a large and prosperous population." "We have in the Colorado an American Nile awaiting regulation," Lippincott had observed, "and it should be treated in as intelligent and vigorous a manner as the British Government has treated its great Egyptian prototype." [11]

At first the city fathers had felt no need to turn to so distant a source, and as late as 1920, they had still believed that the Owens River would take care of their water needs for the foreseeable future. But they had become far less confident about their ability to supply electrical power.

By 1920 the population of Los Angeles was approaching 600,-000, and the city council predicted a doubling of that figure within ten years. But according to the council's calculations, the power supply would remain adequate for only the next three to five years. Alarmed at the threat this scarcity posed to the city's growth, worried council members had brightened when they learned about Davis's plans to develop the Colorado. At the urging of William Mulholland, the nationally famous chief of the city's Bureau of Water Works and Supply, and E. F. Scattergood, the head of the city's Bureau of Power and Light, they had formally announced their interest in the river on August 30, 1920. "The Council of the City of Los Angeles . . . ," they had declared, "does strongly favor the obtaining by the city direct from the Colorado River of such quantity of electric power as . . . will be sufficient for all future needs of its inhabitants. . . . To such end, the council favors and urges the development of

[11] [J. B. Lippincott], "The Colorado River" (1912), p. 9, file 360, Colorado River, Papers of the Los Angeles Department of Water and Power, Los Angeles Department of Water and Power Building. A copy of this report is also in the Joseph B. Lippincott Papers, Water Resources Center Archives, University of California, Berkeley.

the Boulder Canyon Reservoir by the United States Government, or, if that be not provided for, then by the city of Los Angeles." [12]

A year later, when Davis's preliminary report revealed that the government might not be the builder of the dam, city officials moved to protect themselves by filing applications with Arizona, Nevada, and the Federal Power Commission for permission to build the reservoir.[13] The permission of the two states was needed because they owned the bed of the dam site. The Federal Power Commission, created in 1920 and composed of the secretary of war, the secretary of the interior, and the secretary of agriculture, controlled the issuance of licenses for power development on the public lands and navigable rivers.

IV

Vying with Los Angeles for power rights at Boulder Canyon were private firms, especially the Southern Sierras Power Company and the Southern California Edison Company. Southern Sierras Power was a subsidiary of the California-Nevada Electric Corporation, a large holding company which controlled nine firms, including the Imperial Ice and Development Company. Southern Sierras and Imperial Ice had an investment of some $5 million in the Imperial Valley and were naturally interested in the valley's future. But Southern Sierras and its related firms were even more interested in the enormous profits to be made from developing the hydroelectric power potential of the Colorado. Southern Sierras had worked out an agreement with Southern California Edison, the largest power company in the southern part of the state, under which Edison would harness the river and allow Southern Sierras to participate to the extent it wished. Like the city of Los Angeles, Southern California Edison had filed applications with state and federal authorities to build dams at four points on the Colorado, two above the Grand Canyon and two below, one of them at Boulder Canyon.[14] Although the ap-

[12] "Problems of the Imperial Valley and Vicinity," pp. 282–283.
[13] E. F. Scattergood, W. Mulholland, and W. B. Mathews to Los Angeles Chamber of Commerce, August 17, 1921, file 360, Colorado River, Papers of the Los Angeles Department of Water and Power.
[14] Edwin O. Edgerton to Thomas E. Campbell, June 18, 1921, Mechem Papers; John B. Miller to J. G. Scrugham, September 17,

plications had not yet been approved, Edison officials took heart
when Davis's report held out the possibility of private firms either
leasing power privileges or building the dam and power plant
themselves.

Not everyone wanted either Los Angeles or private power
interests to gain a foothold in Boulder Canyon, but to many
there seemed to be no way of keeping them out. This conclusion
was reluctantly reached by Phil Swing, an early advocate of the
All-American Canal and now a newly elected member of Congress who had won his House seat in 1920 on a platform advocating early development of the river. "From my knowledge
of the temperament of Congress and of the people at large,"
Swing told a constituent in the summer of 1921 shortly after
Davis had released his report, "I very gravely doubt the possibility of getting Congress to appropriate money with which to
build this Dam. There is a sentiment sweeping the country expressed in the phrase: 'Less Government in business and more
business in Government.' This sentiment seems to incur a prohibition against the Government doing anything that it is possible
to get private interests to do and would, without doubt, mitigate
against any proposal to have the Government build this Dam,
develope [*sic*] and sell the power." [15]

Swing's assessment of the federal government's chances of
going into the power business was accurate. To be sure, power
was being developed on a number of projects constructed under
the Reclamation Act of 1902, but that development was small
and incidental to the major purpose of the projects—irrigation.
The electricity generated was used for water pumping and other

1921, Scrugham Papers, NHS; House Committee on Irrigation and
Reclamation, *Hearings on Protection and Development of Lower
Colorado River Basin*, H.R. 2903, 68 Cong., 1 sess. (1924), pp. 615,
619, 647. Heightening the competition between Los Angeles and
Southern California Edison at this time was the city's attempt to acquire that portion of the Edison Company's distribution system that
lay within the city. Not until May, 1922, after an eight-year struggle,
did the city acquire the system. For an excellent discussion of this
campaign, see Nelson S. Van Valen, "Power Politics: The Struggle
for Municipal Ownership of Electric Utilities in Los Angeles, 1905–
1937" (Ph.D. diss., Claremont Graduate School, 1963), pp. 56–203.

[15] Phil D. Swing to S. E. Burrows, August 3, 1921, Swing Papers.

needs near the dam, while excess energy was sold and the revenue applied to the cost of the project. In 1906 Congress had gone a step further by authorizing the secretary of the interior to lease the surplus power or the privilege of developing power at federal reservoirs. In response to the insistence of reformers, preference was given to "municipal purposes," such as water pumping and street lighting, but even those uses could not "impair the efficiency of the irrigation project." [16] This policy worked fairly well until the mushrooming demand for electricity and the growing belief that private power companies were charging unfair rates sparked a call for public ownership of generating facilities. Municipalities took the lead in the movement, though following World War I, advocates of large-scale federal involvement also began making themselves heard.[17]

As Swing observed, however, there was in 1921 little public support for the federal government's going into the power business. Some voices were being raised in behalf of transforming the government's nitrate plant at Muscle Shoals on the Tennessee River into a hydroelectric power project, but the voices were few. The Tennessee Valley Authority, the first federal project dedicated primarily to power production, was still more than a decade in the future. For the present, Swing even doubted that Washington would build the dam and allow others to develop the power. "In my opinion," he told a chamber of commerce official in the Imperial Valley, "we have but two chances to build this reservoir within the next five or ten years and that is, —either by making an alliance with the private power companies and allow them the power right under Federal control for a

[16] U.S., *Statutes at Large,* XXXIV: 117; Edwin Vennard, *Government in the Power Business* (New York, 1968), pp. 88–89.

[17] Municipal ownership and operation of electric power facilities actually date from the very beginning of the industry in the late nineteenth century, but the practice grew significantly during the Progressive era, as reformers sought to combat high utility rates and the political influence of private firms. The municipal ownership movement was also a response to private industry's inability to provide power to many small communities. Van Valen, "Power Politics: The Struggle for Municipal Ownership of Electric Utilities in Los Angeles," pp. 11–13; Twentieth Century Fund, *Electric Power and Government Policy* (New York, 1948), pp. 380–383.

limited period of fifty years" or by negotiating a similar agreement with Los Angeles and "various municipalities in southern California." [18]

Many Californians preferred private power interests to the city of Los Angeles. This attitude became readily apparent during a public meeting on the power question called by the Imperial Valley's Associated Chambers of Commerce three weeks after Davis released his report. William Mulholland, E. F. Scattergood, and William Mathews of Los Angeles presented the case for the city, and A. B. West of the Southern Sierras Power Company spoke on behalf of private capital. Many in the assemblage agreed with J. S. Nickerson, the president of the Imperial Irrigation District, who doubted the ability of Los Angeles to handle a major river-control project. For one thing, the city had nearly exhausted its bonding capacity and would have to pass special legislation to obtain needed funds and to spend the money out of state. "The power companies tell me they will build the dam and give us the protection and water," declared Nickerson. "There is no 'mañana' about it. . . . It's all right to talk about fighting corporations but we need this thing now—we can't wait." [19]

Others objected to Los Angeles because they distrusted the city. "I am skeptical of Los Angeles," said a representative from San Bernardino. "She has always been inimical to the interests of the back country when she should be the reverse. . . . The farmers need more power than the city people." [20]

Los Angeles spokesmen tried to persuade the audience that the city was being unfairly maligned. "We are not greedy," protested Mulholland. "That power . . . will be divided among various sections that need it." Moreover, he insisted, Los Angeles could sell the power more cheaply than private firms. Few doubted the last claim, but many, remembering the Owens

[18] Phil Swing to S. E. Burrows, August 3, 1921, Swing Papers. For a careful discussion of the Muscle Shoals question and the origins of TVA, see Preston J. Hubbard, *Origins of the TVA: The Muscle Shoals Controversy, 1920–1932* (Nashville, 1961); see also Jerome G. Kerwin, *Federal Water-Power Legislation* (New York, 1926).

[19] *Brawley News*, July 30, 1921; see also J. S. Nickerson to Phil Swing, July 29, 1921, Swing Papers.

[20] *Brawley News*, July 30, 1921.

Valley episode, were fearful that the city would keep all the power for itself. "I would rather pay $1.27 per kilowat[t] hour and get it than have Los Angeles take it all and we get nothing," declared a Riverside official, whose remarks touched off a round of applause.

V

Joining these Californians in their suspicion of Los Angeles were leaders in Arizona and Nevada, the two states that owned the opposite sides of the Boulder Canyon dam site. These men believed that the location of the site entitled their states to preferential rights to any power that was produced. They acknowledged that the biggest current market for power was in southern California; but they believed that their own needs would soon increase greatly, and they wanted guarantees that they would receive a block of power when they were ready for it. Arizonans wanted electricity to pump groundwater to parched lands and also to expand their copper-mining operations, already among the world's largest. In addition, they had hopes of pumping water to a vast irrigable area in the central part of the state. "You may think when you first read this that we are stark crazy," W. S. Norviel, the Arizona state water commissioner, told Reclamation Service officials in early 1921. "We have in mind . . . a high dam either at Black or Boulder Canyon . . . to raise the water and take our portion out in a high line canal . . . and place it upon lands in the Gila basin and other places, covering thereby in the neighborhood of a million and a half acres." [21]

Nevadans were also interested in cheap power, particularly for working the deposits of borax, gypsum, manganese, and other minerals located near Boulder Canyon. Like Arizonans, they wanted power to pump groundwater to irrigate fertile desert lands, especially the acreage surrounding Las Vegas, a small but ambitious town of some 2,300 that was located less than forty miles from the dam site. To ensure a sufficient power supply, some Nevadans hoped that the compact negotiators would de-

[21] W. S. Norviel to Charles H. Fitch, April 9, 1921, file 032, Colorado River Project, Bureau of Reclamation Papers, Record Group 115, National Archives; "Problems of the Imperial Valley and Vicinity," pp. 302–303.

122 *Power Sets the Stage*

termine rights to electricity as well as to water, but it soon
became obvious that power would have to be dealt with separately.[22] Initially, at least, it would have to go to those capable
of using and paying for it immediately, for only in this way could
the cost of a large reservoir be met. Even so, these leaders
wanted assurances that power would be available for them when
they needed it.

Arizonans and Nevadans were also anxious to collect revenue
from those who would produce power at Boulder Canyon. Southern California Edison, as a private firm, could provide compensation through the taxes levied on its operations, and the city of
Los Angeles promised to provide revenue as if it were a private
corporation.[23] The federal government, on the other hand, might
offer no such return if it built and owned the power plant, for
the state could not tax federal property without the government's
permission. Because of this prohibition and the possibility that
Congress might not authorize federal construction of the dam,
the leaders of Arizona and Nevada studied with great interest
the power applications submitted by Los Angeles and Southern California Edison.

At first both states expressed skepticism about Los Angeles's
financial ability to undertake such a costly project. Like many
others, they also distrusted the city's intentions, and they became
especially resentful when they learned of the attention Davis
had given Los Angeles in his preliminary report. "The Davis
report . . . ," complained Nevada state engineer J. G. Scrugham,
"in effect totally ignores the rights of the various interested states
and proposes to give to the city of Los Angeles the power monopoly of the Southwest." In fact, he declared to Colorado's
Delph Carpenter, another outspoken critic of both Davis's report
and Los Angeles, "the plans outlined by the director . . . show

[22] "Problems of the Imperial Valley and Vicinity," pp. 320–321;
J. G. Scrugham to Key Pittman, June 21, 1921, Scrugham Papers,
NHS; U.S. Bureau of the Census, *Fourteenth Census of the United
States*, I: 255.

[23] Emmet D. Boyle to C. E. Armstrong, August 26, 1921, Emmet
D. Boyle Papers, Nevada State Archives, Carson City; J. G. Scrugham
to John B. Miller, August 26, 1921, Scrugham Papers, NHS; Scrugham to G. C. Ward, August 27, 1921, Scrugham Papers, NHS; J. S.
Nickerson to Phil D. Swing, August 10, 1921, Swing Papers.

such a gross partisanship and disregard for States' rights that I consider them to be a menace to the proper development of the stream system." [24]

Carpenter delighted in finding allies, and he played upon their resentment in an attempt to sidetrack the efforts of both Los Angeles and the Reclamation Service. He believed that private capital could be more easily controlled—and hence trusted—and he urged Arizona and Nevada officials to try to stop federal engineering activity in the Boulder Canyon area, thus "shutting down . . . such work until such time as the whole matter may be considered in an orderly manner by the compact commission." In giving his advice, he pointedly emphasized his support of Arizona and Nevada's request for a preferential allotment of power, and he warned the two states to be on guard against a federal attempt to bargain away their rights to Los Angeles. "While I am not in position to even suggest the matters of best policy for Nevada and Arizona," he explained, "I conscientiously feel that the first benefits from any reservoir constructed in the Colorado River across your common interstate line . . . should run to the two states whose territory is involved." "Neither state," he offered, "can afford to encourage any construction whereby the power to be developed may be bargained away for the benefit of the territory of some other state." [25]

Despite Carpenter's plea, Arizona and Nevada continued to negotiate with Los Angeles as well as with Southern California Edison. By late summer of 1921 Nevadans, in particular, had begun to waver in their opposition to Los Angeles. The city had promised them revenue and a preferential right to power, though important details remained unsettled. As interest in Los Angeles increased, Nevada officials began to cool in their initial enthusiasm for Southern California Edison, particularly when they learned that the company planned to construct its major power plant at Glen Canyon, a site entirely within Arizona and hence

[24] J. G. Scrugham to Delph Carpenter, July 21, 1921, Scrugham Papers, NHS; Scrugham to Levi Syphus, July 27, 1921, Scrugham Papers, NHS; see also Emmet D. Boyle to H. S. McCluskey, December 6, 1922, Boyle Papers.

[25] Delph Carpenter to J. G. Scrugham, September 15, 1921, Scrugham Papers, NHS.

one that could offer no revenue to Nevada.[26] Many Arizonans
naturally warmed to this possibility, but both states decided to
postpone a decision until the entire matter could be discussed
more fully.

An opportunity for such a discussion was planned for December, 1921, at a hearing on the Davis report in San Diego. Secretary of the Interior Albert B. Fall had scheduled the hearing
as soon as he had learned of the strong objections to Davis's
recommendations. In fact, he, too, had been unhappy with the
report, especially with Davis's failure to recommend only federal construction and ownership of the dam.[27] He had told the
Reclamation Service chief that he believed the project was too
big and the international and interstate issues too complex for
agencies other than the federal government to undertake the program.

Davis needed little convincing. He had all along favored such
a course; and if Fall provided the backing of his office, he believed that Congress might very well endorse the project. Both
men agreed to withhold announcement of this major modification
in the preliminary report until the public hearing scheduled for
December.

VI

But more than one meeting was planned for December. Arnold
Kruckman, secretary-treasurer of the League of the Southwest,
wanted the league to continue playing the role of harmonizer
in Colorado River matters; and he called for a meeting in Riverside, California, on December 8–9, 1921, only a few days before
the San Diego hearing scheduled by Fall.

Few greeted the announcement with enthusiasm. Kruckman
had already irritated some people with publicity releases that
had so exaggerated the imminent construction of storage on the
Colorado that state and federal officials were flooded with job

[26] J. G. Scrugham to John B. Miller, August 26, 1921, Scrugham
Papers, NHS; J. G. Scrugham to Levi Syphus et al., August 31, 1921,
Scrugham Papers, NHS; Emmet D. Boyle to C. E. Armstrong, August
26, 1921, Boyle Papers; Emmet D. Boyle to *Los Angeles Evening
Herald,* November 26, 1921, Boyle Papers.

[27] "Problems of the Imperial Valley and Vicinity," pp. 234, 243–
244.

requests. When challenged, he defended his actions in the name
of "poetic license" and the need "to popularize the subject." [28]
Many now sharply criticized the meeting he had scheduled for
Riverside as another unnecessary exercise in propaganda, and
some bluntly told him that they would attend but not participate.
"Unless it is one of the rules of your convention that delegates
have to earn admission by agreement to talk when they get in,"
wrote Governor Emmet D. Boyle of Nevada to Kruckman, "I
cannot see that our delegation will have anything in particular
to say." In fact, announced Boyle, "we [will] have nothing to say
until the official meeting is held in San Diego." [29]

Kruckman tried desperately to persuade Boyle and others that
the meeting had an important purpose: "to promote better understanding and to secure unified action along broad lines for the
utilization of the resources of the river." [30] All agreed that these
were laudable aims, but most believed that more effective ways
now existed for achieving them. The upcoming San Diego meeting was one and the Colorado River Commission being created to
draft a compact was another—indeed, the most important. What
Kruckman failed to realize was that the league, in fathering the
movement for a compact, had undermined what had become its
major reason for existence.

Though the league had lost much of its earlier importance, it
still remained a highly visible organization, now claiming a
membership of 3,000 separate civic and commercial groups. It
also possessed a powerful propaganda machine. Such an organization could not be ignored, particularly since it would hold its
meeting only days before the San Diego hearing. Delph Carpenter

[28] Reclamation Service memo, April 22, 1921, file 032, Colorado
River Project, Bureau of Reclamation Papers.

[29] Emmet D. Boyle to Arnold Kruckman, November 30, 1921,
Boyle Papers.

[30] Arnold Kruckman to Frank C. Emerson, December 1, 1921,
Papers of the Wyoming State Engineer, Wyoming State Archives,
Cheyenne; Arnold Kruckman to Merritt C. Mechem, October 31,
1921, Mechem Papers; Arnold Kruckman to Emmet D. Boyle, November 24, 1921, Boyle Papers. Kruckman also urged Mexico to send
representatives to the meeting. Kruckman to J. Alonzo Ulloa, November 28, 1921, Papers on the Comisión Internacional de Límites entre
México y los Estados Unidos, file 42 (iii), Archives of the Secretaría
de Relaciones Exteriores, México, D.F.

succinctly expressed the concern of most other basin leaders. "We are all convinced that the . . . [Riverside] meeting is in the nature of propaganda to influence the San Diego meeting," he wrote to Nevada's J. G. Scrugham, "and therefore believe it advisable for the States to be pretty well represented, especially upon the resolutions committee, to prevent any action which will be adverse to the general welfare of the Colorado River adjustment." [31]

VII

When Carpenter arrived in Riverside, he found his worst fears confirmed. Californians had taken advantage of the home ground by packing the convention with a delegation larger than that from any other state and dominated by those favoring municipal construction of the power plant and preferential power arrangements with municipalities and other public agencies. Though many advocated federal construction of the dam, others hoped that the city of Los Angeles might build the dam as well as the power-generating facilities. The private power interests naturally opposed such a plan.

Despite the presence in the California delegation of a vocal minority favoring private development, Carpenter feared that the more numerous supporters of public construction would push through resolutions unfavorable to the upper states. He was also greatly worried by the implications of President Harding's delay in announcing the name of the federal representative to the compact commission. Some now wanted the league to take the initiative and recommend a candidate to the president. Carpenter feared that the California-dominated convention would name someone unsympathetic to the upper states.[32]

[31] Delph Carpenter to J. G. Scrugham, November 26, 1921, Scrugham Papers, NHS; Arnold Kruckman to Emmet D. Boyle, October 31, 1921, Boyle Papers.

[32] L. S. Ready, "Report by L. S. Ready on Meeting of League of the Southwest, Riverside, December 8th, 9th and 10th, 1921, and Hearing by Secretary of the Interior A. B. Fall on Colorado River Development, San Diego, December 12th, 1921," typescript, Engineering Library, Stanford University, Stanford, Calif., pp. 2, 15 (hereafter cited as Ready, "Report"); Carpenter, "Colorado River

To neutralize California's numerical strength, Carpenter and his upper-basin allies set out to reform the convention's ground rules. They introduced a motion to suspend the league's bylaws so that voting would be only by states, with one vote to each state. Since league members had unanimously agreed to this practice at two previous meetings, Carpenter did not think the request was unusual.

But on this occasion the stakes were higher, and the motion produced a heated debate that found all the basin states except California firmly on Carpenter's side. Thoroughly persuaded that the interstate nature of the river made voting by states the only fair way to approach the problem, Carpenter and his allies issued an ultimatum: if their request for a vote change were not granted, they would walk out. The demand incensed those Californians favoring public ownership, but it also revealed wide differences between the municipal and private power advocates within the California delegation. The champions of private power threw their support behind the attempt to change the rules because they believed such a change would weaken Los Angeles's position and strengthen their own. The fierce infighting finally led Californians to ask for a day's postponement of a vote on the motion so that they could seek to resolve their differences.

VIII

As the Californians were caucusing, other events of major importance to Colorado River development occurred. These

Compact," pp. 36–37, file 1-M/366, Hoover Papers; *Riverside Enterprise,* December 9, 1921; *Los Angeles Examiner,* December 9 and 10, 1921; *Los Angeles Times,* December 11, 1921; *Riverside Daily Press,* December 10, 1921; *Denver Post,* December 9, 1921; *Santa Fe New Mexican,* December 9, 1921; Tucson *Arizona Daily Star,* December 9, 10, and 11, 1921; Salt Lake City *Deseret News,* December 10, 1921; *Los Angeles Herald,* December 8, 1921. Mexico sent representatives to keep informed of developments in the United States. For a careful Mexican description of what occurred at Riverside and later at San Diego, see M. Balarezo to Secretario de Relaciones Exteriores, December 20, 1921, and Federico Ramos to Secretario de Relaciones Exteriores, January 14, 1922, Papers of the Comisión Internacional, file 42 (iii).

events took place following the arrival in Riverside of Secretary
of the Interior Albert Fall and Reclamation Service Director
Arthur Powell Davis. Both had decided to stop off at the league
meeting before proceeding to the hearing in San Diego.

On their arrival, the two men went immediately to the conference hall, where they arrived in time to hear L. Ward Bannister, a Colorado lawyer and a representative of Denver civic
and commercial interests, announce his strong opposition to
federal development of the river. Alluding to the problem on
the upper Rio Grande following the 1906 treaty with Mexico,
Bannister warned against permitting a similar occurrence on the
Colorado. He also sharply criticized those federal officials who
claimed that the unappropriated waters of unnavigable western
rivers belonged to the federal government. So far as Bannister
was concerned, the Colorado was unnavigable, but he believed
its waters "belonged to the people of the States," who should
devise an "equitable division" among themselves before anyone
—particularly the federal government—developed the river. Bannister also denounced the "purported agreement" between the
Reclamation Service and Los Angeles, which allegedly gave the
city special advantages on the lower river and cast a "black
cloud" over the entire Colorado River question.[33]

Fall listened quietly from his seat on the same platform where
Bannister was speaking until he heard the Coloradoan accuse
the government of entering into a preferential agreement with
Los Angeles. Then, no longer able to contain himself, he broke
into Bannister's speech. "No such agreement is in force," he
snapped, "nor will be in the future." [34] He also emphasized his
support of the movement to achieve a compact, but he left no

[33] Ready, "Report," p. 23; *Los Angeles Times,* December 10, 1921;
Los Angeles Examiner, December 10, 1921.

[34] *Los Angeles Times,* December 10, 1921; *Los Angeles Examiner,*
December 10, 1921. A Los Angeles official subsequently admitted
that a "paper had been drawn" between the city and the Reclamation
Service, but he insisted that "it was never intended as a contract and
was simply designed for the purpose of ascertaining what could be
done under existing acts; that it was never presented to the city of
Los Angeles and that it need not be a matter for concern on the part
of Colorado or any other State." Ibid.; see also Ready, "Report," p.
23.

doubt about where he stood on the question of who had final jurisdiction over the river.

"The ultimate authority to deal with the Colorado River problem is the United States," he declared, and "I believe that the United States is the only instrumentality that can properly protect the interests of the seven States" and Mexico. What this authority means, he explained, is that the federal government "will maintain its control over the waters of the Rio Colorado until . . . matters are all considered and adjusted in the proper way." "I cannot see," he asserted, "how it will be possible for the city of Los Angeles, the Southern California Edison company or any other private interests or corporation to promote so stupendous a project that involves or will involve so many controversies." [35]

Because the river was at least technically navigable and also an international stream, Fall believed that his views were constitutionally sound, but he candidly admitted that his opinions were his own and not necessarily those of the administration. "This matter has not been the subject of any Cabinet discussion, or any discussion by an executive agency of this government. These are my individual views . . . [but] I am accustomed to insisting on them." [36]

Fall's sentiments were echoed by Davis, who also assured Bannister and others that the Reclamation Service would not assert rights to the river's unappropriated waters. The service, he promised, would "proceed as would a private corporation and comply with State laws regarding the appropriation of water." In addition, he explained, he planned to prepare a proviso protecting "the upper districts" and insert it into all lower-basin contracts for water from the Boulder Canyon reservoir.[37]

Davis's promises seemed encouraging, especially because he had already offered the upper basin protection of another sort in his preliminary report. In that document he had recommended

[35] *Riverside Daily Press*, December 9, 1921; *Los Angeles Times*, December 10, 1921; Tucson *Arizona Daily Star*, December 10, 1921; Ready, "Report," p. 23.

[36] *Los Angeles Times*, December 10, 1921; *Los Angeles Examiner*, December 10, 1921; Tucson *Arizona Daily Star*, December 10, 1921.

[37] *Los Angeles Times*, December 10, 1921; Ready, "Report," p. 24.

giving irrigationists priority over power developers, a recommendation that the major power interests had incorporated into their own proposals.[38]

Davis's and Fall's announcements did not eliminate upper-basin fears, but they did lessen them. The audience interpreted their remarks to mean that the Federal Power Commission, of which Fall was one of three members, would grant no permits for either private or public development until a compact had been negotiated.[39] This understanding represented a blow to the advocates of municipal dam construction and also to Southern California Edison, but it pleased upper-river men who wanted their rights secured before any downstream development.

Fall went even further in lessening upper-river apprehension when he called together the basin's principal water leaders and told them that President Harding had decided on a federal representative to the Colorado River Commission. The president, he explained, had already asked Secretary of Commerce Herbert Hoover to take the assignment, and Hoover had accepted.[40] This news eliminated the debate among league members over who the federal representative should be. But most important, it meant that the last obstacle to compact negotiations had been removed.

The promise of imminent negotiations greatly pleased the upper-basin representatives, but Hoover's name generated no feeling of excitement. Despite his cabinet position and his fame as food administrator during the First World War, Hoover had not been the prime candidate of any basin water leader. Delph Carpenter would have preferred Elihu Root or "a big man of this type" who was "entirely apart from the Reclamation or Power Services" and "thoroughly advised on matters of inter-

[38] "Problems of the Imperial Valley and Vicinity," p. 242; "Statement Made by John B. Miller, President, Southern California Edison Co.," August 3, 1921, Swing Papers; E. H. Shoemaker to William Mulholland, December 5, 1921, file 360, Colorado River, Papers of the Los Angeles Department of Water and Power.

[39] *Los Angeles Times,* December 10, 1921; *Los Angeles Examiner,* December 10, 1921.

[40] Carpenter, "Colorado River Compact," p. 37, file 1-M/366, Hoover Papers. Hoover was not officially appointed until a week later, on December 17, 1921. "Hoover Dam Documents," *H. Doc.* 717, 80 Cong., 2 sess. (1948), p. 19.

state and international law." Wyoming and Nevada water men agreed, sharing also Carpenter's preference for someone who "should not come from any of the public land states" and "who is in no way interested in the Western States." [41] As an adopted Californian and an engineer rather than an international lawyer, Hoover obviously failed to meet these requirements.

Not even fellow Californian Phil Swing considered Hoover the ideal candidate, but he believed the secretary's basic honesty and international reputation would benefit the commission. "While he would not be my first choice," Swing told a constituent, ". . . still his understanding would be such that no one could question his intended fairness." "And, in addition to that," noted Swing, "being a member of the Cabinet, [he] might be of value in helping to attract the attention of the administration to this big constructive project." [42]

Most agreed with Swing on Hoover's value as a member of the Harding administration. In fact, Wyoming's Mondell had specifically urged the president to appoint a cabinet member, and Secretary Fall had endorsed Hoover, in large part because of his reputation as an engineer. Hoover's identification with California continued to worry some, especially in the upper basin, but most saw an element of truth in Swing's assessment: "Although he is a Californian, technically speaking, yet as a matter of fact he is really a citizen of the world." [43]

IX

The possibility of early compact negotiations and the promises

[41] Delph Carpenter to J. G. Scrugham, August 15, 1921, Scrugham Papers, NHS; Delph Carpenter to Thomas Campbell, September 15, 1921, Scrugham Papers, NHS; Deputy State Engineer to Frank C. Emerson, June 16, 1921, Papers of the Wyoming State Engineer.

[42] Phil Swing to Cora M. Long, November 21 and 23, 1921, Swing Papers. Swing had learned before the Riverside meeting that Hoover might be the appointee.

[43] Ibid., November 21, 1921; Swing to F. H. McIver, January 14, 1922, Swing Papers; Colorado River Commission, "Minutes of the First Meeting" (Washington, D.C., January 26, 1922), p. 2, file 032, Colorado River Project, Bureau of Reclamation Papers; Carpenter, "Colorado River Compact," p. 35, file 1-M/366, Hoover Papers.

made by Fall and Davis that river development would not violate the rights of the states proved pleasing. But such assurances did not lessen upper-basin determination to change the league's voting regulations. Nor did they cause most Californians to soften their resistance to such a move. Californians returned from their caucus still divided, but the overwhelming majority was dead set against any change in the rules. The advocates of public ownership urged a compromise proposal that would prohibit the enactment of any resolutions and turn the meeting into a forum for general discussion of Colorado River problems. The other delegates balked at this proposal, however, and thus forced a showdown on the motion to suspend the bylaws. When the vote was finally ordered, the numerically superior advocates of public development in the California delegation defeated the resolution.[44]

Though angered by their setback, upper-basin leaders still hoped to heal the breach and frame a declaration on which all could agree. On the morning of the final day of the meeting, they persuaded representatives from six of the basin states and some Californians to meet in another part of the city and draft a series of resolutions to be brought before the convention. In the early afternoon they sent word that they had nearly reached agreement. The news upset many Californians who believed that the resolutions were aimed primarily at protecting upper-basin interests. Rather than provide a forum for their opponents, some disgruntled Californians moved to adjourn the meeting. Attendance at the time was poor, since most league delegates expected no important business until later in the day. Despite the outcries of a few angry dissenters, the Californians successfully adjourned the meeting.[45]

The bitter debate over voting regulations and the abrupt adjournment left the league in a shambles. It never fully recovered from the fight in Riverside, and its influence in Colorado River matters plummeted thereafter. Yet it had played a critical role in river affairs, and if nothing else, its Riverside conference had dramatically emphasized the difficulties of trying to harmonize basin interests.

[44] Ready, "Report," p. 24; *Los Angeles Times*, December 11, 1921.
[45] *Los Angeles Times*, December 11, 1921; Ready, "Report," pp. 24, 28.

X

Secretary of the Interior Albert Fall had sensed the ominous implications of the Riverside fiasco. On December 12, two days after that meeting, as he gaveled to order the hearing in San Diego on Arthur Powell Davis's preliminary report, he was determined to lessen tensions, though not at the expense of removing the federal government from Colorado River development. This determination became clearly evident after he asked Davis to take the floor and describe the major ways in which he planned to modify his earlier report.

One modification prompted virtually no discussion. This was Davis's decision to place the entire burden of paying for the project on the power consumers. Interested states would, however, still be permitted to contribute to the construction expense and receive in return a block of power at cost. Independent study had led Davis to agree with the protesters from the Coachella Valley who believed that power sales could and should finance the entire project. This move would relieve the irrigation and flood-control interests of any burden. But, as Davis noted, those same interests would also be power consumers; hence, in the final analysis, they would help to underwrite the dam with "the money they pay for the power." [46] No one objected to this modification, particularly since the municipal and private power interests had already concluded that electricity sales could easily pay for the project. [47]

The other major change proposed by Davis attracted considerably more attention. By announcing that the federal government alone should "construct, own, and perpetually control any dam," he affirmed what Fall had already intimated at the Riverside meeting. In short, he declared that he was eliminating from his recommendations the option that would permit nonfederal agencies to undertake the project. He admitted that he had ear-

[46] "Proceedings of the Conference on the Construction of the Boulder Canyon Dam, Held at San Diego, Calif.," in *S. Doc. 142*, 67 Cong., 2 sess. (1922), p. 247 (hereafter cited as "Proceedings of the San Diego Conference").

[47] "Statement Made by John B. Miller, President, Southern California Edison Co.," August 3, 1921, Swing Papers; E. H. Shoemaker to William Mulholland, December 5, 1921, file 360, Colorado River, Papers of the Los Angeles Department of Water and Power.

lier included such an option only because he did not think that
Congress would appropriate the necessary funds. He now believed otherwise. In view of Fall's support and "the approaching
success of . . . reduction of armament," he explained, "I think
the chances are excellent that Congress will provide for . . .
the construction." "If the program for the reduction of navies
alone, to say nothing of armies, . . . should be carried out," then
"the Boulder Canyon Dam and several more could be constructed
in the time it would take to build one dam on that river." [48]

Because of the recent imbroglio between the private and municipal power interests, some in the assemblage greeted Davis's
remarks with warm applause. There still remained, however, the
question of who would generate the power at the dam site. Fall
indicated that many parties could participate in that undertaking.
"There will be plenty of places for power plants at the Boulder
damsite, and I personally have no objection to permitting private
interests to construct power plants at the dam." But, he cautioned, "they would have to compete with the government in the
sale of power." [49] Just what he meant by this statement he did
not make clear, but he seemed to imply that the federal government's interest in hydroelectricity might be more than merely
incidental, as it had been in the past.

The question of federal construction of the dam caused many
Arizonans and Nevadans to accept Fall's and Davis's remarks
with something less than enthusiasm. Neither state would be
able to tax federally owned works without special authorizing
legislation, but each registered its strong determination to obtain
needed hydroelectricity from whoever would produce it. "The
State of Arizona is committeed [sic] to any policy and any program that shall meet with the approval of the Secretary of the
Interior," Arizona's Richard E. Sloan assured Fall, but "if the
plan suggested by the director be adopted," then "I think . . .
that we should be safeguarded in some contract" that will protect "our preferential right to the use of such power as we may
legitimately use and need . . . so that when we do want it we
will be able to get it." [50]

[48] "Proceedings of the San Diego Conference," pp. 243–244; *San
Diego Sun*, December 12, 1921; *San Diego Tribune*, December 12,
1921; *Los Angeles Times*, December 13, 1921.

[49] *San Diego Sun*, December 12, 1921.

[50] "Proceedings of the San Diego Conference," pp. 302–303.

Nevada's Governor Emmet Boyle agreed. "There appears to be done all that we can do except to promote the activities of the Department of the Interior," Boyle declared shortly after the San Diego meeting. "We must thereafter trust to the good-will and generosity of the Government in seeing that this State is not deprived of any of its rights in the premises." [51]

Upper-basin spokesmen also resigned themselves to Fall and Davis's decision. Like most others at the hearing, they realized that if they hoped to see their own portion of the basin developed in a reasonable amount of time, they would have to accept Davis's recommendations—at least for the present. Most important in the thinking of upstream leaders, however, were Fall's and Davis's assurances of support for the principles behind the compact movement and their pledge to prevent on the Colorado a repetition of the upper Rio Grande and North Platte situations. Indeed, the government had already taken steps to lift the embargo on the headwaters of the North Platte, and Fall now promised to look personally into the Rio Grande problem. "It may be," he admitted, "that the Reclamation Service has been dilatory in not having ascertained and reported heretofore that there was sufficient water falling within that basin" for additional lands in the United States. "I have suggested as much myself, and it shall be my pleasure to see that at an early date a report is made upon this proposition." He then won a round of applause with his final promise: "[It is] my determination . . . to see that no such disagreements or controversies may arise in the future" on the Colorado.[52]

Also helping to quiet upper-basin apprehension were the peaceful overtures of lower-basin representatives, especially those from California, many of whom now sought to change

[51] Emmet D. Boyle to A. Boyer, January 4, 1922, Boyle Papers. See also J. G. Scrugham to Colorado River Development Commission of Nevada, December 20, 1921, Boyle Papers; and "Proceedings of the San Diego Conference," pp. 319–321. Nevadans eventually concluded that private firms would take too long—possibly fifteen or twenty years—to complete construction of storage and power works in Boulder Canyon. Colorado River Commission, "Hearings" (Denver, April 1, 1922), pp. 22–23, file 032, Colorado River Project, Bureau of Reclamation Papers.

[52] "Proceedings of the San Diego Conference," pp. 318–319, 324; *Santa Fe New Mexican*, December 13, 1921.

the unsavory image they had acquired as a result of their actions in Riverside. "We wish to affirm in the strongest possible manner that we recognize the equitable, moral, and legal right of the States upstream to be guaranteed the . . . fullest opportunity of development of their own projects," declared R. D. McPherrin of the Imperial Irrigation District. Other Californians made similar statements, as did representatives from the two other lower-basin states, Nevada and Arizona. They pointedly emphasized "the justice of the position assumed by the States to the north of us." "We not only recognize that," asserted Arizona's Sloan, "but we stand ready to pledge . . . that no adverse rights to the use of water may be permitted to be developed to the prejudice of the people of these Northern States pending the solution of the question of the equitable distribution of the waters of the Colorado by the Colorado River Commission." [53]

Such declarations were soothing. "I am glad that the spirit manifested here is entirely different from that which seemed to come out of the Riverside meeting," stated Frank C. Emerson, state engineer of Wyoming. The other representatives agreed, and they could only hope that Emerson was right when he predicted that a compact would "be worked out" and "our differences . . . buried." [54]

Fall adjourned the meeting on this optimistic note, and the delegates returned home to prepare for the compact negotiations scheduled to begin in a month. They were confident about the future, but most sensed that the real battle had only begun.

Much had happened in the sixteen months following the Denver meeting of the League of the Southwest. The seven basin states and the federal government had easily endorsed the call for diplomacy issued at that conference in August, 1920; the president had appointed a high-ranking cabinet member to the Colorado River Commission charged with drafting a compact; and Davis had released a report, albeit a preliminary one, formally affirming the feasibility of a high dam in the Boulder Canyon area.

On a more ominous note, a harsh dispute between private and

[53] "Proceedings of the San Diego Conference," pp. 251, 302, 320, passim.
[54] Ibid., p. 324.

municipal power interests had permanently crippled the League of the Southwest and exacerbated tensions throughout the basin just at the moment when the states needed to cooperate. The loss of the league was not critical, however, for it had already served its purpose by paving the way for the upcoming negotiations. More serious had been the bitter intrabasin rivalry that had left the league in a shambles. That rivalry was softened by the promises of Davis and Fall to protect the interests of all the states. And this they seemed more capable of doing once they made up their minds to support federal construction of the Boulder Canyon dam.

Indeed, perhaps the most significant development during the months following the Denver conference had been the decision of Fall and Davis to advocate only a federally constructed project. Davis's initial hesitation in his preliminary report had helped precipitate the struggle between the municipal and private power interests. His return to his earlier position now aided in quieting that same dispute. Never again would he hesitate, but never again would the private power interests remain as silent as they had been. They might acquiesce in federal dam construction, but when forceful attempts would be made during the next decade to put the federal government into the business of producing and selling power at Boulder Canyon, Muscle Shoals, and elsewhere, they would strike back in force on local, regional, and national fronts.

But even now distrust of the federal government and interstate jealousy over water and power rights were strong in the Colorado River Basin. Just how strong would become readily apparent when diplomats from the basin undertook their most formidable task—the drafting of a treaty.

6

Stalemate

In his welcoming speech on January 26, 1922, Herbert Hoover emphasized to the assembled commissioners the need to settle their differences quickly so that the great task of harnessing the Colorado and developing the Southwest's economic resources could begin. "I consider it a great honor . . . to represent the Federal Government in so great an undertaking," one that will "prevent endless litigation" and the "delays and costs" that would "be imposed upon our citizens through such conflicts." [1]

Hoover's hopes were, of course, those of everyone seated around the conference table in Washington, and his listeners reciprocated his warm greeting by unanimously electing him chairman of the Colorado River Commission. Their show of unanimity was deceptive, however, for they would agree on little else during the next few weeks. Even their selection of him as chairman was misleading. Some seriously questioned the wisdom of having a federal official preside over a conference dealing with a matter principally of interest to the states. Others resented

[1] Colorado River Commission, "Minutes of the First Meeting" (Washington, D.C., January 26, 1922), p. 2, in file 032, Colorado River Project, Bureau of Reclamation Papers, Record Group 115, National Archives.

the way in which he took for granted that he would be chairman as soon as he had learned that President Warren Harding had appointed him to the commission. At one point during the preceding year, some had recommended Delph Carpenter for the chairmanship, though they apparently had done so as much to neutralize the "very good talker" from Colorado as to honor him.[2] But Carpenter had no wish to be hampered by the obligations of the position. Moreover, on reflection, most of his fellow conferees agreed that it would be unwise to name someone from a basin state. As much by process of elimination as by any other method, Hoover emerged as the logical candidate.

I

The representatives from the seven "high contracting powers" whom Hoover welcomed to Washington were a talented, if not always harmonious, group. As expected, Colorado had sent Delph Carpenter, the principal advocate of the compact idea and perhaps the shrewdest water-rights lawyer in the United States. His cleverness and diplomatic skills had prompted a friend to dub him the "Silver Fox of the Rockies," a title that his fellow commissioners considered apt.[3]

Carpenter came with the knowledge that his state's future was inseparably linked to the undeveloped water resources of the "western slope," that third of Colorado lying west of the continental divide and within the Colorado River Basin. There the rains and snows on the high mountains assure an abundant water supply, and by 1920 it was being used to irrigate about 740,000 acres, though thousands of additional acres awaited development.[4] East of the continental divide the acreage possible for

[2] W. S. Norviel to J. G. Scrugham, August 30, 1921, J. G. Scrugham Papers, Nevada Historical Society (hereafter cited as Scrugham Papers, NHS); R. E. Caldwell to Delph Carpenter, December 21, 1921, Papers of the Utah State Engineer, Utah State Archives, Salt Lake City. J. G. Scrugham believed that either Carpenter or Arizona's W. S. Norviel would make a good chairman. J. G. Scrugham to W. S. Norviel, August 12, 1921, Scrugham Papers, NHS.

[3] *Santa Fe New Mexican,* November 17, 1922.

[4] Colorado River Commission, "Hearings" (Denver, March 31, 1922), pp. 12–13, copy in file 032, Colorado River Project, Bureau

irrigation was even greater, but the limited water supply was already largely used and future development sharply circumscribed. Carpenter was in Washington for one major purpose: to obtain assurances that there would be enough water to take care of those lands and to satisfy all the other water needs of Colorado.

Also from the upper basin had come Frank C. Emerson of Wyoming, soon known as the "boy commissioner" because of his youthful looks, and R. E. Caldwell of Utah, who would emerge as a tenacious adversary. Both held the position of state engineer, which included, among other duties, the responsibility of overseeing the administration of water rights in their respective states, a task that had kept them well abreast of developments on the Colorado.

COLORADO RIVER BASIN
AVERAGE CONTRIBUTIONS AND DRAINAGE AREAS OF
PRINCIPAL TRIBUTARIES AS OF 1922

Tributary	Percentage of Total Discharge	Discharge in Acre-feet	Drainage Area in Square Miles	Percentage of Total Area	Acre-feet per Square Mile
Green River	32	5,510,000	44,000	18	125
Upper Colorado[a] (Grand River)	40	6,940,000	26,000	10	267
San Juan River	14	2,700,000	26,000	10	104
Other areas except Gila	8	1,560,000	91,000	39	16
Gila	6	1,070,000	57,000	23	19

[a] Technically a part of the mainstream and, hence, not a tributary.

SOURCE: "Problems of Imperial Valley and Vicinity," *S. Doc. 142*, 67 Cong., 2 sess. (1922), p. 2.

Emerson's primary interest was in the Green River, the Colorado's northernmost and largest tributary, which rose in the Wind River Mountains of southwestern Wyoming and, together with the Little Snake, drained some 19,000 square miles before crossing into Utah and Colorado. Though irrigation along the Green

of Reclamation Papers; Colorado River Commission, "Minutes of the Sixth Meeting" (Washington, D.C., January 30, 1922), p. 70.

had begun in the mid-nineteenth century, development had been slow, largely because most of the arable lands were above 6,000 feet and thus subject to plant-killing frosts and a relatively short growing season. Even so, irrigation had proved successful, and by 1920 about 267,000 acres were being watered, though this area was small in comparison to the acreage that Emerson wanted to see brought under the plow. He also wished to reclaim additional water for Wyoming's valuable livestock industry; and like nearly everyone else in the upper basin, he looked forward to the day when hydroelectric plants would be built along the headwaters and their product used to power railroads and to develop the oil shale, coal, and other rich mineral deposits of the upper basin.[5]

Caldwell of Utah shared Emerson's interest in industrial development and in the Green River, but he was also excited by the prospects along the upper Colorado, or the Grand River as it was known until its recent renaming, which joined the Green River in southeastern Utah.[6] Together the Green and the Grand drained some 40,000 square miles in Utah. Their heavy runoff had made possible the irrigation of 359,000 acres by 1920 and encouraged hopes that thousands of additional acres could be developed, including lands outside of the basin and in the valley of the Great Salt Lake.[7]

The final upper-basin delegate, Stephen B. Davis, Jr., of New Mexico, was concerned primarily with a different set of tributaries, the Gila, the Little Colorado, and the San Juan. Together these rivers drained 23,000 square miles of the western part of

[5] Colorado River Commission, "Hearings" (Salt Lake City, March 28, 1922), pp. 14–15 (Denver, March 31, 1922), pp. 170–171; Colorado River Commission, "Minutes of the Sixth Meeting" (Washington, D.C., January 30, 1922), p. 70; "Problems of Imperial Valley and Vicinity," *S. Doc. 142*, 67 Cong., 2 sess. (1922), p. 3.

[6] Six months earlier, on July 25, 1921, the Grand was officially renamed the Colorado River. Because the change was so recent, many people still used the older designation. Until the renaming, the Colorado did not officially begin until the junction of the Green and the Grand. U.S., *Statutes at Large*, XLII: 146.

[7] Colorado River Commission, "Hearings" (Salt Lake City, March 27, 1922), p. 79, passim; Colorado River Commission, "Minutes of the Sixth Meeting" (Washington, D.C., January 30, 1922), p. 70.

the state and in 1920 contributed water for the irrigation of about 34,900 acres. Since the Gila and Little Colorado were almost entirely Arizona streams and difficult to tap in New Mexico because of the deep canyons along their headwaters, the greatest New Mexican interest was in the San Juan, a river that rose in the mountains of southern Colorado and ran through northwestern New Mexico before crossing into the canyon lands of southern Utah, where it joined the mainstream.[8] For Stephen Davis, an associate justice of the New Mexico supreme court and an expert in water law, the task was to assure New Mexico all the waters of the San Juan and the other tributaries that she could put to use.

COLORADO RIVER BASIN DRAINAGE: AREA BY STATES
(In Square Miles)

Wyoming	19,000
Colorado	39,000
New Mexico	23,000
Arizona	103,000
Utah	40,000
Nevada	12,000
California	6,000
Total area in the United States	242,000
Area in Mexico	2,000
Grand total	244,000

SOURCE: "Problems of Imperial Valley and Vicinity,"
S. Doc. 142, 67 Cong., 2 sess. (1922), p. 3.

From the lower basin came an equally determined group of negotiators. They realized that they wanted far more water than their states contributed to the river, but this discrepancy in no way inhibited them in their demands. Among those who would emerge as the most tenacious was Arizona's Winfield S. Norviel,

[8] Colorado River Commission, "Hearings" (Denver, April 1, 1922), pp. 6–10; Colorado River Commission, "Minutes of the Sixth Meeting" (Washington, D.C., January 30, 1922), p. 70; S. B. Davis, Jr., to James F. Hinkle, January 5, 1923, James F. Hinkle Papers, New Mexico State Archives, Santa Fe.

the state water commissioner and a man who prided himself on his ability to avoid publicity, something he would now find increasingly difficult to escape.[9] About 90 percent of Arizona's 114,000 square miles lay within the Colorado River Basin.[10] This fact, together with that state's strong desire for hydroelectric power, helped guarantee unusually deep interest among Arizonans in the compact deliberations. It also complicated immensely the task of arriving at a policy on which most Arizonans could agree.

Representing the two remaining lower-basin states were their state engineers. California dispatched W. F. McClure, a sober— indeed sour-looking—man who invariably managed to wear a scowl whenever a cameraman was present. McClure, a former lay minister with a penchant for quoting the Bible, was given more to a careful weighing of the recommendations of others than to formulating or arguing for proposals of his own. Some Californians attributed his lack of aggressiveness to the fact that he was from the northern part of the state; and despite some earlier work in the Owens Valley, he was not as familiar with conditions along the lower Colorado as he should have been. He "was a fine man," recalled one southern Californian, "but who, I thought, never knew there was a Colorado River." [11]

More expansive than McClure was Nevada's James G. Scrugham, who, like Emerson of Wyoming, later became a governor of his state. Scrugham, unlike the other negotiators, was primarily interested in hydroelectric power. Only a relatively small amount of Nevada's parched acreage could be watered by the Colorado River, and most of this land was along the lower reaches of the Virgin River, which joined the mainstream near the great bend in the river in southern Nevada and northwestern Arizona.[12]

[9] Colorado River Commission, "Hearings" (Phoenix, March 17, 1922), p. 13; *Santa Fe New Mexican,* November 17, 1922.

[10] "Problems of Imperial Valley and Vicinity," p. 3.

[11] *Santa Fe New Mexican,* November 17, 1922; William J. Carr, "Memors" (Oral History Project, University of California, Los Angeles, 1959), p. 141; see also Frank Adams, "Frank Adams, University of California, on Irrigation, Reclamation and Water Administration" (Regional Cultural History Project, University of California, Berkeley, 1959), p. 374.

[12] Colorado River Commission, "Hearings" (Denver, April 1, 1922), pp. 21–22.

California, on the other hand, wanted significant amounts of both water and power—water for the Imperial, Coachella, and Palo Verde valleys and power for Los Angeles and other fast-growing southern California cities and agricultural communities. Unlike Arizona and the upper-basin states, California and Nevada contributed little water to the Colorado. State leaders fully realized, however, that they would benefit enormously from the Reclamation Service's Boulder Canyon project and were anxious to open negotiations in Washington. They were especially pleased, therefore, when Hoover adopted a position that favored their interests.

II

"This Commission," Hoover announced in greeting the delegates, "has been established primarily to consider and if possible to agree upon a compact . . . providing for an equitable division of the water supply of the Colorado and its tributaries." But, he cautioned, "the problem is not as simple as might appear on the surface." "While there is possibly ample water in the river . . . , there is not a sufficient supply . . . to meet all claims unless there is some definite program of water conservation." In short, he explained, "the Commission will . . . inevitably be driven into the consideration of a program looking further than the immediate legalistic relationship of the states if it is to find a solution to the problem." [13]

Such a statement so early in the deliberations proved especially encouraging to lower-basin representatives, particularly to Californians who had begun lobbying with Hoover as soon as his appointment had been announced. Only a few days earlier, Phil Swing had gone to the secretary of commerce and given him California's side of the story. The response had elated him. Not only did Hoover believe in the necessity of a federally built dam on the lower river, but he had also expressed a desire to have the Colorado River Commission itself supervise construction of the works. "Confidentially," wrote Swing in summarizing his impressions of the conversation for an official of the Imperial Irrigation District, "I want to assure you that Secretary Hoover is in

[13] Colorado River Commission, "Minutes of the First Meeting" (Washington, D.C., January 26, 1922), p. 2.

earnest about this work and is already setting about to line up sufficient influence to warrant its being done. It seems to me that the thing for us to do is to get back of him and help him put it over." [14]

McClure had been sent to Washington to "put it over." He found strong support among the other lower-basin representatives, who joined him in endorsing the secretary's suggestion to expand the commission's responsibilities to include storage. Far less enthusiastic, however, were spokesmen from the headwaters, especially Colorado's Carpenter and New Mexico's Davis, who believed that Hoover was rushing matters. "The extent to which this Commission may go in side-recommendations as to the place and position of various structures," declared Carpenter, "is a matter that some of us feel should be developed later as the case proceeds." Davis agreed. "We will have a much simpler task," he explained, "if we . . . lay down a general plan" rather than attempt "to work out an entire scheme." For now, he said, "I would very much like . . . to get the facts before us" and "after that is done it seems to me that we can act more wisely as to what will give the best final results." [15]

Hoover took the hint. There was no sense pushing the issue now and creating hard feelings. He dropped it with the warning, however, that circumstances would probably force a later reconsideration. He also reaffirmed his own strong personal interest in major river development. "I do not at all contest the notion that we are under limitations as to action," he acknowledged, "but at the same time . . . our opportunity to advance national thought on what is one of the greatest assets of the United States should not be missed." [16]

III

The brief discussion of storage dramatized for the delegates the conflicting priorities of the states, especially California's over-

[14] Phil Swing to F. H. McIver, January 14, 1922, Phil D. Swing Papers, Department of Special Collections, University of California, Los Angeles.

[15] Colorado River Commission, "Minutes of the First Meeting" (Washington, D.C., January 26, 1922), pp. 16, 19–20.

[16] Ibid., p. 18.

riding desire for storage and power and the upper basin's equally strong wish to protect itself. With such issues clearly in mind, the commissioners turned soberly to the principal job ahead of them—dividing the waters. Their first and most formidable task was the establishment of criteria that would assure a fair amount of water for each state.

The delegates tried initially to determine the water needs of each state as measured by its irrigable acreage. The approach seemed reasonable, since agriculture represented the greatest consumer of water; and each state planned to devote most of its future water resources to irrigation. Power production required the *use*, but not the *consumption*, of water to turn the turbines; and domestic needs, they believed, would remain relatively small for years to come. The commissioners consequently turned their attention to tables prepared by Arthur Powell Davis depicting the lands that could be watered from the Colorado River.

Davis calculated the total irrigable area at 6,923,000 acres, of which 2,654,000 were currently being irrigated. The number of acres already developed caused no dispute, but there was considerable disagreement over what constituted the future irrigable area. Davis estimated it at 4,349,000 acres, but the states responded with claims totaling 7,160,000 acres, a figure nearly double the Davis estimate. Only California accepted without question the Reclamation Service findings, but she was, of course, anxious for a quick settlement so that river development could begin immediately.

The dissension greatly disturbed Davis, not only because it represented a challenge to his professional competence, but also because any attempt to negotiate a compact based on acreage would be jeopardized by such demands. "Assuming . . . that somehow the water is actually placed upon the acreages claimed," Davis told Hoover, "there would be considerable shortage in some years." [17] In effect, there was not enough water to meet the claims of the states.

The commissioners recognized the predicament in which they

[17] Arthur Powell Davis to Herbert Hoover, February 3, 1922, file 1-M/315, Herbert Hoover Papers, Hoover Presidential Library, West Branch, Iowa; S. B. Davis, Jr., to M. C. Mechem, February 11, 1922, Merritt C. Mechem Papers, New Mexico State Archives, Santa Fe.

ACREAGE ESTIMATES SUBMITTED AT
COLORADO RIVER COMMISSION MEETING,
WASHINGTON, D.C., JANUARY, 1922

State	Irrigated in 1920	Additional Acreage (A. P. Davis Estimate)	Additional Acreage (Estimate of Basin States)
Wyoming	367,000	540,000	580,000
Colorado	740,000	1,018,000	1,825,000
Utah	359,000	456,000	1,000,000
New Mexico	34,000	483,000	1,400,000
Nevada	5,000	82,000[a]	82,000
Arizona	501,000	676,000	1,172,000
California	458,000	481,000	481,000
Total U.S.	2,464,000	3,739,000	6,540,000
Mexico	190,000	610,000	620,000
Grand total	2,654,000	4,349,000	7,160,000

[a] Davis's original estimate was 2,000 acres.

SOURCE: Colorado River Commission, "Minutes of the Sixth Meeting" (January 30, 1922), pp. 70, 77, in file 032, Colorado River Project, Bureau of Reclamation Papers, Record Group 115, National Archives.

had placed themselves, and each tried to persuade Davis that the claim, at least for his particular state, was fair. Davis remained unmoved. Only in the case of Nevada did he eventually agree to modify his estimate, but this concession did nothing to undermine his report because Nevada's claims were the smallest of all the states. Nevada was currently irrigating some 5,000 acres with Colorado River water, and she estimated her future irrigable acreage at only 82,000. Davis had placed it at 2,000.[18] By acknowledging Nevada's larger claim, however, he was admitting that she could irrigate a grand total of 87,000 acres, a

[18] Arthur Powell Davis attributed the incorrectness of his estimate to Nevada's failure to supply him with its acreage claim before the meeting. Had Nevada done so, as the other states did, he contended, there would have been no discrepancy. A. P. Davis to Herbert Hoover, February 3, 1922, file 1-M/315, Hoover Papers; Colorado River Commission, "Hearings" (Phoenix, March 15, 1922), pp. 44–47.

pitifully small amount when compared with the 939,000 acres demanded by California, the state with the next smallest claim.

While Californians were willing to negotiate on the basis of Davis's figures, their request was small compared with the total irrigable area of 1,673,000 acres insisted upon by Arizona, the 2,565,000 acres claimed by Colorado, the 1,359,000 acres wanted by Utah, or the 1,434,000 acres demanded by New Mexico. Not only were the claims of these four states larger, they were based on data that was admittedly inadequate. "Personally, I believe that the acres that have been submitted" by the states "are in excess of what can actually be developed," conceded Utah's Caldwell. "The estimate . . . by the Reclamation Service may be somewhere near right and may ultimately be all that any State will wish . . . to reclaim [but] I am not prepared to conclude on that basis." [19]

Neither were any of the other states except California and Nevada. Behind the opposition was fear—fear that Davis might be mistaken in his projections. Save for the minor exception of Nevada, none of them demonstrated that the reclamation chief was in error; but neither could they point to studies made by their own engineers that corroborated his findings. Though all intended to make such studies—and some were in the process of doing so—none had completed them and few expected to have them in the near future. Faced with uncertainty, they adopted the only safe approach: they claimed an amount great enough to offset their fears.

Hoover realized that careful studies by the states would take years to complete and even then there would be no assurance of agreement. Fearful that the talks were becoming deadlocked, he tried to engineer a compromise by asking whether the states would accept an allocation based on Davis's figures if assurances were given that the allocation could be modified after twenty years.[20]

The question cleared the air, but at the expense of revealing just how far apart the states were. New Mexico and Wyoming expressed approval of a reallocation in twenty years, but they

[19] Colorado River Commission, "Minutes of the Seventh Meeting" (Washington, D.C., January 30, 1922), pp. 92–93.

[20] Ibid., pp. 92, 94.

opposed any allocation based on Davis's figures. Norviel of Arizona, on the other hand, indicated a willingness to negotiate a settlement based on Davis's figures, but only if provision was made for storage and the Gila River was exempted from the terms of the agreement. Most of the Gila's waters were already used by Arizona, and Norviel believed they should belong solely to that state. But his proposal, as well as Hoover's less complicated suggestion, met vigorous opposition from upper-basin representatives, especially those from Utah and Colorado, who now decided to denounce the "whole acreage idea."

"I do not favor getting together in any conclusive way here on the basis of acreage," Caldwell of Utah bluntly announced. Acreage might turn out to be the key to a solution, he admitted, but he could not agree to any such arrangement until after he had consulted with state officials and had personally assured himself that no Utah lands would be left dry. "I think it is my duty as a Commissioner from the State of Utah to determine to my own satisfaction the acreage in our State," he declared firmly.[21]

Carpenter of Colorado was equally adamant. If the states insisted on negotiating on the basis of acreage, he explained, then Colorado "would be compelled" to claim an amount "far in excess of anything that has already been considered." The reasons were both political and geographic. Colorado's lands "are so isolated, so cut up by mountains, so scattered and limited in areas" that, in order "to fix a safe limitation upon her acreage," she would have to demand considerably more acreage than "will ever be . . . reclaimed." "Otherwise," he said, "her limitation of area would be so out of proportion to her water supply that we could expect no other than an unfavorable view by her legislature and ultimate defeat of the present objective." [22]

Despite his opposition to an agreement based on Arthur Powell Davis's estimates, Carpenter accepted Davis's claims about the adequacy of the water supply. Logically his position was indefensible: he could not reasonably accept Davis's conclusion about water supply and at the same time deny the acreage estimates on which that conclusion rested. But he used this weak position to justify a compact proposal of his own, which he introduced on the last day of talks.

[21] Ibid., pp. 92, 93.   [22] Ibid., pp. 112–113.

IV

Carpenter's proposal took the form of a resolution asking the lower basin to assume the risks of an inadequate water supply: "the high contracting parties . . . agree . . . that the construction of any and all reservoirs or other works upon the lower river shall in no manner arrest or interfere with the subsequent development of the territory of any of the upper states." [23] In short, he would reject the principle of priority and remove restrictions on upper-basin water use. "The whole problem rests on the amount of water," he explained. "If there is truth in the statement that there is ample water supply," then "there is no need of any . . . limitation" on the upper states.

Carpenter might have added that if there was sufficient water, the upper basin need not fear development below. He skirted the obvious, however, preferring to emphasize the innocuousness of his proposal. "The typography and configuration of the mountainous states of origin are such," he contended, that they "will never be able to beneficially use even an equitable part of the waters rising and flowing within the respective territory of each." Thus, he concluded, his plan provided for "a natural apportionment of benefits." [24]

As an added fillip, Carpenter claimed that his proposition asked for nothing more than the federal government and the private power interests had already promised at the League of the Southwest meeting in Riverside and at the hearings presided over by Secretary of the Interior Albert Fall in San Diego. "At Riverside and later at San Diego," he reminded his fellow commissioners, "Director Davis of the Reclamation Service stated it to be substantially his position . . . that works . . . on the lower river should be constructed upon the principle of noninterference with the Upper Territory." Moreover, he noted, "at the same time and places, the power interests came forward with a similar statement." [25] Carpenter then produced a corroborative memo signed by R. H. Ballard, vice-president and general manager of the Southern California Edison Company.

Challenges came immediately. "That statement of Director Davis," declared Hoover, "is based on his conclusions as to the

[23] Ibid., p. 105.   [24] Ibid., pp. 105, 109, 138.
[25] Ibid., p. 118.

area of irrigable lands. Yet we have before us estimates of the
. . . Upper States which exceed Director Davis' estimate." "In
fact," he declared, that estimate is "practically doubled." "I doubt
whether" Davis or the private power interests "would form that
declaration again on the basis of such a claimed acreage as
that." [26]

Lower-basin spokesmen strongly backed Hoover's assessment.
"Mr. Carpenter seems to me," grumbled McClure of California,
"to take the position that Colorado must be protected to an extent
which would make her absolutely safe, regardless of other interests." Norviel of Arizona agreed and accused Coloradoans of re-
turning "always to the same point—we cannot be limited by
anything but the natural limitation that the Maker of the World
has given us." [27]

Nor did Carpenter's critics fail to note that his claims about
the adequacy of the water supply were belied by the acreage
estimates submitted by each of the states. So long as there were
any doubts about the water supply, they observed, it would be
impossible to persuade anyone to invest money in lower-basin
reclamation projects. Nevada's Scrugham succinctly summed up
the problem and his solution for it. "The fundamental objection
is that projects on the lower river can not be successfully financed
unless Mr. Carpenter's proposal is materially modified." [28]

But Carpenter refused to modify his proposition, and he was
staunchly supported in his resistance by Caldwell of Utah. The
upper basin was not united, however. Representatives from the
two other upstream states of Wyoming and New Mexico agreed
with those on the lower river that Carpenter was being unreasonable, but their views had no effect on the Coloradoan.

Because of the dissension among the upper-basin commissioners, Scrugham of Nevada thought that a compromise might be
possible. "Would you accept a change in your proposal," he
asked Carpenter, whereby "the construction of . . . reservoirs
or other works in any State upon the stream shall in no manner
arrest or interfere with the subsequent development of the territory of any of the other States . . . for a period of twenty
years?" [29] What Scrugham had in mind was obvious to everyone.
He was willing to allow the upper basin to develop as much as

[26] Ibid., p. 119.   [27] Ibid., p. 122.   [28] Ibid., p. 123.
[29] Ibid., p. 126.

possible—but only for a limited time. Twenty years was his offer.

While Carpenter saw merit in the proposal, he thought twenty years was not long enough to ensure full development in the upper basin. Full development, he insisted, would take at least fifty years.

"If the time limit is made for fifty years," snapped Scrugham, "it would be a serious bar to financing. I even question the wisdom of a twenty year time allowance."

Carpenter was adamant, but he held out the prospect of changing his mind. "I will be glad to consider it further," he stated, "but not at this time would I like to render my opinion." [30]

The negotiations were obviously heading for a deadlock. Hoover sensed what was happening and in desperation returned to the issue he had raised at the outset: the need to conserve the waters going to waste and threatening to inundate the valleys along the lower river. Would the delegates, he asked, be willing to agree on the construction "at the earliest possible moment" of a lower-basin dam? "We ought not to let this meeting break up," he pleaded, "without bringing in a broad visioned constructive plan in general terms so as to advance the whole subject, at the same time not asking anyone to commit himself as to water division." [31]

The reaction of the upper basin was instantaneously hostile. Even the moderate representatives from Wyoming and New Mexico, who were willing to yield to some restrictions on their development, objected. "We are not here to jump in a bandwagon with California," fumed Emerson. "If Wyoming is to make any commitment to development on the lower river," he declared, "we want at the same time a reasonable agreement as to the protection of our rights." New Mexico's Stephen Davis agreed. "I see nothing that the Upper States are going to get out of this . . . except possibly in the . . . use of power in the dams of the lower River"—and that, he contended, was nowhere near enough compensation.[32] He wanted water.

The negotiations had reached a deadlock. Some insisted that the commission admit defeat and disband. "We have split on the underlying and fundamental principles as to whether there

[30] Ibid., p. 127.   [31] Ibid., pp. 95–96.   [32] Ibid., pp. 101, 104.

will be any limitations stated in this compact," bitterly noted New Mexico's Stephen Davis. "I feel that if we can't agree now, we can't agree at all, and it seems to me useless to have a further meeting." [33]

Most others disagreed, Colorado and Utah as strenuously as the rest. "I think it would be the height of crime to the people who sent us here to adjourn permanently now," protested Carpenter. "It may not be near so hopeless as you think," Caldwell told Davis of New Mexico. "In fact, I never felt qualified to come to an agreement on this important matter at this time." [34] Carpenter and Caldwell urged their fellow commissioners merely to recess the meeting so that time could be spent carefully studying the various proposals that had been made. They strongly hinted that they might modify their own position.

This assurance was enough to win approval of future negotiations. The delegates also agreed to schedule a series of public hearings so that they might become better informed about the needs and wishes of people throughout the basin. Finally, on January 30, after a half week of frustrating talks, they left for home.

While Hoover was disappointed with these negotiations, he hoped that the hearings might produce strong public pressure for a settlement. He presided personally over hearings in Phoenix (March 16–17), Los Angeles (March 20), Salt Lake City (March 28), Grand Junction (March 29), Denver (March 31–April 1), and Cheyenne (April 2). He also arranged for the commission to tour the Boulder Canyon site and the Imperial Valley.

Hoover hoped that the hearings would soften the attitude of Caldwell and especially Carpenter, whom he considered the major obstacle to an agreement. He even asked New Mexico's Stephen Davis to go to Denver and reason with the Coloradoan.[35] As an upper-basin delegate and an expert in water law, Davis might be able to make headway with Carpenter in private conversations.

[33] Ibid., p. 147.   [34] Ibid., pp. 142, 150.

[35] S. B. Davis, Jr., to Merritt Mechem, February 11, 1922, Mechem Papers; Clarence Stetson to Ralph Merritt, February 14, 1922, file 1-M/310, Hoover Papers; S. B. Davis to Delph Carpenter, April 26, 1922, Delph Carpenter Papers, in possession of Judge Donald Carpenter, Greeley, Colo.

None of the ploys worked. Davis got nowhere with Carpenter; and Hoover, for his efforts, was accused of showing favoritism to Californians, an accusation that bothered President Warren Harding.[36] Most disturbing was the failure of the hearings to produce a consensus. Instead, they served merely to stiffen upper-basin resistance and to interject other elements into the controversy that left the states even further apart than before.

V

At first Hoover, Arthur Powell Davis, and the lower-basin commissioners hoped that the hearings would persuade Carpenter and Caldwell to agree at least to a twenty-year waiver of water rights. Scrugham had suggested such a settlement in Washington; and Carpenter, however cool to the idea, had agreed to consider it. Such a proposal, though offering no permanent solution, would allow the Boulder Canyon project to be constructed and would afford at least some protection to the upper basin. In effect, the waiver would suspend the principle of priority for two decades, thus permitting the upper states to make limited development without worrying about earlier uses established downstream as a result of a Boulder Canyon reservoir. But the proposal was firmly rejected by Carpenter as soon as the hearings began in Phoenix in March, two months after the Washington negotiations. "We have the mountains and the valleys, and . . . it would probably be a century before that country would reach its normal development," he explained.[37]

A waiver for a century was out of the question so far as the lower-basin representatives were concerned. Not even Arthur Powell Davis's offer of a compromise at the hearings a few days later in Los Angeles could bridge the gap that had developed between the basins. Though it was rejected, his proposition contained novel elements that would turn up again and eventually find their way into the compact negotiated by the states.

Davis suggested that everyone acknowledge what the debates had already made obvious: the commissioners were unlikely to

[36] Herbert Hoover to Warren G. Harding, April 8, 1922, file 1-M/318, Hoover Papers.

[37] Colorado River Commission, "Hearings" (Phoenix, March 17, 1922), p. 35.

agree on apportionments to each individual state; and the major disagreement was between the basins, not among the states within each basin. Starting from this premise, he recommended that the basin be divided into two separate sections for the purpose of water apportionment. Among other considerations, he pointed out, topography suggested such an approach. The deep canyons of northern Arizona and southern Utah naturally divided the states into an upper section, where most of the water originated, and a lower section, where the demand for water exceeded the supply. He proposed that both basins be permitted unrestricted development for perhaps fifty years. At the end of that time, the uses in the two areas should be recognized as rights, with this important proviso: the lower basin's rights would be secondary to those in the upper basin. Thereafter, however, new uses in the lower basin would be accorded rights "prior to anything subsequent in either basin." [38]

The proposal, would, in effect, grant prior rights to all upper-basin uses established during the next fifty years. Despite the concession, the upper states remained unmoved. They were simply not confident that they could make significant strides in fifty years. And this view was now shared by others besides Carpenter. After consultations with officials in their respective state capitals, the other upper-basin commissioners also concluded that a time-limit proposal would not work to their advantage. Governor Merritt Mechem of New Mexico spoke for them all when, in the name of his own state, he declared at the hearings in Denver: "New Mexico . . . could not accept unrestricted development during a limited period of time, unless the limit would be set ahead so far in the future as to be practically no limit at all." [39] The waiver proposal was dead.

Some basin leaders now tried to revive the idea of a compact based on the irrigable acreage within each state, but Colorado and Utah rejected the idea, just as they had at the Washington meeting, by insisting that they would accept no limitation on their future development. Their intransigence met head-on the lower states' equally stubborn refusal to agree to unlimited de-

[38] Colorado River Commission, "Hearings" (Los Angeles, March 20, 1922), pp. 100–111.

[39] Colorado River Commission, "Hearings" (Denver, April 1, 1922), p. 2.

velopment on the headwaters. To a large extent, the intensity with which each side adhered to its position was a product of newer questions introduced at the hearings.

VI

Among the most troublesome of the issues that emerged during the hearings was the interbasin transfer of water—that is, the transfer of water from the Colorado River Basin to other watersheds. Especially interested in such transfers were Colorado and Utah, which were diverting part of the river's flow out of the basin to the fast-growing areas around Salt Lake City and Denver. Such transfers were viewed suspiciously by the lower-basin states, which realized that water taken from the Colorado Basin would produce no return flow for their later use. Also contributing to their uneasiness was their recognition that Arthur Powell Davis's claim about the adequacy of the water supply was based only on his investigation of lands *within* the basin. The diversions to other watersheds were presently small, and most officials in Colorado and Utah insisted that they would remain nominal. Testimony during the hearings, however, caused many in the lower basin to become skeptical about such assurances and to demand restrictions on upper-basin development.

At the Washington meeting, Carpenter had estimated Colorado's future water transfers at 310,000 acre-feet. During the hearings in Denver, however, others raised the figure considerably. R. I. Meeker, deputy state engineer of Colorado, estimated the future diversions at 500,000 acre-feet, while L. Ward Bannister, a Denver lawyer and spokesman for the Denver Civic and Commercial Association, claimed that transfers would amount to 500,000 acre-feet for agriculture *plus* an additional unspecified amount to meet Denver's future needs. Others placed no limit on the water that would be needed on Colorado's eastern slope. "We claim the right," candidly declared a group of farmers who lived along the Arkansas River, "to take" as much from the Colorado River "as can feasibly be diverted across the continental divide." [40]

Utahns expressed similar opinions. Presently they were divert-

[40] Colorado River Commission, "Hearings" (Denver, March 31, 1922), pp. 15, 88, 155.

ing only a small amount—and this through their Strawberry Project—to the basin of the Great Salt Lake, but they planned to increase those diversions and to develop newer transfer routes, like the so-called Provo-Weber project. Some predicted that future diversions would never exceed 200,000 acre-feet, but others placed the estimate as high as 500,000 acre-feet.[41]

Coloradoans and Utahns believed that their desire for inter-basin transfer of water was not unusual or unfair. They delighted in reminding Californians that such transfers had made possible the development of the Imperial Valley. The valley, they noted, was technically not in the basin, since runoff there drained into the Salton Sea rather than into the Colorado River.

Californians responded by arguing that the Imperial Valley situation differed significantly from that upstream in Colorado and Utah. The valley, they pointed out, was the last place along the river where water could be diverted for use within the United States; hence diversions there, even if out of the basin, deprived no American lands of water. But Californians also contended that the valley was part of the basin. "California does not for a moment concede that the Imperial Valley is not within the basin of the Colorado River," declared W. F. McClure at the hearings in Cheyenne in April. "The mere incident of the Colorado having built a temporary barrier does not eliminate that valley from the basin. Regardless of what man may have done during the past twenty-five years—had man never touched it from an enterprising view point, an agricultural view point, the rich valley of Imperial years ago would have been filled with water to the Gulf of California." [42]

Though wrangling continued over whether the valley was in the basin, in the meantime farmers near Denver had become alarmed as they reflected on the city's growth from only 134,000 in 1900 to 256,000 in 1920. This development threatened to precipitate a conflict between the farmers and the city over the limited water supply on which both groups depended. "The most serious problem that confronts us at this time," explained W. F. R. Mills of Denver's Board of Water Commissioners at the hearings

[41] Colorado River Commission, "Hearings" (Phoenix, March 17, 1922), pp. 49–50 (Salt Lake City, March 28, 1922), p. 37, passim.

[42] Colorado River Commission, "Hearings" (Cheyenne, April 2, 1922), pp. 54–55.

in Denver, "is the future city water supply. Unless a construction program is formulated . . . that will bring to Denver and the agricultural communities surrounding it more water . . . , any great future growth in Denver's population must be made at the expense of the agricultural communities surrounding it." [43]

The problems of eastern Colorado had also disturbed many elsewhere in the state, especially those on the western slope of the Rockies near Grand Junction. Residents there reacted with dismay to the talk about increased diversions out of the watershed, since they viewed such transfers as a threat to their own future development. Carpenter was aware of their fears; and when he learned that the Colorado River Commission had scheduled hearings for Grand Junction, he tried to quiet their anxiety. In particular, he worried that the dissidents would ally themselves with lower-river interests who also looked with disfavor on interbasin transfers. "Unless every . . . objection by Grand Junction people against possible future tunnel diversions by Denver can be eliminated," Carpenter told a friend, "it would be suicidal to hold [the] Grand Junction hearings." [44]

But the hearings were held as scheduled, primarily because Carpenter took the precaution of persuading the protesters that he would reject all plans that limited the state's use of Colorado River water. Some western Coloradoans at the Grand Junction hearings actually urged him to take a more moderate position in the compact negotiations, but others strongly agreed with J. J. Tobin, a state senator from the western slope. "It would be an utter impossibility . . . to get the Legislature of this State to pass any act that would appropriate or allow to Colorado only a certain amount of water." [45]

[43] Colorado River Commission, "Hearings" (Denver, March 31, 1922), p. 70.

[44] Delph Carpenter to J. E. Morehead, March 20, 1922, Records Center Container (hereafter RCC): 5, Oliver H. Shoup Papers, Colorado State Archives, Denver.

[45] Colorado River Commission, "Hearings" (Grand Junction, March 29, 1922), pp. 76–77. See also Grand Junction *Daily Sentinel,* March 29, 1922; Grand Junction *Daily News,* March 30, 1922; James W. McCreery, *Interstate Waters and the Colorado River Commission* (n.p., 1922), pp. 20–21; Delph Carpenter to Charles E. Hall, April 8, 1922, Carpenter Papers.

VII

Interbasin transfer of water was not the only issue that figured prominently in the hearings and frustrated attempts at a settlement. Another involved the activities of an Arizona faction that used the hearings as a vehicle for propagandizing about special plans of its own.

The leader of the Arizona dissidents was George H. Maxwell, a headstrong man who served as executive secretary—and virtual boss—of the National Reclamation Association. Maxwell had long promoted irrigation development in the arid western states, particularly in Arizona and California, where he believed the combination of soil and climate were more promising than anywhere else. His latest interest was a scheme known as the "Arizona High Line Canal," a project that called for the irrigation of some 2,500,000 acres in the central part of the state. From a reservoir in the Boulder Canyon–Black Canyon area, Maxwell proposed to divert water hundreds of miles by means of pumping stations, aqueducts, and tunnels.

Very much aware of Maxwell's plan, but not at all enthusiastic about it, was W. S. Norviel. In the spring of 1921, he had appointed Harry F. Blake, formerly with the U.S. Geological Survey, to make a preliminary study of the feasibility of a canal from the Boulder Canyon area. Blake's report of December, 1921, had proved discouraging. "Diverting and carrying water across a hot, arid country without crossing any large bodies of irrigable land until a point 470 miles south of its diversion is reached, would be a very precarious undertaking. In fact, it could not be considered feasible unless these lands under irrigation were of such value that cost could not be considered. This," he had concluded, "is not the case . . . in Arizona." [46]

Since Blake's survey had been conducted hurriedly, Norviel decided in 1922 to put into the field another reconnaissance team, this one under the leadership of E. C. LaRue, a well-known Colorado River expert and a hydraulic engineer for the U.S. Geological Survey. LaRue promised to begin the investigation

[46] Harry E. Blake, "Reconnaissance Report on Colorado River," in Harry E. Blake to W. S. Norviel, December 1, 1921, Arizona Colorado River Commission Papers, Office File, Arizona State Archives, Phoenix.

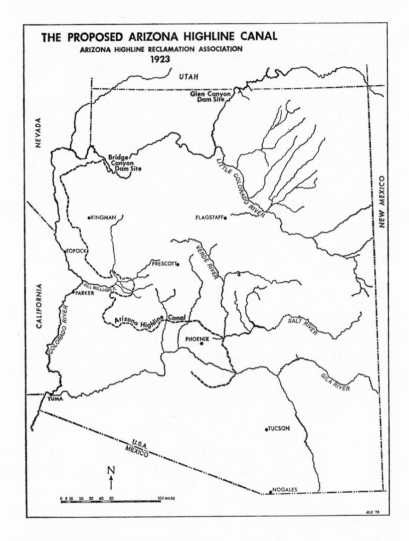

THE PROPOSED ARIZONA HIGHLINE CANAL
ARIZONA HIGHLINE RECLAMATION ASSOCIATION
1923

as soon as he had completed an assignment for the federal government.[47]

But Norviel did not expect LaRue's findings to differ appreciably from those of Blake, in part because he knew that in

[47] W. S. Norviel, "Report of W. S. Norviel, Colorado River Commissioner, State of Arizona," n.d., file 1-M/315, Hoover Papers; W. S. Norviel to George W. P. Hunt, March 26, 1923, box 3, folder 7, George W. P. Hunt Papers, Arizona State University Library, Tempe.

1921 the Reclamation Service had also looked into the canal scheme and had concluded that its cost would be prohibitive. Norviel's attitude had become clear to everyone at the Washington negotiations of the Colorado River Commission when he had submitted a compact proposal that made no allowance for the highline canal.

When Maxwell learned about this omission, he bitterly denounced the Arizona commissioner. At the hearings in Phoenix on March 15, he accused Norviel of advocating "an absolute surrender" of Arizona's rights.[48] He also used the opportunity to lobby for his canal scheme, but on this occasion he modified his plan by suggesting that the water be diverted from the river at a higher contour than he had earlier recommended. He now felt justified in calling for further studies to analyze his latest proposal. And while the investigations were being made, he argued, the basin states should forget about trying to negotiate a compact. They should instead concentrate their efforts on the flood problem, which could be eliminated by two "comparatively inexpensive" dams—one on the Gila at Sentinel, and the other on the Colorado at Bulls Head—and a large 700-foot-high dam at Glen Canyon. The structure at Glen Canyon, he claimed, need be only "a rock-fill dam built high enough to store one year's flood of the Colorado River. That will assure to the River an even flow through the year." [49]

Arizonans other than Norviel joined with federal engineers to challenge Maxwell. G. E. P. Smith, a professor of irrigation engineering at the University of Arizona, believed it to be "absolutely impossible to build any sort of storage dam" at either Sentinel or Bulls Head because there was no bedrock on which to anchor such a structure. As for a 700-foot-high rock-fill dam in Glen Canyon, he was blunt: "My engineering instincts rebel when I try to contemplate it." Nor was the highline canal plan in the realm of possibility. "To my mind," he insisted, "it is an absurdity so long as economic conditions continue measurably as they are today." [50]

48 Colorado River Commission, "Hearings" (Phoenix, March 15, 1922), p. 61.

49 Ibid., p. 53.

50 Colorado River Commission, "Hearings" (Phoenix, March 16, 1922), pp. 2, 8, 12. Though Smith challenged the feasibility of the canal, he believed that it would have to be taken into consideration

Arthur Powell Davis was equally adamant. "The exact project, as outlined by Mr. Maxwell today, has not been presented to the Reclamation Service until this forenoon," he explained, but "money expended upon the investigation of that project . . . would not be wisely expended." The new plan, he argued, was not appreciably different from the earlier one that had been considered and found inadequate. "We . . . estimated the distance which a canal would have to follow . . . as between four hundred and four hundred and fifty miles, most of which is heavy mountain country. . . . The great length of this canal, and the character of the country which it was to pass, struck me and all other engineers . . . as being so far beyond the realms of possibility as to be a waste of our money and time, and I am still of that opinion." [51]

Maxwell remained unconvinced. Not only did he continue to insist that his proposal was sound, but he also claimed that it would eliminate difficulties with Mexico. There would be no return flow from the waters diverted to central Arizona; hence, there would be little water available for the "American speculators" and their coolie laborers in Mexico. "If . . . Arizona is deprived of this great reclamation resource . . . ," he warned, then "the water must inevitably go down to lands in old Mexico . . . which are being colonized by Asiatics." [52]

Davis rejected this contention with as much vigor as he had denied the other claims. "That water . . . could not . . . be

in determining Arizona's water rights if the upper states continued to insist on their inflated acreage claims.

[51] Colorado River Commission, "Hearings" (Phoenix, March 15, 1922), pp. 100–102; see also A. P. Davis to Carl Hayden, March 4, 1922, box 598, folder 9, Carl Hayden Papers, Arizona State University Library, Tempe. Though on this occasion Davis did not challenge the feasibility of a rock-fill dam in Glen Canyon, he did so three months later, claiming that it would be unsafe. House Committee on Irrigation of Arid Lands, *Hearings on Protection and Development of Lower Colorado River Basin, H.R. 11449,* 67 Cong., 2 sess. (1922), p. 25.

[52] Colorado River Commission, "Hearings" (Phoenix, March 15, 1922), p. 87. See also the introductory chapter in Maxwell's manuscript, "Golden Rivers—The Colorado—The Nile of America," in the Maxwell Papers, Western History Research Center, University of Wyoming, Laramie.

appropriated under the laws of Mexico, in my judgment." Moreover, with the completion of American reclamation projects, "we can at any time shut off and dry up the river below the line." [53] G. E. P. Smith agreed. "Mexico is not going to acquire water rights on the strength of great expenditures made by this country at Boulder Canyon or at any other site," he contended. "Furthermore," he offered, "we can turn the natural flow down to them and drown their delta lands for ten days, during the annual flood, every June, until they remove the menace of Asiatic Colonization from our doors." [54]

But Maxwell persisted, driven by his conviction that the high-line canal scheme was sound and that there was not enough water to meet everyone's needs. "We hear . . . that there is plenty of water for all," he noted, "but that is not true unless Arizona is eliminated from the reckoning." Arizona, he claimed in his calmer moments, could best be protected by maintenance of the principle of priority on interstate streams. When he was excited, however, his demands escalated sharply. "Our position is this," he exclaimed at one point during the hearings in Phoenix. "We insistently stand upon the legal, constitutional, moral, equitable and physical condition and right that, as the water has been for ages coming through to the North line of Arizona, we are entitled to have it continue to come." [55]

"If you are going to stand on that contention," replied Hoover, "then there can be no possible agreement that the states would ratify. . . . Now, I am only putting to you the facts of the practical question whether or not in your view it is worth while for this Commission to proceed?"

"It is," responded Maxwell, "provided this Commission proceeds to investigate and gather the facts. . . ."

"Well, now," asked Hoover, "if we knew all of the facts in the world with regard to the river below the Arizona line . . . , would it alter your contention that the full flow of water should come across that line?"

[53] Colorado River Commission, "Hearings" (Phoenix, March 16, 1922), pp. 60–61.

[54] Ibid., p. 4.

[55] Colorado River Commission, "Hearings" (Phoenix, March 15, 1922), pp. 64–65, 70. In this instance Maxwell was obviously invoking riparian law, a doctrine not recognized in Arizona.

Maxwell's response was direct: "Not the slightest in the world."
"Well, then," snapped Hoover, "why should we continue to argue the question." [56]
Maxwell's attitude and the vocal following that he was developing in Arizona left upper-basin leaders uneasy. To most of them, he was a crackpot. They also resented the insinuation that their crops were inferior to those grown in the lower basin or more costly to produce. Most were relieved by the refusal of Norviel and other prominent Arizonans to endorse the highline canal, but the discussion of the scheme only increased their resolve to obtain a compact that protected their future development.

VIII

There was still another Arizona scheme that gained considerable attention during the spring of 1922 and complicated the attempt to negotiate a compact. Primarily responsible was James P. Girand, a businessman who wished to build a power dam with private funds at Diamond Creek on the Colorado in northern Arizona.

Acting on behalf of Arizona copper interests, in 1913 Girand had filed an application to produce power at the site. Two years later he had received a preliminary permit and a request by federal authorities for detailed information about his plans. By the time he had submitted the necessary data, the Federal Power Act of 1920 had created a new agency, the Federal Power Commission, which wanted more information. The commission issued another preliminary permit in 1921, but only on condition that he produce the data within a year. He did so, but when he filed his application in February, 1922, he ran into new problems. Since the compact negotiations were then under way, the Federal Power Commission refused to issue a license until it had cleared the matter with Hoover and his fellow conferees. [57]

The delay prompted a protest from Arizona officials, who asked that the application be approved immediately. The upper-

[56] Ibid., pp. 78–79.
[57] O. C. Merrill to Herbert Hoover, March 5, 1922, copy in Colorado River Commission, "Minutes of the Eighth Meeting" (Phoenix, March 15, 1922), pp. 3–4; Colorado River Commission, "Hearings" (Santa Fe, November 9, 1922), pp. 4–7.

basin states, on the other hand, urged delay. Though not opposed to private development of the river, they objected to any action until their rights had been secured by compact. The two lower-basin states of Nevada and California issued even stronger protests. Nevadans objected because they would be unable to levy taxes on a project, like the Diamond Creek venture, built wholly within Arizona. But the principal complaint of both Nevadans and Californians was succinctly stated by Arthur Powell Davis: "It would kill the Government development in Boulder Canyon." Davis explained that a reservoir at Diamond Creek would be too small to provide flood relief. Its only purpose would be to produce power, but "such development would so fill the power market . . . that it would make for a long time to come unfeasible the financing of any other large power scheme on the river." [58]

These protests made the Federal Power Commission uneasy. It had already issued Girand a preliminary permit, and he claimed to have spent about $100,000 in obtaining the information requested by the federal government. O. C. Merrill, executive secretary of the commission, believed that Girand had built up "equities" in the case, but he and the commission bowed to the protests and to a request from President Harding that a final decision on the application be postponed while compact negotiations were in progress.[59] Even so, Merrill's sympathy for the application and the warm support given Girand by Arizonans served to feed rather than lessen anxieties in the other basin states.

IX

The discussion of the Girand application, the Maxwell scheme, and interbasin transfer of water increased doubts about the adequacy of the water supply. During the talks in Washington, most spokesmen had believed that Davis's estimates of acreage and

[58] Colorado River Commission, "Hearings" (Los Angeles, March 20, 1922), pp. 102–104. See also O. C. Merrill to O. H. Shoup, March 21, 1922, RCC:5, Shoup Papers; Phil Swing to Cora M. Long, March 23, 1922, Swing Papers; Colorado River Commission, "Hearings" (Santa Fe, November 9, 1922), pp. 20–24.

[59] O. C. Merrill to Herbert Hoover, March 3, 1922, copy in Colorado River Commission, "Minutes of the Eighth Meeting" (Phoenix, March 15, 1922), pp. 3–4; Colorado River Commission, "Hearings" (Santa Fe, November 9, 1922), pp. 15–16.

water supply were probably correct, but by the time the hearings ended in April, 1922, the skeptics had grown in number. Arizona's Maxwell was among the most straightforward, but Charles E. Beveridge from Wyoming's Green River Basin was equally forceful in expressing his opinions: "The evidence presented so far rather tends to show there is not enough water." And "if there is not enough water," he asked, "why . . . not say so in some definite terms?" [60]

The commission refused to say so in "definite terms," but its inability to reach an agreement was significant to observers. Even Arthur Powell Davis felt compelled to issue a public warning about his own estimate—an estimate based only on projected uses *within* the basin. "There . . . seems to be some foggy ideas concerning . . . [my] statement that there is water enough for all the lands inside of the basin," he explained at the hearings in Los Angeles. "It would not be wise to make any hard and fast agreement, lasting for all time, on that basis. . . . Economic as well as other conditions are liable to change." [61]

Davis also recognized the serious implications posed by inter-basin transfers. "The areas that might be irrigated, outside of the basin, *if* the water could be put over there, are practically unlimited." His apprehensions were revealed at the Los Angeles hearings when he suggested that a limit be placed on water transfers from upper-basin states—transfers that he conceded could often be justified on economic and other grounds. "I believe the uses outside of the basin might be, in some cases, superior to those inside,—for municipal uses—and in streams where we are sure we can pick up all the return seepage which is not the case with the water supplied to the Imperial Valley." But, he continued, "I would suggest . . . a limit" of possibly 400,000 or 500,000 acre-feet "which might be written into the compact." [62]

[60] Colorado River Commission, "Hearings" (Denver, March 31, 1922), p. 172. For some other expressions of doubt about the adequacy of the water supply, see Colorado River Commission, "Hearings" (Los Angeles, March 20, 1922), p. 96; (Salt Lake City, March 27, 1922), p. 7; (Grand Junction, March 29, 1922), pp. 139–140; (Cheyenne, April 2, 1922), pp. 14, 16.

[61] Colorado River Commission, "Hearings" (Los Angeles, March 20, 1922), p. 99.

[62] Ibid., p. 98.

Colorado and Utah objected, just as they had earlier, to any limitations on their future development. Instead, they doggedly insisted that their diversions from the basin would remain small and that there would always be plenty of water for those downstream.

Early in the hearings Carpenter had believed that he and his upper-basin colleagues were making headway in their fight. "Various suggestions of limitation of our development either by acreage, time, or quantity of water," he had told Governor Oliver Shoup of Colorado in mid-March, "are gradually giving way to the conception that no matter what we may do our consumption will never equal an equitable part of the waters of the stream." [63] By the time the hearings ended in April, however, everyone felt that Carpenter and his allies had failed.

Also, every attempt at compromise had failed. James D. Fredericks of the Los Angeles Chamber of Commerce had offended the states-rights sensibilities of most commissioners when he suggested that the federal government divide the waters. No more successful were two engineers of the U.S. Geological Survey, Nathan Grover and John Hoyt. They proposed that the water be apportioned between the basins, 65 percent going to the lower states and 35 percent to the upper basin. They could say little in defense of the proposition other than that the allotments "appeared to be a fair percentage." [64] Numerous other suggestions were made, many by the commissioners themselves, but all were rejected.

Hoover's exasperation mounted as the compromise proposals were defeated. "If there is to be maximum development of the Colorado river and cooperation in the West," he declared irritably in Denver when the hearings were nearly over, "it becomes the serious business of sane men and women to put down all ex-

[63] Delph Carpenter to Oliver H. Shoup, March 17, 1922, RCC:5, Shoup Papers.

[64] James D. Fredericks to Herbert Hoover, March 31, 1922, file 1-M/300, Hoover Papers; S. B. Davis, Jr., to Clarence Stetson, May 3, 1922, file 1-M/300, Hoover Papers; J. G. Scrugham to Clarence Stetson, May 3, 1922, Scrugham Papers, NHS; Colorado River Commission, "Hearings" (Phoenix, March 16, 1922), pp. 23–34; George Otis Smith to Hoover, February 28, 1922, Papers of the Wyoming State Engineer, Wyoming State Archives, Cheyenne.

tremists and prepare to cooperate." He named no names, but everyone knew that he had primarily Carpenter in mind. Privately he left no doubts, confiding to Wyoming's Frank Mondell that Carpenter was "impossible." [65]

Once the hearings had come to an end in Cheyenne on April 2, Hoover admonished the delegates to spend the next few months deliberating on the costly and time-consuming legal battles that would result if they failed to reach an agreement. Those considerations alone, he continued to hope, would eventually compel the writing of a compact. "There is a sad lack of understanding . . . in the relation of the upper basin to the lower basin," he lectured the commission. "But in time the relative weight of the different engineering principles [and] the different legal processes that may follow from failure to make [a] pact . . . will all contribute to drive these states . . . to some solution." [66]

Time would prove Hoover correct in more ways than he now suspected.

[65] Colorado River Commission, "Hearings" (Denver, April 1, 1922), p. 26; Frank W. Mondell to Frank C. Emerson, May 22, 1922, Papers of the Wyoming State Engineer.

[66] Colorado River Commission, "Hearings" (Cheyenne, April 2, 1922), p. 66.

7

Dividing the Waters

Colorado and Utah resisted for months any settlement that limited their use of Colorado River water. By mid-summer of 1922, however, their attitudes were changing. Prompting their shift in policy was pressure from the Department of the Interior, from California, and, most important, from the United States Supreme Court. That pressure compelled them to soften their positions and to take the lead in the negotiation of the long-sought interstate treaty.

I

Strong pressure from the Interior Department came as early as February, 1922, when Secretary of the Interior Albert Fall and Reclamation Service Director Arthur Powell Davis issued their final report on the problems of the lower Colorado River. This "Fall-Davis Report," as it came to be known, had been authorized by the Kinkaid Act of 1920. Though the final draft contained no surprises, it reaffirmed the necessity of taking quick remedial action against the floods threatening the lands along the lower river.

Fall and Davis, as expected, urged "the construction with Government funds of a reservoir at or near Boulder Canyon" and

the building of "a high-line canal"—an All-American Canal—
"from Laguna dam to the Imperial Valley." Federal expenditures
for the reservoir were "to be reimbursed by the revenues from
leasing the power privileges," and the cost of the canal was to be
repaid "by the lands benefited," a provision entirely satisfactory
to the canal's Imperial and Coachella valley advocates.[1]

Among the Californians responding warmly to the report was
Phil Swing, the Imperial Valley congressman, who was now serving his second year in the House of Representatives. Even before
the document was distributed, Swing was preparing legislation
to implement its recommendations.[2] He also was lining up support in Congress, going first to Hiram Johnson, California's powerful senior senator.

While Johnson was sympathetic, as a veteran of many political
battles he recognized the serious obstacles that the inexperienced
and enthusiastic Swing only dimly perceived. Putting a fatherly
hand on Swing's shoulder, he told him, "Phil, you go ahead and
put it through the House and when it comes over here, I will put
it through the Senate."[3]

At first Swing, too, had doubts about how successful he would
be, particularly if he introduced his bill before the Colorado River
Commission had been given sufficient time to negotiate a treaty.
He had spoken to the commissioners at their Washington meeting
in January and had told them of his strong support for their
efforts. Even after they had failed to reach agreement during their
initial sessions, he had remained optimistic, predicting to a friend
that a compact would be drafted at the Phoenix meeting in
March.[4] But failure on that occasion and at subsequent hearings

[1] "Problems of Imperial Valley and Vicinity," S. Doc. 142, 67 Cong.,
2 sess. (1922), p. 21.
[2] Phil Swing to Cora M. Long, March 10, 1922, Phil D. Swing
Papers, Department of Special Collections, University of California,
Los Angeles.
[3] Phil Swing, "The Struggle for Boulder Dam," p. 63, Swing
Papers.
[4] Colorado River Commission, "Minutes of the Second Meeting"
(Washington, D.C., January 27, 1922), pp. 58–59, file 032, Colorado River Project, Bureau of Reclamation Papers, Record Group
115, National Archives; Phil Swing to Cora M. Long, February 25,
1922, Swing Papers.

had left him disappointed. By April his disappointment had turned to despair. On April 25 he introduced a bill calling for construction of the All-American Canal and a dam "at or near Boulder Canyon." On the same day Johnson introduced a similar measure in the Senate, though he advised Swing that the Imperial Valley congressman would have to shoulder the major burden of the legislative fight. Soon, however, he found himself drawn deeply into the struggle and working as hard as Swing for the passage of the bill.[5]

II

This first of many similar Swing-Johnson bills was sharply attacked by the upper states. "We cannot be expected . . . to lend our assistance to the difficulties of others," Wyoming's Frank Emerson told a group in the Coachella Valley, "unless in return we have the reciprocity to which we are reasonably entitled." Emerson and the other upper-basin critics of the bill made clear what they meant by "reciprocity." "Until a reasonable time has been allowed . . . to obtain a compact . . . ," they explained, "support of . . . the Johnson-Swing bill should not be expected." [6]

The upper states won strong support from Arizona and Nevada. "The bill," complained W. S. Norviel to Arizona's Congressman Carl Hayden, "appears to view the whole situation from a California standpoint and to entirely absorb Arizona and its rights in the River." Norviel favored a dam at Glen Canyon, a site wholly

[5] *Cong. Rec.*, 67 Cong., 2 sess. (April 25, 1922), pp. 5929, 5985. Johnson's role in the fight for the Boulder Canyon legislation has generally been downplayed, but there is extensive evidence in the Johnson Papers in the Bancroft Library that he labored as hard as Swing for the bill's passage. See, especially, Johnson's correspondence with George Young, Franklin Hichborn, Charles K. McClatchy, Frank Doherty, and George Norris.

[6] Frank Emerson to Coachella Valley County Water District, May 15, 1922, Papers of the Wyoming State Engineer, Wyoming State Archives, Cheyenne. See also Merritt C. Mechem to H. O. Bursum, June 20, 1922, Merritt C. Mechem Papers, New Mexico State Archives, Santa Fe; R. E. Caldwell to Delph Carpenter, August 4, 1922, Papers of the Utah State Engineer, Utah State Archives, Salt Lake City.

within Arizona, but his major objection to Swing's bill was its
failure to guarantee Arizona a preferred right to the hydroelectric power that would be produced at Boulder Canyon. He also
criticized the measure because it violated Arizona's sovereignty.
"I hold," he informed Hayden, "that the State of Arizona owns the
bed of the stream from high-water mark to high-water mark and
the waters flowing in the stream within the confines of the State
of Arizona. That the right of the State of Arizona is a proprietary
right; that under the laws of the State of Arizona, even the government of the United States must make application to the State
for a permit the same as any individual company or corporation." [7]

Nevadans, unlike Arizonans, favored a dam in Boulder Canyon, but they nonetheless supported Arizona's opposition to
Swing's bill on the grounds that the measure was premature.
"Personally," Samuel S. Arentz, Nevada's sole House member,
told Governor Emmet Boyle, "I deplore the introduction of such
bills, believing they can only delay final action in the Boulder
Canyon matter by awakening the 'get mine' spirit." [8]

But the small southern Nevada town of Las Vegas had other
thoughts. City fathers welcomed the economic windfall that the
construction of a massive dam nearby might bring.[9] Even so, in
view of the hostility elsewhere, their support offered little consolation to Swing and his friends.

Swing had an opportunity to reply to his critics in June, when
he testified before the House Committee on Irrigation of Arid
Lands. At first he attempted to win over opponents by reaffirming
his support for a compact and even promising to incorporate it
into his bill if it were negotiated before Congress had passed his

[7] W. S. Norviel to Carl Hayden, May 6, 1922, copy in file 1-M/
311, Herbert Hoover Papers, Hoover Presidential Library, West
Branch, Iowa. See also Norviel to Clarence Stetson, May 4 and
June 29, 1922, file 1-M/311, Hoover Papers; and Norviel to Carl
Hayden, May 11, 1922, box 598, folder 7, Carl Hayden Papers,
Arizona State University Library, Tempe.

[8] Samuel S. Arentz to Emmet D. Boyle, April 28, 1922, Emmet D.
Boyle Papers, Nevada State Archives, Carson City.

[9] Leslie R. Saunders to J. G. Scrugham, May 24 and August 8,
1922, J. G. Scrugham Papers, Nevada Historical Society, Reno (hereafter cited as Scrugham Papers, NHS).

measure. But he warned that the needs of the "Imperial Valley cannot wait an indeterminate length of time." [10]

Strong support for Swing came from Arthur Powell Davis and Herbert Hoover, who emphasized the need to eliminate the flood menace on the lower river. Though Hoover was careful to point out that his views were his own and not those of the commission that he chaired, he was straightforward in his remarks. "The first step," he told the House committee, "is the construction of a large storage dam somewhere in the neighborhood of Boulder Canyon. . . . The reasons for coming to this conclusion are . . . the immediate importance of control of flood flow . . . and the probability of an early development of a power market" to pay for the project.[11]

"Then it is your view . . . ," pressed California's Congressman John E. Raker, "that this legislation should go forward, notwithstanding the fact that the commission has not finally determined" the water rights of the basin states?

"I think the legislation should go forward," replied Hoover.[12]

[10] House Committee on Irrigation of Arid Lands, *Hearings on Protection and Development of Lower Colorado River Basin, H.R. 11449,* 67 Cong., 2 sess. (1922), p. 18.

[11] Ibid., p. 53. A recent study contends that Hoover "hedged" at this time on whether power should be produced at the Boulder Canyon dam. A careful examination of the hearings reveals that Hoover definitely supported construction of a power plant. "The sale of power," he told the committee more than once, "will be ultimately necessary in order to establish a substratum to finance the operation." (Ibid., pp. 53, 57–62; cf. Beverley Moeller, *Phil Swing and Boulder Dam* [Berkeley and Los Angeles, 1971], p. 32.) Hoover, however, did not believe that the Colorado River Commission was the proper agency for allocating rights to power. Nor did he think that it was necessary at this time to determine just who the purchasers of the power would be. Moreover, though at this time he favored a federally constructed power dam at Boulder Canyon, he did not want nonfederal agencies automatically barred from building power plants at other locations on the lower river. Finally, Hoover, like nearly everyone else, believed that flood control should be the primary concern.

[12] House Committee on Irrigation of Arid Lands, *Hearings on Protection and Development of Lower Colorado River Basin, H.R. 11449,* p. 54.

Hoover realized that his views were not shared by everyone, particularly by the leaders of the upper basin, and he attempted to meet their criticism by suggesting that the bill be modified with a stipulation that storage could create "no water rights as against the upper States." "I do not think the States of the lower basin would raise any objection," he explained. "Some such action should remove any legitimate objection to immediately proceeding with the construction." [13]

Swing eagerly accepted Hoover's suggestion. Not only would he incorporate such a provision into his bill, he would also insert "a paragraph which provided that when the Colorado River Commission reached an agreement that agreement should govern all the works constructed." [14]

But this offer did not satisfy the leaders of the other basin states, many of whom sharply criticized Hoover for siding with Swing. "I am . . . unable to agree . . . with Mr. Hoover in regard to a commitment to the construction of the Boulder Canyon Reservoir," wrote an angry Emerson of Wyoming to Clarence Stetson, executive secretary of the Colorado River Commission. "As I have before definitely expressed myself, I consider the Swing-Johnson Bill premature in the light of the present effort to secure an agreement between interested states." [15]

So did the other upper-basin spokesmen. They found no comfort in the proviso suggested by Hoover for preventing the establishment of rights to storage water. Most believed that such a provision would apply only against the federal government, the builder of the dam, and not against private individuals downstream who could take advantage of the regulated flow to increase their uses. Moreover, despite Davis's testimony, not all upper-basin critics were willing to admit that Boulder Canyon was the appropriate site for the first major dam on the river. Some agreed with Senator Lawrence C. Phipps of Colorado, who objected to "any legislation . . . until the possibilities of other reservoir sites . . . are considered." [16]

[13] Ibid.   [14] Ibid., p. 195.

[15] Frank Emerson to Clarence Stetson, July 22, 1922, file 1-M/300, Hoover Papers.

[16] House Committee on Irrigation of Arid Lands, *Hearings on Protection and Development of Lower Colorado River Basin, H.R. 11449*, pp. 58, 192.

III

Besides confirming the strong distrust that the other basin states had for California, the debates on the Swing-Johnson bill also underscored the increasingly sensitive relationship that had developed with Mexico. During the hearings, some spokesmen, like California's John Raker, argued against neglecting Mexico: "While we are adjusting our complications in our own States, we have a complication below with Mexico that it seems to me can well be adjusted." [17]

Though Raker was apparently unaware of it, his views were shared by Mexican officials. They had nervously watched the events of the last several years and, following the creation of the Colorado River Commission in 1921, had asked to be "represented and given consideration in the studies and projects." [18] The State Department had denied the request, claiming that the commission was concerned only with domestic matters. Mexico found this reply unsatisfactory and in early 1922 pressed again for representation on the commission, arguing that even if only domestic matters were discussed, such discussions would necessarily have international implications.[19]

This time the State Department turned the Mexican request over to Hoover for comment. He simply reaffirmed the American position and contended that Mexico could not "rightly claim any representation in a Commission engaged in domestic considerations." So far as he was concerned, Mexico had nothing to worry about. Its rights to Colorado River water could be determined by treaty between the two governments. "And such

[17] Ibid., p. 19.
[18] Mexican embassy to U.S. Dept. of State, October 15 and 24, 1921, Dept. of State Papers, file 711.1216M/497–498, National Archives.
[19] Matthew E. Hanna to Manuel Téllez, November 9, 1921, Dept. of State Papers, file 711.1216M/497; Téllez to Dept. of State, February 26, 1922, Dept. of State Papers, file 711.1216M/503; Federico Ramos to Secretario de Relaciones Exteriores, February 22, 1922, Papers of the Comisión Internacional de Límites entre México y los Estados Unidos, file 42 (iv), Archives of the Secretaría de Relaciones Exteriores, México, D. F.

treaty rights," he noted, "will override any interstate arrangements." [20]

Hoover's reply was forwarded to Mexican officials, who found it most disappointing. To continue the argument, however, seemed futile, especially because relations between the two countries were already strained by other matters. In 1920 Mexican President Venustiano Carranza, in an attempt to dictate a successor, had become the center of much factional strife and was assassinated. The scramble for power that followed was won by Alvaro Obregón, but the United States had refused to recognize his succession until he had done something about long-standing American claims and about Mexico's constitution of 1917, under which American-owned oil properties and agricultural lands were threatened with confiscation. Even though the two nations had still not reestablished formal diplomatic ties by 1922, Obregón had decided that his country could not stand by idly while the United States evolved a program for developing the Colorado River Basin. In March, 1922, he created a special agency, the Board of International Waters, to study the problem on the Colorado as well as a similar difficulty on the lower Rio Grande. He also sent observers to the public hearings of the Colorado River Commission and directed Armando Santacruz, chief engineer on the Mexican section of the International Boundary Commission, to attend future negotiations of the basin states.[21] Even if Santacruz was banned from the formal talks, as seemed likely, he might still pick up some useful information.

Despite the lack of formal ties with Mexico, many Americans agreed with California's Raker that relations between the countries should be regularized and a Colorado River treaty negotiated. While few doubted the wisdom of a treaty, most water leaders wanted a settlement of their own difficulties before nego-

[20] Herbert Hoover to Charles Evans Hughes, April 20, 1922, Dept. of State Papers, file 711.1216M/506.

[21] Federico Ramos to Subsecretario de Relaciones Exteriores, April 4, 1922, Papers of the Comisión Internacional, file 42 (iv); México, Secretaría de Relaciones Exteriores, *El Tratado de Aguas Internacionales Celebrado entre México y los Estados Unidos el 3 de Febrero de 1944* (México, D. F., 1947), p. 25; *Santa Fe New Mexican,* November 14, 1922.

tiating with Mexico. In fact, Arizona's Carl Hayden opposed any negotiations until the United States had determined conclusively that it could not use all the water itself. "There is no need for haste in arriving at any . . . adjustment with Mexico," he told Raker during the hearings on the Swing-Johnson bill. "We may ultimately treat with Mexico; but so far as I am concerned, I shall oppose any kind of agreement recognizing any kind of a Mexican water right in the Colorado River until it is definitely and finally determined that there is a surplus of water in that stream for which there is no possible use in the United States." [22]

The resistance to a Mexican treaty as well as to the Swing-Johnson bill proved decisive—at least for the time being. Swing's measure was not reported out of committee, but the discussion of it and the Mexican problem served to remind upper-basin leaders of the strong downstream competition that they faced for the waters of the Colorado. The discussion also reawakened their fear of the possibility of sudden and disastrous floods on the lower river that might stampede Congress into approving a Boulder Canyon bill.

But there now seemed to be even more to worry about. Shortly before the hearings had begun on the Swing-Johnson bill, the U.S. Supreme Court had dealt the upper states a blow so severe that it forced a dramatic shift in upper-basin water strategy.

IV

On June 5 the Supreme Court handed down its long-awaited decision in *Wyoming* v. *Colorado*. The justices were finally prepared to say what principle of law applied to disputes over streams shared by states that adhered to the appropriation doctrine.

The Court's response was clear: the rule of priority prevailed. So far as the appropriation states were concerned, the Court sided with those water users who had a head start on their neighbors. Such a finding, stated Justice Willis Van Devanter

[22] House Committee on Irrigation of Arid Lands, *Hearings on Protection and Development of Lower Colorado River Basin, H.R. 11449*, p. 19.

in the unanimous opinion, was completely "consonant with the principles of right and equity." Since both Wyoming and Colorado "pronounce the rule [of priority] just and reasonable" when applying it to waters *within* each state, "the principle . . . is not less applicable to *interstate* streams and controversies." [23]

The Court explicitly denied Colorado's contention that she possessed absolute rights to waters arising within her borders. Labeling such a claim "untenable," the justices reminded Coloradoans that in 1907 a similar plea had been rejected in *Kansas* v. *Colorado.* But the Court did agree with Colorado that water could be diverted from one drainage basin to another. "In neither State," observed the justices, "does the right of appropriation depend on the place of use being within the same watershed." Moreover, "diversions from one watershed to another are commonly made in both States and the practice is recognized by the decisions of their courts." [24] Consequently, concluded the justices, the same practice should be followed for interstate streams shared by both states.

Only when it came to the disputed claims of the federal government did the Court refuse to take a stand. Lawyers from the U.S. attorney general's office had asked the Court to recognize the authority of the United States over the unappropriated waters in the West's unnavigable streams. The justices refused to commit themselves, however, explaining that since "the United States does not now seek to impose any policy of its own choosing on either State, the question whether . . . it might do so, is not here considered." [25]

Though most basin leaders had hoped that the Court would reject the federal government's claims, they were divided on nearly everything else about the decision. The lower states were, of course, delighted with the major thrust of the Court's action. "This decision will be a very great benefit to us in the lower states and should assist us very greatly in reaching an agreement with the northern states," declared Arizona's Norviel. Governor Emmet Boyle of Nevada was even more pleased with the implications of the ruling. "This decision . . . ," he cheerfully told Clarence Stetson, "appears to quite effectually dispose of the

[23] *Wyoming* v. *Colorado,* 259 U.S. 470 (1922), emphasis added.
[24] Ibid., 466.   [25] Ibid., 420, 465.

'unlimited right' theory of our friend, Senator Delf [*sic*] Carpenter." [26]

Even Mexican leaders brightened at the news. "With that decision," noted an official in the Secretaría de Agricultura y Fomento, "the Supreme Court . . . established a preference for priority of use," thereby furnishing "a very efficient base to lean upon in discussing the rights of Mexico . . . over more recent uses . . . in American territory." [27]

In sharp contrast to the attitude of Mexico and the lower basin was the reaction of leaders from upstream. "If they [the lower states] can develope [*sic*] their country under the decision in the Wyoming Colorado case," declared a worried Merritt Mechem, governor of New Mexico, "they do not need any compact." Less convinced of that eventuality but still alarmed was Frank Emerson, who hoped that the decision would "not prevent a reasonable attitude of the lower states towards the interests of the upper river basin." Of one thing he was almost certain, however. The ruling would "temper the attitude taken by certain of the upper states." [28]

That it did, but not everyone in the upper basin considered the decision detrimental or even applicable to the Colorado River situation. L. Ward Bannister, prominent Denver attorney and sometime contender with Carpenter over who could best direct Colorado's water strategy, did not believe that anyone should "be one bit concerned by the decision." The ruling, he maintained in speeches and letters, was not applicable to the Colorado River Basin because the decision on which it was based involved two "Simon-pure priority states." But not every state in the Colorado Basin was a priority state. "California," he reminded the Denver Bar Association in a speech in early August, "is fundamentally a riparian state" where "the appropriation system is only partially in force." "Thus, the case of California as against the upper states

[26] W. S. Norviel to Clarence Stetson, June 14, 1922, file 1-M/311, Hoover Papers; Emmet Boyle to Clarence Stetson, June 22, 1922, file 1-M/295, Hoover Papers.

[27] J. Pedrera Cordova to Secretario de Relaciones Exteriores, June 27, 1922, Papers of the Comisión Internacional, file 42(i).

[28] Merritt Mechem to Clarence Stetson, June 21, 1922, Mechem Papers; Frank C. Emerson to W. S. Norviel, June 15, 1922, Papers of the Wyoming State Engineer.

. . . would be distinguishable from *Wyoming* vs. *Colorado*," and any controversy would have to be settled according to a different rule of law.[29]

The rule that Bannister thought applicable was the principle of "equitable apportionment" laid down by the Supreme Court in *Kansas* v. *Colorado*. According to that principle, a decision would rest on the special circumstances or "conditions" of each individual case. Nevertheless, past experience suggested that even the rule of equitable apportionment could not be applied by the Court without a prolonged legal battle. For this reason Bannister believed that a simpler and wiser solution lay in the negotiation of a compact. The first step in that direction, he argued, would be the abandonment by the upper states of their "unreasonable" claims to all the water rising within their boundaries and their acceptance of a limitation on their uses. "I feel very certain as to the correctness of these views" and "personally believe that Colorado ought to name its quantity of water in order that the other states may know what they may have in order that both public and private capital may know in turn upon what water supply projects may be launched." [30]

V

Bannister's agitation, the Court decision, and the debate over the Swing-Johnson bill had the desired effect. Though Delph Carpenter disagreed with Bannister about the applicability of the Wyoming-Colorado decision—Carpenter, like most others, contended that it left the upper basin "badly exposed"—he realized that he would have to modify his earlier position if the upper states were to obtain a compact protecting them from development below. "We simply *must* use every endeavor to bring about a compact at the next meeting," he told Emerson of

[29] L. Ward Bannister to Ottamar Hamele, June 22, 1922; Bannister to Clarence Stetson, July 5 and August 16, 1922; and Bannister, "A Memorandum on Wyoming vs. Colorado and Kansas vs. Colorado," in Bannister to Stetson, July 11, 1922, all in file 1-M/295, Hoover Papers.

[30] L. Ward Bannister to Clarence Stetson, July 5 and Aug. 16, 1922, file 1-M/295, Hoover Papers; Bannister to Ottamar Hamele, June 22, 1922, file 1-M/295, Hoover Papers.

Wyoming, "otherwise . . . we may never again have a like opportunity." [31]

Also weighing heavily on Carpenter's mind as he pondered ways to devise a satisfactory formula were some proposals of Arizona and California that were offered in the wake of the Court decision. Arizona's Norviel had collaborated with Richard Sloan, a former Arizona territorial governor and associate justice of the territorial supreme court, in resurrecting the idea of a compact based on a time limit. They recommended unrestricted development of both basins for twenty or perhaps thirty years, at the end of which time uses were to be recognized on a basis of parity. Thereafter, rights would be based on priority of appropriation. Transfers of water out of the basin in Utah and Colorado were to be limited to specific amounts, preferably 310,000 acre-feet for Colorado and 190,000 acre-feet for Utah.[32]

This proposal did not please upper-basin leaders any more than earlier and similar propositions had pleased them. Nor did they react favorably to the suggestion of W. F. McClure of California, who recommended simply that "priority of appropriation . . . govern regardless of state lines." McClure did, however, soften his proposal by suggesting the creation of a permanent Colorado River Commission "clothed with full authority to refuse any further appropriation within any state proposing to take what may appear to be an excess." [33]

But Carpenter wished to avoid "super interstate agencies" as

[31] Delph Carpenter to Frank C. Emerson, September 7, 1922, Papers of the Wyoming State Engineer; Carpenter to R. E. Caldwell, July 5, 1922, Delph Carpenter Papers, in possession of Judge Donald Carpenter, Greeley, Colo. Despite his concern, Carpenter was optimistic about what would follow from the *Wyoming* v. *California* decision. He told California's McClure that the decision would make his work "much easier" because the "extreme views" of both basins had now been "more or less modified." Carpenter to W. F. McClure, July 11, 1922, Carpenter Papers.

[32] W. S. Norviel to Clarence Stetson, June 14, 1922, file 1-M/311, Hoover Papers; Norviel to A. P. Davis, June 27, 1922, file 032, Colorado River Project, Bureau of Reclamation Papers; memo from Morris Bien, July 28, 1922, file 032, Colorado River Project, Bureau of Reclamation Papers.

[33] W. F. McClure to W. S. Norviel, August 7, 1922, file 1-M/295, Hoover Papers.

well as time limits, and the only solution seemed to lie in the
upper states' agreeing to a limitation on their water use. In
August he circulated a proposal that eventually became the basis
for the Colorado River Compact. His proposition called for
dividing the Colorado River Basin into two sections and then
allocating the waters equally to each division.[34]

VI

In suggesting an apportionment between the basins rather than
to each state, Carpenter returned to an idea he had discarded at
the Denver meeting of the League of the Southwest in 1920.[35]
It was also an idea that had been proposed five months earlier
by Arthur Powell Davis at the hearings in Los Angeles. Hoover,
too, had recommended such an approach at the hearings in Salt
Lake City, and R. E. Caldwell of Utah was presently working on
a compact proposal that incorporated the same principle.[36]

[34] Delph Carpenter to Frank C. Emerson, August 19, 1922, Papers of the Wyoming State Engineer; Carpenter to W. F. McClure, September 28, 1922, Swing Papers.

In 1951 Hoover claimed in his memoirs that he devised the two-basin formula and that he did so in November, 1922, during the compact negotiations in Santa Fe. Hoover's memory was obviously playing tricks on him, because although he contributed mightily to the success of those negotiations, he did not invent the two-basin concept. Herbert Hoover, *The Memoirs of Herbert Hoover: The Cabinet and the Presidency, 1920–1933* (New York, 1951), p. 116. The discrepancy in Hoover's memoirs was first noted by Beverley Moeller in her *Phil Swing and Boulder Dam*, p. viii.

[35] "Hoover Dam Documents," *H. Doc. 717*, 80 Cong., 2 sess. (1948), 18 n.

[36] Delph Carpenter to Oliver Shoup, August 24, 1922, Carpenter Papers; Carpenter to Lawrence Phipps, July 11, 1922, Carpenter Papers; Colorado River Commission, "Hearings" (Los Angeles, March 20, 1922), pp. 100–101, copy in file 032, Colorado River Project, Bureau of Reclamation Papers; Colorado River Commission, "Minutes of the Eleventh Meeting" (Santa Fe, November 11, 1922), pp. 24–25, copy in file 032, Colorado River Project, Bureau of Reclamation Papers; Clarence Stetson to L. Ward Bannister, March 7, 1923, file 1-M/295, Hoover Papers. At the hearings in Phoenix in March, an engineer of the U.S. Geological Survey had recommended a similar proposal. He suggested that 65 percent of the flow be allotted to

Like most water leaders, Carpenter now believed that the major disagreements were between the basins, not among the states within each basin. Moreover, virtually everyone acknowledged that the commission lacked the precise data needed for working out allocations to each state. In addition, Carpenter's proposal seemed to reflect the geographic and political realities that daily appeared more obvious. "I have no copyright upon the idea" of dividing the water between the basins, he later told his fellow commissioners in an attempt to broaden the appeal of his proposal. "It is a composite expression of various members of this Commission and learned men." [37]

Carpenter recommended that the point of demarcation between the basins be established at Lee's Ferry, an old river-crossing station located in northern Arizona's canyon lands about a mile below the mouth of the Paria River. The upper basin, according to his formula, included parts of Colorado, New Mexico, Utah, Wyoming, and Arizona, while the lower basin embraced parts of three of the same states—Utah, New Mexico, and Arizona—in addition to California and Nevada. While the boundary suggested by Carpenter did not follow state lines, in all subsequent discussions, the term "upper basin" was used to designate the states of Wyoming, Colorado, Utah, and New Mexico, which had the larger part of their territory drained above Lee's Ferry. The expression "lower basin" referred to the states of Arizona, California, and Nevada, which were mostly drained below that point.

---

the lower basin and 35 percent to the upper states. His proposal differed significantly from the later ones, however, in that he went on to specify the amount that he believed should go to each state. Colorado River Commission, "Hearings" (Phoenix, March 16, 1922), first session, pp. 23–34; see also George Otis Smith to Herbert Hoover, February 28, 1922, Scrugham Papers, NHS.

[37] Carpenter also noted that the two-basin idea "was advanced before this Commission by Director Davis; not in the exact form that I have suggested, but division below the mouth of the San Juan was suggested by him." Colorado River Commission, "Minutes of the Eleventh Meeting" (Santa Fe, November 11, 1922), p. 39. See also ibid., pp. 35, 42; House Committee on Irrigation of Arid Lands, *Hearings on Protection and Development of Lower Colorado River Basin, H.R. 11449*, p. 53; Clarence Stetson to Carl Hayden, January 27, 1923, in *Cong. Rec.*, 67 Cong., 4 sess. (1923), p. 2710.

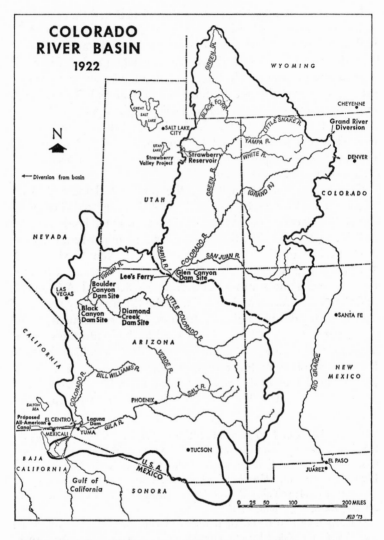

COLORADO
RIVER BASIN
1922

Carpenter based his water-allocation formula on the commonly held assumption that the average annual runoff of the Colorado River was approximately 17,400,000 acre-feet. This volume was determined by the Reclamation Service from measurements made at Yuma. Carpenter proposed that this water be divided equally between the upper and lower basins. The lower basin's share of 8,700,000 acre-feet would consist of water from two sources: lower-basin tributaries, and the deliveries made by the upper basin at Lee's Ferry. He calculated that the lower-basin tributaries annually produced 2,436,000 acre-feet; consequently, he concluded that the upper basin would have to let down 6,264,000 acre-feet in order to provide the lower states with their promised amount of 8,700,000 acre-feet.[38]

Actually Carpenter's proposal did not represent an equal division of the water reaching Yuma. Of the 17,400,000 acre-feet arriving at that point, only about 1,000,000 acre-feet came from the lower-basin tributaries. Though the actual total production of those tributaries was much greater, all the water from them except for about 1,000,000 acre-feet was either diverted by upstream irrigators or lost to evaporation before reaching Yuma. But Carpenter wanted to have the lower states charged for all the water of their tributaries in order to reduce the obligation of the upper basin.

Put succinctly, Carpenter's proposal obligated the upper basin to produce at Lee's Ferry an annual average of 6,264,000 acre-feet, as measured over any ten-year period. (The ten-year average was provided in order to compensate for fluctuations in the stream flow.) The upper states were also obligated to deliver at Lee's Ferry half of any future treaty obligation to Mexico.

Carpenter believed that his proposal would solve many lesser yet still important problems that had vexed the commissioners. "This method . . . ," he told Wyoming's Frank Emerson, "automatically takes care of . . . diversions . . . out of the watershed" since such transfers would simply be "made and cared for at the expense of the division in whch they occur." In addition, "evaporation losses . . . are automatically cared for within each division." But most important, he observed, the formula would establish "a permanent and perpetual status" between the basins, thus eliminating many of the uncertainties found in earlier compact propositions.[39]

[38] Delph Carpenter to Frank C. Emerson, August 19, 1922, Papers of the Wyoming State Engineer; Carpenter to W. F. McClure, September 28, 1922, Swing Papers; Colorado River Commission, "Minutes of the Eleventh Meeting" (Santa Fe, November 11, 1922), pp. 14–23.

[39] Delph Carpenter to Frank C. Emerson, August 19, 1922, Papers of the Wyoming State Engineer.

The reception accorded the proposal during the weeks immediately following its circulation seemed to justify Carpenter's enthusiasm. Arthur Powell Davis believed that the offer contained "more promise of agreement than any I have yet seen." [40] Only leaders of Arizona and New Mexico registered some skepticism about the two-basin idea. They remained hopeful that an allocation to each state might still be achieved. Most other spokesmen, including those in California, found Carpenter's proposition appealing, though Phil Swing thought that the lower basin should seek more water than Carpenter was offering.

Thomas Yager of the Coachella Valley urged Swing to communicate his ideas to McClure, the California member of the Colorado River Commission. Yager had become worried by what he considered McClure's failure to understand thoroughly the situation along the lower river. "Personally," Yager told Swing, "I believe it would be a great advantage if you . . . could advise McClure as to the action he should take, and between you and I [*sic*], he needs this advice." [41]

Swing responded by preparing for McClure an analysis of Carpenter's proposal. He drew special attention to Arizona's acreage claims and noted that they greatly exceeded Davis's estimates. "If the Carpenter proposal is the one to be adopted," he told McClure in a remarkably prescient observation, "I suggest that as far as you can you take the part of Arizona, because if Arizona does not get satisfaction at this time out of the Carpenter agreement, she will try to take it out on California when we come to adjust our differences with her later." The Gila, Swing believed, was the key to the problem. "The effort will be to charge the lower states with more water of the Gila than can be put to a beneficial use. We in turn will have to charge this to Arizona. So we are helping ourselves when we help Arizona. . . ." [42]

But Arizona was not the only matter on Swing's mind as he pondered the Carpenter proposition. Of much greater concern was the Boulder Canyon dam. "It seems to me," he advised

[40] A. P. Davis to V. E. Skiles, August 26, 1922, file 032, Colorado River Project, Bureau of Reclamation Papers; A. P. Davis to Delph Carpenter, October 24, 1922, Carpenter Papers.

[41] Thomas Yager to Phil Swing, October 3, 1922, Swing Papers.

[42] Phil Swing to W. F. McClure, October 28, 1922, Swing Papers. Two letters were written to McClure on the same day.

McClure, "that it might be well to angle for the endorsement of Boulder Dam in return for our agreement to some modified form of the Carpenter proposal. If an endorsement of the whole Commission is not possible, the next best thing would be to get the endorsement of the Commissioner for each of the upper states, as we know we can get that of Nevada." Nevada, of course, had reasons of its own for wanting a high dam in Boulder Canyon.

Though Swing had reservations about the Carpenter proposal, he believed that it deserved a full hearing at the next round of negotiations scheduled for Santa Fe. Those negotiations turned out to be the most significant discussion of water problems so far.

VII

Herbert Hoover and his fellow Colorado River commissioners approached the Santa Fe conference on November 9 with a mixture of seriousness and optimism. The chances of success seemed unusually favorable. The public also sensed that an agreement was near, and scores of newsmen came to the New Mexico capital, creating congestion and the need for additional telegraph lines. The interest was understandable. During the months immediately preceding the meeting, newspapers and national magazines had devoted considerable attention to dramatizing the complex legal and engineering issues that had rocked the basin for so long.[43] The curiosity had been especially strong since midsummer, when this round of negotiations had first been scheduled. They had then been cancelled when major strikes in the railway and coal industries required Hoover's presence elsewhere. Postponement had also seemed advisable because of approaching

[43] See, for example, Clarence C. Stetson, "Making an Empire to Order," *World's Work* XLV (November, 1922): 92–102; *Santa Fe New Mexican*, November 4, 1922; C. E. Grunsky, "International and Interstate Aspects of the Colorado River Problem," *Science* LVI (November 10, 1922): 521–527; Herbert Hoover, "Colorado River Development," *Industrial Management* LXIII (May, 1922): 291; Wayne C. Williams, "A Treaty Among States: How the Southwest Will Regulate and Utilize the Flood Waters of the Colorado River," *Review of Reviews* LXV (June, 1922): 619–622; E. L. Hampton, "The Battle with the Colorado," ibid. LXVI (November, 1922): 525–531.

local and national elections, which might have turned the compact into a political football.[44]

Hoover was especially anxious to keep the pact out of politics,
and he was equally concerned with finding a meeting site where
negotiations might be free from the distractions of the big city.
For that reason he selected Bishop's Lodge, a rather posh dude
ranch with living quarters constructed in an architectural style
evocative of New Mexico's Spanish heritage. Though the lodge
was located only about three and a half miles north of Santa Fe,
it was not easily reached. "To get to the place," observed one unimpressed visitor, "you are obliged to wriggle in an automobile
over a convolution of roads that dizzily swoop up and down like
a switch-back roller coaster and hang so precariously to the steep
sides of the desolate landscape that the passage of a vehicle
makes you think of a fly crawling over an eyebrow." [45]

But the difficulty of access served Hoover's purpose well.
Though he wished to have the public aware of the conference, he
wanted privacy. In fact, he wanted to limit sharply the delegations
from each state. When the manager of Bishop's Lodge overbooked
the accommodations, in some cases placing four people in rooms
intended for two, Hoover reacted swiftly. He ordered the flustered
innkeeper to relieve the congestion in the quarters of the delegates, or he would terminate the conference and move it elsewhere. Clarence Stetson, the secretary of the commission and
Hoover's "polite echo," prepared a list of those who could remain
and then directed the manager to evict the others.[46]

Such tactics left hard feelings, particularly among the Californians who had accepted the crowded quarters without complaint. When seven of them returned from breakfast one morning
to discover, as the maid discreetly put it, that they had "moved,"
they protested bitterly. Though three of them decided to com-
mute daily over the rough road from Santa Fe, the four others
left for home.

[44] Clarence Stetson to L. Ward Bannister, July 24, 1922, file 1-M/
295, Hoover Papers; Stetson to Leslie R. Saunders, August 3, 1922,
file 1-M/296, Hoover Papers; Stetson to Colorado River Commissioners, August 15, 1922, file 1-M/299, Hoover Papers; Stetson to Merritt
C. Mechem, August 15, 1922, Mechem Papers.

[45] Arnold Kruckman, "Inside Story of River Conference," *Saturday
Night* III (November 18, 1922): 5.

[46] Ibid.

ARTHUR POWELL DAVIS   CHARLES R. ROCKWOOD

MARK ROSE   PHIL SWING

THE IMPERIAL VALLEY AREA—The Imperial Valley Area as photographed from Gemini V. The Salton Sea is in the center of the picture, with the Imperial Valley to the right and the Coachella Valley to the left. The Colorado River is in the extreme upper right-hand corner.

DELPH CARPENTER

THE COLORADO RIVER COMMISSION—*Left to right:* Delph Carpenter, Colorado; W. S. Norviel, Arizona; Clarence Stetson, executive secretary of the Colorado River Commission; Herbert Hoover; James Scrugham, Nevada; R. E. Caldwell, Utah; W. F. McClure, California; Stephen B. Davis, Jr., New Mexico; Frank C. Emerson, Wyoming. (*Courtesy of the Herbert Hoover Presidential Library.*)

BISHOP'S LODGE, NEW MEXICO, NOVEMBER, 1922

SIGNING THE COMPACT, NOVEMBER 24, 1922—*Seated:* Herbert Hoover. *Standing, left to right:* Frank C. Emerson, Wyoming; Stephen B. Davis, Jr., New Mexico; W. S. Norviel, Arizona; Delph Carpenter, Colorado; Clarence Stetson, executive secretary of the Colorado River Commission; James Scrugham, Nevada; W. F. McClure, California; R. E. Caldwell, Utah.

Lee's Ferry—the Dividing Point (*Courtesy of the Bureau of Reclamation, U.S. Department of the Interior.*)

George W. P. Hunt

The "Million Acre Feet" Picture—"W. S. Norviel from Herbert Hoover—In tribute to a million acre feet and a fine associate."
Source: Colorado River Commission of Arizona, *Report of the Colorado River Commission of Arizona for Period, February 2, 1933–May 3, 1935* (Prescott, Ariz., May 3, 1935), opposite p. 36.

George Maxwell (*Courtesy of Arizona State University Library.*)

HOOVER DAM (*Courtesy of the Bureau of Reclamation, U.S. Department of the Interior.*)

THE ALL-AMERICAN CANAL (*Courtesy of the Bureau of Reclamation, U.S. Department of the Interior.*)

IMPERIAL DAM AND DESILTING WORKS (*Courtesy of the Bureau of Reclamation, U.S. Department of the Interior.*)

Far less controversial was the decision to hold formal talks in executive session so that each delegate might feel more at ease in speaking his mind or in agreeing to a compromise. Participation in these sessions was limited to the commissioners themselves and to their advisers. Only one legal adviser and one engineering adviser were permitted for each representative. Except for specially invited witnesses, all others were barred. Among those receiving special invitations were the incumbent governors and several new governors-elect from the basin states. Six governors and governors-elect eventually showed up, and among them they represented five states—Arizona, Colorado, New Mexico, Nevada, and Wyoming. One of the governors-elect was James Scrugham, Nevada's Colorado River commissioner. Though Scrugham naturally took an active role in the talks, the other governors and governors-elect seldom spoke, and most attended only one or two of the seventeen negotiating sessions. Nonetheless, the arrival of these officials testified to the importance of the talks, while their silence reflected their decision to leave the technical questions and hard bargaining to their representatives.

For his part, Hoover relied on Arthur Powell Davis's engineering advice and on Ottamar Hamele's legal knowledge. Hamele was chief solicitor for the Interior Department and a strong advocate of federal rights in Colorado River matters. He was determined to make his presence felt at the proper moment.

VIII

The commissioners gathered in the bridal suite at Bishop's Lodge for the first round of negotiations on November 9; what followed during the next two weeks, however, was far from a honeymoon. Each commissioner had been asked to prepare a compact proposal, but discussion centered almost from the beginning on Carpenter's proposition.

Only Davis of New Mexico and Norviel of Arizona sought to resurrect the idea of an apportionment to each state. "All that I can see in the group idea is that we shove off to the future that much responsibility," objected Davis. "It isn't . . . what we were appointed for," agreed Norviel. "It doesn't arrive at any conclusion, and . . . it leaves the two divisions to work out their own salvation." Both quickly bowed to the majority, however, who argued persuasively that the commission lacked the data to make any other kind of adjustment.[47]

Though quick agreement was reached on the matter of a two-basin allocation, other provisions of the Carpenter proposal often produced acrimonious debate. Dominating most of the discussions was Norviel, whose demands played a major role in shaping the treaty that was eventually drafted. His attitudes reflected important recent developments in Arizona, especially the election two days before the conference of a new Arizona governor, George W. P. Hunt.

Though new to office in the sense that he had just defeated the incumbent, Thomas Campbell, Hunt was not new to the governorship. He had been elected governor three times; and in 1916, the last time he had run, he had also defeated Campbell, though on that occasion the initial returns had given the election to his opponent. Nearly a year went by before the results of a recount permitted him to take office. The delay served merely to estrange further the two men, who were already at odds because of the heat generated during the campaign.

In 1922 Hunt had won a clear victory over Campbell, and he had done so on a platform opposing development of the Colorado by "selfish private interests." He emphasized instead Arizona's "superior and natural" rights to "the waters which will be impounded and the hydro electric energy which will be stored within her borders." Of particular significance, however, was his revelation that he had fallen under the spell of George Maxwell, the advocate of a highline canal for Arizona. "Maxwell," he had told supporters less than two weeks before negotiations began in Santa Fe, ". . . has sounded the keynote which should be the aim of our government officials," and "my policy" will be "to work towards the accomplishment of that aim." [48]

As ominous to Norviel as Hunt's election was Maxwell's arrival

[47] Colorado River Commission, "Minutes of the Eleventh Meeting" (November 11, 1922), pp. 33, 34; "Minutes of the Twelfth Meeting" (November 12, 1922), p. 23; "Minutes of the Thirteenth Meeting" (November 13, 1922), p. 2.

[48] George W. P. Hunt to Friend, October 28, 1922, George W. P. Hunt Papers, Arizona State Archives, Phoenix. This was a form letter used during the campaign. See also Phoenix *Arizona Republican,* September 28, 1922.

in Santa Fe. At an open meeting attended by the commissioners before the start of talks, Maxwell had repeated his well-known demands: postponement of the compact and concentration now on relatively small flood-control works. He also again denounced the Boulder Canyon project as a scheme to create an Asiatic colony in Mexico—a scheme that would lead to war. "As between the submergence of the Imperial Valley by floods," he declared, "and the devastation of southern California and Arizona in an Asiatic war, the loss of the Imperial Valley would be the lesser of the two evils." [49]

Maxwell's presence reminded Norviel that a detailed survey of Arizona's irrigable acreage was still not available. The investigating team, headed by E. C. LaRue, had only entered the field in early October. "However," Norviel privately told Stetson, "I feel that our 'guess' will be fairly accurate and we will stay with that until we learn more definitely what can be done." [50]

In Norviel's mind the ideal compact would be one that confirmed the principle of priority and guaranteed to Arizona the kind of hydroelectric power settlement she had all along wanted. He knew that such an agreement was impossible, however, so he concentrated instead on modifying Carpenter's plan, especially the provisions dealing with water allocation.

Norviel flatly refused to accept Carpenter's apportionment formula, claiming that it allocated mostly flood waters to the lower basin. The commissioners of California and Nevada, on the other hand, though opposed to some details of the offer, did not challenge the basic apportionment. McClure, in fact, considered it "a fair basis for discussion." [51] Norviel thus found himself carrying the brunt of the attack, but he did not waver.

At first Hoover steered the discussion toward what he believed were less serious areas of disagreement, hoping that their

[49] Colorado River Commission, "Hearings" (Santa Fe, November 9, 1922), pp. 25–29; *Santa Fe New Mexican,* November 14, 1922; *Los Angeles Times,* November 11 and 16, 1922.

[50] W. S. Norviel to Clarence Stetson, October 31, 1922, file 1/M-310, Hoover Papers; W. S. Norviel, "Report of W. S. Norviel, Colorado River Commissioner, State of Arizona," n.d., file 1-M/315, Hoover Papers.

[51] Colorado River Commission, "Minutes of the Twelfth Meeting" (November 12, 1922), pp. 22–23.

settlement would pave the way for a resolution of the allocation problem. But five days of wrangling over lesser issues convinced him that he would have to tackle head-on the problem of water allocation. Unless it was satisfactorily resolved, virtually no progress would be possible on anything else. Taking the initiative, he offered a compromise proposal that he hoped would satisfy both Norviel and the upper states.

Hoover's suggestion revealed that he agreed with Carpenter about the wisdom of dividing the water between the basins. It also reflected his sympathy for Norviel, for he proposed that the lower basin be given the water of its tributaries *in addition to* half the flow at Lee's Ferry.

The average flow at Lee's Ferry, according to the Reclamation Service, was 16,400,000 acre-feet.[52] Hence, Hoover's suggestion accorded each basin half that amount. For the lower basin this division meant an increase at Lee's Ferry of nearly 2,000,000 acre-feet more than Carpenter was willing to concede. Such an amount, Hoover believed, would be enough to satisfy all future lower-basin needs—needs that Arthur Powell Davis estimated at 7,450,000 acre-feet, a figure that included enough water to irrigate half the estimated 800,000 irrigable acres in Mexico. The surplus, explained Hoover, could be applied to evaporation losses, including those occurring to any share awarded to Mexico between the time that it arrived at Lee's Ferry and the time that it reached the border, some six hundred miles below.[53] To account for the fluctuations in river flow, Hoover suggested that deliveries at Lee's Ferry be calculated over ten-year periods and recommended that the upper states obligate themselves to deliver an average of 82,000,000 acre-feet, as measured over any ten-year period.

Hoover's proposal received a mixed response. Norviel was

[52] It should be noted that in the compact the expression "Lee Ferry" was used instead of "Lee's Ferry." This was a result of the current practice in map-making of dropping the apostrophe and "*s*" off a place name. (Colorado River Commission, "Minutes of the Twenty-second Meeting" [November 22, 1922], Part I, p. 5). Both expressions were used during the negotiations. For the sake of consistency, I have used "Lee's Ferry" except where it appears differently in a quotation.

[53] Colorado River Commission, "Minutes of the Sixteenth Meeting" (November 14, 1922), pp. 25–28.

COLORADO RIVER FLOW AT LEE'S FERRY, 1899–1920

Year	Acre-feet	Percentage of mean
1899	21,700,000	132
1900	16,800,000	102
1901	15,200,000	93
1902	9,110,000	56
1903	11,300,000	69
1904	9,890,000	60
1905	16,000,000	98
1906	17,700,000	108
1907	24,800,000	151
1908	12,600,000	77
1909	25,400,000	155
1910	14,200,000	87
1911	17,600,000	107
1912	18,200,000	111
1913	11,800,000	72
1914	20,200,000	123
1915	12,900,000	79
1916	18,900,000	115
1917	20,000,000	122
1918	13,100,000	80
1919	11,000,000	67
1920	21,100,000	129
Mean	16,400,000	

NOTE: These figures were based on measurements made at Laguna Dam' not at Lee's Ferry. There was no gauging station at Lee's Ferry during these years, but the Reclamation Service believed that the flow at Laguna Dam, near Yuma, was the same as that at Lee's Ferry. Evaporation losses between Lee's Ferry and Laguna Dam, according to the Reclamation Service, were offset by the inflow from tributaries. (The figures on this table do not include the inflow from the Gila, since that tributary entered the mainstream below Laguna Dam. The annual average discharge of the Gila was estimated at 1,070,000 acre-feet.)

SOURCES: "Problems of Imperial Valley and Vicinity," *S. Doc. 142*, 67 Cong., 2 sess. (1922), pp. 2, 5; *Cong. Rec.*, 67 Cong., 4 sess. (1923), p. 2714.

naturally pleased, but the upper states, after caucusing to consider the measure, registered strong disapproval. New Mexico's Stephen Davis singled out the principal objection: the minimum-flow record showed that the upper states would be unable to comply with the proposal without depriving themselves of water. "Taking the measured flow for the . . . lowest ten years for which we have a record . . . ," he explained, "it is apparent . . . that . . . any such guaranty would have been violated." [54]

Davis pointed out that during the first ten years for which measurements were available, the flow at Lee's Ferry was 155,-000,000 acre-feet, of which half was 77,500,000 acre-feet. Consequently, if such a dry period should repeat itself, as was likely, the upper basin would have to cut back on its portion in order to provide the lower states with the 82,000,000 acre-feet required under Hoover's formula.

Davis produced a counterproposal that had been prepared by the upper states during their caucus. The upper basin offered to guarantee delivery of 65,000,000 acre-feet during any ten-year period. "There is a tendency," observed Delph Carpenter in defense of the proposition, "to eliminate arbitrarily the flow of certain [lower basin] streams like the Gila. . . . The figure arrived at is one which takes into consideration those other streams, all of which are for the benefit of the lower territory. . . . In effect, this says that so much water shall pass Lee's Ferry, and leaves all the flow of the lower streams to the territory in which they arise." [55]

Norviel was unimpressed with Carpenter's offer because Hoover's proposal had also awarded the lower states the water of their tributaries. "If that is the attitude . . . [of] the upper division," he snapped, then "we . . . better try out some other proposition, because it would be utterly useless to take this proposition back to our state and expect to have it ratified by the legislature." [56]

Norviel refused to settle for less than half the flow at Lee's Ferry plus the tributaries. All of the water reaching the mainstream from the tributaries, he claimed, was lost to evaporation

[54] Colorado River Commission, "Minutes of the Seventeenth Meeting" (November 15, 1922), p. 2.
[55] Ibid., pp. 5, 6.   [56] Ibid., p. 8.

before it could be put to use. "Also," he argued, "there is no calculation made in the tabulation . . . for any acreage . . . to be irrigated by the Gila River, and I am sure there is abundant acreage to take care of every drop that may come down the Gila. If that is to be considered . . . , then our needs would run far above the needs specified for the upper basin." [57]

No one wished to reopen the Pandora's Box of trying to reach a settlement based on acreage, but the upper states steadfastly refused to grant the 82,000,000 acre-feet that would have satisfied Norviel. Though McClure of California remained silent, Nevada's Scrugham came to Norviel's aid. "If the upper basin will only guarantee sixty-five million acre-feet . . . we might as well abandon the discussion." [58]

"I think we could say the same thing of the lower states," replied New Mexico's Stephen Davis. "If the lower states are set on eighty-two million, we might as well abandon the discussion."

The negotiations, as they had so often before, seemed on the verge of breaking down.

IX

Once again Hoover tried to bring the two sides together. "Of course, the business of the Chairman is to find a medial ground," he explained. "So I am wondering if the northern states will make it" 7,500,000 acre-feet annually, or 75,000,000 acre-feet every ten years? [59] That amount, he believed, would satisfy requirements on the lower river, and it would not obligate the upper states to cut down on their uses if the low-flow period should repeat itself.

Hoover's offer was made in the late afternoon of November 15 and held the promise of resolving the deadlock. The commissioners recessed, split into upper- and lower-basin discussion groups, and studied the proposal through the night. By morning, the worst seemed to be over. "Good prospect for agreement this morning," stated California's McClure in a telegram to Phil Swing.[60]

The meeting that day confirmed McClure's optimism. The commissioners not only approved the Hoover proposition, but

[57] Ibid., p. 12.   [58] Ibid., p. 21.   [59] Ibid., p. 22.
[60] W. F. McClure to Phil Swing, November 16, 1922, Swing Papers.

also made progress on other important points: any future treaty obligation to Mexico would be borne equally by the two basins; priority in the use of water would go, first, to agricultural and domestic purposes; second, to power; and, third, to navigation; and the basin was defined so as to include "all of the territory to which the waters of the river and its tributaries can be beneficially applied within the United States." [61] This last point made it clear that the commissioners approved interbasin transfers of water.

Their discussions also revealed that they were unconcerned about the quality of the waters that they were dividing. The reservoirs would remove troublesome silt by acting as settling basins, and the water supply would be great enough to dilute the saline return flow coming from upriver irrigation projects. Their concern was with quantity, not quality. Norviel expressed it best: "We are perfectly willing to take second-hand water, provided the amount is sufficient." [62]

By mid-afternoon Hoover thought that enough progress had been made so that he could appoint a drafting committee to prepare the formal document. He then broke the news silence covering the negotiations by announcing to reporters that agreement had been "reached . . . upon the main principles of a treaty." Plans were even made to rename the bridal suite the "Treaty Room" and to place there a bronze tablet commemorating the event.[63]

X

The euphoria was short-lived. Three days later, when the commissioners met to approve the work of the drafting committee, the excitement turned to gloom. Although the major reason for

[61] Colorado River Commission, "Minutes of the Eighteenth Meeting" (November 16, 1922), pp. 3, 10, 33, 53. As finally adopted, the wording of the definition of the basin was slightly different, but the intent remained the same. See article II (a) of the compact.

[62] Colorado River Commission, "Minutes of the Thirteenth Meeting" (November 13, 1922), p. 47; see also Colorado River Commission, "Hearings" (Salt Lake City, March 28, 1922), p. 24; Frank C. Emerson, "Report . . . in re Colorado River Compact" (January 18, 1923), p. 15, Papers of the Wyoming State Engineer.

[63] *Santa Fe New Mexican*, November 16 and 17, 1922.

opposition was renewed resistance from Norviel, he was not alone. Others quickly raised additional questions that threatened to destroy the accord. The debate ranged over a wide variety of issues, but three were particularly important: the status of the lower-basin tributaries, the responsibility for supplying Mexico, and storage in the lower basin.

Norviel almost innocently precipitated this latest crisis when he asked that the wording in the compact be made to specify that the lower basin would receive 7,500,000 acre-feet *in addition to* the flow of its own tributaries. He believed that he was asking merely for a clarification of a point upon which agreement had already been reached. Hoover's first offer, as well as the upper basin's proposition for 6,500,000 acre-feet, had utilized that principle. Norviel assumed that Hoover's latest compromise proposal for 7,500,000 acre-feet had incorporated the same principle. "Mr. Carpenter," he recalled, "made the statement that they [the tributaries] were ours utterly to use as we saw fit." [64]

"No I didn't," replied Carpenter to a shocked Norviel. The upper-basin proposition had been based on such an understanding, admitted Carpenter, but not Hoover's latest proposal.

Before Hoover could say anything, Stephen Davis of New Mexico widened the breach.

"Irrespective of what Mr. Carpenter said," declared Davis, "I think it is incorrect to say we have arrived at any point, —if you mean by that *All* the northern states, because we have arrived at nothing."

"Then we will have to start all over," snapped Norviel.

Norviel's concern derived primarily from his belief that if Carpenter and Davis had their way, then the lower states would be prevented from using the entire 7,500,000 acre-feet that was to be delivered at Lee's Ferry. His reasoning was easy to follow. He believed that uses on the Gila and other lower-basin tributaries would eventually amount to as much as 3,000,000 acre-feet. This meant, he concluded, that the lower states would be able to use only 4,500,000 acre-feet of the water arriving at Lee's Ferry before they would have reached 7,500,000 acre-feet, their maximum allotment.

"There will be remaining . . . ," stated Norviel, "something

[64] Colorado River Commission, "Minutes of the Nineteenth Meeting" (November 19, 1922), Part I, p. 4.

like 3,000,000 acre-feet of that 7,500,000 acre feet . . . to which
we could not obtain any priority of right and you are asking us
. . . to put that back into the general jackpot and divide it up
again." [65]

The wrangling continued for three days until Norviel, who
stood alone in his opposition, finally buckled under the pressure
and agreed to a compromise offered by Scrugham of Nevada.
Scrugham suggested that 7,500,000 acre-feet be allocated to each
basin, with an additional 1,000,000 acre-feet going to the lower
states to appease Norviel.[66] This additional 1,000,000 acre-feet—
which were provided for in article III (b) of the compact—
represented a considerable volume of water, but the amount was
still only about a third of what Norviel expected the lower basin
to take from its tributaries. To be more precise, it represented
only about a third of what Arizona expected to take from the
tributaries, since nearly all of the tributary water came from her
territory. In agreeing to Scrugham's proposition, Norviel was
obviously backing down substantially from his earlier demands.

The precise reasons for Norviel's retreat do not appear in the
minutes of the Colorado River Commission because most of the
bargaining that led to his decision took place in private conversations and during subcommittee meetings for which no
record was kept. But there is other evidence that seems to explain Norviel's action. In view of the later controversy over the
meaning of the compact—and over the meaning of article III
(b) in particular—this evidence deserves careful scrutiny. The
most telling document is the report that Norviel prepared—
shortly after leaving Santa Fe—for Hunt, Arizona's newly elected
governor.[67]

[65] Ibid., p. 8.

[66] Scrugham actually suggested a number of ways to satisfy Ari-
zona's objections. These suggestions were turned over to a subcom-
mittee, which settled upon the proposal that was finally adopted.
Colorado River Commission, "Minutes of the Twenty-second Meeting"
(November 22, 1922), Part I, p. 3; "Minutes of the Twenty-first
Meeting" (November 20, 1922), Part II, p. 15.

[67] W. S. Norviel, "Report of W. S. Norviel, Colorado River Commissioner, State of Arizona," n.d., file 1-M/315, Hoover Papers.
Though this copy of the report is undated, there is evidence in the
files of the Arizona Colorado River Commission that Norviel submitted

A reading of Norviel's report reveals that his decision rested heavily on another compact provision—article III (d)—which obligated the upper states to deliver 75,000,000 acre-feet every ten years. Norviel realized that this requirement provided the lower states with an average annual delivery of 7,500,000 acre-feet. The amount might vary during individual years; yet with storage the variations would be slight. But most important, the delivery requirement had to be met regardless of the volume of water taken from the lower-basin tributaries. Not even "the fullest use made of all the available waters in Arizona from any and all streams," he observed, would "affect in any way the said amount of water to pass Lee Ferry." [68] The only restriction was that the water had to be "reasonably . . . applied to domestic and agricultural uses" [69]—and that requirement posed no problem. In other words, even if lower-basin uses eventually amounted to 10,500,-000 acre-feet (7,500,000 acre-feet at Lee's Ferry plus 3,000,000 acre-feet from the tributaries), the upper basin would still be obligated to send down 75,000,000 acre-feet every ten years. Of course, the advantage provided the lower basin by this arrangement was more apparent than real. Article III (d) seemed to guarantee the lower basin 7,500,000 acre-feet annually plus the flow from tributaries, but in fact it did no such thing: the compact, regardless of the effect of some of its provisions, gave the lower basin a *right* to only 8,500,000 acre-feet (7,500,000 acre-feet allocated by article III [a] and 1,000,000 acre-feet allocated by article III [b]). Uses in excess of that amount—whether the uses were of mainstream water or tributary water—would have no legal standing until recognized by a future compact.

---

the report to Hunt on January 19, 1923. See W. S. Norviel to George W. P. Hunt, January 19, 1923, Arizona Colorado River Commission Papers, Office File, Arizona State Archives. A copy of Norviel's report is also in box 22, Northcutt Ely Papers, Stanford University. See also W. S. Norviel, "The Colorado River Compact Means Much to Southwest," *Arizona Mining Journal* VI (January 15, 1923): 34–35, 59–61; Richard E. Sloan, "Pact Criticism Is Largely on What It Does Not Say," ibid., pp. 29, 31, 58–59.

[68] Norviel, "Report," p. 12, file 1-M/315, Hoover Papers. Hoover made this same point about the same time. *Cong. Rec.*, 67 Cong., 4 sess. (1923), p. 2711.

[69] See article III (e) of the compact.

Though this consideration was important, it did not deter Norviel from accepting Scrugham's compromise proposal. Even if the lower states did not have rights to all the waters of their tributaries, they did have assurances of 75,000,000 acre-feet at Lee's Ferry every ten years. And so far as the tributary water itself was concerned, they would obtain through Scrugham's proposal firm rights to 1,000,000 acre-feet. That amount, in Norviel's view, represented a significant "concession," particularly since the upper states had at first refused to provide any compensation for the lower-basin tributaries.[70]

Still, Norviel remained uneasy about his decision to compromise, and this uneasiness becomes nowhere more apparent than in his report. At the time that he was drafting it, he was under stinging criticism from fellow Arizonans who believed that the state's tributaries—especially the Gila—should have been excluded from the compact and given without reservation to Arizona. He responded to their criticism by claiming that the compromise embodied in Scrugham's article III (b) accomplished that goal. "As the Gila River is estimated to produce between 1,070,000 and 1,100,000 acre-feet per annum on an average over a long period of records," he observed, "Section (b) was written into the Compact, it being understood, though not expressed, that it would practically take care of or offset all the water produced in this state." [71]

Norviel was exaggerating. To begin with, he had made it clear during the negotiations that he believed there were probably 3,000,000 acre-feet in Arizona's tributaries, not 1,000,000. Moreover, his estimate of 1,070,000 or 1,100,000 acre-feet in the Gila accounted only for the Gila water then reaching the mainstream. It did not take into consideration an additional 1,000,000 acre-feet that was consumed upstream on the Gila and never reached the mainstream. Nor did it account for still another 1,000,000 acre-feet that the Reclamation Service believed was entering the mainstream from lower-basin tributaries other than the Gila. Thus, if the negotiators had actually wanted, in Norviel's words, to "take care of . . . all the water produced" by Arizona, they

[70] Norviel, "Report," p. 12, file 1-M/315, Hoover Papers.

[71] Ibid.; see also W. S. Norviel to Carl Hayden, February 16, 1926, box 598, folder 7, Carl Hayden Papers, Arizona State University Library, Tempe.

would have had to increase considerably the amount covered by
article III (b).[72] Indeed, Norviel's fellow Arizonan and legal
adviser, Richard Sloan, believed that the Gila River alone produced 2,350,000 acre-feet, an estimate more than twice as large
as that given by Norviel in his report.[73]

Additional evidence that Norviel exaggerated in his report is
found in a statement made about nine years later by Delph Carpenter. "At the time the Compact was being drafted," observed
Carpenter in a letter written to explain the meaning of article
III (b), "Arizona suddenly awakened to the fact that the Gila is
a tributary of the Colorado River and after much argument it was
finally decided to increase the apportionment to the Lower
Basin to 8,500,000 acre feet on account of *then present estimated
consumptive uses on the Gila.*" [74]

Though Norviel's report exaggerated, there is no gainsaying the
fact that the additional 1,000,000 acre-feet provided by article III
(b) made the compact considerably more palatable to him. Moreover, as Arizonans were to argue years later, the negotiators
doubtlessly intended for the entire 1,000,000 acre-feet to be given
to Arizona when the lower-basin states eventually divided their
share of water among themselves. Though the minutes of the
negotiations are silent on this point, the fact that article III (b)

[72] Colorado River Commission, "Minutes of the Nineteenth Meet-
ing" (November 19, 1922), Part I, p. 8; "Minutes of the Sixteenth
Meeting" (November 14, 1922), pp. 17–19; Delph Carpenter to
Frank C. Emerson, August 19, 1922, Papers of the Wyoming State
Engineer; A. P. Davis to Frank Emerson, January 30, 1923, file 032,
Colorado River Project, Bureau of Reclamation Papers.

[73] Sloan, "Pact Criticism," p. 58. Lack of precise data made it
impossible for the commissioners to state with precision the amount
of water in the tributaries. Though, as indicated, some estimates ran
as high as 3,000,000 acre-feet, others were lower. Carpenter, for
example, believed the amount to be 2,436,000 acre-feet. Despite
the differences, no one else placed the estimate as low as Norviel
did in his report. In 1933 Thomas Maddock, an engineer and the
secretary of Arizona's Colorado River Commission, estimated the
volume of water in the lower-basin tributaries at more than 2,500,000
acre-feet. Maddock to George W. P. Hunt, April 2, 1933, Maddock
Papers, Arizona Historical Society, Tucson.

[74] Delph Carpenter to Thomas H. Gibson and Ray L. Sauter,
March 2, 1931, Carpenter Papers. Emphasis added.

was added as a result of Norviel's protests lends strong support to the later Arizona contention. Unfortunately, such an understanding could not be written into the compact because the commissioners had already agreed to apportion water only to basins, not to individual states. If an exception was made for Arizona, the other states would demand similar treatment; and all hope for a settlement would be lost.

But the negotiations did not collapse, for Norviel accepted Scrugham's compromise proposal. His decision to do so was also influenced by his belief that Arizona had nothing to fear from the other lower-basin states—Nevada and California. Nevada's water requests, as everyone admitted, were minimal and could be met almost entirely by diversions from the Virgin River, a small lower-basin tributary. Since the Virgin entered the mainstream below Lee's Ferry, Nevada's diversions from it would obviously not deplete the 75,000,000 acre-feet promised by the upper states every ten years.

California, on the other hand, planned to use much of the water delivered by the upper basin, but this intention did not bother Norviel or his adviser, Sloan, because they believed that California's "ultimate development" was already "definitely well-known" and that it posed no threat to Arizona. Sloan calculated that the future uses of the lower basin—including Arizona's projected uses along the Gila—would total 7,450,000 acre-feet. Since Scrugham's compact proposal was for 8,500,000 acre-feet (7,500,-000 acre-feet at Lee's Ferry plus an additional 1,000,000 acre-feet from other sources), there would be a "margin of safety" of 1,050,000 acre-feet.[75]

[75] Norviel, "Report," p. 6, file 1-M/315, Hoover Papers; Sloan, "Pact Criticism," p. 58. Sloan's assessment of future lower-basin uses seems to square with the views of the other members of the Colorado River Commission. At the time of the Santa Fe negotiations, Arthur Powell Davis offered a similar assessment, which was probably the basis of Sloan's estimate. (Colorado River Commission, "Minutes of the Sixteenth Meeting" [November 14, 1922], pp. 25–28.) California had all along accepted Davis's figures. Nevada had challenged his initial estimate of that state's irrigable acreage, but Nevada's demands were very small. While Sloan's assessment of lower-basin needs was in general agreement with the estimates of others, his assessment of upper-basin needs was not. Nor was his description of the compact negotiations an accurate one. Sloan claimed that the negotiators devised a simple formula for allocating the water. They

Also undoubtedly persuading Norviel to accept Scrugham's water allocation formula was the unsympathetic attitude of the other commissioners. The upper-state representatives were openly hostile; Hoover was at best tolerant; and the delegates from California and Nevada were indifferent. McClure of California ignored the advice given by Swing before the negotiations and left Norviel to fight alone his battle for the tributaries. That the Arizonan was able to win an additional 1,000,000 acre-feet testified to his tenacity and led Hoover to describe him as "the best fighter on the Commission."

"Arizona should erect a monument to you," he told Norviel, "and entitle it 'One Million acre feet.' " Arizona erected no such monument, but Hoover prepared a symbolic monument of sorts. He sent Norviel a picture of himself, which he warmly inscribed: "W. S. Norviel from Herbert Hoover—In tribute to a million acre feet and a fine associate." [76]

But the battle over the tributaries was not the only issue that disturbed the conference. Norviel raised other serious objections. The most disturbing involved Mexico.

XI

Norviel and his fellow commissioners had earlier—and rather quickly—agreed that any future treaty obligation to Mexico

---

determined the "known requirements" of each basin—according to him, about 7,500,000 acre-feet for the lower basin and 6,500,000 acre-feet for the upper basin—and then merely added to each basin's requirements an additional 1,000,000 acre-feet as a "margin of safety." Sloan's explanation obviously ignores the complicated give-and-take of the actual negotiations, and his estimate of the upper-basin's requirements was derived from Reclamation Service studies that the upper states had steadfastly refused to accept. Doubtlessly, Sloan prepared an explanation of the negotiations calculated purposely to leave the impression that the compact rested on unquestioned scientific data and made undeniably fair allocations of water to each basin. When he offered this explanation, he did so in an article that was written to combat criticism of the pact that had developed in Arizona.

[76] Herbert Hoover to W. S. Norviel, November 26, 1922, in *Report of the Colorado River Commission of Arizona for Period, February 2, 1933–May 3, 1935* (Prescott, Ariz., 1935), p. 36. The autographed photograph is reproduced in ibid. between pages 36 and 37.

should be supplied from surplus water. If the surplus proved insufficient, then the burden was to be shared equally by the two basins.[77] Though Norviel approved of this solution in principle, he did not think that it went far enough.

Of special concern to the Arizonan was the threat that Mexico might pose during the interim between the approval of the compact and the negotiation of a Mexican treaty. As now formulated, the compact obligated the upper basin to share the Mexican burden only *after* a treaty had been obtained. Prior to such an agreement (and a treaty might not be negotiated for years), the lower basin would have to shoulder the entire Mexican obligation. Norviel believed this scheme to be unfair, and he insisted that the upper basin share the present burden as well as any future treaty commitment.

The other commissioners—including those from the lower states of California and Nevada—vigorously objected to saying anything in the compact about a present obligation, arguing that such action would amount to a tacit acknowledgment of Mexican rights to Colorado River water. Such an acknowledgment before any treaty negotiations might prejudice future treaty arrangements.

"We don't want to put anything in here," said Carpenter, "that can be construed in any way as the slightest admission when it comes to matters of the State Department."

Hoover was even more candid: "We do not believe they [the Mexicans] ever had any rights."[78] Despite his disclaimer,

[77] It seems rather clear that this was agreed to with the understanding that the lower basin would be responsible for evaporation losses occurring to the upper basin's share between the time it left Lee's Ferry and the time it arrived at the Mexican border. This was definitely the understanding when Hoover proposed that the flow at Lee's Ferry be divided equally, with 8,200,000 acre-feet being allocated to each basin. (Colorado River Commission, "Minutes of the Sixteenth Meeting" [November 14, 1922], p. 27.) At that time, only Norviel objected. The question was not raised again during the negotiations. Recently, however, it has been merged with other points of contention among the basin states. See chapter 10, below.

[78] Colorado River Commission, "Minutes of the Twentieth Meeting" (November 19, 1922), p. 2; "Minutes of the Nineteenth Meeting" (November 19, 1922), Part II, p. 2.

Hoover's concern was so great that he asked for and received the commission's approval to expunge from the minutes all discussions dealing with Mexico.[79]

Hoover's apprehension about Mexico had several months earlier prompted him to discuss the coming Santa Fe meeting with Secretary of State Charles Evans Hughes. Hughes, citing Harmon's opinion of 1895, had reaffirmed his belief that the United States was free to use all the waters of the Colorado so long as it acted "wholly within United States territory and not along the common boundary line." But he cautioned Hoover against a compact that would deprive Mexico of water. "Considerations of equity and comity would require that the interests of Mexico in the matter should be taken fully into consideration." He reminded Hoover of the 1906 treaty with Mexico on the Rio Grande. On that occasion, the United States had foregone its legal rights and awarded Mexico the maximum volume of water that country had used before the negotiations. In view of such a precedent, Hughes did not believe that the federal government should "become a party in an analogous case for monopolization . . . of the waters of the Colorado River." [80]

Hoover agreed, but he did not want the compact to contain anything that might strengthen Mexico's claims. He and the other commissioners believed that Norviel's request would do exactly that. In particular, they feared that it would give legitimacy to the concession of 1904. This was the contract negotiated between Mexican officials and Imperial Valley settlers that gave Mexico rights to half the water diverted through the Alamo Canal. "If that [contract] is brought into discussion anywhere in this compact," warned Hoover, "we give value to it which we must keep away from with all our might." [81]

[79] Hoover never made the deletions, however. This was probably because the minutes of the last nine meetings were never circulated to the commissioners for approval. Once the pact had been negotiated, there seemed to be no immediate need for a complete set of the minutes. When the need did arise, an official set of the minutes was not available. The set deposited in the Hoover Papers shows lines drawn through the passages that Hoover wished to delete.

[80] Charles Evans Hughes to Herbert Hoover, August 17, 1922, Dept. of State Papers, file 711.1216M/511.

[81] Colorado River Commission, "Minutes of the Nineteenth Meeting" (November 19, 1922), Part II, p. 3.

Hoover's warning had special meaning for those who had read the statements recently issued by Armando Santacruz, the Mexican official who had come to Santa Fe as an observer. Santacruz had told reporters from the *Santa Fe New Mexican* that the contract of 1904 had given Mexico a "prior right" to enough water "to irrigate 400,000 acres . . . or double what is now being irrigated" in Mexico.[82]

Santacruz's announcement and Hoover's warning helped to reinforce the opposition to Norviel's recommendation and assure its defeat. These actions also served to remind Californians of their own special recommendation for solving the Mexican problem: an All-American Canal and a high dam at Boulder Canyon. To McClure of California, the dam was especially important not only for the obvious reasons, but also because of pressure from the large delegation of Californians that had come to Santa Fe from Los Angeles and the Imperial and Coachella valleys. He now responded to this pressure by insisting that the compact make provision for storage.

XII

McClure's approach to the problem was somewhat roundabout. He asked that enforcement of the compact be delayed until storage had been constructed in the lower basin. He preferred a dam in Boulder Canyon; but if the commissioners refused to specify a particular dam, then he indicated his willingness to settle for a provision making the compact dependent simply upon completion of federally built "control works" somewhere on the lower river.[83]

[82] *Santa Fe New Mexican*, November 14, 1922. For Santacruz's description of the Santa Fe meeting, see his report to Federico Ramos, November 30, 1922, Papers of the Comisión Internacional, file 844 (i).

[83] Colorado River Commission, "Minutes of the Twenty-first Meeting" (November 20, 1922), Part I, pp. 14–15. McClure did not press for the All-American Canal, a scheme that he later described as a "monstrosity" and "a purely local or State project." He considered it too expensive, and he did not believe that it would relieve the U.S. of the need to maintain protective works in Mexico. W. F. McClure to Carl Hayden, January 3, 1924, box 600, folder 6, Hayden Papers; and McClure to Frank C. Emerson, April 7, 1924, Papers of the Wyoming State Engineer.

McClure had no sooner made his recommendation than Delph Carpenter jumped to his feet. "To incorporate that as a condition precedent within this compact is something that I for my part would not care to consent to." [84]

"Allow me to become a Californian a minute instead of a Chairman," interrupted Hoover, who came to McClure's aid. "I would like to present one phase of this which we have never considered." During the low-flow season, Hoover explained, the entire river was often diverted by those downstream. But once the compact became effective, those on the lower river would be unable to prevent the upper basin from interfering with the minimum flow. The upper states were merely obligated to supply 75,000,000 acre-feet every ten years; they could, therefore, keep the entire flow during a dry spell and still fulfill their commitment over the ten-year period. This possibility represented the "crux of the anxiety" for those on the lower river, argued Hoover. Only storage would enable them to guard against the loss of water when they needed it most. It would also help them to take care of Mexico's demands during the period before a treaty.[85]

Carpenter remained unmoved. "If we interweave in this compact the idea of predicating it upon flood control someplace, I am free to say that many earnest advocates of construction first and wholly upon the headwaters will immediately enter the arena and present very persuasive arguments in behalf of their plan of development." [86] Carpenter indicated his willingness to support a resolution calling for storage, but he objected to incorporating it into the compact itself.

The other upper-basin commissioners lined up solidly behind Carpenter. Even the Nevada delegate agreed that a separate resolution was the "appropriate" way to handle the matter.[87]

Hoover and McClure immediately sensed the strength of the opposition. They favored a storage provision, but neither was willing to sacrifice the compact in an attempt to get it. They did insist, however, on a provision protecting users along the lower river during the low-flow season: "Nothing in this compact shall limit the legal rights of any state in the lower basin to maintain

[84] Colorado River Commission, "Minutes of the Twenty-first Meeting" (November 20, 1922), Part I, p. 16.
[85] Ibid., pp. 16–17.   [86] Ibid., p. 19.   [87] Ibid., p. 25.

a minimum flow of the Colorado River during the low water season at an average of the past five years." [88]

"Now this is not a guarantee," explained Hoover, "it just simply does not deprive them of such right as they may have to secure that minimum flow. It is not dependent upon construction. It is obvious that the minute there is storage in the river that minimum flow will be maintained without any legal action."

Hoover successfully made his point. "Offhand it seems very reasonable to me," replied Utah's representative. The others agreed. Confident that the worst was over, Hoover for a second time appointed a drafting committee and adjourned the meeting. What he did not know was that the worst was over for everyone except McClure.

XIII

McClure left the meeting disappointed at his inability to secure a storage provision, and he avoided telling the delegation of lobbyists from California about his failure. Less reticent was Nevada's Scrugham. Now that settlement seemed imminent, he believed that the Californians deserved to know how the situation stood.

"I'm sure that McClure has not told you what's going on," he explained to a group of them that he had hastily called together. "I think you're the fellows that are really interested and ought to know. I'm giving you my copy of the draft, and I'm telling him so." [89]

The Californians were astounded at what they read. They immediately wired the bad news to friends back home and sent a formal letter of protest to McClure. "We might have to go ahead and . . . take our licking . . . ," they told him, "but . . . California should let it be understood that we'd never sign that compact until Congress had authorized . . . Boulder Dam and the All-American Canal."

Now it was McClure's turn to act. Stung by the criticism, he went to Hoover and showed him the letter. Hoover was incensed.

[88] Ibid.

[89] William J. Carr, "Memoirs" (Oral History Project, University of California, Los Angeles, 1959), p. 142. The quotations in the next five paragraphs can be found in ibid., pp. 142–144.

Both men believed that they had done all that could reasonably be expected of them. The California delegation, they concluded, needed to be put in its place.

That night Hoover summoned the Californians to his suite at Bishop's Lodge. As they filed into the room and seated themselves in a row of stiff-backed chairs facing Hoover and McClure, they realized that the visit would not be friendly. "Hoover," as one of them noted, "had one of his famous frowns on." None of them, however, was prepared for what actually happened.

"Gentlemen," Hoover announced coldly, "I have just read the communication you sent to Colonel McClure. I think it was a most outrageous, scandalous thing I have ever had called to my attention. And I want to say here and now that unless you gentlemen forthwith and immediately . . . apologize to Colonel McClure, I'm going to disband this conference, announce that [the] Boulder Dam project is dead, and that you are the people who killed Cock Robin."

Immediately Mark Rose, the pioneer advocate of the All-American Canal, jumped to his feet, grabbed his hat, and started for the door. He had to walk directly in front of Hoover; and as he passed the secretary of commerce, he stared at him with utter contempt, almost as if he were going to spit in his face, and snarled, "Aw, Hell!" The other Californians then got up, followed Rose out of the room, and went to Santa Fe, where they made reservations for the next train to Los Angeles.

Hoover quickly realized that he had gone too far, and he tried to persuade the Californians to stay. Most refused, but J. S. Nickerson of the Imperial Irrigation District was less disturbed by what had happened because he believed that Californians in time would get what they wanted. He agreed to sit down with McClure and try to work out a storage provision that would pacify those on the lower river and at the same time not antagonize the upper-basin commissioners.

The task proved difficult, but the two men finally agreed on a proposal that McClure introduced on November 22. It specified that "present perfected rights" were "unimpaired" by the compact and that "whenever works of capacity sufficient to store 5,000,000 acre feet of water have been constructed on the Colorado River within or for the benefit of the lower basin, any rights which the users of water in the lower basin may have against the users of water in the upper basin shall be satisfied thereafter from the waters so stored." [90]

Such wording clearly did not call for anything like the proposed Boulder Canyon dam; in fact, it did not make mandatory storage of any size. But it did provide protection for "present perfected rights," and it also spelled out the minimal amount of storage necessary to supply the lower basin during the low-flow season. The provision proved somewhat more palatable a short time later when the commissioners, as they had promised, approved a separate resolution calling for "the early construction of works . . . to control the floods." [91]

The upper states grudgingly agreed to McClure's proposition. By now everyone knew why it had been introduced and all conceded its necessity, though some did so with obvious reluctance. "I will register my vote as 'yes' on that Article . . . ," announced the commissioner from New Mexico, but "only because to my mind it is the least objectionable of the attempts that have been made to frame the idea expressed in it, and not because I approve of it." [92]

The compact at last seemed a certainty.

XIV

As soon as the commissioners realized that a settlement was imminent on the major issues of water allocation and storage, they easily resolved some of the lesser questions that remained. They quickly agreed, for example, that after forty years either basin, once it had established uses to the waters allocated to it, could ask for an apportionment of the remaining surplus. And no one doubted that a surplus would be available for later distribution.

The commissioners also unanimously rejected Ottamar

[90] Colorado River Commission, "Minutes of the Twenty-third Meeting" (November 22, 1922), pp. 6–7.

[91] Colorado River Commission, "Minutes of the Twenty-seventh Meeting" (November 24, 1922), p. 7.

[92] Colorado River Commission, "Minutes of the Twenty-sixth Meeting" (November 24, 1922), p. 24. The final wording of the resolution was slightly different, but the intent remained the same. See article VIII of the compact.

Hamele's request that the compact be made "subject to all exist-ing rights of the United States." [93] The request seemed innocent enough, but everyone knew that Hamele, who was the solicitor for the Interior Department and Hoover's legal adviser, was among the strongest and most persistent advocates of the idea that the federal government owned the unappropriated waters in the West's unnavigable streams. The commissioners automatically held suspect his recommendations.

"Any paragraph in any way sanctioning the claim of the federal government to all the unappropriated waters," explained Scrug-ham of Nevada, "would cause the compact to be defeated in all the intermountain states."

"This proposal doesn't sanction that claim," replied Hamele.

"It would include it," retorted Carpenter. "You claim that," and "if it were later decided . . . that you are right, then this clause would include all unappropriated waters of the river." [94]

The commissioners were in fact so fearful of federal encroach-ment that they added a provision to the compact making use of the river for navigation subservient to all other uses. Cali-fornians were a little uneasy with this move since they recognized that the federal government's right to control navigation would provide important constitutional grounds on which Congress could justify its dam-building plans. To protect themselves, the Cali-fornians won approval of an additional provision that would allow Congress to reject the navigation provision without voiding the entire compact.[95]

Another question on which the commissioners reached quick agreement involved the Indian. No attempt was made to discover how many Indians were in the basin or what their water needs were. The commission simply assumed that the water rights of Indians were "negligible." Still, since the federal government had

[93] Colorado River Commission, "Minutes of the Twenty-second Meeting" (November 22, 1922), Part I, p. 25; see also Ottamar Hamele, "Memorandum for the Chairman of the Colorado River Commission," January 30, 1922, file 032, Colorado River Project, Bureau of Reclamation Papers.

[94] Colorado River Commission, "Minutes of the Twenty-second Meeting" (November 22, 1922), Part I, p. 30.

[95] See article IV(a) of the compact; see also W. J. Carr to Phil Swing, December 2, 1922, Swing Papers.

treaties with Indians, Hoover believed that it would be unwise to ignore the Indians' rights—whatever they might be.

"You always find some congressmen . . . ," he explained, "who will bob up and say, 'What is going to happen to the poor indian [*sic*]?' We thought we would settle it while we were at it." And the way to settle it, he suggested, was his "wild Indian article": "Nothing in this compact shall be construed as effecting the rights of Indian tribes." The commissioners unanimously approved his suggestion.[96]

XV

By Friday, November 24, after fifteen days of hard bargaining, the commissioners were finally prepared to sign the treaty. Not surprisingly, there were some who sought to take advantage of the relaxed atmosphere of the last day to press for special projects of their own. Norviel was one of them.

Norviel wanted the delegates to advise the Federal Power Commission that they had no objection to James P. Girand's application to build a power plant at Diamond Creek. The application had been laid aside pending a settlement among the basin states. Now that an agreement had been reached, Norviel saw no reason to delay action further. Moreover, he was aware that Hunt, Arizona's newly elected governor, strongly favored the Girand project. Though Hunt had earlier announced his opposition to river development by "selfish private interests," he did not consider Diamond Creek such an undertaking. It was a "minor project," he explained shortly after his election, and would provide "cheaper motor power . . . for operating [the] Arizona mines [which are] . . . the largest investments in the State." [97] In pressing for approval of the Girand application, Norviel was also responding to a disturbing announcement made only two days earlier by Hunt. In a wire to Hoover, which was released to the press, Hunt had declared his support of Maxwell and his

[96] Colorado River Commission, "Minutes of the Twentieth Meeting" (November 19, 1922), pp. 39–40. Delph Carpenter, *Report . . . in re Colorado River Compact* (n.p. [December 15, 1922]), p. 7, copy in file 032 Colorado River Compact, Bureau of Reclamation Papers. The final wording was altered slightly, but not the meaning. See article VII of the compact.

[97] Phoenix *Arizona Republican,* November 17, 1922.

opposition to any compact until more data had been obtained on Arizona's irrigable acreage. "No compact or treaty between the States can be agreed upon by Arizona until this engineering work has been fully completed," he told Hoover.[98] And he predicted that at least two years would be required to finish the investigation.

Norviel believed that such a careful study would vindicate his actions, but he also sensed the need to mollify Hunt and his supporters. The commission's endorsement of the Girand application would help.

But Norviel failed to obtain the endorsement. California opposed the request on the same grounds that Arthur Powell Davis had earlier resisted it: a power plant at Diamond Creek would preempt the power market necessary to finance the Boulder Canyon project. Others, including Hoover, objected because they felt that the matter of power licenses was beyond the jurisdiction of the commission.[99] Norviel would have to go home with far fewer victories than he would have liked.

But Norviel was not alone. Neither he nor anyone else got everything he wanted. Carpenter's original water-allocation proposal had been modified until little more than the idea of a two-basin division remained. Caldwell of Utah, who had come to Sante Fe wanting to limit the lower states to 6,000,000 acre-feet, had agreed to considerably more. The Californians, who had resolved to make the compact subject to completion of a Boulder Canyon dam, had settled for much less.

Obviously the pact represented compromise. "We . . . finally arrived at a compact which everyone feels he could improve upon if he drew it himself," Thomas Yager of the Coachella Valley told Phil Swing. "They all feel that they have conceded a great deal to get it done, but I believe it will operate materially to the interests of all the seven states. . . ."[100]

[98] George W. P. Hunt to Herbert Hoover, November 21, 1922, file 1-M/350, Hoover Papers; Phoenix *Arizona Republican,* November 22, 1922; *Los Angeles Times,* November 22, 1922.

[99] Colorado River Commission, "Minutes of the Twenty-seventh Meeting" (November 24, 1922), pp. 3–5; Colorado River Commission, "Hearings" (November 9, 1922), pp. 20–24.

[100] Thomas Yager to Phil Swing, November 28, 1922, Swing Papers.

Those were the sentiments—certainly, the hopes—of the Colorado River commissioners when they approved the compact on the afternoon of November 24 and then adjourned to Santa Fe for the formal signing in the Palace of the Governors. "We have about completed the task assigned to this Commission," announced Delph Carpenter on that occasion, "which is the first exemplification of interstate diplomacy in the history of the United States on so large a scale. . . . Each of us may take what credit we wish and not feel we have overdone the measure." [101]

The compact represented a most significant event in the history of the West. But time would soon reveal the prematurity of Carpenter's suggestion about taking credit for what had been accomplished. As everyone soon learned, the signing of a treaty was not a guarantee of its ratification.

[101] Colorado River Commission, "Minutes of the Twenty-seventh Meeting" (November 24, 1922), p. 8; *Santa Fe New Mexican*, November 25 and 28, 1922; *Los Angeles Times*, November 25, 1922.

8

Ratification Battles

News of the compact spread quickly through the Colorado River Basin. Though many water leaders were at first guarded in their comments, preferring to say little until they had examined the treaty, most reacted with a sense of relief and pleasure—relief because the struggle finally seemed over and pleasure because river development could, hopefully, now proceed rapidly. Few believed that even Arizona's recalcitrant new governor would openly fight ratification, and most shared the enthusiasm of the *Santa Fe New Mexican*. "The compact is . . . a monumental achievement," declared that newspaper's editors. "It opens the door of Opportunity in the vast undeveloped Southwest and we hesitate to believe that any state involved will close this door." [1]

But some did attempt to "close this door." Ratification, instead of being the formality that most expected, prompted battles that prevented Congress from approving the pact for more than six years. Even then, special steps had to be taken before the agreement could become effective and river development begin. But those steps and the controversy surrounding them set the stage for years of additional strife.

[1] *Santa Fe New Mexican*, November 25, 1922.

I

The movement to approve the compact began as soon as the Santa Fe talks had ended. On December 18, 1922, less than a month after the conference, Frank Mondell of Wyoming introduced a bill to give congressional approval to the treaty, but few expected early action on that measure. Congress had just begun a short session that was scheduled to terminate in March and had given priority to important appropriation bills. Besides, as Reclamation Service official J. F. Beadle noted, Congress was not likely to press for ratification "until sufficient time has elapsed to show what the States are going to do." [2] The action of the basin states would be critical, and attention now naturally shifted to the legislatures that were analyzing the compact and trying to understand the larger meaning behind its technical language.

Among the upper-basin states, Utah and New Mexico proved, at least at first, to be the compact's most sympathetic advocates. Utah's governor and officials were so pleased with the agreement that their enthusiasm worried R. E. Caldwell, the state's Colorado River commissioner. "I have pursued the policy," he told a friend shortly after the pact had been sent to the legislature, "of refraining from making it appear that Utah has great cause to rejoice because of the unfavorable reaction that it may produce upon the other states." [3]

The only Utah skeptic of importance was Congressman Don B. Colton, who urged the state legislature to study the pact "from every angle" before approving it. Though the Salt Lake City *Tribune* endorsed Colton's cautious policy, the legislature ignored him. The lawmakers chose instead to believe Caldwell, who assured them that "there is nothing in this compact that in any way does violence to any of the fundamental water rights . . . in Utah." [4]

[2] *Cong. Rec.*, 67 Cong., 4 sess. (December 18, 1922), p. 660; J. B. Beadle to R. M. Priest, December 8, 1922, file 032, Colorado River Project, Bureau of Reclamation Papers, Record Group 115, National Archives; J. B. Beadle to Milton Calvin, January 30, 1923, file 032, Colorado River Project, Bureau of Reclamation Papers.

[3] R. E. Caldwell to Frank C. Emerson, January 22, 1923, Papers of the Wyoming State Engineer, Wyoming State Archives, Cheyenne.

[4] R. E. Caldwell to Clarence Stetson, January 19, 1923, file 1-M/296, Herbert Hoover Papers, Hoover Presidential Library, West

Caldwell argued that the compact placed no restrictions on upper-state development. Even if the upper basin diverted the entire river, there would still be enough water, in the form of return flow, to satisfy the obligation to the lower basin. "It will be impossible under any conceivable circumstance," he insisted, "for the Upper States to prevent 75,000,000 acre-feet going past Lee's Ferry in any ten year period." [5]

Also gratifying to Caldwell's listeners was his estimate of the river's total water supply. He claimed that the total, or "reconstructed," flow of the river was at least 20,000,000 acre-feet, some 4,000,000 acre-feet more than the amount allocated by the compact. He arrived at this impressive figure by adding together two items: his estimate of current uses in the basin, and the Reclamation Service's estimate of the flow as measured on the mainstream near Yuma. The Reclamation Service estimate was about 17,500,-000 acre-feet, and Caldwell calculated the current uses at 2,500,-000 to 4,500,000 acre-feet. Hence, he believed that the reconstructed flow was somewhere between 20,000,000 and 22,000,000 acre-feet.

Caldwell's reference to the reconstructed flow introduced an important new element into discussions concerning the river. The commissioners had not utilized it in their negotiations because the figure was difficult to determine with precision. To them, the safer approach was to base their calculations on the actual measurements taken at downstream gauging stations. Thus they preferred to rely only on the Reclamation Service estimate of 17,500,000 acre-feet at Yuma and 16,400,000 acre-feet at Lee's Ferry. In attempting to put the compact in the best possible light, however, Caldwell and other basin leaders abandoned their earlier conservative approach and cited the reconstructed flow as clear evidence that there was plenty of water to satisfy both the compact allocation and any future treaty with Mexico. Few people possessed either the technical skills or the detailed knowledge that would permit them to challenge such

---

Branch, Iowa; R. E. Caldwell to Herbert Hoover, February 5, 1923, file 1-M/296, Hoover Papers; *Salt Lake Tribune,* January 26, 1923; R. E. Caldwell to the Utah senate, January 19, 1923, p. 9, file 1-M/296, Hoover Papers.

[5] R. E. Caldwell to the Utah senate, January 19, 1923, pp. 7–8, file 1-M/296, Hoover Papers.

claims. Moreover, of those who were experts, nearly all were treaty advocates who believed that Caldwell's assessment of the pact's larger significance was sound. "The big thing that the compact will do if ratified," he told the legislature, "is to prevent litigation and knit the States together in a close and satisfied relationship working harmoniously and effectively for the full scientific development of all of the resources pertaining to the river." [6]

The legislature was convinced. On January 24, 1923, five days after Caldwell had filed his report and only two months after the compact had been signed, the Utah senate unanimously approved the pact. Two days later the house endorsed it by a vote of fifty-three to one.[7]

New Mexican advocates of ratification found the going as smooth as those in Utah did. Stephen Davis, the state's Colorado River commissioner, assured them that their "principal interest" —the water of the San Juan River—received full protection in the compact. "So far as New Mexico is concerned," he told Governor James Hinkle, "the agreement is especially favorable, as it practically means that we will have the unrestricted use of . . . the San Juan River." Like Caldwell, however, Davis cautioned against displaying too much enthusiasm. "To make a public statement to that effect . . . might have a bad influence elsewhere." [8]

Neither Davis nor the governor had to make such a statement, for the legislature was convinced by Davis's more restrained claim that "the rights of all the states are fully protected." To a considerable degree, the legislature's favorable attitude was the result of another agreement that Davis had brought with him from Santa Fe. While the seven states were hammering out a compact covering the entire basin, he and Delph Carpenter had negotiated a special pact of their own covering the waters of the La Plata, a small tributary of the San Juan that drained only

[6] Ibid., p. 6.

[7] *Senate Journal: Fifteenth Session of the Legislature of the State of Utah, 1923* (Salt Lake City, 1923), p. 125; *House Journal: Fifteenth Session of the Legislature of the State of Utah, 1923* (Salt Lake City, 1923), p. 123.

[8] S. B. Davis, Jr., to James F. Hinkle, December 14, 1922, January 5, 1923, James F. Hinkle Papers, New Mexico State Archives, Santa Fe.

Colorado and New Mexico. The La Plata had been the subject of a long and unpleasant controversy. At Carpenter's suggestion, the two states had been trying for several months to resolve their differences. Buoyed by the successful negotiation of the seven-state treaty on November 24, the men had arrived at an agreement on the La Plata only three days later.[9] Because Davis took time to discuss the La Plata pact with interested New Mexican land-owners, he assured a favorable reception for it and the seven-state agreement. On January 31 the state senate and house unanimously approved the seven-state pact. On the same day they also endorsed the La Plata accord without dissent.[10]

II

In Wyoming the advocates of the compact encountered stiffer resistance than they did in New Mexico and Utah. The strong endorsement given the treaty by state engineer Frank Emerson was enough for many, but it did little to soften the criticism of Nellis E. Corthell, a talented Laramie attorney and former counsel in the *Wyoming* v. *Colorado* case. Corthell launched his strongest attack in January, 1923, at a meeting of the state bar association in Cheyenne. Because of the compact's importance, nearly all members of the state legislature were present and heard him denounce the interstate treaty as ambiguous and based on erroneous assumptions of stream flow.

Specifically, Corthell criticized the agreement for failing to detail the needs of Indians and the responsibility of the two basins in satisfying those needs. He also complained about the compact's failure to fix for each upper state its individual responsibility in meeting the obligation to the lower basin. In addition, he scored the pact because of its failure to recognize Mexico's geographic position in the lower basin and to deduct its water from the lower basin's share.[11] He leveled numerous other charges against the treaty, but his most serious objection dealt with the water supply.

[9] S. B. Davis, Jr., to James F. Hinkle, December 14, 1922, Hinkle Papers.

[10] *House Journal: Proceedings of the Sixth State Legislature—State of New Mexico, 1923* (Santa Fe, 1923), pp. 157, 158; *Senate Journal: Proceedings of the Sixth State Legsilature—State of New Mexico, 1923* (Santa Fe, 1923), pp. 109, 110.

[11] Cheyenne *Wyoming State Tribune,* January 12, 1923.

According to Corthell, the commissioners had grossly over-estimated the water supply. In his preliminary report to the legislature, Emerson had estimated the reconstructed flow of the river at 22,000,000 acre-feet. Corthell maintained that the reconstructed flow was no more than 18,500,000 acre-feet, and he believed that the average flow at Lee's Ferry was only 15,750,000 acre-feet, some 250,000 acre-feet less than "the Commission assumed to apportion." But Corthell questioned whether even the lesser amount would always be available. "The known imperfections of measurement and observation," he told the audience, "as well as the enormous variation in stream flow which is known to occur over long periods of time suggest caution even in ordinary projects." Yet the compact was no ordinary project, he emphasized. "In this case, the apportionment based upon these data is 'in perpetuity' and . . . affects subjects and interests of . . . vast and unknown value." Consequently, "the need of caution is multiplied many fold." "It would be a crime—a crime amounting to treason against the state to let it pass without the most thorough and searching deliberation and criticism." [12]

Many of the state's lawmakers agreed. Worried by the strength of Corthell's challenge, Emerson went before an informal joint session of the state legislature to defend his actions. He reaffirmed his belief that the total flow of the river was 22,000,000 acre-feet, but he acknowledged that evaporation losses would leave only about 20,000,000 acre-feet for actual use. Even so, this amount was far more than was needed to satisfy all upper-basin needs and to meet the lower-basin obligation. Corthell's lower estimate, he explained, was based "upon a misunderstanding of the real meaning of stream flow," for the Laramie attorney had failed to take into consideration the large amount of water already being used. Had he done so, observed Emerson, he would have discovered that the upper basin alone contributed over 18,500,000 acre-feet annually. "All of this amount could be once diverted and the return flow would still be sufficient to supply the specified delivery at Lee Ferry." [13]

[12] Ibid.

[13] Ibid., January 18 and 19, 1923. Emerson also filed an official report, but a fuller explanation of his views can be found in the newspaper accounts. Cf. Frank C. Emerson, "Report," January 18, 1923, Papers of the Wyoming State Engineer.

Emerson also criticized Corthell for his failure to realize that the upper basin was obligated to deliver an average of only 7,500,000 acre-feet at Lee's Ferry, not 8,500,000 acre-feet. To be sure, the lower basin was allowed an additional 1,000,000 acre-feet, but, lectured Emerson, "the additional allowance is patently to come from lower river tributaries." Consequently, the compact's provisions could be fulfilled if only 15,000,000 acre-feet were available above Lee's Ferry (7,500,000 acre-feet for the upper states and 7,500,000 for delivery to the lower basin). Corthell's estimate of 15,750,000 acre-feet at Lee's Ferry obviously indicated that more water was available than was needed.

To strengthen his hand further, Emerson appealed for help to Reclamation Service Director Arthur Powell Davis. The response from Davis was most encouraging. He estimated the total available supply at 20,500,000 acre-feet, half a million acre-feet more than Emerson had thought. Yet even before Davis had replied, most Wyoming lawmakers had decided to support the pact. Their views were succinctly summarized by Wade Fowler, state senator from Converse County. "I admit my ignorance concerning the bill. But I have so much confidence in our state engineer that I feel

RECONSTRUCTED FLOW OF THE COLORADO RIVER:
RECLAMATION SERVICE ESTIMATE, 1923
(In Acre-feet)

Mean flow at Laguna Dam	16,400,000
Past depletion, lower basin above Laguna Dam (20,000 acres at 3 acre-feet per acre)	60,000
Past depletion (approximate), upper basin (1,094,000 acres at 1.54 acre-feet per acre)	1,700,000
Mean flow of reconstructed river at Laguna Dam	18,160,000
Gila, mean discharge at mouth	1,070,000
Gila, present consumption	1,290,000
Total reconstructed flow	20,520,000

SOURCE: Arthur Powell Davis to Frank C. Emerson, January 30, 1923, file 032, Colorado River Project, Bureau of Reclamation Papers, Record Group 115, National Archives.

sure he never would have agreed to the compact if it were not a
square deal for Wyoming." [14]

On January 29, when the compact finally came to a vote in the
state senate, only one dissenter remained. On the following day
the opposition in the house was stronger, but the treaty was still
approved by a margin of forty-three to eleven.[15]

III

In the upper basin some of the strongest opposition to the compact emerged, ironically, in Colorado, the home of Delph Carpenter, the principal architect of the agreement. There, as expected, some denounced the treaty as an infringement upon
Colorado's "sovereignty." As in Wyoming, however, the principal
objection concerned the adequacy of the water supply. Fears were
particularly strong among residents in the western part of the
state, who worried not only about the obligation to the lower
basin, but also about the desire of Denver and the farmers of
eastern Colorado to increase water transfers to areas outside
the basin. When Congressman Edward Taylor from Glenwood
Springs joined those expressing doubts about the pact, Carpenter
realized that he had a fight on his hands.[16]

Like Emerson and Davis, Carpenter insisted that there was
plenty of water and cited as evidence the studies by Ralph I.
Meeker, Colorado's deputy state engineer. Meeker had concluded
that the river's total water supply was 20,500,000 acre-feet. Of
that amount, Carpenter claimed that some 17,500,000 acre-feet
were contributed by the upper basin alone. Though this volume

[14] Frank Emerson to A. P. Davis, January 23, 1923, file 032, Colo-
rado River Project, Bureau of Reclamation Papers; A. P. Davis to
Frank Emerson, January 30, 1923, file 032, Colorado River Project,
Bureau of Reclamation Papers; Cheyenne *Wyoming State Tribune*,
January 29, 1923.

[15] *Senate Journal of the Seventeenth State Legislature of Wyoming, 1923* (Sheridan, Wyo., 1923), p. 126; *Journal of the House of
Representatives of the Seventeenth State Legislature of Wyoming,
1923* (Sheridan, Wyo., 1923), p. 146.

[16] Clarence Stetson to R. E. Caldwell, January 20, 1923, file 1-M/
296, Hoover Papers; W. N. Searcy to J. L. Morrison, January 29,
1923, Delph Carpenter Papers, in possession of Judge Donald Carpenter, Greeley, Colo.; Edward Taylor to Robert Rockwell, February
7, 1923, Carpenter Papers.

was 1,000,000 acre-feet less than Emerson of Wyoming had calculated, Carpenter still believed it was far more than the amount required to satisfy the lower-basin obligation and the future needs of the upper states, even those needs in Colorado outside the basin. The western slope, he emphasized, had nothing to fear. "Colorado cannot divert 5% of its portion of the river flow to regions outside the river basin." [17]

But Carpenter saw the pact as providing numerous other advantages. "Broadly speaking," he told the governor and the legislature, "from a Colorado viewpoint, the compact perpetually sets apart and withholds . . . a preferred right to utilize the waters of the river . . . to the extent of our present and future necessities. It protects our development from adverse claims on account of any great reservoir or other construction on the lower river. It removes all excuses for embargoes upon our future development and leaves us free to develop our territory in the manner and at times our necessities may require." [18]

Carpenter's appeal and Meeker's studies helped quiet the fears of most legislators. So, too, did the strong endorsement given the pact by Colorado's Governor Oliver Shoup and Shoup's successor, William E. Sweet, who took office in January, 1923, shortly before the Colorado legislature took the compact under consideration. Sweet had been at Santa Fe during part of the negotiations, and he used the knowledge gained there to defend the agreement and to win the support of Congressman Taylor.[19] Moreover, both Sweet and Shoup, like most other Coloradoans, were favorably impressed with the settlement on the La Plata that Carpenter had worked out with New Mexico.

Despite such auspicious signs, ratification became doubtful when Carpenter found himself embroiled in a controversy growing out of misunderstandings over certain key compact provisions. The sections causing the most trouble were articles III(b)

[17] Delph Carpenter to Oliver H. Shoup, December 15, 1922, Oliver H. Shoup Papers, Colorado State Archives, Denver. A copy of this letter is in *Senate Journal of the General Assembly of the State of Colorado, Twenty-Fourth Session, 1923* (Denver, 1923), pp. 75–81; see also ibid., pp. 888–895.

[18] Ibid.

[19] William E. Sweet to Edward Taylor, March 14, 1923, Records Center Container (hereafter RCC): 2, William E. Sweet Papers, Colorado State Archives.

and VIII. Critics claimed that III(b)—the provision granting the lower states 1,000,000 acre-feet in addition to the basic allocation of 7,500,000 acre-feet—might someday be construed by the courts as being cumulative in its effect, that is, authorizing the lower basin to increase its uses by an extra 1,000,000 acre-feet *each year*. The same critics argued that article VIII—the provision stipulating that 5,000,000 acre-feet of storage would take care of present rights in the lower basin—might also be interpreted as making a special grant of water to the lower states. Unless a "preamble" or "interpretive clause" were added to the compact, they stated, they would vote against ratification.[20]

Carpenter denied the need for clarification, claiming that the compact's meaning was clear and pointing out the absurdity of believing that article III(b) could be cumulative in its effect. If that were true, he explained, then within a few years the lower states could claim more than the entire flow of the river.

But to those accustomed to complicated legal battles over water, the possibility of losing their rights because of a technicality seemed far from absurd. Besides, the stakes were too high to take a chance. Carpenter understood their concern, but he cautioned against adding explanatory provisos to the pact. Such statements, he believed, would set a dangerous precedent. Other basin states that were then under pressure to make substantive changes in the pact would be encouraged to do so. And if they succumbed to the temptation, he warned, the entire pact would probably have to be renegotiated. In that event, Colorado might end up with a far less favorable settlement.

Despite the vigor of his appeal, Carpenter made little headway until, in early February, 1923, he secured a letter from Herbert Hoover confirming his interpretation of the compact. His hand was further strengthened by similar statements from Arthur Powell Davis; W. F. McClure; and R. T. McKisick, deputy attorney general of California and McClure's legal adviser during the negotiations in Santa Fe.[21]

[20] Delph Carpenter to Clarence Stetson, January 3, 1923, file 1-M/296, Hoover Papers; Carpenter to Hoover, February 11, 1923, file 1-M/296, Hoover Papers.

[21] Herbert Hoover to Delph Carpenter, February 12, 1923, file 1-M/296, Hoover Papers; *Senate Journal: Colorado, 1923*, pp. 893–896.

Nevertheless, many western Coloradoans continued to demand an interpretive preamble. Under the intense pressure, Carpenter began to waver in late February, but he rallied when Hoover urged him to hold fast: "Believe inclusion [of] preamble would be most regrettable owing [to] effect it might have on Arizona legislature which might thereby be led to include in their approval a preamble of exactly contrary interpretation."[22]

Carpenter was aware of the problems that had developed in Arizona, but he had a serious battle to win. Though Hoover sympathized, he was held in Washington by pressing problems of his own and sent Clarence Stetson to Denver to lobby with the state legislature. Strong support also came from Hubert Work, Albert Fall's successor as secretary of the interior, who urged "prompt ratification . . . without preamble or reservation" so as to prevent "years of wasted time over bootless dispute."[23]

The extra effort paid off. Western-slope members of Colorado's upper house finally agreed to forego their demand for a preamble if Carpenter would merely place in the senate journal a supplementary report containing Hoover's interpretation of the disputed compact provisions. When he complied, the senate unanimously approved the agreement. The lower house also endorsed the measure without dissent.[24] Colorado's action meant that the entire upper basin had now ratified the compact.

IV

While Colorado was debating the pact, two of the lower states, Nevada and California, were also acting. On January 27, 1923, Nevada became, in fact, the first basin state to register its approval. Both houses of the state legislature responded unani-

---

[22] Clarence Stetson to Delph Carpenter, February 21, 1923, file 1-M/319, Hoover Papers; Carpenter to Stetson, February 20 and 24, 1923, file 1-M/319, Hoover Papers.

[23] *Denver Post,* March 14 and 29, 1923.

[24] *Senate Journal: Colorado, 1923,* pp. 920–921; *House Journal of the General Assembly of the State of Colorado, Twenty-Fourth Session, 1923* (Denver, 1923), pp. 1184–1185, 1268; *Denver Post,* March 21 and 29, 1923. The La Plata pact was approved unanimously in the senate and with only four dissenting votes in the house.

mously to the appeal of former Governor Emmet Boyle as well
as to that of his newly elected successor, James G. Scrugham,
who had been Nevada's representative at the compact negotiations.[25] For these men and the legislators, the Boulder Canyon
project was the main goal, and they saw the compact as the
shortest route to that goal and to the windfall that it would bring
in the form of construction contracts and revenue from the sale
of hydroelectric power.

Many Californians, on the other hand, doubted the value of
the agreement that W. F. McClure had brought home from Santa
Fe, but they had long acknowledged the necessity of a compact.
Most believed that the Santa Fe document would pave the way
for a Boulder Canyon dam and the All-American Canal, but a
significant minority thought otherwise and was strong enough to
create a heated battle in the legislature.

Among the most outspoken critics was Mark Rose, the Imperial Valley leader who had left Santa Fe embittered because
the Boulder Canyon project had not been made part of the compact. So far as Rose was concerned, the upper states had gotten
all the protection they had wanted without surrendering anything in return. He now resolved to rectify that error. He and his
supporters demanded that the California legislature add a reservation to the compact making ratification dependent upon passage of legislation authorizing the All-American Canal and a
high dam at Boulder Canyon.[26]

Rose received strong support from many quarters, including
the Imperial Valley Farm Bureau, the valley's American Legion
chapter, many Los Angeles owners of valley property, and the
municipal power interests of southern California. E. F. Scatter-

[25] Emmet D. Boyle to H. S. McCluskey, December 6, 1922, Emmet D. Boyle Papers, Nevada State Archives, Carson City; *Journal
of the Assembly of the Thirty-First Session of the Legislature of the
State of Nevada, 1923* (Carson City, 1924), pp. 38, 87; *Journal of
the Senate of the Thirty-First Session of the Legislature of the State
of Nevada* (Carson City, 1924), p. 39.

[26] *Los Angeles Examiner*, November 26, 1922; Clarence Stetson
to Ralph Merritt, January 20, 1923, file 1-M/310, Hoover Papers;
Stetson to W. F. McClure, January 22, 1923, file 1-M/307, Hoover
Papers.

good, the chief engineer of the Los Angeles Bureau of Power and Light, was as outspoken as Rose in his criticism. "The terms of the pact . . . are all one-sided," he complained to Phil Swing, the Imperial Valley congressman who, along with Hiram Johnson, was still pressing for a Boulder Canyon bill. "Full Boulder Canyon development . . . is much desired by us," but "from what I have heard from Mr. Rose, some . . . [upper basin] senators are now working against us in Washington, as they were last June and July. . . . In view of these things, it is manifestly foolish for the southern states to approve the pact except they are absolutely assured, in fact, of Congressional authorization for the full development proposed at Boulder Canyon." [27]

Swing was in complete agreement. To him, not even the compact provision stipulating the need for 5,000,000 acre-feet of storage gave the lower states anything. "This is like giving up a bird in the hand for one in the bush," he told a friend, "for what becomes of the water right which has thus shifted to . . . a 5,000,000 acre foot reservoir when that reservoir shall have silted up, which it will, according to Government figures, at the end of 56 years." [28]

Swing's own strategy was similar to Rose's. Swing planned to continue agitating in Congress for his Boulder Canyon bill while also urging the California legislature to add a reservation to the pact that would prevent the treaty from taking effect until his bill had passed. At first he refrained from taking a public stand on the pact, preferring to wait until the other six states had acted so as not to encourage them to add reservations of their own. Arizona's leaders, in particular, had come to worry him as they had Hoover and Carpenter. "Our discussing a reservation," he cautioned his brother, Ralph, a newly elected member of California's upper house and his spokesman in the legislature, "will promptly suggest the same idea to Arizona, which state . . . would adopt a different reservation from ours, I fear,—for instance, a reservation that the compact shall take effect . . .

[27] E. F. Scattergood to Phil Swing, January 19, 1923, Phil D. Swing Papers, Department of Special Collections, University of California, Los Angeles; see also W. F. McClure to Clarence Stetson, January 22, 1923, file 1-M/307, Hoover Papers.

[28] Phil Swing to W. J. Carr, December 13, 1922, Swing Papers.

when the Government authorizes a project for the special benefit of Arizona. This, of course, would be unfortunate from our standpoint." [29]

But advances made by advocates of the pact finally forced Swing to speak out publicly. Even then, however, he remained hopeful that most people, particularly those in the upper states, would accept his course as reasonable. "I cannot see how any of the upper stream states, or how Mr. Hoover even, could object to this reservation," he told a California state senator, W. J. Carr, "because they all have given us assurances verbally that if the pact is ratified, they will then be for the Boulder Dam. The reservation merely takes them at their word." [30]

Swing guessed incorrectly, and he realized his mistake when Hoover as well as upper-state spokesmen roundly denounced the California attempt to add a reservation. They cited, among other reasons, the one given so often before: if California added a reservation, then the other states would be encouraged to do the same. In view of Rose's attitude in Santa Fe, Hoover had anticipated an attempt to modify the compact, and that expectation had been a major reason for the secretary's decision to visit the state in early December, 1922. He had campaigned strongly for the treaty in San Francisco, Los Angeles, and the Imperial Valley, and had been encouraged by the warm reception given him. Now, six weeks later, the situation had changed, but the issues, to Hoover at least, remained the same. Reservations mean delay, he declared in a telegram to the California legislature, and "I . . . deplore anything that would delay the ratification of the Colorado River compact because I have the feeling that it is the

[29] Phil Swing to Ralph Swing, January 20, 1923, Swing Papers. At this time Hiram Johnson remained aloof from the battle over the compact, confessing to friends that his knowledge about the agreement was "so limited" that he preferred they contact Swing, "who has an intimate knowledge of the subject." Johnson did, however, play a major role in the fight for the Boulder Canyon legislation. Hiram Johnson to John Francis Neylan, February 9, 1923, Hiram Johnson Papers, Bancroft Library.

[30] Phil Swing to W. J. Carr, January 15, 1923, Swing Papers; *Imperial Enterprise*, January 25 and 31, 1923; *El Centro Press*, January 30, 1923.

first step in securing . . . the protection of the Imperial Valley and other works for California." [31]

Swing and his supporters disagreed, and none more vehemently than Mark Rose, who publicly accused Hoover of hypocrisy and of wanting only a small flood-control dam. Hoover countered by insisting that he favored the larger project, but he found it difficult to defend himself because of statements he had recently made to Phil Swing and other Imperial Valley leaders. In those conversations, he had suggested a course different from that favored by most Californians. He had proposed that initial construction consist of a small dam, though one designed with a base on which a larger structure could later be built. Such an undertaking, he believed, stood less chance of arousing eastern and upper-basin opposition. Moreover, a project of smaller magnitude could escape the tight control of national government agencies or private power interests. Instead, the farmers, through their irrigation districts, could be in charge, a possibility that appealed to his preference for local control. But he had not been adamant in his views, and he resented Rose's implication that he had been. "The only suggestion I made," he declared in response to Rose's attack, "was that it might be worth while . . . taking the project at two bites in order to gain three or four years time, and at the same time provide both the engineering and financial foundations upon which the whole development could march to ultimate completion under the direction of the water users themselves instead of either power interests or government." [32]

Hoover made an even stronger personal appeal to Swing. "Please don't hold the idea that I have ever suggested an abandonment of an ultimately and definitely completed construction program that would secure full power, river control or protection from foreign interference. I did suggest to you and to some of the Valley people an alternative idea for discussion that might secure all these things and possibly secure their march through

[31] Herbert Hoover to Isaac Jones and J. J. Prendergast, January 19, 1923, file 1-M/344, Hoover Papers; *Los Angeles Examiner,* December 6 and 8, 1922.

[32] Herbert Hoover to Tax Payers' Association of Imperial County, December 30, 1922, file 1-M/348, Hoover Papers; *Los Angeles Times,* December 8 and 9, 1922.

this vale of thorns a few years earlier," he admitted, "but you and
the people in the Valley are the only ones who can decide." [33]

Swing had decided. He wanted a high dam and an All-American Canal; he wanted both now; and he wanted the federal government to construct them. So, too, did Mark Rose and his followers, including Scattergood of the Los Angeles Bureau of
Power and Light. "The Hoover idea . . . is not satisfactory,
even as a first step," Scattergood told Swing. "The . . . program
is one contemplating the making of profits out of power" and
"holding out such a sop to irrigation districts." But Hoover
"knows perfectly well," observed Scattergood cynically, "that the
districts will never enjoy that profit but private interests will." [34]

Though many shared Scattergood's view of Hoover's proposal,
they also saw merit in approving the compact without reservations. They had the support of the governor, the state attorney
general, and such powerful southern California interests as the
Los Angeles Times and the Los Angeles Chamber of Commerce.
Those who opposed reservations had varied reasons for their
stand. Some believed that a "clean ratification" would be the
quickest way to achieve public development of the river. Others
looked upon it as a means of promoting private development.
Still others, like Harry Chandler of the Los Angeles Times,
viewed reservations as support for the All-American Canal, a
project they considered either too expensive or a threat to
American-owned lands in Mexico, or both. Thus, though their
motives differed, a large number of prominent Californians had
concluded that reservations should be avoided. [35]

Possibly the strongest boost to the anti-reservation campaign
resulted from infighting among Imperial Valley leaders. Though
many naturally supported Mark Rose's demands for reservations,
other valley spokesmen, including J. S. Nickerson, president of
the Imperial Irrigation District's board of directors, vigorously
opposed them. Nickerson, in fact, favored a river-development
bill similar to that suggested by Hoover. "The Northern States

[33] Herbert Hoover to Phil Swing, December 27, 1922, file 1-M/348,
Hoover Papers.
[34] E. F. Scattergood to Phil Swing, January 19, 1923, Swing
Papers.
[35] El Centro Imperial Valley Press, January 25, 1923; Los Angeles
Times, January 25 and 31, 1923.

. . . ," he told Swing only a few days after the compact had been signed, "will absolutely not stand for your Bill as it is, asking for the $80,000,000 for the Boulder Dam and all American Canal. . . . If we build a storage and power dam they fear we will acquire the water right by usage before this pact becomes effective. . . . But they do say that they will get behind and instruct their congressmen to help us in the way of a flood control dam, that would cost in the neighborhood of $25,000,000. Now, Phil, my best judgment is for you to either amend that bill or draw a new one. . . . I know your bill is alright [*sic*] and I am for it from start to finish, but it's going to be impossible to get it." [36]

Swing disagreed, but he had to face more than just the opposition of Nickerson. Four of the five members of the Imperial Irrigation District's board of directors favored ratification of the compact without reservations. Rose was the lone dissenter. "The compact in itself has no connection with [the] Swing Johnson bill now pending in Congress," declared the majority on the board in a telegram to the California legislature, and "we . . . believe that neither this bill nor any other bill proposed for our benefit will have any chance to pass unless and until the compact has been first ratified by all of the signatory states and by Congress." [37]

Because of the Imperial Irrigation District's importance in valley affairs, its views won the support of George Davis, the valley's representative in the state assembly and the chairman of the assembly's important Federal Relations Committee, the committee then holding hearings on the compact. On January 24 the committee voted unanimously for ratification, and one day later the assembly approved the pact without dissent. In the state senate, Ralph Swing followed the advice of his brother and urged delay so that the compact "might be used as a club to get the support of some of the up-river states to the Swing-Johnson bill." But the senators rejected his motion to postpone action by a vote of twenty-nine to ten. In view of the size of the vote against him,

[36] J. S. Nickerson to Phil Swing, November 28, 1922, Swing Papers.
[37] Imperial Irrigation District to California Senate Committee on Federal Relations, as quoted in Imperial Irrigation District Board of Directors, "Minutes" (January 30, 1923), copy in Swing Papers; *Imperial Enterprise,* January 21, 1923.

he decided to resist no longer. On February 1 the senate unanimously endorsed the pact.[38]

Now that California appeared to be securely among the compact states, attention focused on Arizona, where an even more heated battle over ratification was being waged. News of that fight sounded ominous.

V

When George W. P. Hunt, Arizona's newly elected governor, told Hoover in November, 1922, that he would be unable "to consent to any compact" for at least two years, most believed that the Arizona legislature would ratify the treaty anyway. Those who held this view completely underestimated Hunt.

Self-educated, distrustful of both big business and the federal government, and always alert to a good political issue, George Hunt had developed a large following as a result of his programs championing labor and the less privileged. He had been Arizona's first governor following statehood; and though occasionally turned out of office, he would eventually serve a total of seven two-year terms. His popularity was due in large measure to his down-to-earth—at times ungrammatical—language and his talent for demagoguery. But he had made solid achievements in a number of areas, including penal reform and highway development. Having worked his way up from the station of waiter in mining-camp restaurants to that of successful merchant as well as politician, he also understood the problems of business. He might distrust Arizona's mining corporations and rail at them in his bid for the popular vote, but he never forgot that mining was the mainstay of the state's economy.[39]

[38] *Journal of the Assembly: Forty-Fifth Session of the California Legislature, 1923* (Sacramento, 1923), pp. 203, 215; *Journal of the Senate: Forty-Fifth Session of the California Legislature, 1923* (Sacramento, 1923), p. 275; George H. Davis to Herbert Hoover, January 27, 1923, file 1-M/344, Hoover Papers; J. J. Prendergast to Hoover, February 2, 1923, file 1-M/344, Hoover Papers.

[39] Madeline Paré and Bert M. Fireman, *Arizona Pageant* (Phoenix, 1965), pp. 263–265; John S. Goff, *George W. P. Hunt and His Arizona* (Pasadena, Calif., 1973), passim.

Hunt fully realized that Arizona's present prosperity depended on the success of the mines, but he also knew that some day the mineral wealth would be exhausted. Before it was gone, he believed that Arizona should accelerate the development of its other resources, the most important of which was its water— water for agriculture and water for hydroelectric power. For this reason, George Maxwell's highline canal scheme sounded especially appealing. It was also for this reason that Hunt offered in November, 1922, to send Maxwell to Santa Fe as his representative when he heard that the Colorado River commissioners were about to put their signatures to the compact.[40]

Hoover ignored the offer. He considered Maxwell a crackpot, and he had no wish to jeopardize the agreement that had been all but signed. On November 22 he sent Hunt a telegram, assuring him that "Arizona's interests" had been protected and the state "represented with very great zeal." [41] Two days later the compact was signed.

Hunt refused to comment publicly on Hoover's reply and the signing of the pact, but his attitude was reflected in a single cryptic entry in his diary: "Hoover will run up against a brick wall." [42]

Maxwell took the initiative in constructing that "brick wall." He embarked on speaking engagements throughout the state, wrote articles denouncing the pact, and harassed political leaders on all levels of government. The compact, he lectured President Harding, "is a carefully camouflaged effort to hamstring Arizona and . . . to establish a great Asiatic city and state in [the] Colorado River delta . . . inevitably resulting . . . in a war with Asia in which Arizona and California would be the shock country as was Belgium in the World War." Hoover came in for special criticism for having used his "general prestige . . . to misguide the public." But, stated Maxwell, "as soon as Arizona

[40] Phoenix *Arizona Republican*, November 22, 1922. For Hunt's fears about the future of the mining industry and his desire to develop the state's water resources, see his remarks in *Journal of the Senate: Sixth State Legislature of Arizona, 1923* (Phoenix, 1923), p. 22.

[41] Phoenix *Arizona Republican*, November 22, 1922.

[42] Diary of George W. P. Hunt, entry for November 29, 1922, Arizona State University Library, Tempe.

can get these facts before the people every true hearted American will join hands to prevent this war." [43]

Neither Hoover nor the president permitted themselves to be drawn into a public debate with Maxwell. "My recommendation," Hoover told Harding's secretary, "is to ignore the gentleman. He is a demagogue of the first water and has already been pretty well squelched in his own state." [44]

Hoover was wrong. Some Arizonans, including Winfield Norviel, the state's Colorado River commissioner, had tried to "squelch" Maxwell, while others, including incoming Governor Hunt, clearly had not. Moreover, Norviel himself was now being accused of dereliction of duty for having signed the pact before E. C. LaRue had filed his report on Arizona's irrigable acreage. Even so, Hoover remained optimistic about ultimate ratification by the Arizona legislature. So, too, did Richard Sloan, Norviel's legal adviser at the compact negotiations, who was cheered by the strong support given the pact by the *Arizona Republican,* a powerful Phoenix newspaper owned by Dwight Heard. By late November only the Phoenix *Gazette* seemed to oppose the agreement, but neither this opposition nor Maxwell's campaign discouraged Sloan. "Maxwell is holding nightly meetings at the

[43] George H. Maxwell to Warren Harding, November 24 and 25, 1922, file 1-M/366, Hoover Papers; George H. Maxwell, "Shall America Be Developed? The Truth About the Compact," *Arizona Mining Journal* VI (January 15, 1923): 33; *Maxwell's Talisman* XV (February, 1923); National Reclamation Association, News Bulletin, February 7, 1923, file 032, Colorado River Project, Bureau of Reclamation Papers; George H. Maxwell to E. C. LaRue, Porter J. Preston, and H. E. Turner, April 9, 1923, box 600, folder 6, Carl Hayden Papers, Arizona State University Library, Tempe. Maxwell also tried to win support among Californians by telling them that the compact would deprive them of water that could be carried to the southern California coastal plain. Arthur Powell Davis, while admitting that a southern California aqueduct might some day be practical, believed that Maxwell's scheme would not be economically possible for years. A. P. Davis to Carl Hayden, May 12, 1923, box 598, folder 9, Hayden Papers.

[44] Herbert Hoover to George B. Christian, Jr., December 12, 1922, file 1-M/366, Hoover Papers; Clarence Stetson to Delph Carpenter, December 15, 1922, file 1-M/296, Hoover Papers.

rooms of the Chamber of Commerce," Sloan told Hoover. "Of course, he is meeting with some temporary success, but I do not believe that he is making such an impression as may not be overcome when the true nature of the Pact is made clear, as it will be." [45]

Just as he had in California, Hoover lent his personal support to the campaign to reveal the pact's "true nature." On December 8 he visited the state capital at Phoenix and delivered a public address before a crowd of some 1,500 at a local theater. He praised the pact and denounced its critics, especially Maxwell, though he mentioned no one by name. "It was the belief of the Commission and the unanimous testimony of the many hundreds of witnesses who came before the Commission, including every witness from your State except one," he emphasized, "that the future of your state and of America rested upon the development of homes out under the blue sky rather than in the development of great industrial centers." The applause was strong. The audience also enthusiastically greeted Hoover's claim that there was "but one [compact] provision in connection with Mexico," and that provision had been added "for the protection of the states of the lower basin, your state." "If the United States government shall at any time admit the right of Mexico to any of the water of the Colorado River, the burden of supply of that water shall fall equally on the upper basin as well as upon the lower basin." [46]

In combating the pact's critics, Hoover conveyed the impression that the fight was between the forces of good and evil. "There are many selfish interests that will develop or have developed," he explained, but "there are no proponents of this compact except the people of this basin who wish to have the right thing done, and have it done now." "Infinite opponents . . . will grow up to the right and to the left of you," he warned his listeners, "and I do implore you when you listen to that opposi-

[45] Richard E. Sloan to Herbert Hoover, November 29, 1922, file 1-M/350, Hoover Papers; see also W. S. Norviel to Carl Hayden, January 26, 1923, box 598, folder 7, Hayden Papers.

[46] Herbert Hoover, *The Colorado River Pact: Address of Herbert Hoover* (n.p. [Dec. 8, 1922]), p. 5; *Los Angeles Times,* December 9, 1922.

tion to search carefully in your mind to find if that opposition is
as disinterested as the services of these men who have indited
this compact." [47]

Hunt resented Hoover's remarks. After meeting with the secretary of commerce, he announced that his position on the compact
remained "unchanged." He also came away from the meeting unimpressed with Hoover's personality. "He seems quite nice" and
"studious," Hunt noted in his diary, "but I did not notice any
dynamic force." [48]

Hoover did not allow his visit with Hunt to upset him. He was
pleased with the public reception accorded him in Phoenix and
also encouraged by the support given the compact by many state
legislators, particularly those representing Yuma and Mohave
counties, areas which stood to benefit significantly from a major
dam on the lower river. Yuma, like the Imperial Valley, would
receive relief from floods, while Mohave County, not far from the
proposed dam site, expected to obtain cheap power to work the
many mines in the area. The Mohave County town of Kingman,
like Las Vegas in Nevada, also hoped to become a supply point
for the construction of the dam. "The signing of the pact," declared the state legislators from Mohave County, "is the entering
wedge for the starting and carrying to completion the greatest
enterprise ever undertaken in the West, and Arizona gets its full
share of the cream." [49]

VI

During the next few weeks, Governor-elect Hunt quietly bided
his time. He had said little since the signing of the agreement in
Santa Fe, but by January, 1923, when he finally took office, he
was ready to speak out. His remarks disappointed those who had
hoped that his views might have softened.

"The most important problem before this Legislature," he said

[47] Hoover, *Colorado River Pact*, p. 8.

[48] Diary of George W. P. Hunt, entry for December 8, 1922; Tucson
Arizona Daily Star, December 9, 1922; Phoenix *Arizona Republican*,
December 9, 1922.

[49] Phoenix *Arizona Republican*, November 29, December 9, 1922,
February 21, 1923; C. C. Lewis to Clarence Stetson, February 21,
1923, file 1-M/310, Hoover Papers.

on January 8 in his first message to the state's lawmakers, "is . . . whether or not it is advisable for Arizona to enter into the compact." He left little doubt about where he stood. Though he carefully avoided an outright rejection of the pact, he opposed ratification during the present session of the legislature. His major objection continued to be the "regrettable" lack of information about future irrigation possibilities, but his remarks also revealed Maxwell's heavy influence.

"If it is at all practicable," Hunt told the legislature, "and men who have studied the proposition carefully say that it is, to utilize the waters of the Colorado River to irrigate over two million acres of land in Arizona, then we should bend every energy toward the achievement of this purpose." No other course, he emphasized, was safe. "Arizona cannot afford to give away her greatest natural resource . . . and she cannot afford to plunge blindly into a contract that may be unfair to her." "We must know," he declared, "how much water can be used in Arizona, how many acres can be irrigated, and what steps are necessary to secure the quantity needed for the adequate development of our State." [50]

Heightening Hunt's concern was his belief that the heyday of mining, the state's major industry, was about over. "Before many years have passed," he observed, "some of the great mines . . . which are now bearing the major portion of taxation will in all probability be depleted and remain but a memory." Consequently, "it is imperative that we look into the future and plan the development of other resources to take the place of those industries." But, he cautioned, "we have no unlimited field from which to choose. We have a vast potential resource still undeveloped in the Colorado River which offers great possibilities toward the irrigation of our arid land, and the almost unlimited creation of cheap electrical power for the operation of our industries." [51]

Despite Hunt's admitted lack of "sufficient data" about the Colorado, he nevertheless believed he knew enough to call the "special attention" of the legislature to "several matters" concerning the compact. He claimed that the pact's allocation to the upper basin "would reduce the potential power resources of the river to an extent which would appear to be an economic waste."

[50] *Journal of the Senate: Arizona, 1923*, pp. 22–23.
[51] Ibid., p. 22.

He also suspected that the inclusion of the Gila in the pact did "a grave injustice to Arizona." Equally disturbing was the aid given Mexico by the agreement. "The pact provides for an estimated surplus of six million acre-feet of water, capable of irrigating over a million acres of land, which is to be permitted to flow to the sea or to be used in Mexico for a period of forty years." This situation constituted a menace, he believed. "It is apparent that, as a matter of equity, which is tentatively suggested by the pact itself, . . . water rights . . . may be obtained by Mexico, because of that country having first put the waters to beneficial use." "I am not an alarmist," he emphasized in a statement reminiscent of Maxwell, "but I think it well to call your attention to the fact that American land speculators are seeking to reap huge profits from Japanese financiers interested in lands in Lower California." [52]

Two weeks later, on January 23, when Hunt formally submitted the compact to the legislature, he stressed again "the necessity of . . . taking such time as may be necessary to secure accurate and adequate information" so that "you, as the representatives of the people of Arizona," may "act wisely upon this most important subject." [53] He then noted that LaRue's report would not be ready for another five months. Though he said little more, no one missed his point: the legislature should take no action.

Many Arizona lawmakers concluded otherwise, however, and they insisted upon ratification. They were aided in their efforts by Norviel; his adviser, Sloan; former Governor Campbell; the American Legion; and even by James P. Girand, who saw ratification of the compact as the best way of securing a permit from the Federal Power Commission for his Diamond Creek project.[54] Strong support also came from such periodicals as the *Arizona Mining Journal*, which described itself as the "only publication in the Southwest devoted to mining" and which was interested in cheap power. "Some pact is necessary," declared its

[52] Ibid., pp. 23–24.

[53] Ibid., p. 131; Phoenix *Arizona Republican*, January 24, 1923.

[54] *Arizona Mining Journal* VI (January 15, 1923): 19–20, 34–35, 59–61, passim; Clarence Stetson to W. S. Norviel, February 16, 1923, file 1-M/297, Hoover Papers; Tucson *Citizen*, March 7, 1923; *Journal of the House of Representatives of the Sixth State Legislature of the State of Arizona, 1923* (Phoenix, 1923), p. 555.

editors in a special issue devoted to the interstate agreement, "before Arizona can step out much farther in industrial development." [55]

Offering even stronger encouragement to the compact's advocates was Dwight Heard, whose Phoenix *Arizona Republican* spearheaded the fight for ratification. Several times a week, sometimes even daily, Heard, a staunch Republican and supporter of former Governor Campbell during the last campaign, ran feature articles and editorials urging the Arizona legislature not to delay approval. "The [federal] government is going to establish flood control on the Colorado," he predicted. "That is going to be done, compact or no compact. And without a compact," he warned, "we have reason to believe that it will be done with scant regard for the interests of Arizona in the waters of the Colorado, either for irrigation or power." [56]

VII

Despite such support, the compact met resistance in the legislature. The opposition, however, lacked unity. Many agreed with Hunt about the need for delay, while others called for repudiation of the treaty. These differences in goals weakened the opponents, forcing them early in the debate to change their tactics and to adopt a strategy that promised a broad appeal. They introduced reservations calculated either to make the agreement more palatable or, if necessary, to kill it.

The new approach proved more successful. It attracted many who favored the pact, but believed it had shortcomings. Some insisted that the treaty should have pegged Mexico's share, while others expressed uneasiness about the fact that Arizona's tributaries, especially the Gila, had been included in the waters apportioned by the agreement. To Arizona's powerful mining interests, the compact was seriously flawed by its failure to deal with the question of hydroelectric power. They particularly regretted the omission of a provision specifying the amount of the royalty to be collected by the state from those producing power at plants like those envisaged for the Boulder Canyon area. Their attitude was understandable, for such revenues, they hoped,

[55] *Arizona Mining Journal* VI (January 15, 1923): 27.
[56] Phoenix *Arizona Republican,* January 30, 1923, passim.

would lighten their tax burden.[57] Of course, royalties would also mean higher prices for power. But, at first anyway, Californians would be buying most of the electricity and hence indirectly providing most of the revenue. The net result for Arizona would be decidedly favorable.

Taking the lead in attempting to modify the compact was the lower house of the Arizona legislature. At the urging of Representative Lewis Douglas, son of millionaire mineowner James S. Douglas, the house took under consideration an amendment leveling a royalty of five dollars per horsepower a year on all electricity produced with Colorado River water. "Under this plan," claimed Douglas, "the revenue from [the] power royalty would be sufficient to meet all the running expenses of the government," thus completely freeing the mineowners from their present tax load. Moreover, observed Douglas, such an amendment represented "the most effective way of protecting for the State of Arizona, and the people thereof, their right in power sites." [58]

Despite warnings about the possible effect of reservations on Congress and the other states, house members approved the royalty proviso as well as another reservation stipulating that Mexico could receive no more than 2,000,000 acre-feet, an amount believed to be the safe maximum for that country. In addition, they tried to allay their fears concerning the Gila by specifying that it "be not included, considered, or involved in any way with the so-called Colorado River Compact." [59]

News of the reservations alarmed Hoover, who urged their rejection. So, too, did Carl Hayden, Arizona's sole member of the House of Representatives and, like Hunt, a Democrat, though the two Arizonans differed sharply on the compact. To the legislature Hayden sent a telegram that repeated almost verbatim what Hoover had told him: "Approval of the Colorado River compact

[57] Tucson *Citizen*, February 9 and 10, 1923.

[58] *Journal of the House: Arizona, 1923*, pp. 210–212, 246–247; Tucson *Citizen*, February 10, 1923; Lewis Douglas to John C. Greenway, February 8, 1923, box 85, Lewis Douglas Papers, University of Arizona, Tucson; see also H. A. Elliott and Lewis Douglas to George W. P. Hunt, April 3, 1923, George W. P. Hunt Papers, Arizona State University Library, Tempe.

[59] *Journal of the House: Arizona, 1923*, pp. 210–212, 221–222, 246–247.

. . . with reservations or amendments is, in fact, no approval at all." [60]

George Maxwell was incensed. "Don't be another Old Dog Tray," he scolded Hayden. "Get a grip on yourself and stand fast for Arizona. . . . Those urging the pact are urging Arizona to commit harikari." [61]

Hayden refused to back down. He had decided to support the pact after carefully studying the detailed responses that Hoover and Arthur Powell Davis had made to elaborate questionnaires he had prepared in January. He was convinced that the upper basin would never consume its share, and he told engineer E. C. LaRue that he had "been unable to come to any other decision than that the water supply is ample for all purposes even including the irrigation of the lands which might be served, at a reasonable cost, by the Arizona High Line Canal." [62] So far as he was concerned, the determination of Mexico's share fell properly within the responsibility of the federal government, and the question of royalties on power production could be handled by separate legislation. The Gila, he believed, should have been eliminated from the pact during the talks at Santa Fe, but he had no intention of jeopardizing ratification by now insisting on an amendment to exclude it. Besides, he asked LaRue, "if the State of Arizona asks that the waters of the Gila Basin be excluded from the Colorado River system will not the Colorado Legislature have

[60] Carl Hayden to Kean St. Charles, February 7, 1923, in Phoenix *Arizona Republican,* February 8, 1923; Clarence Stetson to Hayden, February 7, 1923, file 1-M/301, Hoover Papers.

[61] George Maxwell to Carl Hayden, February 8, 1923, box 598, folder 5, Hayden Papers.

[62] Carl Hayden to E. C. LaRue, February 12, 1923, box 598, folder 3, Hayden Papers. Hayden's questionnaires and the responses of Hoover and Davis can be found in *Cong. Rec.,* 67 Cong., 4 sess. (1923), pp. 2710–2717. "Any fair-minded person," Hayden told a constituent, "must conclude that Arizona alone cannot undertake the development of that great river without the consent of the United States, and without an understanding with the other States of the Colorado River Basin, all which leads to the inevitable conclusion that sooner or later the Colorado River Compact must be approved by the State of Arizona." Carl Hayden to W. C. Hyatt, May 21, 1923, box 598, folder 2, Hayden Papers; see also Hayden to Albert D. Leyhe, February 20, 1923, box 598, folder 3, Hayden Papers.

the same right to insist that the tributaries in that State be like-
wise eliminated?" [63]

Those elsewhere in the basin could not help but note the irony
created by the furor over the Gila. Observed Wyoming's Frank
Emerson to Clarence Stetson: "Norviel had good reason for trying to get away with the Gila during our negotiations at Santa
Fe." Stetson agreed. "Norviel did have good reason. . . ." [64]

But Norviel had not gotten away with the Gila, and this fact,
as well as the concern over Mexico and power royalties, weighed
heavily on the Arizona legislators. The battle that erupted was
not along strict party lines, for the two camps were nearly equal
despite the fact that about 90 percent of the legislature was
Democratic. On February 15 an attempt in the house to strike all
reservations failed, twenty-three to twenty-two. The amended
compact then passed by a vote of twenty-eight to seventeen and
went to the senate for confirmation. [65]

The senate proved less receptive to amendments—that is, less
receptive to all amendments but one. By the narrow vote of ten
to nine, it endorsed the compact with a proviso specifying that
each state retained "the full and unrestricted right of taxation
by way of the imposition of a royalty upon electrical power
generated from any structure within the . . . State." [66] Though
the senate did not stipulate a specific royalty, the purpose of the
reservation was the same as that offered by the house: to assure
Arizona the necessary authority to collect royalties from both
federal and private producers of power at Boulder Canyon or at
any other site in the state or on its borders.

[63] Hayden to E. C. LaRue, February 12, 1923, and Hayden to
W. A. Killinsworth, June 10, 1924, box 598, folder 3, Hayden Papers; Dwight Heard to Herbert Hoover, May 29, 1923, file 1-M/350,
Hoover Papers. Within a few years Hayden would become greatly
concerned about the status of the Gila, but for the present he was
optimistic, and he devoted his energies to trying to quiet the fears
of his fellow Arizonans. For his later views, see *Cong. Rec.*, 70 Cong.,
2 sess. (1928), pp. 171, 175, 335–336, 459, 466–468, passim.

[64] Frank Emerson to Clarence Stetson, February 13, 1923, file
1-M/300, Hoover Papers; Stetson to Emerson, February 17, 1923,
file 1-M/297, Hoover Papers.

[65] *Journal of the House: Arizona, 1923*, pp. 299–300.

[66] *Journal of the Senate: Arizona, 1923*, p. 613; "Hoover Dam
Documents," *H. Doc. 717*, 80 Cong., 2 sess. (1948), p. 35.

Most Arizona legislators obviously disagreed with Hayden and other pact supporters who believed that the royalty question could be handled later with separate legislation. Arizona house member Lewis Douglas summed up their views: "If such a reservation is not attached to the Pact and instead is ennunciated [*sic*] by act of the Legislature, there would be a very serious doubt, from a legal point of view, as to whether or not such an act of a State Legislature could be made applicable to the Federal Government. . . ." [67]

Though the two Arizona houses acknowledged the need for a reservation covering royalties, they could agree on nothing else. After prolonged discussion, the senate bill died in the house, and the house bill died in the senate. On March 8 the compact's friends in the house made a final effort to secure unconditional ratification. They failed because of a tie vote (twenty-two to twenty-two) and then gave up—at least for that session of the legislature. [68]

VIII

Most water leaders elsewhere in the basin interpreted Arizona's refusal to ratify the pact as not particularly serious. They were relieved that ratification with reservations had been avoided, and they were confident that the Arizona legislature as well as Governor Hunt would soon reconsider. No major development could take place in Arizona or anywhere else, they believed, without federal help, and the federal government was unlikely to do anything until the states had agreed among themselves. In a telegram to Delph Carpenter, Clarence Stetson made an optimistic prediction: "Special session [of the Arizona legislature is] probably to be called before July or after September when absolutely clean action [is] anticipated as public sentiment will demand it." [69]

[67] Lewis Douglas to John C. Greenway, February 8, 1923, box 85, Douglas Papers. Douglas believed that the compact "was written with the objective of completing finally and ultimately the nationalization of the Colorado River for power purposes." Douglas to Marcus A. Smith, April 6, 1923, box 85, Douglas Papers.

[68] *Journal of the House: Arizona, 1923*, p. 570.

[69] Clarence Stetson to Delph Carpenter, March 10, 1923, file 1-M/ 319, Hoover Papers.

Federal officials actively encouraged that public demand. In late February, while the Arizona legislature was still pondering the compact, President Harding and his cabinet had announced that the administration would support no plan for river development until the basin states had either approved the pact or entered into some comparable agreement.[70] For Arizona's James P. Girand, the announcement was especially disappointing because the freeze extended even to his relatively small project. But the upper states greeted the policy warmly. "If the Federal Government will but continue its announced policy of granting no licenses until the compact is ratified," declared Colorado's L. Ward Bannister to Secretary of Agriculture Henry C. Wallace, "there is not the slightest question but that Arizona will ratify." [71]

But Bannister and others miscalculated the impact of such pressure on Hunt. Coercion merely intensified his resistance—a resistance that he had now come to believe was not unlike the position already taken by the upper states. "As I understand the matter," he wrote to Colorado's Governor William E. Sweet on May 14, "the reason for the Compact in the first place is caused by the self interest of the States in the upper basin . . . to be given assurance that the development of the river in the lower basin will not hamper the development of Colorado and the other upper States." "Arizona," he emphasized, "occupies relatively the same position as Colorado occupies as between the upper and lower basins. California and *Mexico* will inevitably be developed earlier than Arizona because of the way nature made the country. Insofar as the citizens of Arizona are concerned who are opposing the compact, they are trying to do for Arizona in the lower basin what you are trying to do for your State." [72]

[70] Phoenix *Arizona Republican,* February 24, 1923; Clarence Stetson to F. M. Feiker, April 18, 1923, file 1-M/297, Hoover Papers.

[71] John B. Kendrick to William B. Ross, April 21, 1923, RCC:2, Sweet Papers; L. Ward Bannister to Clarence Stetson, May 1, 1923, file 1-M/295, Hoover Papers; Bannister to Henry C. Wallace, April 20, 1923, file 1-M/295, Hoover Papers; U.S. Federal Power Commission, *Third Annual Report* (Washington, D.C., 1923), pp. 139, 155.

[72] George W. P. Hunt to William E. Sweet, May 14, 1923, RCC:2, Sweet Papers; see also H. S. McCluskey to J. G. Scrugham, May 21, 1923, file 1-M/316, Hoover Papers; George W. P. Hunt to L. Ward Bannister, October 24, 1923, box 3, folder 7, Hunt Papers.

Actually Hunt was trying to do even more. The scope of his efforts became apparent in early May at a two-day conference he called to devise an Arizona Colorado River policy. The tenor of the meeting was determined by his selection of participants: about three dozen prominent Arizonans, nearly all of whom were opposed to the compact. They listened approvingly as Hunt denounced the pact, claiming that it "would be overwhelmingly defeated if submitted to the people." [73] A few in the audience, most notably Carl Hayden, disagreed; but their remarks were immediately challenged, and none of them made any headway with the governor or his supporters.

To Hunt, the best approach was a state-controlled project. He suggested that Arizona issue bonds and then build a dam of its own in Glen Canyon as the first step in a comprehensive program of development. Obviously, despite his earlier claims that Arizonans possessed insufficient information to decide about future water projects, he had virtually made up his mind.

Many approved of Hunt's suggestion, but Anson Smith, the Mohave County editor and long-time advocate of damming the Colorado, insisted that Arizona would never be able to meet the interest payments on the bonds. Even Thomas Maddock, a highly respected engineer who candidly admitted favoring a "selfish attitude" for Arizona, objected to Arizonans paying for a dam that would provide flood control for Californians. Still others, particularly those who had favored a private development scheme, such as the one proposed by James P. Girand, were distressed by Hunt's desire to have the state develop the river.

Hunt said little publicly about his ideas, but privately he confessed that he was motivated as much by a concern for hydroelectric power as for water. "The control of the power of the Colorado in Arizona," he noted in his diary at the end of the first day of the conference, "is the biggest thing that will ever come up in Arizona but I am skeptical of the outcome." He feared that private interests—the "Power trust" he called them—might defeat him. Those interests, he observed, "will never [permit] a

[73] "Colorado River Conference Held at Phoenix, Arizona, May 8th and 9th, 1923," RCC:2, Sweet Papers; see also Carl Hayden to J. G. Scrugham, May 12, 1923, box 598, folder 6, Hayden Papers; Phoenix *Arizona Gazette*, May 9, 1923; and George W. P. Hunt to Lewis Douglas, April 18, 1923, box 85, Douglas Papers.

state to produce power if they can help it." "With their immense
resources," they "can back us [or] beat us but we can make a
fight." [74]

To help in that fight and to devise a plan on which Arizonans
could unite, Hunt appointed a subcommittee of nine to work out
the details of an Arizona reclamation project.

IX

While Hunt's subcommittee considered the options open to the
state, E. C. LaRue and his fellow engineers completed their survey
of Arizona's water needs. Their report, filed on July 5, proved
encouraging to Hunt, but not for the reasons that he had anticipated.

The main portion of the report was disappointing. It merely repeated what Norviel and others had all along maintained: a highline canal to irrigate 2,000,000 acres in the central portion of the
state was possible, but economically impractical. Of far more
interest to the governor was a separate report prepared only by
LaRue and appended to the longer document. In it the engineer
raised serious doubts about Arizona's future if economic conditions were to change. Specifically, he noted that if the highline
canal should someday "be proven feasible," then "the annual water
supply would be deficient." The lands irrigable under the canal,
together with other irrigable lower-basin lands in the United
States and Mexico, would require 16,000,000 acre-feet, far more
water than would be available under the compact. "While larger
irrigation projects on the lower river in Arizona and California
may not be feasible at this time," he emphasized, "these projects
may be feasible 20 or 30 years from now." [75]

LaRue's implied criticism of the compact came as no surprise
to those who knew the engineer. He had been upset with the
compact ever since the Colorado River Commission had neglected
to consult him or even to consider his ideas for an interstate
treaty. As a well-known government engineer who had devoted
years to studying the Colorado River, he felt that he had merited

[74] Diary of George W. P. Hunt, entry for May 8, 1923.

[75] Arizona Engineering Commission, *Report Based on Reconnaissance
Investigation of Arizona Land Irrigable from the Colorado River*
(n.p., July 5, 1923), pp. 40–41, copy in file 1-M/350, Hoover Papers.

such courtesies, and he attributed the failure of the commission to seek his advice to the machinations of Arthur Powell Davis, a man with whom he had had personal differences and for whom he confessed "no great love." But personal considerations notwithstanding, he had issued a statement in support of the compact in early 1923, though he had done so with obvious lack of enthusiasm. "Inasmuch as the seven states have agreed to something," he had announced, "I suppose the Compact should be ratified." But to Carl Hayden he privately explained: "In making that statement it was necessary for me to swallow a lump. If you want to know my honest opinion of the Compact I can give it in one word, 'Rotten.'" [76]

LaRue disagreed with those who insisted that there was a five to seven million acre-foot surplus. He believed that "practically all the flow of the river has been allocated," and he also believed that the compact was unenforceable. "It is a practical impossibility to determine at any time how much water is being consumed in the upper basin," he told Hayden in February, 1923, and even "if it were possible to determine how much water was being consumed and it was determined that the lower basin was being deprived of water unlawfully, it would require the service of several divisions of the United States Army to compel the people in the Upper Basin to turn any more water down." [77]

LaRue's reconnaissance report of July did not reflect all his fears, but it did raise doubts about the adequacy of the future water supply. These doubts were enough to disturb Governor Hunt, who now felt even more justified in resisting the pact. Others, notably Maxwell, had made claims similar to those of LaRue, but they did not have his credentials. Also greatly encouraged by LaRue's observations was Fred T. Colter, an Arizona state senator who believed that the highline canal was practical from both an engineering and economic point of view. In 1923 he and a few like-minded friends created the Arizona Highline Reclamation Association and then filed on behalf of the state for all the Colorado River water flowing through Arizona. As presi-

[76] E. C. LaRue to Carl Hayden, February 20, 1923, box 598, folder 4, Hayden Papers; Carl Hayden to Mulford Winsor, February 12, 1923, box 598, folder 12, Hayden Papers.

[77] E. C. LaRue to Carl Hayden, February 20, 1923, box 598, folder 4, Hayden Papers.

dent of the association, he waged for decades a campaign that had as its goals a dam at Glen Canyon to provide flood control and another dam at Bridge Canyon for generating power to pump water into a highline canal.[78]

But others reacted much differently to LaRue's report. Norviel, whom Hunt had forced out of office three months earlier, responded with anger. He claimed that LaRue's calculations were incorrect and that the other states would never permit Arizona to have all the water it wanted even if the highline project did become feasible. "The High Line Canal with the dams, tunnels and other structures," he complained to Hoover, "cannot be constructed for double or trebble [*sic*] the money its proponents say the cost will be." Clarence Stetson agreed. "LaRue's special report . . . ," he told Governor J. G. Scrugham of Nevada, "looks to me like an attempt to delay matters in Arizona." James P. Girand thought it signified even more. "LaRue . . . is a political engineer," he fumed, "thus adding another class of engineers to the already numerous kinds. . . . It seems that about the time we get ready to do something, for it is currently reported that the special session of the Legislature is imminent, Mr. LaRue comes to the front with . . . his peculiar ideas." [79]

Hunt had no intention of calling a special session. Instead, encouraged by LaRue's report, he met with the subcommittee of nine that had been appointed in May, hammered out the details of a plan for river development in Arizona, and arranged for a meeting in September with the Federal Power Commission, where he would press his views.

Hunt told the Federal Power Commission that Arizona would never consent to the compact. What the state wanted, he explained, was "a state owned, operated and controlled enterprise, in co-operation with the United States of America, through . . . its Federal Power Commission." He proposed that an Arizona State Power Corporation oversee the construction of major works

[78] Arizona Highline Reclamation Association, *Highline Book* (Phoenix, 1923; 1934); Richard E. Sloan and Ward R. Adams, *History of Arizona*, 4 vols. (Phoenix, 1930), III: 570–573.

[79] W. S. Norviel to Herbert Hoover, November 6, 1923, file 1-M/350, Hoover Papers; Clarence Stetson to J. G. Scrugham, August 14, 1923, file 1-M/316, Hoover Papers; James B. Girand to Hubert Work, August 31, 1923, file 1-M/350, Hoover Papers.

within Arizona, the first to be a high dam at Glen Canyon. Though the Girand application was for a privately built power dam, he did not oppose it, and he saw no inconsistency in not doing so. As he had earlier noted, the Diamond Creek facility would be a relatively small project. Moreover, Arizona could eventually acquire it "by negotiation or by condemnation proceedings as provided by Section 14 of the Federal Power Commission Act." "The more commercially feasible sites . . . ," concluded Hunt in the brief he filed with the commission, "are entirely within our State, and . . . we want only a square deal." [80]

The Federal Power Commission was unimpressed. So, too, were the representatives from the other basin states, who repeated their now standard objection to the issuance of licenses until the compact had been ratified by all the states. Even George Maxwell opposed the Diamond Creek application, arguing that the water released from turbines there would provide a regulated flow aiding the American speculators in Mexico who were driving an "Asiastic wedge . . . into the heart of America." [81] Maxwell and Hunt did not see eye to eye on all matters, though they continued to agree on what had become to both a major test of loyalty: opposition to the compact.

X

Lack of sympathy on the part of federal officials and warnings from LaRue were not the only considerations that encouraged

[80] Arizona Colorado River Conference Committee, "Statement before the Federal Power Commission by the Arizona-Colorado River Conference Committee Concerning the Development and Utilization of the Resources of the Colorado River," September 24, 1923, pp. 2, 5–6, file 1-M/295, Hoover Papers; see also "Hearing before Federal Power Commission Relative to the Development of the Colorado River," September 24–25, 1923, copy in box 96, folder 8, Douglas Papers.

[81] House Committee on Irrigation and Reclamation, *Hearings Before the Federal Power Commission: Information in Connection with H.R. 2903*, 68 Cong., 1 sess. (1924), p. 101; U.S., Federal Power Commission, *Fourth Annual Report* (Washington, D.C., 1924), pp. 66–67, 90; see also Clarence Stetson to Carl Hayden, October 15, 1923, box 598, folder 10, Hayden Papers.

Hunt's resistance to the compact. He also reacted angrily to
California's continued pressure for the Swing-Johnson bill. For
a time he believed the bill had suffered a major setback when
Hubert Work, Fall's successor as secretary of the interior, had
dismissed Arthur Powell Davis as director of the Reclamation
Service in June, 1923. Work, reflecting views popular at the time,
believed the operations of the service should be in the hands of a
businessman instead of an engineer. Besides dismissing Davis, he
dramatized his action by changing the name of the agency to the
Bureau of Reclamation.

Though gratifying to Hunt, Davis's dismissal shocked Swing
and his allies, for it meant that they had lost their most powerful
friend in the administration, a man who was an effective spokesman for development of the lower river and whose name was
synonymous with the Boulder Canyon project. But the setback, to
Swing's relief and Hunt's chagrin, turned out to be less serious
than they had at first thought. Work pointedly announced that
"the resignation of one or more employees need not affect the
policy," and within a short time the secretary was among the
strongest advocates of the Boulder Canyon project.[82] His endorsement encouraged Swing, who continued to lobby constantly for the compact as well as for the bill, even taking his case
in June to a sparsely attended meeting of the League of the
Southwest in Santa Barbara. Though he admitted that the pact
did not contain everything that California "would like . . . to
have," he argued for its ratification as well as for a Boulder
Canyon dam.[83]

Hunt tried to check the activities of Swing and his supporters.
In pamphlets, private conversations, and public speeches, he
lashed out at California's "desire for plunder" and at "the ruth-
less manner in which the Swing-Johnson bill now pending in the
Congress of the United States attempts to dispose of Arizona's
rights in the Colorado River." [84] He took consolation in the

[82] Hubert Work to Benjamin Fly, June 26, 1923, Swing Papers.

[83] *Los Angeles Times*, June 9, 1923; *Los Angeles Examiner*, June
9, 1923.

[84] George W. P. Hunt, *Why I Oppose the Approval of the Colorado
River Compact* (n.p. [1923]), passim; House Committee on Irrigation and Reclamation, *Hearings before the Federal Power Commission*,
p. 192, passim.

failure of Swing's bill to be reported out of committee, but he became uneasy in December, 1923, when Swing and Hiram Johnson once more introduced similar companion measures at the beginning of the Sixty-eighth Congress. He became more fearful when hearings on those bills confirmed rumors of a new threat to Arizona's plans, the most serious so far. California had increased its demands for Colorado River water. "I am here," William Mulholland announced to the House Committee on Irrigation and Reclamation on February 15, 1924, "in the interest of a domestic water supply for the city of Los Angeles; and that injects a new phase into this whole matter." [85]

Mulholland's announcement fell like a bombshell. It further divided Californians and Arizonans, as citizens of both states recoiled at the implications of the new demands. At first Mulholland requested 1,000 second-feet to supplement Los Angeles's water supply, but in June, 1924, the city filed for 1,500 second-feet for itself as well as for other communities on southern California's coastal plain. In September a Colorado River Aqueduct Association was founded, and plans were publicized to construct a 268-mile aqueduct "to bring to this Southland the much needed waters of the Colorado River." [86] Because enormous amounts of power would be required to pump the water over the 1,400-foot barrier separating the river from the coastal communities, the demand for Boulder Dam power increased as dramatically as the demand for water.

California's announcement played easily into the hands of the compact opponents in Arizona. Now more than ever they saw themselves in a position analogous to that of the upper states—though with one major difference. The compact, if approved, would repeal the law of prior appropriation between the basins, thus protecting the upper states from faster developing California. But the compact would offer no such protection to Arizona. The law of prior appropriation would continue to operate within

[85] House Committee on Irrigation and Reclamation, *Hearings on Protection and Development of Lower Colorado River Basin*, H.R. 2903, 68 Cong., 1 sess. (1924), p. 97. For a sampling of earlier discussions of Mulholland's plan to bring Colorado River water to Los Angeles, see *Los Angeles Examiner*, October 24, 1923.

[86] *Riverside Enterprise*, September 18, 1924; "In Union There Is Strength," *Intake* I (November, 1924): 25.

each basin. California would, therefore, be in a position to establish rights to the lion's share of the lower-basin water before Arizona could assert its own claims. By the time California and Mexico got what they wanted, little would remain for Arizona.

Also strengthening the hand of the Arizona compact opponents was California's refusal to negotiate a special lower-basin agreement. Such a settlement had been urged as early as 1923 by Dwight Heard, the owner of the *Arizona Republican*. Hunt had responded favorably to Heard's suggestion, and he had thought that he could perhaps persuade Nevada and California to join him in opposing the compact. In October, 1923, he had written to the governors of California and Nevada to propose a tri-state conference. Though James G. Scrugham of Nevada liked the idea, Friend Richardson of California rejected the proposal, insisting that it would be unwise "to attend any conference which is not participated in by all of the States." Hunt feared that such a conference would merely become a vehicle to pressure Arizona into approving the compact. Though he dismissed the idea of a basin-wide meeting, he went ahead and appointed a commission to meet with representatives from California and Nevada. The move was a calculated one. Governor Richardson of California, as expected, refused to appoint delegates, thus giving Hunt an opportunity to denounce the insult publicly. "To read the propaganda sent out by . . . California . . . ," complained Hunt, "one would think . . . that the dam sites and power sites were all located in the back yard of Los Angeles." [87]

The rebuff by California and the plans of Los Angeles to divert water helped Hunt to maintain his political hold on Arizona. Despite strong pleas from many Arizonans that he accept the compact and concentrate his energies on achieving a lower-basin agreement with California, most voters continued to

[87] Hunt's correspondence with the two governors and his opinion of Richardson's letter can be found in House Committee on Irrigation and Reclamation, *Hearings before the Federal Power Commission*, pp. 192–199; see also Hunt, *Why I Oppose*, passim; and H. S. McCluskey, comp., *Compiled Messages of Geo. W. P. Hunt and Thos. E. Campbell, Governors of Arizona from 1912 to 1928 Inclusive*, 2 vols. (n.p., n.d.), II. For Dwight Heard's proposal for a lower-basin agreement, see the enclosure in Heard to Lewis Douglas, September 22, 1923, box 85, Douglas Papers.

support him. In November, 1924, they reelected him by a narrow but decisive margin over Dwight Heard.[88] To most observers, the election signified that Arizona would probably never ratify the pact as long as Hunt was governor. Many basin leaders now began looking for a way to circumvent Arizona.

XI

Hunt's reelection proved especially disconcerting to the upper states. They had followed a hands-off policy, believing that Arizonans would eventually succumb to pressure and ratify the pact; but "the policy of 'watchful waiting,'" as one upper-basin leader ruefully concluded two weeks after Hunt was returned to office, had "served its usefulness." [89] The state of Colorado took the lead in trying to find a solution to the problem. At first its officials considered an appeal to the U.S. Supreme Court, and Governor William E. Sweet ordered an investigation into the possibility of persuading the Court to adjudicate "the rights of the several states and of the two groups of states on the basis of the terms and provisions of the Compact." The governor also directed an emissary, L. Ward Bannister, to ascertain whether the other states would join in such a suit.[90]

Delph Carpenter opposed the plan. "The object of the compact," he told Sweet, "was to avoid litigation." Even if all six states agreed to initiate a lawsuit, there would still be "no assurance that all of them would remain parties during the long period of years which would be involved in trying the case." [91] To Carpenter, a much more satisfactory approach lay in winning approval of a six-state compact. Those states that had already approved the pact could merely take additional "legislative action

[88] Ellen Lloyd Trover, ed., *Chronology and Documentary Handbook of the State of Arizona* (New York, 1972), p. 25.

[89] Fred S. Caldwell to William E. Sweet, November 17, 1924, RCC:2, Sweet Papers.

[90] Delph Carpenter to L. Ward Bannister and Fred S. Caldwell, November 20, 1924, RCC:2, Sweet Papers.

[91] Memo from Delph Carpenter to Herbert Hoover, in Carpenter to J. O. Seth, January 19, 1925, A. T. Hannett Papers, New Mexico State Archives, Santa Fe; Delph Carpenter to R. T. McKisick, December 23, 1924, Hannett Papers.

making the compact effective when ratified by six *or more*." This step would provide the upper states with some protection—at least more than they would have with no agreement—and it would permit Arizona "to enter at her leisure." "We would prefer that the compact be ratified by all seven of the states . . . ," he told a California official, but "if . . . the compact were agreed to as binding upon the United States and the six states which have already ratified, it would in large measure serve the desired purposes, particularly in view of the fact that the entire cañon in Arizona is one great Federal Power Reserve."[92]

Carpenter's reasoning proved persuasive, not only to Governor Sweet, who now abandoned his earlier policy, but also to Herbert Hoover, to whom he unveiled the plan during a conference in Washington, D.C., in December, 1924. With Hoover's help and that of other upper-basin spokesmen, he submitted a draft resolution to the basin states for action.

Ratification of the six-state agreement proceeded smoothly in most of the states. The most active champion of the six-state formula was naturally Carpenter himself. Though now wracked by Parkinson's disease and hardly able to write his own name, his mind remained as keen as ever. He forced himself to visit doubtful state capitals, where he lobbied for his proposal and won over most key legislators. Many in the upper states, especially in Wyoming, expressed concern about ratifying an agreement to which Arizona would probably not be a party, but most agreed with Carpenter that there seemed to be no practical alternative. In view of the increased demands for water in Arizona and California, they concluded that it would be folly to renegotiate the pact. A new agreement as favorable as the present one seemed out of the question, and by mid-March, 1925, all the upper states had approved the six-state arrangement.[93]

[92] Delph Carpenter to R. T. McKisick, December 23, 1924, Hannett Papers; Carpenter to Reuel Olson, July 30, 1925, Carpenter Papers; Carpenter to William E. Sweet, December 23, 1924, Carpenter Papers.

[93] The vote was unanimous in both houses of all upper-basin state legislatures, except for the lower house of Wyoming, which approved the pact with eleven dissenting votes. *House Journal of the General Assembly of the State of Colorado, Twenty-Fifth Session, 1925* (Denver, 1925), pp. 432–433; *Senate Journal of the General Assembly of the State of Colorado, Twenty-Fifth Session, 1925* (Den-

Both Nevada and California were expected to give their approval, but Nevada at first rebuffed the six-state idea. Governor Scrugham preferred to try diplomacy on Hunt in an attempt to win him over to the pact and thus strengthen the hand of Nevada and Arizona in any fight for royalties. After a conference with the Arizona governor in January, 1925, however, he abandoned that idea, confessing to Carpenter that an early settlement with Hunt appeared unlikely. On March 18 Nevada approved the six-state idea, leaving California the only state yet to ratify.[94]

In California the Carpenter proposal sparked a fierce battle over the pact. Phil Swing, Mark Rose, and their supporters took advantage of the request for the six-state waiver to agitate once more for a reservation for a high dam. This time they had the vigorous support of leaders from southern California's coastal communities as well as firm backing from Imperial Valley settlers, including A. C. Finney, a lawyer-farmer who was also a representative in California's lower house. Finney prepared the reservation and introduced it on March 5, 1925.[95]

---

ver, 1925), pp. 440–441; *Senate Journal: Sixteenth Session of the Legislature of the State of Utah, 1925* (Salt Lake City, 1925), pp. 612–613; *House Journal: Sixteenth Session of the Legislature of the State of Utah, 1925* (Salt Lake City, 1925), p. 583; *House Journal: Proceedings of the Seventh State Legislature, State of New Mexico, 1925* (Santa Fe, 1925), p. 433; *Senate Journal: Proceedings of the Seventh State Legislature, State of New Mexico, 1925* (Santa Fe, 1925), p. 268; *Journal of the House of Representatives of the Eighteenth State Legislature of Wyoming, 1925* (Cheyenne, 1925), p. 592; *Journal of the Senate of the Eighteenth State Legislature of Wyoming, 1925* (Cheyenne, 1925), p. 323.

[94] J. G. Scrugham to Herbert Hoover, December 30, 1924, January 18, 1925, file 1-M/350, Hoover Papers; Delph Carpenter to Herbert Hoover, February 7, 1925, Papers of the Wyoming State Engineer; *Journal of the Senate of the Thirty-Second Session of the Legislature of the State of Nevada, 1925* (Carson City, 1925), p. 141; *Journal of the Assembly of the Thirty-Second Session of the Legislature of the State of Nevada, 1925* (Carson City, 1925), p. 275; *Nevada Revised Statutes*, chap. 538.010.

[95] *Journal of the Assembly: Forty-Sixth Session of the California Legislature, 1925* (Sacramento, 1925), pp. 613, 983–984; *Los Angeles Examiner*, March 14, 19, and 20, 1925.

Lined up against his proposal were private power companies
and opponents of the All-American Canal, including members of
the Colorado River Control Club, an organization formed a year
earlier to promote flood control on the river, but not the canal.
But the most serious objections came from several state political
leaders, particularly from the former Colorado River commissioner, W. F. McClure; the state attorney general, U. S. Webb;
and a deputy state attorney general, R. T. McKisick. Just as
they had done in 1923, they argued that ratification with a
reservation would be tantamount to no ratification at all. Unless
the pact were approved "cleanly," they predicted strong upper-
basin opposition to the Swing-Johnson bill.[96]

Hoover seconded their views, and he invoked the name of the
president in an attempt to win unqualified endorsement of the six-
state compact. "President Coolidge assures me," he declared on
March 16 in a telegram to the state legislature, that "he will . . .
recommend to Congress the construction of a dam in the Colorado
River to stabilize the flow and eliminate [the] flood menace.
. . . I believe Congress will give it support provided our western
states give it united support." But, he emphasized, "if [the]
proposed reservation is put on by California, it will . . . destroy
the unity of the northern states." [97]

Hoover's message backfired. The proponents of the reservation
noted that he had said nothing about a large, publicly owned,
power-producing dam like that advocated by Swing, and they
cited his telegram as evidence that he favored only a flood-control dam. To offset this impression, Hoover immediately sent
another telegram, protesting the distortion of his views. "I favor
the construction of works which will not only control [the] flood,"
he stated, "but [which will] develop full irrigation and water
power resources of [the] lower river. . . . I trust you will correct the misimpression." [98]

[96] *Los Angeles Examiner,* March 14, 15, 17 and 20, 1925; *San
Diego Sun,* March 20, 1925; *Brawley News,* March 16, 1925; W. F.
McClure to Herbert Hoover, December 24, 1925, file 1-I/195, Hoover
Papers.

[97] Herbert Hoover to George H. Davis, March 16, 1925, file 1-M/
350, Hoover Papers.

[98] Herbert Hoover to M. L. Requa, March 29, 1925, file 1–M/
350, Hoover Papers.

Hoover's telegram failed to satisfy the reservation advocates, who insisted that the only realistic way to obtain storage—and they wanted a reservoir with a capacity of at least twenty million acre-feet—was to amend the compact. The earlier failure to do so, they insisted, had got California nowhere. Their argument prevailed. On March 19 the California assembly approved the pact as modified by Finney by a vote of fifty-seven to fifteen. Two weeks later the state senate concurred by a vote of twenty-nine to eleven.[99]

Thus, California accepted Carpenter's six-state proposal, but it did so with the understanding that the compact—whether ratified by six states or seven—"shall not be binding or obligatory upon" California "until the President of the United States shall certify and declare (a) that the Congress of the United States has duly authorized and directed the construction by the United States of a dam in the main stream of the Colorado River, at or below Boulder Canyon, adequate to create a storage reservoir of a capacity of not less than twenty million acre-feet of water; and (b) that the Congress of the United States has exercised the power and jurisdiction of the United States to make the terms of said Colorado River Compact binding and effective as to the waters of said Colorado River."

Upper-basin reaction to the California action was what Hoover had predicted it would be. "The attitude of . . . Los Angeles and the Imperial Valley," declared Wyoming's Emerson to Delph Carpenter, "has placed the Upper States more than ever upon the defensive, and . . . our opposition to the construction of large works upon the Lower River must be even more insistent." Carpenter agreed and at Hoover's suggestion called an upper-basin conference to counter the "agitators in Southern California." That conference, held on August 28 and 29 in Denver, unanimously approved a resolution opposing all new development on the river until the compact had been approved.[100]

[99] *Journal of the California Assembly, 1925,* p. 1031; *Journal of the Senate: Forty-Sixth Session of the California Legislature, 1925* (Sacramento, 1925), pp. 1135–1136.

[100] Frank Emerson to Delph Carpenter, May 16, 1925, Papers of the Wyoming State Engineer; Delph Carpenter to A. T. Hannett, August 22, 1925, Hannett Papers; Tucson *Arizona Daily Star,* August 30, 1925; *Denver Post,* August 30, 1925.

XII

The Denver conference revealed other sources for upper-basin uneasiness besides California's resolution. Recent events in Arizona were also alarming, particularly since California's action had shown that a six-state compact would be as difficult to obtain as a seven-state agreement. Girand and his supporters were again pressing for a license from the Federal Power Commission. In addition, Arizonans had finally responded to the attempt of the other states to circumvent them. In March, 1925, the legislature had approved the pact—but with reservations of its own. It had ratified the agreement on condition that the lower states enter into a supplementary pact allocating "exclusively" to Arizona the 1,000,000 acre-feet embraced by article III(b) of the compact. It had also added the important proviso "that said right shall . . . be held to completely exhaust the right to the use of waters of the Colorado River System entering the Colorado River within the State of Arizona below Lee Ferry." [101] In short, Arizona wanted all its tributary waters, and it also wanted to be charged for no more than 1,000,000 acre-feet of such waters even if it used more than that amount. As for the water remaining in the mainstream, the legislature had offered to divide it equally with California after Nevada had taken the small amount she needed.

Hunt had vetoed the legislature's action, arguing that the compact should be rejected even with such reservations. Many legislative leaders believed the veto had no effect, however, since the pact had been approved by a concurrent resolution, which, they argued, did not require the governor's approval.

The upper states were little concerned with Arizona's internal squabbles, but they were greatly worried by the refusal of both Arizona and California to give an unqualified endorsement to the pact. They also regretted the inability of leaders from the lower states to work out a lower-basin agreement among themselves. The first attempt to negotiate such a settlement—on August 17 in Phoenix—had ended almost as soon as it had begun.

[101] *Journal of the Senate: Arizona, 1925*, pp. 410–411, 527; *Journal of the House of Representatives: Seventh State Legislature of the State of Arizona, 1925* (Phoenix, 1925), pp. 526, 535–536; Raymond Dyas to Herbert Hoover, February 28, 1925, file 1-M/350, Hoover Papers; *Los Angeles Examiner*, March 12, 1925.

Californians had taken the initiative in suggesting the Phoenix meeting because they believed that a conference might help win Arizona support for the Swing-Johnson bill. The chances for such support were slim, but Phil Swing thought an attempt should be made to secure "a reasonable agreement with Arizona," especially now that California had succeeded in antagonizing the upper states with the Finney resolution. "We need . . . [Arizona's] support," Swing told Charles Childers, the legal counsel for the Imperial Irrigation District. "California must make a gesture of good will to Arizona, perhaps a resolution—but a step further—provide a commission. . . ." [102] The California legislature agreed that a commission held the best promise of success. Among the members appointed were Swing's brother, Ralph; A. C. Finney; and Arthur Powell Davis, now chief engineer and general manager of the East Bay Municipal Utility District in Oakland, California.

The conference in Phoenix was opened by Governor Hunt, who got matters off to a poor start by refusing to specify Arizona's water needs and by denouncing the compact. "If you ask me specifically what we want," he declared, "I reply to you frankly, without any apology, that we do not know because we have not sufficient data available to determine what is . . . practicable to develop." Even so, stated Hunt, "we are fully satisfied with the present laws as interpreted by the United States Supreme Court. . . . We do not fear development in California or in the upper basin if the law, of priorities based upon appropriation for beneficial use, remains in full effect. But . . . if Arizona signed the Colorado River Compact in its present form we would be signing away our future right to utilize the resources of the river without recompense." [103]

Though Hunt was unprepared to specify Arizona's water demands, he was clear about the matter of power royalties. "Arizona expects to derive revenue from every unit of electrical energy generated in this State that is utilized in other states." "You gentlemen did not come to Arizona looking for charity," he chided the delegates. "If we have something you want and can utilize, economic justice dictates that it be paid for."

[102] Phil Swing to Charles Childers, April 4, 1925, Swing Papers; Phil Swing to Ralph Swing, July 31, 1925, Swing Papers.

[103] Arizona, *Official Report of the Proceedings of the Colorado River Conference* (Phoenix, August 17, 1925), pp. 4, 6.

Nevada naturally agreed that revenue should go to the states in which the power was produced, but it joined California in protesting the tone of Hunt's opening remarks and his refusal to accept the basic compact allocation. Both states also made a demand of their own. "The basis of all negotiations in this conference as far as Nevada is concerned," declared Charles Squires of Las Vegas, "must be the recognition of the immediate necessity for a dam at or near Black or Boulder Canyon on the Colorado River. That, gentlemen, is the position which Nevada takes in this matter." [104]

California adopted the same position, but Arizona's representatives balked; and the meeting ended in failure.

Subsequent conferences during the next few months proved no more successful. At some of them, like that in December, 1925, Arizona indicated a willingess to accept the compact if it could obtain a water-allocation and power settlement to its liking; but sharp differences, especially with California, continued to prevent agreement.[105]

The dispute between California and Arizona heightened anxieties in the upper states; but these tensions lessened a bit in October, 1925, when Arizona officials decided to oppose Girand's latest application to the Federal Power Commission. Hunt now believed that there should be no private development at Diamond Creek. Ostensibly he took that position because state law, he maintained, would prevent Arizona from collecting royalties. But rather than advocate a change in the law, he preferred to have the site owned outright by the state.[106] His opposition to the Girand

[104] Ibid., p. 11.

[105] Colorado River Commission of California, "Text of Proposed Agreement for Division of Water and Power from the Colorado River among Arizona, California and Nevada," December 1, 1925, copy in Arizona State Archives, Phoenix; "Plan of Development of the Colorado River Submitted by Arizona Delegation to California and Nevada Delegations, December 14, 1925," in McCluskey, *Compiled Messages of Hunt and Campbell*, II:2–4; Colorado River Commission of California, *Colorado River and the Boulder Canyon Project* (Sacramento, 1931), pp. 327–328.

[106] *Journal of the Senate: Arizona, 1925*, p. 18; U.S. Federal Power Commission, *Sixth Annual Report* (Washington, D.C., 1926), pp. 72–73.

application signaled the death of that project. Its end naturally pleased the upper states, but it represented only a minor consolation that they quickly forgot as California and Arizona continued to squabble.

XIII

By 1927 leaders of the upper states were in despair. More than four years had passed, and still the compact was not ratified. Seven-state ratification seemed completely out of the question, and a six-state agreement appeared nearly as hopeless. Several events now dramatized their frustration; the first was Utah's move in January to repeal its approval of the six-state compact.

Though disturbing, Utah's action was not a great surprise. It reflected the fear of many in the upper states that even a six-state agreement offered no real protection. This fear had been growing in intensity ever since California had attached reservations to its ratification of the six-state compact in 1925.[107] Many now believed that California would probably obtain the Boulder Canyon project—the *quid pro quo* for its approval of the pact—and then establish uses to nearly all the lower basin's water. If that happened, Arizona would be compelled to look elsewhere for water. As a nonsigner of the compact, it would be free to encroach on the upper basin's share, establishing prior uses which the courts might recognize as rights.

But there were also other, and special, reasons for Utah's action. Leaders in Utah believed that the Boulder Canyon bill threatened state sovereignty, especially Utah's right to the bed of the Colorado River. The desire of Utahns to exploit power sites as well as oil deposits in the channel of the Colorado near Moab was a major reason for this attitude. Significantly, it prompted them not only to view themselves as holders of a special position but also to look at Arizona's intransigence in a different light. "If you have followed the discussions in detail," explained Utah's Governor George Dern to the other upper-basin governors,

[107] Nellie Tayloe Ross, George H. Dern, and Clarence J. Morley to the people of Colorado, New Mexico, Utah, and Wyoming, August 29, 1925, file 1-M/344, Hoover Papers; George M. Bacon to Elmer Leatherwood, February 9, 1926, Papers of the Utah State Engineer, Utah State Archives, Salt Lake City.

"you have doubtless observed that Utah, although she is an upper basin state, is in some respects in a different position than the rest of the upper basin states. Indeed, in some particulars the interests of Utah and Arizona are common. Practically all of the power possibilities on the Colorado River are in Arizona and Utah, and when I make a careful analysis of our position I am inevitably led to a considerable sympathy with conclusions that Arizona reached long ago. The ownership of the bed of the river by the state is held to be of tremendous importance by the State of Utah, both on account of its control over power resources and on account of its potential value as oil producing ground." The implications for Utah of such measures as the Swing-Johnson bill, still being pressed in Congress, were serious, he emphasized: "If these two states own the river bed, certainly the Federal Government cannot come in and build a dam in one of them without its consent." [108]

But there were also partisan considerations that weighed heavily on the minds of Governor Dern and William R. Wallace, Utah's Colorado River commissioner. "Wallace and I," Dern confided to Delph Carpenter in early January, 1927, "are a couple of lonesome Democrats completely surrounded by an overwhelmingly Republican legislature, which always has an eye on the political aspects of any question. The result is that I fear we are going to have some difficulty in controlling the actions of our legislature. A lot of propaganda has been started in favor of repealing Utah's ratification of the six state compact, and it now

[108] George Dern to William H. Adams, March 19, 1927, box 76, George H. Dern Papers, Utah State Archives, Salt Lake City; Dern to F. B. Balzar, March 22, 1927, box 76, Dern Papers; Dern to Frank C. Emerson, March 19, 1927, box 77, Dern Papers; Dern to R. C. Dillon, March 19, 1927, R. C. Dillon Papers, New Mexico State Archives, Santa Fe; see also Dern to George W. P. Hunt, March 18, 1927, box 78, Dern Papers; Dern to C. C. Young, March 18, 1927, box 80, Dern Papers; Dern to Delph Carpenter, February 1, 1927, Carpenter Papers; Delph Carpenter to Herbert Hoover, January 13, 1927, file 1-M/344, Hoover Papers; Dern to R. C. Dillon, January 30, 1928, Dillon Papers; "Amended Report of Subcommittee to Advisory Committee of the Governor of the State of Utah on Colorado River Pact and Swing-Johnson Bill," January 17, 1927, box 77, Dern Papers; *Salt Lake Tribune,* December 29, 1926.

looks as if that action would be taken whether Mr. Wallace and I favor it or not." [109]

Dern proved correct. In mid-January, 1927, the Utah legislature repealed its approval of the six-state ratification and then about a month later passed legislation asserting the state's right to the bed of the river.[110] Since the validity of this claim rested on the Colorado's being considered a navigable stream, the legislature took the additional step of asserting the river's navigability. This move alarmed many in the upper basin because it seemed to challenge the compact itself. That document had specifically proclaimed that the river had "ceased to be navigable."

The Utah action only added to the worries of the other upper states, and Governor Frank Emerson of Wyoming openly chided Dern in a letter that he circulated to others. "Even though personally I have felt that we were not ready to see the Swing-Johnson Bill pass Congress," Emerson told Dern, "I have regretted that Utah felt it advisable to repeal her ratification of the plan of the six state acceptance of the Compact." Moreover, he declared, "the other Utah act, whereby the Colorado River and the Green River in Utah are declared to be navigable and the state asserts title to the bed of these rivers and their tributaries amounts, in my opinion, to a reservation to the seven state Compact and therefore nullifies to some extent Utah's favorable action in its original ratification of the Compact. These matters give me

[109] Delph Carpenter to George Dern, January 11, 1927, box 76, Dern Papers; see also Dern to L. Ward Bannister, December 13, 1926, box 76, Dern Papers.

[110] *Senate Journal: Seventeenth Session of the Legislature of the State of Utah, 1927* (Salt Lake City, 1927), pp. 52–57, 94–95, 212; *House Journal: Seventeenth Session of the Legislature of the State of Utah, 1927* (Salt Lake City, 1927), pp. 85, 323–324. Dern had mixed feelings about Utah's rejection of the six-state pact. "That action," he told Delph Carpenter, "was taken at the united request of our Congressional delegation and was entirely beyond my control. I had some misgivings about the widsom of taking that step, but if it will have the affect of delaying action on the Swing-Johnson Bill and yet keeping that bill alive until the next session of Congress, perhaps it will do just what we have been striving for." Dern to Carpenter, February 1, 1927, box 76, Dern Papers; see also Dern to Frank Emerson, January 20, 1927, box 77, Dern Papers; Dern to Addison T. Smith, February 5, 1927, box 80, Dern Papers.

much concern for it seems to me that they tend to confuse the issue. The situation is now becoming so involved that there appears grave danger of losing the whole Compact matter." Colorado's Delph Carpenter agreed, and in a private conversation with Dern he told the Utah governor that Utah was "defeating its own purpose," for the federal government might use navigability as an excuse to "claim the whole river." [111]

Most upper-basin leaders shared the fears of Carpenter and Emerson. Already alarmed by the continuing controversy in the lower basin, they responded warmly to Utah's request for a seven-state governors' conference to be charged with "working out a mutually satisfactory solution of the whole problem." That conference, which met on August 22 in Denver, determined to make one last attempt "to bring about seven state ratification of the Santa Fe Compact." [112]

Governor Dern of Utah, the chairman of the conference, opened the meeting by emphasizing the need of the basin states to settle their differences before the federal government took control of the river and forced a settlement on them. All agreed about the danger of federal interference, and they believed that their best hope lay in helping the lower states settle their differences. Arizona's Governor Hunt lifted the spirits of everyone present when, in his first speech to the conferees, he announced his willingness to abide by the Santa Fe agreement—"if and when . . . supplemented by a subsidiary compact, which will make definite and certain the protection of Arizona's interests." [113]

But the achievement of such a supplementary pact proved impossible, largely because of irresolvable differences between Arizona and California. California insisted on the necessity of a dam at Boulder Canyon, while Arizona countered with a demand for

[111] Frank Emerson to George H. Dern, April 13, 1927, box 77, Dern Papers; Dern to Delph Carpenter, July 21, 1928, Carpenter Papers; Carpenter to Dern, January 17, 1927, box 76, Dern Papers.

[112] George Dern to R. C. Dillon, March 19, 1927, Dillon Papers; "Proceedings of the Colorado River Conference" (Denver, 1927), I: ii, copy in Arizona State Archives.

[113] "Proceedings of the Colorado River Conference" (Denver, 1927), I: 48. For a detailed description of the meeting by a reporter for the *Salt Lake Tribune*, see Oliver J. Grimes, *The Colorado River Problem* (Salt Lake City [1927]).

revenue from power produced within the state. Representatives from the two states also refused to agree on the critical question of water allocation. Though both accepted Nevada's small demand for 300,000 acre-feet, they could agree on nothing else.

Arizona wanted all its tributary waters and half the water remaining in the mainstream after Nevada had received its share. California's representatives responded by demanding 4,562,000 acre-feet from the mainstream and offering Arizona 2,637,400 acre-feet from the main river plus the waters of that state's tributaries. Californians also insisted on a provision stipulating that after twenty years any apportioned water not being used could be acquired by either state.

Arizona flatly rejected the California proposal, especially the provision for the twenty-year waiver, since few Arizonans believed they would be using all their water in such a short period of time. Faster developing California would obviously receive an unfair advantage and get the lion's share of the lower-basin allocation.[114]

The upper-basin governors tried to mediate the dispute by preparing a compromise proposal of their own. Of the 7,500,000 acre-feet available on the average at Lee's Ferry, they recommended 300,000 acre-feet for Nevada; 4,200,000 acre feet for California; and 3,000,000 acre-feet for Arizona. In addition, Arizona was to receive 1,000,000 acre-feet "to be supplied from the tributaries . . . before the same empty into the main stream." [115] The last provision obviously referred to the water embraced by article III(b) of the compact.

Both states balked at the offer. California refused to modify its earlier demands, except to extend the waiver for protected rights from twenty to thirty-six years. Arizona expressed satisfaction with most of the proposal, but withheld complete acceptance unless its tributaries were exempted from any future Mexican burden and its power interests were protected. Despite a recess and then days of further hard bargaining, neither side would give in; and the conference ended in failure on October 4.

The only accomplishment of the meeting was passage of a

[114] "Proceedings of the Colorado River Conference" (Denver, 1927), I: 34–42, 46–50, 160–161, 311–315, passim.

[115] Ibid., II: 45–47, 459–461; see also "Hoover Dam Documents," p. 38.

resolution proclaiming the "rights of the states . . . to demand
and receive compensation for the use of their lands and waters."
This resolution, introduced by Senator Key Pittman of Nevada,
also stipulated that the "state or states upon whose land a dam
. . . is built by the United States Government . . . are entitled
to the preferred right to acquire the hydro-electric energy so
generated." Arizona and Nevada—and now Utah, in view of the
reasons for its recent rejection of the six-state compact—naturally
favored the resolution; but so did nearly all of the states, for
they saw in it an opportunity to promote "the cause of States'
rights." [116] Only Californians refused to endorse the proposition.
They feared it would lessen their chances to secure passage of the
Swing-Johnson bill. They also doubtlessly saw it as an attempt
to charge them more for power and possibly even to deprive them
of needed electricity.

XIV

Failure of the governors' conference bitterly disappointed leaders of the upper states. When several subsequent meetings between Arizona and California proved no more successful, upper-
basin leaders decided that their only real hope for protection now
lay in Congress. The Swing-Johnson bill would have to be modified in such a way as to guarantee them the safety that had thus
far eluded them.

The decision of most upper-state leaders to concentrate their
efforts on the Swing-Johnson bill seemed to be the only reasonable alternative remaining to them. They realized that pressure
for that measure had been building in Congress, and they acknowledged the necessity of controlling the river before cata-
strophic floods struck. They also believed they were merely
being realistic in recognizing that Congress would have to authorize more than just a flood-control dam. To do otherwise
would mean that California's Finney resolution would absolve
that state from the requirements of the compact. And California
had to be made subject to the compact at all costs, for even a
flood-control structure would help it establish rights against the

[116] "Proceedings of the Colorado River Conference" (Denver, 1927),
II: 162–165, 465–466; L. Ward Bannister to Herbert Hoover, October 8, 1927, file 1-M/344, Hoover Papers.

upper basin. New Mexico's interstate stream commissioner summed up the general attitude in a letter to Congressman John C. Tilson. "I have noticed a tendency to attempt to divert Congress from the main purposes of the Boulder Dam Project . . . and to plant . . . the idea of the construction of a flood control dam as a substitute," he wrote. "California would not accept such a dam in lieu of the storage project, and thus would not ratify the Compact." "Under such conditions . . . ," he explained, "there would be . . . no protection to the Upper Basin States." [117]

Though resigned to the eventual passage of the Swing-Johnson bill, the upper states were determined to mold it to their interests. Swing and Johnson had already made important concessions. In 1925 they had incorporated the compact into the provisions of their third bill. They did so again in December, 1927, in the fourth bill. That later measure was also modified to provide for royalties—37.5 percent of power profits in excess of the amount needed to amortize construction—to be divided equally between Arizona and Nevada in lieu of the taxes that those states might collect if the project were built by private capital. Arizona wanted a larger royalty, but Nevada settled for the arrangement.[118] So, too, did the upper states, which were especially pleased that the bill now acknowledged the principle of revenue for the states in which a project was constructed. The upper states were also pleased by the addition of a provision authorizing $250,000 for the investigation of feasible reclamation projects in every basin state except California.

Californians further sought to placate the upper basin by agreeing that anyone wishing water from Boulder Canyon storage would first have to obtain from the secretary of the interior a

[117] Francis C. Wilson to John C. Tilson, November 22, 1927, Dillon Papers; L. Ward Bannister to George H. Dern, October 30, November 15, and December 31, 1926, box 76, Dern Papers; cf. George Dern to John C. Tilson, December 1, 1927, box 80, Dern Papers; Dern to Francis C. Wilson, December 1, 1927, Dern Papers; Dern to John B. Kendrick, February 23, 1928, box 78, Dern Papers; Frank Emerson to Wilson, November 28, 1927, Carpenter Papers.

[118] Hiram Johnson to C. K. McClatchy, March 17, 1928, Johnson Papers; Carl Hayden to George Dern, March 26, 1928, Carpenter Papers.

contract that would be subject to the compact. In addition, they accepted an amendment that reflected the states' rights sensibilities of most basin representatives: "Nothing herein shall be construed as interfering with such rights as the States now have either to the waters within their borders or to adopt such policies and enact such laws as they may deem necessary with respect to the appropriation, control, and use of waters within their borders, except as modified by the Colorado River compact or other interstate agreement." To satisfy those who were worried about Mexico, they agreed to a stipulation that the waters to be reclaimed were for use "exclusively within the United States." Arizonans responded to this final provision by arguing that Mexico's rights should be determined by treaty before a major dam was constructed. But so far as Californians were concerned, a treaty more favorable to the United States could be obtained as soon as the dam and the All-American Canal were built. Most congressmen agreed.[119]

But the most important concession obtained by the upper states directly involved California—and the compact. Upper-basin leaders recognized that Arizona would probably continue to withhold its approval of the pact. Despite this probability, most of them agreed to the Boulder Canyon legislation, but only on condition that the act not become effective until at least six states had ratified the pact. In addition, they insisted that California would have to be one of the ratifying states and that it would have to limit itself to a specific amount of the 7,500,000 acre-feet allocated to the lower basin by article III(a) of the compact.

Upper-state representatives believed their demands were reasonable. They realized they could not force Arizona to ratify the pact and acknowledge their claims. With the cooperation of California, however, they believed they could minimize the Arizona threat. If they could induce California to limit its uses so that

[119] House Committee on Irrigation and Reclamation, *Hearings on Colorado River Basin, H.R. 6251 and H.R. 9826,* 69 Cong., 1 sess. (1926), pp. 82, 120, 161, 163, 177–180; *Cong. Rec.,* 70 Cong., 2 sess. (1928), pp. 169, 474, 593, 603, passim; *Cong. Rec.,* 70 Cong., 1 sess. (1928), p. 10262; Senate Committee on Irrigation and Reclamation, *Hearings on Colorado River Basin, S. 728 and S. 1274,* 70 Cong., 1 sess. (1928), pp. 441–444, passim.

Arizona might be satisfied from the lower basin's share, then they could breathe more easily. "The States of the upper basin much prefer a 7-State compact," explained Senator Lawrence Phipps of Colorado, "but they desire a compact of some kind, and with a provision under which one of the lower basin States—California —practically steps into the position of guarantor, so that the upper basin [states] would be reasonably assured . . . that they could go ahead safely in developing their irrigation enterprises." [120]

Congress settled finally on 4,400,000 acre-feet for California's share. This pleased neither Californians, who wanted at least 4,600,000 acre-feet (the amount they had demanded at the governors' conference in Denver), nor Arizonans, who insisted that the limitation be 4,200,000 acre-feet. But Californians had fought too long for the Boulder Canyon legislation to see it slip from their grasp now, and so they reluctantly agreed to the proposal.

Congress, however, went even further in trying to resolve the water dispute that had rocked the lower basin for so long. Exasperated by the failure of Arizona and California to resolve their differences, Nevada's Key Pittman suggested an amendment to the bill spelling out the details of a lower-basin pact. His amendment would give prior congressional approval to a lower-basin agreement allocating 300,000 acre-feet to Nevada; 4,400,000 acre-feet to California; and 2,800,000 acre-feet to Arizona. In addition, Arizona would receive exclusive rights to its Gila River water—water that "shall never be subject to any diminution whatever by any . . . treaty" with Mexico. Surplus waters unapportioned by the Colorado River Compact were to be divided equally between Arizona and California.

Californians only grudgingly accepted the amendment. They especially disliked the section exempting the Gila from any future Mexican burden, but when Pittman assured them that his amendment should not be construed as "the request of the Congress," they agreed to it. Arizona's Carl Hayden, now a member of the Senate, objected to the amendment for just the opposite reason. He wanted the bill written in such a way as to require California to concede the demands of Arizona and Nevada.[121]

[120] *Cong. Rec.*, 70 Cong., 2 sess. (1928), pp. 382, 389; Richard C. Dillon to W. H. Adams, May 7, 1928, Dillon Papers.

[121] *Cong. Rec.*, 70 Cong., 2 sess. (1928), pp. 459, 466–468, 472.

While some congressmen thought that Congress was infringing upon states' rights by even suggesting a lower-basin pact, Pittman strenuously disagreed. "If California and Nevada and Arizona do not like this agreement," he explained, "they do not have to approve it." "All I have in mind," he protested, is "trying to save six or seven months' time." If the lower-basin states were to enter into an agreement that already had congressional approval, he observed, then they would not have to return later to Congress for approval. "I may not be accomplishing anything; but Arizona seems to be wedded to a certain plan. If the California Legislature does not like it, it does not put us in any worse fix than we are in if we do not adopt it." [122]

Congress agreed, and Pittman's proposal was incorporated into section 4(a) of the bill. Thirty-five years later the U.S. Supreme Court would misconstrue this action and decide that the Boulder Canyon Act provided a statutory apportionment of the waters of the lower Colorado. In 1928, however, Congress appeared confident that it was merely suggesting a way in which the lower states *might* settle their problem themselves.

XV

Despite the attempt to facilitate a lower-basin agreement and to quiet upper-basin fears, many still resisted the Boulder Canyon

[122] Ibid., pp. 470, 471. Two months later, Pittman reaffirmed his views with unequivocal explicitness. "There is no attempt on the part of the Federal Government to apportion the waters," he told Utah's Governor Dern, "but the Government does decline to have the bill go into effect and to build the dam unless California voluntarily limits its sovereignty over the waters of the Colorado River to the extent of 4,400,000 acre feet of water." (Key Pittman to George Dern, February 19, 1929, box 79, Dern Papers.) To a Nevada official Pittman wrote: "The four million four hundred thousand acre feet is not allocated to California. California simply agrees not to attempt to appropriate or use any more than such amount." Pittman to George W. Malone, February 23, 1929, box 79, Dern Papers. See also Key Pittman to George W. Malone, February 12, 1929, box 79, Dern Papers; Henry F. Ashurst and Carl Hayden to John C. Phillips, December 21, 1928, Thomas Maddock Papers, Arizona Historical Society, Tucson; Charles E. Winter to Charles B. Stafford, January 31, 1929, Papers of the Wyoming State Engineer.

bill. Some opposition came from easterners who looked upon the massive project as unnecessary special-interest legislation for westerners. Farmers outside the West also believed that the bill would add to the agricultural surplus already depressing farm prices. Speculators in land on the Mexican delta resisted the bill's All-American Canal provision, and they were joined by some Imperial Valley farmers who argued that the canal was too expensive and not a suitable substitute for a Mexican treaty. Still others hammered away at the bill's engineering and economic features, claiming that they were impractical.[123]

Among the most powerful opponents were state and private power interests, which for years had fought the Boulder Canyon project because it would allow the federal government to enter the hydroelectric power business in a massive way. The critical word here was "allow," for though the Swing-Johnson bill stipulated that the federal government was to build the dam, it did not require the government to build and operate the power plant. Several options were possible, and the secretary of the interior was free to choose among them. The federal government could construct the plant and then lease the facility (or part of it) to state, municipal, or private agencies; it could merely lease storage water to the other agencies and permit them to build and operate the plant; or it could construct and operate the plant itself.

The last possibility, in particular, was anathema to spokesmen for private power interests who objected to the federal government competing with private industry and who feared that passage of the bill would represent a dangerous precedent and serve to encourage congressmen agitating for federal power development at Muscle Shoals—the future Tennessee Valley Authority. "The power monopoly," Nevada's Senator Key Pittman told Governor George Dern of Utah, "is not interested much in the Boulder dam, but it is deeply interested in the precedent that may be established in the legislation relative to the subject." [124]

The bill also proved unpopular with many state leaders, especially in Arizona and Utah, who wanted power plants placed under the control of the states in which they were located. Among

[123] House Committee on Irrigation and Reclamation, *Hearings on Colorado River Basin, H.R. 6251 and H.R. 9826,* passim.

[124] Key Pittman to George Dern, December 14, 1927, box 79, Dern Papers.

Arizona critics, the most vocal were the utilities, most of which were owned by such powerful out-of-state interests as the Cities Service Company and Electric Bond and Share Company. The chief opponent, however, was a publicly chartered agency, the Salt River Valley Water Users' Association, which claimed that it alone could handle Arizona's power needs.[125]

Despite the strong opposition both inside and outside the basin, the Swing-Johnson bill picked up the support needed for passage. The royalties conceded to Arizona and Nevada helped to mollify many of the advocates of state-controlled power plants. Also helpful were the endorsements provided by such well-known spokesmen as conservationist Gifford Pinchot and reformers Robert La Follette and George Norris. In the Senate Norris lent particularly strong support to the bill as a way to keep the "Power Trust" in check and further his own plans for public power development at Muscle Shoals.[126]

Considerable sentiment in favor of the Boulder Canyon project also resulted from the public reaction to a disastrous flood on the Mississippi River in 1927. Even if the Boulder dam would lead to the production of crops that competed with southern and eastern produce, declared George Norris, the structure was necessary "to save Imperial Valley."[127]

[125] Though it was a publicly chartered irrigation district, the Salt River Valley Water Users' Association, in its capacity as a producer of hydroelectricity, operated essentially as a private utility company. For a discussion of its unusual role, see N. D. Houghton, "Problems in Public Power Administration in the Southwest—Some Arizona Applications," *Western Political Quarterly* IV (1951): 124, 126 n; see also "Boulder Canyon Project," *H. Rept. 918*, 70 Cong., 1 sess. (1928), Part 2, pp. 15–16; U.S. Federal Power Commission, "National Power Survey: Principal Electric Utility Systems in the United States, 1935," *Power Series No. 2* (Washington, D.C., 1936).

[126] Gifford Pinchot, "Who Owns Our Rivers?" *The Nation* CXXVI (January 18, 1928): 64–66; *Los Angeles Examiner*, April 26, 1928; Richard Lowitt, *George W. Norris: The Persistence of a Progressive, 1913–1933* (Urbana, 1971), pp. 352–353, passim; Preston J. Hubbard, *Origins of the TVA: The Muscle Shoals Controversy, 1920–1932* (Nashville, Tenn., 1961), p. 236, passim.

[127] *Cong. Rec.*, 70 Cong., 2 sess. (1928), p. 594; Lowitt, *Norris*, p. 353.

Even stronger support for the bill followed disclosures by the Federal Trade Commission about the lobbying activities of private power firms. In the spring of 1928, the FTC issued reports revealing that private power interests were annually spending more than a million dollars through such powerful organizations as the National Electric Light Association and the National Utilities Associations to promote private ownership of utilities and to defeat the Muscle Shoals and Boulder Canyon bills. Some $400,000 had been raised and earmarked specifically for the defeat of the Swing-Johnson bill. Former Colorado River Commissioner Stephen B. Davis of New Mexico had received nearly $29,000 from private utilities since June, 1927. The law firm in which Merritt C. Mechem, former governor of New Mexico, was a partner had been paid more than $5,000 "in return for services rendered in watching and reporting . . . on the conferences of Western Governors attempting to reach an agreement on the Boulder Dam Bill." At the time that Mechem was engaged in "watching and reporting," he had also been a member of New Mexico's official delegation to the conferences. James Scrugham, former Nevada governor and Colorado River commissioner, had also been on the utilities payroll, receiving his money from a "special fund" handled by Stephen Davis.[128]

These and other disclosures received ample national publicity in the Hearst and Scripps-Howard newspapers. They also provided grist for the propaganda mills of the Boulder Dam Association, created in 1923 by southern California interests, and the National Boulder Dam Association, created by the same interests in 1926 and headquartered in Washington, D.C., where it was run vigorously by Harry Slattery, former secretary of Gifford Pinchot and an outspoken conservationist.[129]

Strong support for Boulder Dam also came in December, 1928, when Congress received a report from a group of engineers and geologists under the chairmanship of Major General William L.

---

[128] *Los Angeles Examiner,* April 20, 25, 26, and 27, 1928; see also Hubbard, *Origins of TVA,* pp. 238–240; Beverley Moeller, *Phil Swing and Boulder Dam* (Berkeley and Los Angeles, 1971), pp. 111–112.

[129] See the Boulder Dam Association and National Boulder Dam Association files in the Swing Papers; see also *Washington Herald,* May 26, 1928; *San Diego Sun,* May 31, 1928.

Sibert. This Colorado River Board, or "Sibert board," as it was better known, had been created the preceding May to settle questions raised about the project's engineering and economic features. The board strongly endorsed the project, but in doing so it also made observations about the water supply that left many uneasy: "the original estimates for the flow at Black Canyon are exceedingly uncertain, and in the opinion of the board are too high." [130]

Sibert and his colleagues calculated that the reconstructed flow of the river at the canyon was about 15,000,000 acre-feet, an amount more than 1,000,000 acre-feet less than the Reclamation Service had estimated in 1922. The error was attributed to two major considerations: the use of poor gauging equipment at Yuma (measurements there were used as the basis for the estimate of the flow in the canyon), and the Reclamation Service's failure to take adequately into account the years of unusually low flow prior to 1905. As early as 1909, noted the board, an engineer of the U.S. Geological Survey had urged the use of "improved methods" for measuring the flow at Yuma, but such techniques had not been adopted until 1918. Then another eight years had passed before the "best modern methods" had been utilized in 1926.[131] No explanation was offered for the delay in installing the better equipment, though lack of funds was apparently the principal reason.

The board also attributed the errors in the earlier river-flow estimates to the fact that they rested primarily on data gathered after 1905, when the flow of the river was unusually heavy. The board acknowledged that it could not demonstrate its contention with precision because of the faulty equipment and because no "actual current meter gaugings" were made at Yuma until 1902. But "gauge heights" for the river at Yuma had been made since 1878, and that evidence, together with rainfall records and stream-flow measurements taken from nearby streams, suggested that the two decades before 1905 were years when the flow was "much below the average." "Records also show," warned the board, "that periods of high and low flow occur in cycles of very uncertain magnitude and duration. A low period similar to that

[130] "Report of the Colorado River Board on the Boulder Dam Project," *H. Doc. 446*, 70 Cong., 2 sess. (1928), p. 9.
[131] Ibid., pp. 9, 12.

which occurred from 1886 to 1905 is sure to recur, and may be expected at any time." [132]

The warning came too late to change many minds about the Swing-Johnson bill. The Sibert board made its report about two weeks before the Christmas recess. The pressure to pass the bill and to clean up other last-minute business provided little time to reflect on the board's report. Moreover, only about two and a half months remained in the session, and Congress was anxious to turn its full attention to several major appropriation bills that would take precedence over the Boulder Canyon measure. Then, too, despite the reduced stream flow, the Sibert board believed there was sufficient water to justify the dam and to placate the upper states. Its estimate of 15,000,000 acre-feet in the Boulder–Black Canyon area, it noted pointedly, was equivalent to "the amount apportioned by the seven States compact for division at Lees Ferry." [133] This finding more than satisfied Wyoming's Governor Frank Emerson, who believed that the Sibert board's estimates of water supply were overly conservative. "I do not hesitate in giving you my continuing conviction," Emerson, one of the drafters of the compact in 1922, told Utah's Governor Dern, "that the Upper States are safe within all reasonable limits. . . . My own conclusion has been supported by several other engineers well versed in water supply matters and possibly better qualified through virtue of their practical experience to pass upon such questions than . . . the engineers rendering the Sibert report. . . ." [134]

Though encouraging to some, Emerson's assurances failed to quiet the fears of those worried about Mexico. Nor did his claims or the findings of the Sibert board satisfy those, especially in the lower basin, who envisaged projects requiring more water than was apportioned by the compact. But by the time protesters were able to organize their forces, Congress had already acted.

On December 14, 1928, only a week and a half after the Sibert board had released its report, the Senate passed the Swing-Johnson bill by a vote of 64 to 11. The House had already approved the bill seven months earlier, but its version, unlike the Senate measure, did not contain all the amendments demanded by the

[132] Ibid., pp. 9, 11.   [133] Ibid., p. 12.

[134] Frank Emerson to George Dern, January 4, 1929, box 77, Dern Papers.

upper states. Consequently, House members had to register their approval of the Senate bill. This they did by a vote of 167 to 122 only four days after the Senate had acted. On December 21 President Calvin Coolidge signed the Boulder Canyon bill into law.[135]

XVI

But congressional approval did not put into effect either the compact or the Boulder Canyon Act. Still necessary was the ratification of the compact by the seven states or by six states including California. If seven-state approval were not obtained within six months, then the six-state option could be invoked. When the bill was passed in December, 1928, only four states had already endorsed without reservations both a seven- and six-state compact. Attention now focused on the three remaining states— Arizona, California, and Utah.[136]

Californians wasted little time now that they had the Boulder Canyon project nearly within their grasp. Less than three weeks after President Coolidge had signed the Swing-Johnson bill, the California legislature unanimously passed an emergency measure approving the pact, and Governor C. C. Young quickly ratified the legislature's action. Californians understandably hesitated to ratify immediately the six-state formula and limit themselves to

[135] *Cong. Rec.*, 70 Cong., 1 sess. (1928), p. 9990; *Cong. Rec.*, 70 Cong., 2 sess. (1928), pp. 603, 837–838; U.S., *Statutes at Large*, XLV: 1057–1066.

[136] Though most attention centered on California, Arizona, and Utah, some basin leaders also nervously eyed an attempt to repeal the six-state pact in Wyoming, where many had become alarmed by the reduced stream-flow estimates of the Sibert board and by California's growing demands. Other objections were voiced, most of which were similar to those offered in 1923. The repeal attempt was defeated when Governor Frank Emerson successfully persuaded the legislature to stand by its earlier action. Wyoming, he argued, would get its share of water "when the time was right." Charles E. Winter to Charles B. Stafford, January 31, 1929, Papers of the Wyoming State Engineer; Stafford to Winter, February 5, 1929, Papers of the Wyoming State Engineer; Cheyenne *Wyoming State Tribune*, February 2, 1929; *Journal of the Senate of the Twentieth State Legislature of Wyoming, 1929* (Sheridan, Wyo., 1929), pp. 123, 379–384, passim.

the 4,400,000 acre-feet specified by Congress until all hope for an Arizona ratification had faded. By early March the continued opposition of Governor Hunt and other Arizona leaders had convinced them that it was futile to wait longer. On March 4 they approved the six-state pact and enacted the necessary legislation. Specifically, they limited themselves to 4,400,000 acre-feet of "the waters apportioned to the lower basin states by paragraph 'a' of article three of the . . . Colorado river compact, plus not more than one-half of any excess or surplus waters unapportioned by said compact." [137]

In limiting themselves, Californians also hoped to undercut strong opposition that had developed in Utah to both the compact and Boulder Dam. Despite the concessions wrung from California during the congressional debates, many Utahns still believed that a six-state compact did not afford them enough protection. The Sibert board's doubts about the adequacy of the water supply worried them, as did the protests of two of their congressmen, Senator Reed Smoot and Representative Elmer Leatherwood.

Smoot and Leatherwood had been among the most outspoken opponents in Congress of the Swing-Johnson bill. Like Arizonans, they claimed the measure was "uneconomic" and would aid development in Mexico. Moreover, they insisted that the legislation, by permitting the compact to take effect without Arizona's approval, would "establish the theory that the Government owns and controls the unappropriated waters of the streams in the arid-land States, and that hereafter the Federal Government will allocate the waters of said streams, by legislative fiction if necessary, and deny all ownership by the States in the unappropriated waters of streams within their borders." [138]

[137] *Journal of the Senate: Forty-Eighth Session of the California Legislature, 1929* (Sacramento, 1929), pp. 72, 118, 457–458; *Journal of the Assembly: Forty-Eighth Session of the California Legislature, 1929* (Sacramento, 1929), pp. 97, 574–576; *Calif. Stats.* (January 10, 1929), chap. 1, pp. 1–7; ibid. (March 4, 1929), chaps. 15–16, pp. 37–39.

[138] *Cong. Rec.*, 70 Cong., 2 sess. (1928), p. 836; see also Reed Smoot to Calvin Coolidge, November 26, 1928, box 57, Reed Smoot Papers, Brigham Young University, Provo, Utah; George M. Bacon to William R. Wallace, November 27, 1928, Papers of the Utah State Engineer; *Salt Lake Tribune*, December 4, 1928.

The bill's proponents had challenged these claims, especially the last, for they had no intention of passing legislation that would violate their concept of states' rights. Ironically, another Utah congressman, Senator William King, was among those who issued the strongest challenge to Smoot and Leatherwood's view. "I deny the proposition," declared King, an advocate of the Swing-Johnson bill, "that the Federal Government may go into a stream . . . and put its powerful hands down upon the stream and say, 'This is mine; I can build a dam there and allocate water to whom I please.' " [139]

Neither King nor the bill's other friends believed that the compact would deprive Arizona of its rights. If Arizona did not approve the pact, then it could not be bound by it. As a nonsigner, explained Representative Charles Winter of Wyoming, Arizona would remain "master and arbiter" of its water uses.[140] Indeed, the realization of that fact had prompted the demand that California enact self-limitation legislation.

Such responses made little headway with Smoot and Leatherwood. Nor did they persuade the two men to abandon another of their major objections. "This bill," declared Leatherwood, who was believed by Swing to be in league with private power interests, "means that the Government is going into the power business. . . . When this project is authorized, . . . the Government has on its hands a glorified Muscle Shoals—a source of administrative worry, of congressional debate, of interstate conflict, of international conflict, for the next 20 years." Smoot remained equally adamant. He had personal reasons for being stubborn, for he was the president of the Electric Company of Provo, Utah, which had connections with the Utah Power and Light Company, the Electric Bond and Share Company of New York, and the Electric Power and Light Corporation of New York. Hence, his warning to the *Salt Lake Telegram* came as no

---

[139] *Cong. Rec.*, 70 Cong., 2 sess. (1928), p. 169. King provided a lengthy description of his attitude to the Swing-Johnson bill in William H. King to George Dern, December 22, 1928, box 78, Dern Papers.

[140] *Cong. Rec.*, 70 Cong., 1 sess. (1928), p. 9654. Winter did believe, however, that the federal government, through its control of the public lands over which Arizona would have to divert its waters, could compel Arizonans to abide by the compact.

surprise: "Nothing but trouble, danger and great expense to our Government is ahead if this unwise power project is begun." [141]

Many Utah legislators shared Smoot's fears, but their opposition to the project was less intransigent than his. To be sure, they remained vitally interested in obtaining confirmation of their state's right to the beds of the Colorado and Green rivers, a confirmation that would be valid only if those streams were held to be navigable where they flowed within the state. But Utah's Governor Dern, who sympathized with this view, had concluded that the question of navigability could be settled satisfactorily by nothing short of a Supreme Court decision. Rather than force the issue now, he told his followers that the state should bide its time and then, when a favorable judicial decision seemed likely, appeal to the Supreme Court.[142]

[141] *Cong. Rec.*, 70 Cong., 2 sess. (1928), p. 836; Reed Smoot to *Salt Lake Telegram*, December 22, 1928, box 57, Smoot Papers; Smoot to Ralf Woolley, January 7, 1929, box 57, Smoot Papers; Phil Swing to D. F. McGarry, March 22, 1927, Swing Papers; Loren B. Chan, *Sagebrush Statesman: Tasker L. Oddie of Nevada* (Reno, Nev., 1973), p. 136; *Who's Who in America, 1928–1929* (Chicago, 1928), p. 1937.

[142] In 1931 the federal government took the initiative in this matter and asked the Supreme Court to declare unnavigable the Green and Colorado rivers within Utah. The Court rendered a mixed decision; it found certain sections of the rivers navigable and other stretches unnavigable. As expected, the Court declared that the bed of the navigable portions belonged to the state of Utah. Though this seemed to be an important—if partial—victory for Utah, the impact of the victory was weakened by a proviso added by the Court: "The United States of America shall in nowise be prevented from taking any such action . . . as may be necessary to protect and preserve the navigability of any navigable waters of the United States of America." The force of this proviso became readily apparent in another decision handed down at the same time. In *Arizona* v. *California et al.* (1931), Arizona had sought to prevent the construction of Hoover Dam on the grounds that the state owned half the river bed on which the dam was to rest (the other half belonged to Nevada) and it had not approved construction. Though the Supreme Court did not deny the state's claim to half the river bed, it refused to prevent construction. It rested its argument on the grounds that Congress had stipulated in the Boulder Canyon Act that one of the purposes of the dam was the improvement of navigation. And "the improvement of navigation," declared the Court, falls "clearly within

Most Utah lawmakers recognized the wisdom of this approach, but many of them were also intensely interested in obtaining dams of their own, especially at Flaming Gorge and Dewey. Some urged reservations that would require California to "agree not to interpose any objection" to reservoirs at those sites. But Governor Dern persuaded the legislature to reject these suggestions, since reservations would require reconsideration of the pact by Congress and the other ratifying states.[143] The results of that move would be confusion, rancor, and, doubtlessly, no compact at all.

For a while Utahns resisted the six-state compact as strongly as they opposed reservations. Reed Smoot encouraged them to hold out for nothing less than a seven-state pact which protected Utah "in all of her rights." "Utah and Arizona," he told the president of the Utah senate, "have at all times asserted that the waters in their streams were subject to appropriation under State law. For either one of them to approve the Colorado River Compact on a six-state basis is a repudiation of that principle and an admission that the Federal Government has supreme control of the waters of streams in public land States." [144]

Many Utahns challenged Smoot, and they were joined by others who believed that even if he were correct, the state would

the powers conferred upon Congress." Thus, even though the states owned the beds of navigable rivers, they could not prevent the federal government from building dams on those rivers. *Arizona* v. *California et al.*, 283 U.S. 456–457 (1931); *U.S.* v. *Utah*, 283 U.S. 64, 804 (1931). See also chap. 8 below.

[143] *Senate Journal: Eighteenth Session of the Legislature of the State of Utah, 1929* (Salt Lake City, 1929), pp. 680–681; *House Journal: Eighteenth Session of the Legislature of the State of Utah, 1929* (Salt Lake City, 1929), pp. 362–389; *Salt Lake Tribune*, January 24, 1929; George Dern to Delph Carpenter, February 7, 1929, box 76, Dern Papers; Dern to William H. King, February 19, 1929, box 78, Dern Papers; William R. Wallace to Dern, January 17, 1929, box 80, Dern Papers; Ralf Woolley to Reed Smoot, February 13, 1929, box 57, Smoot Papers; L. Ward Bannister to Herbert Hoover, March 9, 1929, file 1-E/99, Hoover Papers; Frank C. Emerson to John A. Whiting, February 20, 1929, Papers of the Wyoming State Engineer.

[144] Reed Smoot to Hamilton Gardner, January 28, 1929, box 57, Smoot Papers.

be better off with a six-state compact than no compact at all. After two months of deliberation, the Utah legislature arrived at the same conclusion: a pact in which California limited itself and thereby weakened the threat from Arizona seemed to be as much as Utah could expect.

On March 6, two days after California passed its self-limitation act, Utah approved the six-state pact. Then, on June 25, 1929, newly elected President Herbert Hoover, after waiting the six months required by the Boulder Canyon Act, issued a proclamation declaring the act effective.[145]

The compact had at last won approval—if only from Congress and six of the seven basin states.

[145] The Utah house approved the pact by a vote of forty-six to seven, while the senate endorsed it by a vote of fourteen to one. *House Journal: Utah, 1929,* p. 513; *Senate Journal: Utah, 1929,* pp. 701–702; George Dern to Delph Carpenter, February 11, 1929, Carpenter Papers; U.S., *Statutes at Large,* XLVI: 3000.

9

Arizona v. California

With the Boulder Canyon legislation a reality, Arizona redoubled its efforts to obtain a satisfactory lower-basin agreement. Even before California and Utah had approved the six-state compact, Arizona had met once again with lower-basin representatives in an attempt to resolve their differences. That conference, held in Santa Fe in February and March, 1929, was significant primarily for defining newer issues of conflict that would trouble the lower states for more than three decades and produce three appeals to the U.S. Supreme Court.

I

The Santa Fe conference began on an optimistic note. There was considerable hope that the water-allocation formula suggested in section 4(a) of the Boulder Canyon Act would pave the way for a quick settlement. That hope quickly faded, however, as each state tried to amend the congressional proposal to satisfy its own self-interest.

The basic problem was created by ambiguities in both the Boulder Canyon Act and the Colorado River Compact. As already noted, the compact allocated an additional 1,000,000 acre-feet to the lower basin in article III (b). Though the evidence suggests that the additional water was intended for Arizona, the compact could not specifically say so, since allocations were made to basins, not to individual states. This ambiguity was complicated by another one in the Boulder Canyon Act.

Congress, in suggesting a division of the flow available to the lower states, had mentioned three classes of water: (1) the 7,500,000 acre-feet allocated by article III (a) of the compact; (2) surplus water unapportioned by the compact; and (3) Gila River water. Congress had suggested that Arizona receive 2,800,-000 acre-feet of the III (a) water; half the surplus; and all the Gila River water within its boundaries.[1] Unfortunately, however, Congress had said nothing about the 1,000,000 acre-feet allocated by article III (b) of the compact or about the relationship of that provision to Arizona's uses of Gila River water or its uses of water from any of its other tributaries.

The lack of precision was understandable, since the formula in section 4(a) had been added at the last minute during floor debate in the Senate. It had not been the product of hearings on the bill, where amendments are usually the result of more deliberate action. Nor had there been an opportunity to subject it to the scrutiny of a joint House-Senate conference committee. To save time and to preclude the necessity of further Senate debate if the bill was changed in conference, Swing had persuaded House leaders to vote at once on the Senate version of the measure.[2] The result of this action had been approval of a bill containing an ambiguity that Arizonans and Californians now sought to turn to their own respective advantages.

Arizona opened the Santa Fe talks by submitting a proposition that reflected its continuing interest in the highline canal scheme. The state believed that it needed about 3,500,000 acre-feet of mainstream water in order to justify construction of the canal. The method its spokesmen now devised to get this water was simple. Since the meaning of III (b) was unclear, they "clarified" it by insisting that both it and article III (a) referred only to mainstream water. Those two articles apportioned 8,500,000 acre-

[1] U.S., *Statutes at Large*, XLV: 1058–1959.

[2] Phil D. Swing, "The Struggle for Boulder Dam," pp. 80–81, Phil D. Swing Papers, Department of Special Collections, University of California, Los Angeles.

feet to the lower basin. Of that amount Arizonans demanded
3,500,000 acre-feet *plus* everything in their tributaries. To be
more precise, they demanded their tributaries; 2,800,000 acre-feet
of the III (a) water; and 700,000 acre-feet of III (b) water. To
Nevada they offered 300,000 acre-feet of the III (a) water; and
to California they conceded the balance of the III (a) water plus
300,000 acre-feet of the III (b) water, for a total of 4,700,000
acre-feet.[3]

Californians rejected the offer. On this occasion, they conceded to Arizona its tributaries and also 2,800,000 acre-feet of
III (a) water. They agreed, in addition, that III (b) should be
construed as applying to the mainstream, but they wanted more
of that water than Arizona had offered. They wanted nearly all
of it, and there was one way that they might be able to get their
wish. If the III (b) water was made subject to the law of prior
appropriation, then faster developing California would probably
establish rights to most—perhaps all—of it. This rationale became the basis for California's offer to Arizona: permit the III
(b) water to go to those first using it.[4]

Arizonans naturally turned down the offer. The negotiations
also foundered because of disagreement over the All-American
Canal and rates for water and power. Rumors were circulating
that California wanted to use the All-American Canal—which
had been authorized by the Boulder Canyon Act but still not
built—to compel Mexican landowners to help pay for the aqueduct and for flood-control works. According to the rumors, Californians planned to construct a bypass near the aqueduct's head-
gates and then send water to Mexico—but only for a price. The
news angered Arizonans, who accused Californians of wanting to

[3] Charles B. Ward, John Mason Ross, and A. H. Favour, *Proposals
as to a Basis for a Lower Basin Compact, Submitted at Santa Fe
Conference by the Colorado River Commission of Arizona, March 3,
1929* (Albuquerque, New Mex. [1929]), copy in Swing Papers; *Cong.
Rec.*, 71 Cong., 2 sess. (1930), pp. 11770–11771.

[4] John L. Bacon, W. B. Mathews, and Earl C. Pound, *California's
Reply to Arizona's Proposals as to a Basis for a Lower Basin Compact,
Submitted at Tri-State Conference by the Colorado River Commission
of California, March 7, 1929* (Albuquerque, New Mex. [1929]), copy
in Swing Papers; see also *Cong. Rec.*, 71 Cong., 2 sess. (1930), pp.
11771–11772.

sell water that did not belong to them. To guard against the threat, they insisted that the All-American Canal "not, directly or indirectly, carry any water to or for the use of any lands in Mexico." [5]

Power, too, continued to be a major concern to Arizona. Its negotiators used the conference as an opportunity to demand higher royalties and also a two dollar per acre-foot charge on all water diverted to southern California's coastal plain. The charge for water would help produce "excess revenues" for distribution to Arizona and Nevada. In addition, Arizonans demanded a five-year option, during which time Arizona and Nevada could obtain a preferred right to 75,000 horsepower.

Californians were no more amenable to these requests than to those for water. To modify the revenue and power provisions of the Boulder Canyon Act, they declared, would be "unjust and unreasonable" and "no doubt would antagonize Congress and cause rejection of the Compact." "As to the proposal that the All-American Canal be not used for delivery of water for Mexican use," they curtly replied, "that is not a proper subject of concern." [6] Despite the intervention of a federal mediator, William J. Donovan, a former U.S. assistant attorney general, the two states failed to resolve their differences. This conference, like so many before it, ended in failure.

II

When subsequent meetings in 1929 proved no more successful, Ray Lyman Wilbur, who became secretary of the interior following Herbert Hoover's election to the presidency in 1928, decided that he could no longer hold up construction of the Boulder Canyon project. In September, 1929, he invited applications from those wishing to purchase Boulder Dam power. Until power contracts that guaranteed repayment in a fifty-year period were signed, Congress would not fund the undertaking. By April, 1930, after considerable hard bargaining, Wilbur had worked out with

[5] Ward, Ross, and Favour, *Proposals as to a Basis for a Lower Basin Compact*, p. 2.

[6] Bacon, Mathews, and Pound, *California's Reply to Arizona's Proposals*, pp. 2, 3.

the power applicants the general guidelines to be followed. The federal government would build the power plant and then lease operating rights to two agents, the city of Los Angeles and the Southern California Edison Company, which agreed to underwrite construction by purchasing all the power not contracted for by others. In addition, Wilbur reserved the right to draw back 36 percent of the power for use in Arizona and Nevada at any time during the next fifty years that the two states might need it. Californians resisted this reservation clause, and Arizonans and Nevadans protested that the arrangement was too generous to California, but Wilbur believed that the guidelines were fair.[7]

The discussion of contracts for power invariably raised questions about water. Those wishing to purchase electricity pointed out that they could not obligate themselves to do so unless they also obtained a contract for water. The Metropolitan Water District of Southern California, for example, needed large amounts of hydroelectricity to pump water through its aqueduct, but it could not bind itself to purchase the energy without assurance of the water that it wished to pump. Secretary Wilbur thus found himself in a delicate situation. He could not authorize construction of the dam without power contracts, and he could not secure the power contracts without also negotiating water contracts.

If California and Arizona could settle their differences, the contract problem would be resolved, but the two states continued to wrangle. When their leaders met again in January and February, 1930, Californians adopted a tactic that soured the talks at the outset. They insisted that Arizona be charged for all the waters in its tributaries, a move calculated to maximize the amount of mainstream water available to California. The response from Arizona was predictable. "Arizona from the first," grumbled its spokesmen, "has tried to make it clear that we can not and will not discuss a division of our tributary waters or the water of the Gila. We have insisted and still insist that if any division of water is to be made it must be confined to water

[7] "Hoover Dam Documents," *H. Doc. 717*, 80 Cong., 2 sess. (1948), pp. 65–69; Loren B. Chan, *Sagebrush Statesman: Tasker L. Oddie of Nevada* (Reno, Nev., 1973), pp. 138–139; Paul L. Kleinsorge, *The Boulder Canyon Project* (Stanford, Calif., 1941), p. 149.

actually reaching and flowing in the main stream." [8] Faced with such obstinancy, Californians agreed to let Arizona have its tributary water; but this concession proved meaningless, since the two states continued to disagree sharply over how to divide the water in the mainstream.

Now convinced that a lower-basin pact was out of the question for the foreseeable future, Wilbur proceeded to draw up the necessary water contracts with California. In doing so he carefully avoided specifying how much water was covered by article III (a) or III (b) or how much water might have to come from surplus. He did, however, stipulate that the California contracts —which eventually totaled 5,362,000 acre-feet—were "subject to all the terms and provisions of the Colorado River Compact and of the Boulder Canyon Act." [9] Wilbur wished to avoid responsibility for settling the dispute between Arizona and California, but his decision nevertheless angered Arizonans, who observed bitterly that the secretary, who was a Californian, was playing favorites.

Wilbur's decision also created a significant measure of uncertainty within the Interior Department. The problem involved the legal status of the contracts. In negotiating them, Wilbur usually tried to avoid any suggestion that he was conferring a water right. Congress had not authorized the secretary to make such a determination; and according to current legal opinion, rights to the waters of interstate streams could be determined in only two ways: by a treaty among the states involved, or by Supreme Court decision. Wilbur and his colleagues acknowledged these views by announcing that the contracts had "no bearing on the allocation of water." But Wilbur could not be blind to reality. He recognized that as the official responsible for operating the reservoir, he would be compelled to make administrative decisions about the release of waters and about water-delivery charges. These considerations prompted one of his advisers to note that while the secretary could not make a

[8] William Donovan's report to Secretary Wilbur describing these negotiations can be found in *Cong. Rec.*, 71 Cong., 2 sess. (1930), pp. 11778–11781; Senate Committee on Appropriations, *Hearings on Second Deficiency Appropriation Bill, 1930*, 71 Cong., 2 sess. (1930), pp. 173–185, 192–193.

[9] "Hoover Dam Documents," pp. A487–A489, passim.

"determination" of water rights, he could "designate the owner-ship of waters released from storage." [10] In short, Wilbur and his fellow officials tried to distinguish between the creation of water rights and the practical necessities dictated by the administration of the dam.

At times the distinction was lost. The most telling example of this occurred in 1931, when some Californians who opposed the aqueduct sought by the Metropolitan Water District claimed that the district's contract did not provide clear title to water. To support their contention, they cited a letter from Reclamation Commissioner Elwood Mead in which he had stated that "the Secretary of the Interior has no authority to designate the owner-ship of waters released from Hoover Dam." Alarmed when he learned of the threat his letter posed to the aqueduct project, Mead told MWD officials that he had been referring only to the "unregulated flow" of the river, not to "water stored in Hoover Dam," and he criticized those "casting doubt on the water right conferred by your contract." [11]

Such statements reflecting the Interior Department's confusion alarmed many states' rights advocates, and none more than those in Arizona. Unable to obtain a favorable lower-basin settlement and angered by the contracts California was obtaining from Wilbur, Arizonans turned to the Supreme Court for redress.

III

Arizona filed suit in the Supreme Court in October, 1930, asking the Court to declare unconstitutional the Boulder Canyon Act and the compact. The state accused the federal government of violating its "quasi-sovereign rights" by "building . . . a dam, half of which is to be in Arizona," without its permission. More-

[10] Memo from E. B. Debler to Northcutt Ely, August 14, 1931, file 032, Colorado River Project, Papers of the Secretary of the Interior, Record Group 48, National Archives; Ray Lyman Wilbur to George L. Ulrick, June 4, 1931, file 032, Colorado River, Papers of the Secretary of the Interior; memo from Commissioner of Reclamation to Secretary of the Interior, January 18, 1930, file 032, Colorado River Compact, Bureau of Reclamation Papers, Record Group 115, National Archives.

[11] Elwood Mead to W. P. Whitsett, August 25, 1931, file 032, Colorado River, Papers of the Secretary of the Interior.

over, it argued, Congress's claim that the Boulder Canyon Act is for the improvement of navigation is "a mere subterfuge and false pretense." The river was not navigable, Arizona claimed, but "even if said river were navigable, the diversion, sale and delivery of water therefrom, as authorized in said act, would not improve, but would destroy, its navigable capacity." [12]

Arizonans also contended that the Boulder Canyon Act did the state "irreparable injury," since it required Secretary Wilbur "to permit no use or future appropriation" of storage water within Arizona "except subject to the conditions and reservations contained in the Colorado River Compact; . . . the Act thus attempts to enforce . . . against Arizona . . . the compact which it has refused to ratify." Thus, the Court should declare "unconstitutional, void, and of no effect" the compact and the Boulder Canyon legislation and enjoin Wilbur from carrying out his "pretended contracts" with California.

But Arizonans did even more in their plea to the Court. They leveled against the compact a detailed attack—an attack which revealed that their criticism continued to extend beyond the issues of Wilbur and California. At times in the past, they had indicated a willingness to accept the basic compact allocation, but on this occasion they showed no desire to compromise. The pact "attempts to apportion" to the upper states far more than "an equitable share of water," since the lower basin "can put to beneficial use more than twice the quantity of water" needed by the upper states. Indeed, Arizona alone "can put to beneficial use more than the total quantity of water which the . . . compact attempts to apportion to . . . [the] entire Lower Basin." Moreover, the pact injured Arizona by including the Gila within the waters being apportioned. "The effect of including the Gila River . . . ," they declared in an argument reminiscent of Arizona's position during the compact negotiations eight years earlier, "would be to reduce by 3,000,000 acre-feet annually the quantity of water now subject to appropriation in Arizona."

The Court was unmoved by Arizona's plea. On May 18, 1931, in an eight-to-one decision, the justices rejected the suit, claiming that the Boulder Canyon Act represented a "valid exercise of Congressional power" and in no way abridged Arizona's rights.

[12] *Arizona v. California*, 283 U.S. 439, 444, 450, 455 (1931); Arizona, *Arizona v. California: Bill of Complaint* (n.p., n.d.), pp. 18–40.

On the question of navigability, the Court cited evidence that the river had been used for navigation in the past, and it refused to inquire "into the motives which induced members of Congress" to approve the Boulder Canyon bill: "Whether the particular structures proposed are reasonably necessary is not for this Court to determine." [13]

The justices expressly denied that the Boulder Canyon legislation or the compact impaired Arizona's water rights. "On the contrary," they noted, "section 18 [of the Boulder Canyon Act] specifically declares that nothing therein 'shall be construed as interfering with such rights as the States now have either to the waters within their borders or to adopt such policies and enact such laws as they may deem necessary with respect to the appropriation, control, and use of water within their borders, except as modified' by interstate agreement. As Arizona has made no such agreement," explained the Court, "the Act leaves its legal rights unimpaired." [14]

Nor did the justices believe that Wilbur's water contracts with California violated Arizona's rights. Some nine million acre-feet of river water were still flowing unused into Mexico, noted the Court. Hence, there was no reason "for determining now Arizona's rights to interstate or local waters which have not yet been, and which may never be, appropriated."

Less than a month after Arizona's defeat in the Supreme Court, workmen began excavating the diversion tunnels for the huge dam that became known at first as Hoover Dam and then Boulder Dam, before Congress in 1947 ended the confusion by reaffirming Hoover Dam as the correct name. But confusion extended to more than the dam's name. Despite the publicizing over the years of Boulder Canyon as the likely site, the dam was actually built in Black Canyon, a narrow gorge some twenty miles farther downstream where the bedrock conditions were more suitable.

IV

Regardless of the dam's location or name, Arizonans bitterly resented its construction. They spent the two years following their

[13] *Arizona v. California*, 283 U.S. 464, 455, 456 (1931).
[14] Ibid., 462–464.

court defeat in fruitless bargaining with California. Continued failure to reach an agreement finally prompted the state to open negotiations with the secretary of the interior for a water-delivery contract. If Arizona could not get what it wanted from California, perhaps it could get the next best thing—a favorable contract.

That hope, too, was dashed. Secretary Wilbur offered to deliver 2,800,000 acre-feet annually from the mainstream; but as he had in the California contracts, he insisted that the agreement be made subject to the compact. He also refused to specify which part of the water was covered by articles III (a) and III (b) of the compact or which part, if any, was to come from surplus. "Differences of opinion may exist between the State of Arizona and other contractors," he observed in his offer of February, 1933. "Accordingly, . . . this contract is without prejudice to relative claims of priorities as between the State of Arizona and other contractors with the United States, and shall not otherwise impair any contract heretofore authorized by said regulations." [15]

Arizonans rejected the offer. Disappointed at the failure of their latest gambit, they carefully reassessed their position and then decided to turn once more to the Supreme Court. This time their ambitions were more modest, though their approach was not.

In February, 1934, Arizonans asked the Court to "perpetuate," or certify for later use, some oral testimony that they planned to introduce in a future action. This was the first time that such a request had come before the Supreme Court. Arizonans made the unusual plea because they believed they could produce witnesses who would prove that the 1,000,000 acre-feet covered by article III (b) were meant "exclusively" for Arizona. The witnesses that they had in mind were those members of the Colorado River Commission who were still living—Herbert Hoover; Delph Carpenter; James G. Scrugham; R. E. Caldwell; Clarence Stetson; W. S. Norviel; C. C. Lewis (one of Norviel's advisers during the negotiations); and Thomas Campbell, the former Arizona governor who was present at the Santa Fe talks. Their testimony,

[15] Ray Lyman Wilbur, "Regulations: Delivery of Water in Arizona," February 7, 1933, file 032, Colorado River, Papers of the Secretary of the Interior. These regulations and the proposed Arizona contract can also be found in "Hoover Dam Documents," pp. A551–A557.

argued the Arizona attorneys, would show that the compact negotiators intended that the III (b) water be awarded to Arizona in any future lower-basin settlement. That water, they insisted, was to go to Arizona as compensation for inclusion of the Gila within the provisions of the compact. Arizona's attorneys had no documentary proof to substantiate their claim, but they had interviewed Norviel, Lewis, and Campbell—all of whom agreed that the 1,000,000 acre-feet was intended for Arizona.[16] The attorneys hoped that the other drafters of the compact would support their claim.

Had Arizonans been successful in locating a copy of the minutes of the compact negotiations, they would have found corroboration for their claim. The minutes, as noted earlier, reveal that article III (b) was added in response to Norviel's protests concerning the lower-basin tributaries, especially the Gila. The minutes do not, however, contain any discussion of a future lower-basin pact allocating the III (b) water to Arizona. But omission does not mean that such a pact was not discussed. A reading of the minutes indicates that most of the bargaining that culminated in the acceptance of article III (b) took place during informal talks for which no record was kept.

Despite the lack of a detailed record, the negotiators undoubtedly intended that the water covered by III (b) should be awarded to Arizona. Norviel had nearly single-handedly waged the fight for the lower-basin tributaries. California's W. F. McClure had done almost nothing to help him and, in fact, had been willing to negotiate on the basis of a compact draft that contained no compensation for the tributaries.[17]

But Arizonans overstepped themselves in one particular. They contended that Arizona should never be charged for using more than 1,000,000 acre-feet of Gila River water. This, they suggested,

[16] Arizona, *In the Supreme Court of the United States, . . . State of Arizona vs. State of California et al., Bill to Perpetuate Testimony* (n.p., n.d.), pp. 13, 65–67; Colorado River Commission of Arizona, *Report of the Colorado River Commission of Arizona for Period, February 2, 1933–May 3, 1935* (Prescott, Ariz., 1935), pp. 27–28, 37–54.

[17] Colorado River Commission, "Minutes of the Twelfth Meeting" (Santa Fe, November 12, 1922), pp. 22–23, passim, file 032, Colorado River Project, Bureau of Reclamation Papers.

was also part of the understanding reached by the negotiators.[18] The minutes and other available documents dealing with the Santa Fe meeting do not support such a contention. To be sure, Norviel had tried to obtain compensation for the water of the Gila and the other lower-basin tributaries, but in those attempts he believed he was asking for 3,000,000 acre-feet.[19] Obviously, when he agreed to settle for only the 1,000,000 acre-feet of article III (b), he was settling for much less water than he thought was in the tributaries or even in the Gila alone.[20]

But the Court refused to give Arizona an opportunity to detail fully its arguments or even to present its witnesses. The "proposed testimony," it declared in a unanimous ruling on May 21, 1934, was not "relevant." "The meaning of the Compact . . . can never be material . . . since Arizona refused to ratify." Even if Arizona had ratified and the testimony were relevant, explained the justices, the evidence to be submitted "would not be competent." "There is no allegation that the alleged agreement between the negotiators made in 1922 was called to the attention of Congress in 1928 when enacting the [Boulder Canyon] Act; nor that it was called to the attention of the legislatures of the several States." [21]

This second rejection of an Arizona appeal to the Supreme

---

[18] Arizona, *In the Supreme Court of the United States, . . . Bill to Perpetuate Testimony*, pp. 11, 66.

[19] Colorado River Commission, "Minutes of the Nineteenth Meeting" (Santa Fe, November 19, 1922), Part I, p. 8.

[20] In January, 1923, Arthur Powell Davis estimated the reconstructed flow of the Gila at 2,360,000 acre-feet. He arrived at this figure by combining the mean discharge of the Gila at its mouth (1,070,000 acre-feet) with the amount of water then being consumed upstream (1,290,000 acre-feet). A. P. Davis to Frank Emerson, January 30, 1923, file 032, Colorado River Project, Bureau of Reclamation Papers. Davis also estimated that an additional 1,000,000 acre-feet entered the mainstream from lower-basin tributaries other than the Gila. Colorado River Commission, "Minutes of the Sixteenth Meeting" (November 14, 1922), pp. 17–19. In 1933 Thomas Maddock, an engineer and the secretary of Arizona's Colorado River Commission, estimated the volume of the lower-basin tributaries at more than 2,500,-000 acre-feet. Maddock to George W. P. Hunt, April 2, 1933, Thomas Maddock Papers, Arizona Historical Society, Tucson.

[21] *Arizona v. California et al.*, 292 U.S. 342, 343, 360 (1934).

Court left the state's leaders embittered. Though George W. P. Hunt was no longer governor, his successor, Benjamin B. Moeur, who had taken office in 1933, was as determined an opponent of California as his predecessor.[22] Two months before the Supreme Court handed down its decision, he ordered the Arizona National Guard to prevent the erection of Parker Dam, a proposed structure 150 miles downstream from Hoover Dam that was to serve as the diversion point for California's Metropolitan Water District aqueduct. The presence of about a hundred guardsmen and an Arizona "navy" of one ferryboat proved sufficient force to prevent construction.[23]

The Justice Department then turned to the Supreme Court and asked for an injunction against Arizona. But in April, 1935, the Court denied the request, pointing out that Congress had never specifically authorized construction of Parker Dam. Four months later, when Congress remedied that oversight, Arizona had to permit construction of the Parker Dam diversion works.[24]

Arizonans did not give up entirely, however. In November, 1935, they again appealed to the Supreme Court, this time naming the other basin states as defendants and asking the Court to determine "Arizona's equitable share of the water." They also spelled out some of the elements that would make for an "equitable share": California should "be barred from having or claiming any right" in excess of its self-limitation act, and California should be made liable for any increase in Mexican water use that resulted from "works being constructed by or for California." [25] The implications of Arizona's second demand were obvious, but those of the first were less so.

The Court, however, refused to offer an interpretation. In May, 1936, the justices threw out the case, explaining that the United

[22] Hunt was governor until 1929, when he was succeeded by John C. Phillips, who had defeated him for reelection. Hunt was then reelected in 1930 and remained in office until Moeur took over in 1933.

[23] Clayburn C. Elder, "Clayburn C. Elder, Hydrographic Engineer" (Oral History Program, University of California, Los Angeles, 1969), pp. 88–90; Remi Nadeau, *The Water Seekers* (New York, 1950), p. 233.

[24] *U.S.* v. *Arizona*, 295 U.S. 174 (1935); "Hoover Dam Documents," pp. 131–132.

[25] *Arizona* v. *California et al.*, 298 U.S. 559, 560 (1936).

States government, which had vital interests in the river, should have been made a party to the suit. The Court left little doubt, however, that its action would have been the same even if the United States had been a party. As it had done in 1931 following Arizona's first appeal, the Court explained that a "justiciable controversy" would exist only if Arizona could show that its rights were actually being violated and its uses restricted. By noting that there were still millions of acre-feet of water flowing unused in the river, the Court seemed to imply that Arizona would find it difficult to prove that it was being harmed.[26]

V

Though disappointed in court, for eight more years Arizonans stubbornly resisted the compact and continued their futile attempts to reach agreement with California. Then, on February 24, 1944, state leaders performed an about-face and unconditionally ratified the compact. Two weeks earlier, on February 9, they had negotiated a water contract with the secretary of the interior. The contract had left unsettled the dispute with California. It provided for the delivery to Arizona of 2,800,000 acre-feet from the mainstream plus half of "any excess or surplus . . . to the extent such water is available for use in Arizona under . . . [the] compact." The contract, however, did not specify "what part, if any, is excess or surplus waters unapportioned by said Compact." [27] Arizona had tried to get a contract favorable to its interests, but Harold Ickes, now secretary of the interior, had refused to give it to the state. Like his predecessor, Ray Lyman Wilbur, he believed that Arizona and California should settle their differences themselves or get the Supreme Court to do it for them.

[26] Ibid., 562, 567, 570, 572.

[27] Memo from Harold L. Ickes, February 9, 1944, file 032, Colorado River, Papers of the Secretary of the Interior. A copy of the Arizona contract can be found in "Hoover Dam Documents," pp. A559–A565. See also memo from H. W. Bashore, May 22, 1943, file 8.8, Colorado River, Bureau of Reclamation Papers; memo from H. W. Bashore to Secretary of the Interior, April 26, 1943, file 032, Colorado River Compact—Arizona Ratification, Bureau of Reclamation Papers; memo from S. O. Harper, April 20, 1943, file 032.5, Colorado River, Bureau of Reclamation Papers.

Arizonans were disappointed by Ickes's attitude, but several recent developments had persuaded them that they had no choice but to join the other states in approving the compact. One of these developments had been the negotiation of a treaty between the United States and Mexico covering the waters of the Colorado River.

On February 3, 1944, only three weeks before the Arizona legislature ratified the pact, the United States had signed a treaty awarding Mexico 1,500,000 acre-feet. This was far more water than many basin leaders, particularly those in California, believed Mexico deserved. Californians claimed Mexico deserved only 750,000 acre-feet, the maximum amount that it had used prior to the completion of Hoover Dam in 1936. This was also the amount offered Mexico during futile negotiations in 1929 and 1930, and it was the amount that Californians believed Mexico could be forced to accept once the All-American Canal was completed. That aqueduct had finally been finished in 1940.[28]

But State Department officials contended that the larger amount was fair, and cited as evidence their belief that Mexico was presently using 1,800,000 acre-feet, 300,000 acre-feet more than was awarded by the treaty. They also emphasized the harm that would be done to the Good Neighbor Policy if the United States forced Mexico to accept a smaller amount of water. The repercussions of such a move would be especially serious now because Mexicans, not American capitalists, were farming the lands of the Mexicali Valley. Most of the acreage belonging to the Chandler syndicate had been expropriated by the Mexican government in 1938 and the remainder disposed of in 1944.

Most of the basin states agreed with the State Department's assessment of the situation. Their support, together with pressure from President Franklin D. Roosevelt and his successor, Harry S. Truman, proved decisive. On April 18, 1945, the United States Senate approved the treaty by the overwhelming vote of seventy-six to ten.[29]

[28] For a discussion of the treaty and negotiations with Mexico over the Colorado River, see Norris Hundley, jr., *Dividing the Waters: A Century of Controversy Between the United States and Mexico* (Berkeley and Los Angeles, 1966).

[29] *Cong. Rec.*, 79 Cong., 1 sess. (1945), pp. 3491–3492; see also Carl Hayden to Thomas Maddock, February 5, 1945, box 2, folder 2,

Though Arizonans were among those recognizing the necessity of the treaty, they realized that it represented a heavy drain on the river. Unless they ratified the compact and took steps to develop their lands, they might find that California and Mexico would leave them little or no water. This point was dramatically made during the hearings on the Mexican treaty when the Bureau of Reclamation issued a report on the future water supply of the lower basin. That report, drawing upon more accurate gaugings made since the compact was negotiated, revealed that the water supply was even less than the Sibert board had calculated in 1929. During a future dry decade, such as the one that had occurred between 1931 and 1940, the volume of water available below Hoover Dam would be less than 7,000,000 acre-feet annually. This amount would obviously not be enough to satisfy the lower-basin demands on the mainstream, which now totaled 8,462,000 acre-feet (Arizona, 2,800,000 acre-feet; Nevada, 300,000 acre-feet; and California, 5,372,000 acre-feet). Then, too, there was the new Mexican burden, half of which had to be supplied by the lower states. Many argued that Mexico's share could be met mostly with return flow that would cross the border regardless of what the United States might do. Even so, calculations revealed that during a future drought, there would be a shortage. Though the shortage could be temporarily met by extra releases from Hoover Dam storage, the drawdown on the reservoir would result in power losses; and if the drought lasted more than thirteen years, the reservoir would be exhausted.[30]

But long before the Reclamation Bureau issued its report, Arizonans had begun facing an internal crisis that caused them to change their minds about the compact. During the previous two decades, the state's population had increased from 334,000 in 1920 to 500,000 in 1940, a jump of 67 percent. Nearly all of this growth took place in the central Arizona counties of Maricopa

Thomas Maddock Papers, Arizona State University Library, Tempe. Many Americans also favored the treaty because it divided with Mexico the waters of the lower Rio Grande, thus resolving a long-standing dispute over that river.

[30] Senate Committee on Foreign Relations, *Hearings on Water Treaty with Mexico,* 79 Cong., 1 sess. (1945), p. 1760; "Water Supply Below Boulder Dam," *S. Doc. 39,* 79 Cong., 1 sess. (1945), part I, pp. 6–8.

and Pima, where Phoenix and Tucson are located. By 1944, the year that Arizona approved the compact, the state's population had increased by an additional 200,000. This growth in numbers was serious enough, but it had been accompanied by a declining water supply. Though the Gila represented a vital resource for central Arizona, most of the state's water came from wells that were rapidly nearing exhaustion. Moreover, the years from 1938 through 1940 were among the driest on record, and Arizona's dams were left nearly empty.[31]

The decline in stream flow increased the demands on the limited groundwater supply, dealt agriculture a severe blow, and created a critical power shortage that threatened both industry and the vital water-pumping operations. In 1939 the Bureau of Reclamation constructed an emergency line bringing in electricity from Hoover Dam, but the power crisis nevertheless did not abate until the heavy rainfall of 1941.[32]

The decision by Arizona to accept Hoover Dam energy, even though only on an emergency basis, represented a major step in its move to accept the compact. Arizona and Nevada had been guaranteed an allotment of power by the secretary of the interior, but Arizona had thus far steadfastly refused to negotiate the necessary contract. Its refusal reflected not only its distaste for the Boulder Canyon Act and the compact, but also the vigorous opposition of the state's power companies to the sale of cheap Hoover Dam electricity within Arizona. But the power shortage and the fact that Arizona's power rates were among the highest in the nation caused most Arizonans to doubt the wisdom of their stand on the pact.[33]

[31] U.S. Bureau of the Census, *Sixteenth Census of the United States: 1940—Population,* vol. I, *Number of Inhabitants* (Washington, D.C., 1942), pp. 89–91; idem, *Statistical Abstract of the United States, 1952* (Washington, D.C., 1952), p. 11; Senate Committee on Irrigation and Reclamation, *Hearings on Arizona Water Resources,* S. *Res. 304,* 78 Cong., 2 sess. (1945), pp. 1, 42, passim.

[32] U.S. Secretary of the Interior, *Annual Report, 1939* (Washington, D.C., 1930), pp. 195–196; U.S. Federal Power Commission, *Arizona Power Survey* (Washington, D.C., March 1942), p. 11.

[33] N. D. Houghton, "Problems in Public Power Administration in the Southwest—Some Arizona Applications," *Western Political Quarterly* IV (1951): 124; Twentieth Century Fund, *Electric Power and Government Policy* (New York, 1948), p. 212.

Taking the lead in persuading the legislature to reverse its stand on the compact was Governor Sidney P. Osborn, a Democrat who felt no obligation to maintain the tradition of opposition established by former Democratic Governor Hunt. Osborn also believed that Arizona had exhausted its legal remedies and had no chance of settling satisfactorily its differences with California. Under the circumstances, the wisest course seemed to lie in ratification of the compact and then an appeal to Congress for funds to bring in needed Colorado River water to supplement the already overdrawn local supply and to develop new lands. "With the passage by Congress of the Boulder Canyon Project Act in 1928," Osborn told the state legislature in 1943, "the era of theorizing about the Colorado's riches ended. Whatever our previous opinions about the best place or the best plan for utilizing its water or the fairest basis for dividing its power, we now can only recognize that the decisions have been made, and dam has been constructed." [34]

Despite the strong opposition to Osborn's advice from the state's utility companies and Fred Colter's Highline Reclamation Association, the legislature approved the compact by wide margins in 1944. Only two members of the state senate and six of the house voted against it.[35]

VI

Arizona's approval of the compact represented a dramatic step in basin politics. The move, however, did not assure Arizona any water. Congress would first have to authorize the necessary dams and canals. For a time, prospects looked good. The Reclamation Bureau reexamined earlier proposals to divert water to the central part of the state and in December, 1947, unveiled its plan for an enormous undertaking, the Central Arizona Project (CAP).[36]

[34] *Journal of the Senate: Sixteenth Legislature of the State of Arizona, 1943* (Phoenix, 1943), pp. 89–90.

[35] *Journal of the Senate: First Special Session—Sixteenth Legislature of the State of Arizona, 1944* (Phoenix, 1944), pp. 38–39; *Journal of the House of Representatives: First Special Session—Sixteenth Legislature of the State of Arizona, 1944* (Phoenix, 1944), p. 60.

[36] "Central Arizona Project," *H. Doc. 136*, 81 Cong., 1 sess. (1949), pp. 131 et seq.

A resurrection of the old highline canal scheme, this billion-dollar proposal was now thought to be economically feasible. It called for the construction of a 241-mile-long aqueduct to bring some 1,200,000 acre-feet of water from Lake Havasu behind Parker Dam to the fast-growing Phoenix and Tucson areas.

But the secretary of the interior also noted that, if Arizona's claims to mainstream water were not valid, then "there will be no dependable water supply available from the Colorado River for this diversion." [37] Despite the warning, Arizonans introduced a bill to authorize the CAP, but that measure as well as similar bills introduced during the next three years failed to win congressional approval. Stiff resistance came from those believing the project was an extravagance and an unwarranted drain on the national treasury to help farmers who had overextended themselves. But the major opposition came from Californians, who argued that Arizona was attempting to use water that did not belong to it. Faced with the conflicting claims of the two states, Congress refused to authorize the CAP on the grounds that it would be foolish to invest in a project for which no water might be available.[38]

Congress's refusal to act proved bitterly disappointing to Arizonans, especially now that they also had the upper basin on their minds. In 1948 the upper states had negotiated a supplementary agreement dividing among themselves the water apportioned to them by the compact. Because of their slower development, they had not immediately felt the necessity to divide their share of the water. Before 1946, only one major project, the Colorado–Big Thompson, had been initiated in the upper basin. In 1946, however, the Reclamation Bureau, following an inventory of potential projects, had formally announced that there would be insufficient water for all of them. Until the states had divided the water among themselves, no new projects would receive the bureau's approval.[39]

[37] J. A. Krug to Hugh Butler, September 16, 1948, box 38, folder 27, Carl Hayden Papers, Arizona State University Library, Tempe; "Central Arizona Project," p. 3.

[38] House Committee on Interior and Insular Affairs, *Hearings on the Central Arizona Project, H.R. 1500 and H.R. 1501,* 82 Cong., 1 sess. (1951), pp. 739–756, passim.

[39] U.S. Bureau of Reclamation, *The Colorado River: A Comprehensive Departmental Report on the Development of the Water Re-*

In July, 1946, representatives of the upper states had met at Cheyenne, Wyoming, to plan their strategy. During the next two years, they had gathered technical data and held field meetings to obtain the opinions of local water users. Then, in July, 1948, during a three-week conference in Vernal, Utah, they had hammered out the major provisions of a tentative agreement allocating 51.75 percent of the upper-basin share to Colorado, 11.25 percent to New Mexico, 23 percent to Utah, and 14 percent to Wyoming. Percentages had been adopted because of the uncertainty over how much water would remain after the upper basin had met its obligation to the lower states. Only Arizona, which had a small part of its territory in the upper basin, had received a flat grant of 50,000 acre-feet a year. The agreement had gone significantly beyond the compact of 1922 by providing for "an interstate administrative agency"—the Upper Colorado River Commission—composed of a representative from each upper-basin state and the federal government. The agency was charged with determining the use of each state and with curtailing water use, if that became necessary, to meet the obligations of the 1922 compact or the treaty with Mexico. The tentative agreement had then been circulated among leaders within each of the states before being officially signed in Santa Fe on October 11, 1948. By early 1949 it had been ratified by all five states and Congress.[40]

Though Arizonans approved the upper-basin pact, they recognized that it would pave the way for the upper states to use all their water. No surplus could be expected from that quarter. This realization prompted Arizonans to intensify their appeal for congressional approval of the Central Arizona Project. "Without water from the Colorado River," declared Senators Carl Hayden and Ernest W. McFarland of Arizona in a joint appeal to their Senate colleagues, "Arizona is doomed to wither away to the point of disaster. This is a crisis for our state." [41] Most congress-

sources of the Colorado River Basin for Review Prior to Submission to the Congress (Washington, D.C., 1946), p. 21.

[40] Jean S. Breitenstein, "The Upper Colorado River Basin Compact," *State Government* XXII (1949): 214–216, 225; "Hoover Dam Documents," pp. 30–31; House Committee on Public Lands, Subcommittee on Irrigation and Reclamation, *Hearings on the Upper Colorado River Basin Compact,* 81 Cong., 1 sess. (1949), pp. 78–80.

[41] Carl Hayden and Ernest W. McFarland to U.S. senators, April 8, 1949, box 38, folder 25, Hayden Papers.

men were sympathetic, but they refused to approve the Arizona project until lower-basin water rights had been settled. Finally, in 1952 Arizonans decided that the only way they could get the water they needed was to appeal once more to the Supreme Court.

VII

When Arizona filed suit in 1952, the amount of water in the river still exceeded current uses. But Arizonans believed they had evidence to demonstrate the harm that would be done them if the Court refused to settle the dispute with California. Any delay, they insisted, would aid Californians, who were now diverting water in excess of 4,400,000 acre-feet.

The Court agreed to take the case under submission. The subsequent trial proved to be among the most complicated and hotly debated in Supreme Court history. It involved the earlier dispute over the status of Arizona's tributaries as well as such other important questions as water for federally owned lands.[42] The federal government intervened to defend its interests and also to protect the rights of Indians living on some twenty-five reservations in the lower basin. Largely ignored heretofore, the Indians had attracted attention following the Second World War, as many white Americans became more conscious of the social and economic inequities in the status of the country's ethnic minorities. The federal government reflected the growing national awareness by urging the Court to determine Indian water rights so that significant development could take place on the reservations. Much to the chagrin of the attorneys from Arizona, where most of the reservation land was located, the federal lawyers asked that the Indians be assured enough water to develop all their irrigable lands, not just the acreage then in cultivation.

The case was long and expensive as well as hard fought. It lasted eleven years, required the services of a special master, cost nearly $5 million, and prompted important shifts in position as the two states jockeyed for advantage. Some 340 witnesses testified and nearly fifty lawyers participated before the opinion was

[42] Simon H. Rifkind, *Report of the Special Master on Arizona v. California* (n.p., December 5, 1960), pp. 1–6, 254, passim.

finally announced on June 3, 1963, followed by the decree on March 9, 1964.[43]

The decision represented a tremendous victory for Arizona and a lesser, though nonetheless important, one for the Indians. Though the Court refrained from adjudicating the rights of the Indians living along the lower-basin tributaries, it sustained completely the federal government's claims for the five reservations along the mainstream—Chemehuevi, Cocopah, Yuma, Colorado River, and Fort Mohave. Citing as a precedent the 1908 case of *Winters v. U.S.*, the Court declared that "these reservations . . . were not limited to land, but included waters as well. . . . It is impossible to believe that when Congress created the great Colorado River Indian Reservation and when the Executive Department of this Nation created the other reservations they were unaware that most of the lands were of the desert kind—hot, scorching sands—and that water from the river would be essential to the life of the Indian people and to the animals they hunted and the crops they raised." The Court agreed with the special master that the Indians possessed rights to "enough water"—about a million acre-feet—"to irrigate all the practicably irrigable acreage on the reservations" and that "all uses of mainstream water within a State are to be charged against that State's apportionment." [44] The Court also stipulated that the rights of the Indians dated from the creation of the reservations and were superior to later non-Indian rights, even if those rights were based on uses initiated *before* the Indians had begun diverting water. Since some of the Indian lands had been set aside as early as 1865 and none later than 1917, this announcement of the Court strengthened considerably Indian rights to Colorado River water.[45]

[43] *Arizona v. California et al.*, 373 U.S. 546 (1963), 376 U.S. 340 (1964); Rifkind, *Special Master*, pp. 1–3; Erwin Cooper, *Aqueduct Empire: A Guide to Water in California—Its Turbulent History and Its Management Today* (Glendale, Calif., 1968), p. 312.

[44] *Arizona v. California et al.*, 373 U.S. 596, 598–601 (1963); cf. *Winters v. U.S.*, 207 U.S. 564 (1908). See also *Arizona v. California et al.*, 376 U.S. 344–345 (1964).

[45] But it did not strengthen them as much as the Indians would have liked. Originally the U.S. attorney general had petitioned the Court to declare the Indians' rights "prior and superior to the rights" of all non-Indians. Under lower-state pressure, however, he deleted

But Arizona won the greater victory, though it did so in a way that took nearly everyone by surprise. Cutting through the extensive testimony and legal technicalities, the Court grounded its opinion not on the compact, but rather on the thirty-five-year-old Boulder Canyon Act. In that measure, declared the Court in a five-to-three decision, Congress "intended to and did create its own comprehensive scheme for . . . apportionment." According to the justices, Congress in 1928 had done more than merely *suggest* a lower-basin compact in section 4(a) of the act. It had actually *authorized* the secretary of the interior to use his contract power to implement a lower-basin pact—a pact "leaving each State its tributaries" and a pact in which "Congress decided that a fair division of the first 7,500,000 acre-feet of . . . mainstream waters would give 4,400,000 acre-feet to California, 2,800,000 to Arizona, and 300,000 to Nevada." [46] In addition, claimed the Court, the secretary possessed the authority to determine how future surpluses and shortages would be divided among the states.

Arizonans were elated. By obtaining 2,800,000 acre-feet plus their tributaries, they acquired virtually everything they had been fighting for. The victory even seemed to soften the heavy loss of water to the Indians. Though the Court said nothing about the compact's controversial article III (b), its decision had the effect of awarding to Arizona the 1,000,000 acre-feet embraced by that provision. Indeed, the decision actually had an even more far-reaching effect. It distinctly implied that article III (b) and Arizona's tributaries were one and the same, despite the fact that the article mentions only 1,000,000 acre-feet, whereas Arizona's tributaries have a total runoff of considerably more water. [47]

---

these words from his petition. William H. Veeder, "Federal Encroachment on Indian Water Rights and the Impairment of Reservation Development," in U.S. Congress, Joint Economic Committee, "Toward Economic Development for Native American Communities," *Joint Committee Print*, 91 Cong., 1 sess. (1969), p. 513.

[46] *Arizona* v. *California et al.*, 373 U.S. 564, 565 (1963).

[47] The estimate of the water in Arizona's tributaries has varied significantly over the years. As noted earlier in this study, some experts, at the time that the compact was being negotiated, placed the figure as high as 3,000,000 acre-feet. It is interesting to observe that Californians, who naturally wanted to charge Arizona for as much of

Californians were naturally critical of the decision, and they were joined by many others who accused the Court of misreading the intent of Congress, a charge that has been corroborated in a detailed analysis of the decision.[48] They also denounced the Court for eroding the rights of the states, since the decision represented the first time that the Court had discovered a device, congressional apportionment, for decreeing rights to interstate streams. Heretofore, water rights had been determined only by interstate compact or by the Supreme Court itself. Now a third way had been discovered; and though it had taken the Court thirty-five years after Congress had acted to make this "discovery," the results were nonetheless of great significance.

Also of far-reaching importance—indeed, according to most legal scholars, "the real bombshell"—was the Court's decision on how shortages and surpluses were to be handled. Not only had the secretary been authorized by Congress to allocate shortages and surpluses among the states, announced the Court, he had also been empowered to make such allocations among the water users *within* each state.[49] This finding marked a sharp break with the past, for previously each state had determined who could legally use water within its boundaries. This state authority had followed logically from the long-established practice of allowing states to determine the water laws that would govern their citizens. Now, however, according to the Court, the secretary had been empowered by Congress to abrogate state water law in

_____

her tributary water as possible, suggested a considerably smaller figure during the trial in the 1963 *Arizona* v. *California* case. They stated that the total "dependable supply" available to Arizona from the lower-basin tributaries was 1,797,500 acre-feet. California, *In the Supreme Court of the United States, . . . Arizona v. California, . . . Opening Brief of the California Defendants in Support of Their Exceptions to the Report of the Special Master* (Los Angeles, 1961), p. 22.

[48] Norris Hundley, jr., "Clio Nods: *Arizona* v. *California* and the Boulder Canyon Act—A Reassessment," *Western Historical Quarterly* III (1972): 17–51.

[49] Naturally, if it wished, Congress could tell the secretary how to apportion water in the event of a shortage or surplus. Several years later, in the Colorado River Basin Project Act of 1968, it did just that by instructing the secretary on how to handle lower-basin shortages. U.S., *Statutes at Large*, LXXXII: 888.

those instances where water had been secured by contract from federal reclamation projects. Essentially what it all meant was that henceforth Congress, not state law, could determine priorities to Colorado River water within each lower-basin state. Equally important, if Congress could exercise such authority on the Colorado, it could also do so on other streams where there were federal reclamation projects.

Though the justices stated that Congress derived its new authority over apportionment from the navigation clause of the constitution, they also hinted that Congress could invoke the "general welfare" clause, and thereby divide the waters of non-navigable as well as navigable streams.[50] In short, by this action Congress's authority over the West's water courses increased by a quantum jump. "This decision," affirmed legal experts, "represents a monumental victory for advocates of national control" and "a major departure from principles and practices of long standing." [51]

The most immediate effect of the decision, however, was also the most obvious: the Arizona-California controversy seemed to be over at last.

[50] *Arizona* v. *California et al.*, 373 U.S. 587 (1963). Law professor Frank J. Trelease suggests that Congress might also divide waters by merely asserting authority over the waters stored in federally constructed dams. Congress might also do the same thing by invoking the war power, the power over international streams, or the right to improve public lands. See Frank J. Trelease, "Arizona v. California: Allocation of Water to People, States, and Nation," in Philip B. Kurland, ed., *The Supreme Court Review, 1963* (Chicago, 1963), p. 181.

[51] Joseph L. Sax, "Problems of Federalism in Reclamation Law," *University of Colorado Law Review* XXXVII (1964–1965): 55; David Haber, "Arizona v. California—A Brief Review," *Natural Resources Journal* IV (1964–1965): 21; Trelease, "Arizona v. California," p. 184; Charles J. Meyers, "The Colorado River," *Stanford Law Review* XIX (1966–1967): 64; Edward W. Clyde, "The Colorado River Decision—1963," *Utah Law Review* VIII (1962–1964): 312; cf. Mark Wilmer, "*Arizona* v. *California*: A Statutory Construction Case," *Arizona Law Review* VI (1964–1965): 40–64.

10

Epilogue

The 1963 decision of the Supreme Court settled the major water-supply controversy over the lower Colorado, but the irony in the Court's action was unmistakable. The compact had been advocated as a way to avoid costly and time-consuming litigation, yet on three different occasions Arizona had gone to the Supreme Court for redress. The compact's proponents had also seen it as a means of preventing federal encroachment in Colorado River matters, yet it had been a principal cause for the 1963 decision, which gave Congress powers that would have shocked the negotiators in 1922 as well as the proponents of the Boulder Canyon Act in 1928. The decision would have even surprised earlier Supreme Court justices, for when the Court had rejected Arizona's second appeal in 1934, it observed that the Boulder Canyon Act did "not purport to apportion [water] among the states of the lower basin." [1]

I

There is still another irony—perhaps the most striking of all. The upper states had promoted the compact as a means of assur-

[1] *Arizona* v. *California et al.*, 292 U.S. 357 (1934).

ing themselves of unrestricted development. By the time the Court acted in 1963, it was clear that development in the upper basin would be restricted—perhaps even more than that in the lower basin. Data accumulated by the special master for the 1963 decision revealed that the reconstructed, or virgin, flow of the Colorado River at Lee's Ferry is about 14,000,000 acre-feet. This is the runoff as measured between 1922 and 1956, a period when improved gauging equipment was used at major stations along the river. Measurements made since 1956 indicate that the runoff has remained approximately the same.[2] This news represents a serious setback for the upper states. Such a conclusion is made clear by a glance at article III (d) of the compact. According to that provision, the upper basin cannot "cause the flow of the river at Lee Ferry to be depleted below an aggregate of 75,000,-000 acre-feet for any period of ten consecutive years." This statement essentially means, of course, an annual delivery of 7,500,000 acre-feet.[3] But if the upper states contribute only 14,000,000 acre-feet annually to the mainstream, they will obviously have to limit considerably their future consumptive uses in order to fulfill their obligation to the lower basin. They can, it should be noted, improve their situation through water-salvage programs devised to capture some of the runoff from up-river tributaries that is now lost to evaporation and has not been counted in calculations of reconstructed stream flow at Lee's Ferry. But these steps offer little real consolation. New Mexico state engineer S. E. Reynolds estimates that even with additional storage facilities the upper

[2] Simon H. Rifkind, *Report of the Special Master on Arizona v. California* (n.p., December 5, 1960), p. 118; John W. Mueller, acting regional director, Upper Colorado Regional Office, U.S. Bureau of Reclamation, to the author, October 24, 1973; Myron B. Holburt, chief engineer, Colorado River Board of California, to the author, September 29, 1973.

[3] It should be noted that delivery of 7,500,000 acre-feet at Lee's Ferry does not mean that there will be that much water available for use in the lower basin. Considerable water is lost to evaporation between Lee's Ferry and the downstream diversion points. Some of the losses are offset by inflow below Lee's Ferry, but the net loss is approximately 500,000 acre-feet. "Water Supply below Boulder Dam," S. *Doc.* 39, 79 Cong., 1 sess. (1945), part 1, p. 8; interview with Vernon E. Valantine, principal hydraulic engineer, Colorado River Board of California, October 23, 1974.

states will be limited to about 6,600,000 acre-feet, nearly a million acre-feet less than anticipated.[4]

Indeed, the upper states may eventually have to curtail their uses even more in order to share the burden of the Mexican treaty. According to article III (c) of the compact, if there is not enough surplus water to supply Mexico, then each basin must supply half the Mexican obligation. This obligation, however, is easier to describe than to carry out, for the two basins disagree over how to determine the existence of a surplus. At the root of their disagreement is a variation on the decades-old controversy over the status of the lower-basin tributaries.[5]

The lower states, especially Arizona, are informally insisting that the lower-river tributaries should not be counted in determining a surplus. If these tributaries are excluded, explain the lower states, then the upper basin's share of the Mexican burden is approximately 900,000 acre-feet (half the total treaty obligation of 1,500,000 acre-feet plus 150,000 acre-feet for evaporation losses).[6] The lower states cite as support for their position the 1963 decision of the Supreme Court, which, according to their interpretation, stipulates that Congress, in ratifying the compact, excluded the lower-river tributaries.[7] Not surprisingly, Californians have joined Arizona in advancing this contention, even though it has meant adopting a position in direct contrast to the one California held for years. The explanation for the reversal is self-evident: once Californians had lost their fight with Arizona, they teamed up with their *former* enemy against the *common* enemy—the upper basin.

The upper states naturally reject the lower basin's position. The

[4] S. E. Reynolds to the author, September 12, 1973.

[5] Much of the discussion which follows is based on information provided the author by Wesley E. Steiner, state water engineer of Arizona; Myron Holburt, chief engineer of the Colorado River Board of California; Northcutt Ely, attorney for California and long-time prominent figure in Colorado River matters; S. E. Reynolds, state engineer of New Mexico; William R. Kelly, a Greeley, Colorado, attorney prominent in upper-basin water development; and Floyd Bishop, state engineer of Wyoming.

[6] Myron Holburt to the author, March 28, 1969.

[7] Northcutt Ely to the author, May 14, 1969, July 19, 1972; Wesley E. Steiner to the author, May 26, 1969, January 16, 1973.

RECONSTRUCTED FLOW OF THE COLORADO RIVER AT LEE'S FERRY, 1922–1972

Year	Acre-feet	Year	Acre-feet
1922.	18,305,000	1949.	16,376,000
1923.	18,269,000	1950.	12,894,000
1924.	14,201,000	1951.	11,647,000
1925.	13,033,000	1952.	20,290,000
1926.	15,853,000	1953.	10,670,000
1927.	18,616,000	1954.	7,900,000
1928.	17,279,000	1955.	9,150,000
1929.	21,428,000	1956.	10,720,000
1930.	14,885,000	1957.	20,095,000
1931.	7,769,000	1958.	16,489,000
1932.	17,243,000	1959.	8,609,000
1933.	11,356,000	1960.	11,263,000
1934.	5,640,000	1961.	8,457,000
1935.	11,549,000	1962.	17,299,000
1936.	13,800,000	1963.	8,450,000
1937.	13,740,000	1964.	10,156,000
1938.	17,545,000	1965.	18,913,000
1939.	11,075,000	1966.	11,208,000
1940.	8,601,000	1967.	11,907,000
1941.	18,148,000	1968.	13,664,000
1942.	19,125,000	1969.	14,386,000
1943.	13,103,000	1970.	15,405,000
1944.	15,154,000	1971.	14,846,000
1945.	13,410,000	1972.	11,905,000
1946.	10,426,000		
1947.	15,473,000	Mean.	13,790,900
1948.	15,613,000		

SOURCES: Simon H. Rifkind, *Report of the Special Master on Arizona v. California* (n.p., December 5, 1960), p. 118; John W. Mueller, acting regional director, Upper Colorado Regional Office, U.S. Bureau of Reclamation, to the author, October 24, 1973; Myron Holburt, chief engineer, Colorado River Board of California, to the author, September 29, 1973.

Supreme Court, they admit, awarded Arizona the water of its tributaries in its dispute with California, but, they insist, it did not eliminate the tributaries from the compact itself. They ground their argument on the language of the compact, especially in articles I and II. Those articles specify that the waters being divided belong to the "Colorado River System," which is defined as "that portion of the Colorado River *and its tributaries* within the United States of America." [8] Hence, insist the upper states, the lower-basin tributaries must be counted in determining a surplus. If those tributaries are counted, then the upper states may be required to contribute little or nothing to the Mexican obligation. According to their computations, the tributary water, when added to the flow arriving at Lee's Ferry, is virtually sufficient to satisfy the lower basin's share and also to meet the entire Mexican obligation.

Should the conflicting parties—or the Supreme Court, if the dispute is taken before it—decide to abide by the intentions of the compact's negotiators, then the upper basin's position would prevail. There are several reasons, other than the ones currently offered by the upper states, for arriving at this conclusion. The documentary record of the compact negotiations reveals that no Colorado River waters were excluded from that agreement. Time and again, Norviel had tried to exclude Arizona's tributaries, but had failed; he had settled, finally, for article III (b), the grant of only an additional 1,000,000 acre-feet to the lower basin. But even that additional water was not to be excluded when calculating whether a surplus existed. The compact itself made this fact clear in article III (c), where the word "surplus" was defined as those "waters . . . over and above the aggregate of the quantities specified in paragraphs (a) *and* (b)." [9]

Herbert Hoover also made public statements in support of this view. On January 27, 1923, only two months after the compact had been negotiated, he responded to a query from Arizona's Carl Hayden with unequivocal explicitness. "This term [Colorado River System] is defined in article II as covering the entire river and its tributaries in the United States. No other term could be used," insisted Hoover, "as the duty of the commission was to divide *all* the water of the river. It serves to make it clear that this was what the commission intended to do and prevents any state from contending that, since a certain tributary rises and empties within its boundaries and is therefore not an interstate stream, it may use its waters without reference to the terms of

[8] Emphasis added.
[9] Emphasis added.

the compact. The plan covers *all the waters of the river and all its tributaries,* and the term referred to leaves that situation beyond doubt." [10]

But if the Supreme Court is asked to decide this matter, it may, as it has before, ignore the intentions of the compact's negotiators or misconstrue the views of the advocates of the Boulder Canyon Act. To second-guess the Court or the states themselves as they grapple with this problem is a fruitless exercise, however. The options are simply too numerous. But even if all parties should agree to count the tributaries in determining a surplus, they would still have to face the question of just *how much* water is in those tributaries. This issue could be a major stumbling block to settlement, since over the years basin leaders have disagreed sharply about not only the amount of tributary water but also the scientific method to be used in determining that amount. More to the point is the fact that much has happened since 1922, and greater injustice might be done by adhering to a strict interpretation of the compact than by seeking a different solution that would reflect today's needs and the sharply reduced estimates of stream flow.

II

The surplus question is not the only point of disagreement between the basins. Another area of contention involves the meaning of the compact phrase "beneficial consumptive use." Though the drafters of the pact apportioned water to each basin for "beneficial consumptive use," they neglected to say how such use was to be measured. According to many lower-basin officials, especially Californians, use should be determined merely by deducting the volume of return flow from the volume of the total diversions made. The upper states insist that a different technique of measurement should be employed. They contend that the upper basin should be charged only for the amount of water by which it "depletes" the flow of the river at Lee's Ferry. In other words, they do not wish to be charged for water captured upstream that would otherwise be lost to evaporation before reach-

[10] Herbert Hoover to Carl Hayden, January 27, 1923, in *Cong. Rec.,* 67 Cong., 4 sess. (1923), p. 2710 (emphasis added).

ing Lee's Ferry. Just how much additional water they could salvage and use in this fashion is uncertain, but some estimates run as high as 200,000 acre-feet.[11] Naturally Californians, whose state contributes little water to the river and therefore cannot benefit by application of the depletion theory, demand that the upper basin be charged for its actual uses, wherever they occur.

Arizonans now support California's demand, although before the last *Arizona* v. *California* case, they had often joined the upper basin in advancing the depletion theory. They did so because, like the upper states, they had tributaries of their own; and they understandably wanted to be charged only for the amount by which their uses depleted the mainstream, not for their actual consumptive uses, which were considerably greater. Now that they believe that the Supreme Court has excluded their tributaries from the compact, however, they see their position as similar to California's. In other words, they believe that at least so far as the compact is concerned, Arizona, like California, possesses no tributaries. Future Court decisions may reveal that they have erred in this interpretation of the Court's decision and that their tributaries have not been exempted from the compact's provisions. Until then, however, their interests, as opposed to those of the upper basin, appear to be similar to California's; and thus they have joined Californians in resisting the depletion method for measuring water use.

Though the compact itself is silent about how "consumptive use" is to be measured, there seems little doubt that the drafters intended for each basin to be charged for *all* uses, regardless of where they take place in the basin. The debate over the Gila during the compact negotiations in 1922 seems to testify to such an interpretation. So, too, do the compact provisions and Hoover's statement indicating that the commissioners were dividing the waters of the entire river *system*, not just the flow reaching Lee's Ferry. Moreover, the negotiators of the compact were rather explicit about their intentions. In his report of December 15, 1922, to the Colorado legislature, Delph Carpenter, the father of the

[11] House Committee on Public Lands, Subcommittee on Irrigation and Reclamation, *Hearings on the Upper Colorado River Basin Compact*, 81 Cong., 1 sess. (1949), pp. 92–95, 100, 147; John W. Mueller, acting regional director, Upper Colorado Regional Office, U.S. Bureau of Reclamation, to the author, October 24, 1973.

compact and the principal upper-basin spokesman, defined beneficial consumptive use as most lower-basin spokesmen are now
defining it—diversions minus the return flow. "It means the
amount of water consumed and lost to the river during uses of
the water diverted," explained Carpenter. "Generally speaking,
it is the difference between the aggregate diverted and the aggregate return flow. It is the net loss occurring through beneficial
uses." [12]

Regardless of the meaning of "consumptive use," however, it
is clear that the compact negotiators, in their haste to settle the
question of apportionment, failed to consider adequately the
enormity of the measurement problem. The difficulty is especially
serious in the upper basin, where, according to a Colorado official,
"there are literally thousands of diversions, many of which are
on tributaries and of very small quantities. To require installation
of automatic measuring devices on each headgate . . . is to be
utterly unrealistic and impractical." [13]

Perhaps the increasing value of water will eventually make
feasible—even mandatory—the installation of measuring devices.
On the other hand, the two basins may be able to work out a
compromise solution. But whatever the outcome, there seems
little doubt that the dispute will occupy the attention of water
leaders for some time to come.

[12] Delph Carpenter to Oliver H. Shoup, December 15, 1922, Oliver
H. Shoup Papers, Colorado State Archives, Denver. A copy of this
report is in the *Senate Journal of the General Assembly of the State
of Colorado, Twenty-Fourth Session, 1923* (Denver, 1923), pp. 75–
81, esp. 78; see also ibid., p. 892. Arthur Powell Davis gave a definition similar to Carpenter's. *Cong. Rec.*, 67 Cong., 4 sess. (1923),
p. 2714.

[13] Jean S. Breitenstein, "The Upper Colorado River Basin Compact," *State Government* XXII (1949): 216; House Committee on
Public Lands, *Hearings on the Upper Colorado River Basin Compact*, p. 109. The upper basin succeeded in writing its definition of
consumptive use into the upper basin compact of 1948, but the House
and Senate committees that held hearings on the pact approved a
statement stipulating that "Congress, by giving its consent to the
Upper Colorado River Basin Compact, does not commit the United
States to any interpretation of the Colorado River Compact." *Cong.
Rec.*, 81 Cong., 1 sess. (1949), p. 2758.

III

Besides the disagreements over the Mexican burden and the measurement of use, water quality has also emerged as a major issue—an issue not anticipated by the negotiators of the compact and for that reason all the more difficult to settle. The decline in the water supply has led to a conservation program that has created its own problems. Waste of water is looked upon as a cardinal sin, and each acre-foot is used as many times as possible before it is allowed to go downstream. Such intensification of use, combined with high rates of evaporation from reservoirs, has caused the salt content in the river to rise steadily. In 1940 the salinity level at Lee's Ferry was 500 parts of salt per million parts of water (ppm); by 1970 it exceeded 600 ppm. Studies indicate that unless corrective measures are taken, the salt content of the water will continue to rise, going beyond 800 ppm by the year 2000.[14]

Such saline flow sharply increases costs through corrosion of metal pipes and heaters, added soap consumption, increased water-softening costs, and more expensive treatment of water for drinking and industrial purposes. Farmers are especially hard hit, since salt-laden water must be diluted with fresh runoff or used in large quantities in order to maintain a proper salt balance and prevent crop damage. But these options do not please the lower-basin states, for such practices require the application of more water to grow the same crops that were produced with less water a few years earlier.

Many basin spokesmen are urging Congress to assume financial responsibility for costly desalination plants, while others, espe-

[14] Colorado River Board of California, *Need for Controlling Salinity of the Colorado River* (n.p., August, 1970), pp. 24–25, 35, 38. In 1970 the salt content at Imperial Dam was 897 ppm; and at the international boundary above Morelos Dam, it was 1,140 ppm. Maurice N. Langley of the Bureau of Reclamation to the author, February 1, 1973. See also U.S. Dept. of the Interior, Federal Water Pollution Control Administration, *Colorado River Basin Water Quality Control Project, The Mineral Quality Problem in the Colorado River Basin: Appendix B—Physical and Economic Impacts* (Denver, Colo., January, 1970); U.S. Bureau of Reclamation, *Colorado River Water Quality Improvement Program* (Washington, D.C., February, 1972).

cially in the lower states, have tried to alleviate the problem through the use of tile drains, better crop selection, and a host of other techniques. But some lower-basin leaders are also questioning whether the compact cannot be invoked to assert rights to water of a specific quality as well as quantity. They believe that as a minimal concession, the lower states should receive good quality water for the rights that they had already established at the time the compact was ratified. By "good quality" they mean water as good as that which they were using in the 1920s. To support their claim, they cite article VIII of the pact, which stipulates that "present perfected rights . . . are unimpaired" by the agreement.[15] Of course, when that provision was added, the negotiators were not thinking of water quality. They realized that increased uses would bring increased salinity, but as noted earlier in this study, they believed that the water supply would always be great enough to prevent serious deterioration in quality.

Efforts to read a water-quality standard into the compact have been resisted by the upper states, which have received some encouragement from the way the United States has handled a similar difficulty with Mexico. The treaty of 1944 guaranteed Mexico a specific quantity of water, but the agreement said nothing about quality. In 1961, when water containing 2,700 ppm was delivered to Mexico, the Mexican government reacted angrily, claiming a violation of the treaty and insisting on water as good as that which was being used when the treaty was signed. State Department officials expressed regret over reported crop losses in Mexico, but they maintained that the treaty imposed no obligation "with respect to the quality of the water." Nonetheless, in August, 1973, after lengthy negotiations between the two countries, the United States agreed to build a desalination plant at Yuma and to construct other facilities designed to provide a "permanent and definitive solution" to the salinity problem. Though the agreement represents a major step forward, only the future will reveal whether it will bring about the desired results. Skepticism remains because ten years ago, in March, 1965, the United States and Mexico had also reached an agreement that was supposed to have provided for a "permanent and

[15] See, for example, Northcutt Ely to the author, May 14, 1969, and January 15, 1973. For demands that Congress fund the needed desalination plants, see Salt Lake City *Deseret News*, November 28, 1973.

effective solution" of the salinity dispute. If the present agreement is no more successful than the earlier one, this difficulty will continue to sour relations between the two countries. A recent optimistic sign was the overwhelming approval by Congress in June, 1974, of a bill authorizing construction of the projects needed to improve the quality of Mexico's water. The same measure also provided for upstream salt-control projects in Nevada, Utah, and Colorado. In signing the bill, however, former President Richard Nixon declared that "the financial arrangement for the development of these projects is, to a large extent, contrary to those policies established by this Administration and the Congress." Those policies, he explained, called "for placing most of the financial responsibility for pollution abatement on those who are causing the pollution problem, or, in the case of natural pollution, placing the cost of water purification on the water users." He noted ominously that as soon as a national program for controlling pollution had been devised, it might be necessary to "recommend to the Congress that these Colorado River projects be altered." It is too soon to know whether such alterations will be made and, if so, whether they will affect adversely the situation on the lower Colorado.[16]

IV

Other disagreements have emerged over the meaning of the compact, and the future will doubtlessly reveal even more. Of one thing we can be reasonably certain. Most major problems will be traceable to the same root cause: lack of sufficient water.

[16] For information on the water-quality problem, see, among others, *Los Angeles Times*, August 31, 1973; cf. *Los Angeles Times*, March 23, 1965; Colorado River Board of California, *Salinity Problems in the Lower Colorado River Area* (Sacramento, September, 1962), p. 15; Norris Hundley, jr., *Dividing the Waters: A Century of Controversy Between the United States and Mexico* (Berkeley and Los Angeles, 1966), pp. 172–180; *Los Angeles Times*, September 13, November 24, 1970, October 25, November 5, 1972, May 14, 1973, March 6, 1974; "Pollution and Political Boundaries: U.S.–Mexican Environmental Problems," *Natural Resources Journal* XII (October, 1972); Colorado River Board of California, "Chief Engineer's Monthly Report" (July 5, 1974), 5–6, Papers of the Colorado River Board of California.

Some basin leaders have responded to the shortage by calling for a reexamination—perhaps even a rewriting—of the compact. Particularly outspoken are the upper states. The shortage they face is part of the reason, but their attitude is also influenced by the enormous oil reserves that they possess. These reserves— possibly the world's largest—are locked up in vast shale deposits, which contain an estimated 600 billion to 3 trillion barrels of high-grade petroleum. For years the cost of extracting this oil prohibited development, but sharp increases in the demand for fuel and the escalating price of oil produced outside the United States have helped create the current fuel crisis and drastically change the situation. In November, 1973, the federal government, which owns between 70 and 80 percent of the oil-shale lands, agreed to initiate a prototype program by leasing some of its holdings to private developers.[17]

The government's move threatens to precipitate a new crisis, for the processing of shale requires enormous quantities of water —eventually more water than the upper basin has earmarked for that purpose. Adding to the water deficit would be the extraction and conversion of such other upper-basin resources as natural gas and coal, which are increasingly attracting the interest of developers. One solution, which the upper states have thus far rejected, calls for them to divert to energy production some of their water now required for other projects. Many are instead advocating that the upper basin bargain some of its oil for lower-basin water, and they have suggested a reconsideration of the compact as a first step towards achieving such an arrangement. "The potential impact of the demand for energy production on the available water supplies of the Colorado River can become enormous," recently announced ex-Governor John Vanderhoof of Colorado, the state possessing the richest parcels of oil-bearing land. "This demand was never contemplated by the Colorado River Compact. If the Upper Basin states are to furnish energy for the rest of the United States, then the already depleted water allocations may have to be re-examined." [18]

[17] Salt Lake City *Deseret News,* November 28, 1973; *Salt Lake Tribune,* November 28, 1973; *Time* (December 10, 1973), p. 44.

[18] "Remarks of John D. Vanderhoof . . . before the Thirtieth Annual Session of the Colorado River Water Uses Association" (November 26, 1973), p. 2, copy in Papers of the Colorado River Board of California, Los Angeles; *Los Angeles Times,* November 27, 1973.

Lower-state leaders have thus far resisted these overtures from America's "new Arabia," but they recognize that the energy crisis and the demands for national self-sufficiency may force a modification of traditional positions. Even so, few are predicting harmony between the basins and some fear monumental conflicts.

Also among those expressing concern are many preservationist groups which believe that oil-shale production will destroy the natural beauty of large parts of the West. In an attempt to quiet criticism, the Secretary of the Interior recently insisted that the government had devised "rigorous and comprehensive environmental controls," but even he admitted that "risks" are involved. One of the biggest problems is how to dispose of thousands of tons of waste shale. The removal of oil leaves pulverized rock with a volume at least 12 percent greater than that of the shale before it was processed. Moreover, according to findings made in 1974 by a team of scientists at the University of Denver, the "spent" shale contains cancer producing substances that "reach levels of intensity more than double the levels known to induce malignancy in laboratory animals." Environmentalists are also worried about some of the techniques for removing the oil-shale from underground. According to the U.S. Atomic Energy Commission, the use of nuclear explosions to help extract the oil "would require accepting the risk of some leakage of radioactivity during the first few detonations." [19] Other critics are alarmed about the possibility that some developers will employ the open-pit mining method, in which huge machines peel back the grass and sagebrush covering thousands of acres and then gouge out the oil-bearing rock.

But mining techniques aside, oil-shale development would have other consequences. "Such an industry," predicted economist Morris Garnsey more than twenty years ago, "would create whole cities where today there is only desert, and would add at least a half million persons to the population of the region. . . . The oil-shale industry, alone," he observed, "is capable of bringing an industrial revolution to the undeveloped West." [20] While westerners, as well as Americans elsewhere in the country, are divided on the wisdom of ushering in such a revolution, they agree that

[19] *Los Angeles Times,* April 28 and May 12, 1974; *Time* (December 10, 1973), p. 44.

[20] Morris Garnsey, *America's New Frontier: The Mountain West* (New York, 1950), p. 61.

the oil-shale industry would alter radically the face of the American West.

V

In the meantime, efforts are being made to augment the Colorado River basin's water supply. Cloud-seeding experiments have attracted interest, but so far the experiments have failed to produce significant results; and even if they do, there would still remain large parts of the Southwest with few clouds to seed. Major advances have been made in desalting sea water, but the cost is still too expensive for agriculture—and the ocean, too far away from much of the Southwest.[21] Important research is being done on ways to exploit geothermal resources, but a major breakthrough is still years away. According to geologist Robert W. Rex, formerly of the University of California at Riverside and now head of Republic Geothermal, Inc., there are sufficient geothermal resources beneath the Imperial Valley alone to produce not only twenty to thirty thousand megawatts of electricity but also some five to seven million acre-feet of nearly salt-free distilled water, "an ideal blending material for augmentation and quality maintenance of Colorado River water." Rex also believes that major geothermal reserves can be found in all the western states, but he and other scientists admit that there are still "many obstacles to . . . development, some technical, some political, and some economic." [22]

Many westerners are advocating the importation of water into the Colorado River Basin from elsewhere—possibly from the watershed of the Columbia River or even from as far away as

[21] Among those who are optimistic about the future of desalination is A. D. K. Laird, a professor at the University of California and an expert in sea water conversion. He predicts that "real progress will be made by early in the next century," by which time he believes that "desalted water will be cheaper than other means of water-supply augmentation." A. D. K. Laird, "Desalting Technology," in David Seckler, ed., *California Water: A Study in Resource Management* (Berkeley and Los Angeles, 1971), p. 160.

[22] Robert W. Rex, "Geothermal Resources in the Imperial Valley," in Seckler, ed., *California Water*, pp. 197, 199, 204; see also *Los Angeles Times*, January 23, 1974.

coastal Canada and Alaska. Stoutly resisting these schemes are many preservationist groups that believe that such interbasin transfers of water will cause ecological disaster. They have been joined by residents of the Pacific Northwest, who are determined not to surrender their water.[23] A few years ago, their cry was "let the people come to where the water is," but with today's emphasis on zero population growth, they are not anxious to have newcomers join them; and they are even more concerned than before with the environmental consequences of interbasin transfers of water. What the future holds in the way of such transfers is far from certain.

Many Californians have also begun to question their earlier obsession with growth and the water imperialism that has sustained that growth. Nevertheless, state leaders in 1973 celebrated completion of an aqueduct bringing additional water to the southern part of the state from the more humid northern portion. Though more than two million acre-feet will eventually reach the southland when the so-called State Water Plan is in full operation, officials claim that it will not lessen the area's reliance on the Colorado River or preclude the necessity of developing still newer sources of water. "This northern water . . . ," they stated recently, "is expected to take care of our growth for perhaps the next generation, but as growth continues, the time will come when still greater quantities of water will be needed, from still more distant sources." [24]

Some Californians, living as they do near the Pacific Ocean,

[23] See, for example, Robert H. Boyle, John Graves, and T. H. Watkins, *The Water Hustlers* (San Francisco, 1971), pp. 10–14; *Los Angeles Times,* November 6, 1965. A physicist has suggested building a dam across the shallow fifty-six-mile wide Bering Strait. The dam, he claims, would keep cold Arctic water out of the Pacific Ocean and thereby "raise the rainfall in the American Southwest and other areas along the Pacific." Because of the plan's cost and the unpredictability of its effects on the environment, it has found few supporters. *Los Angeles Times,* January 27, 1973.

[24] *Los Angeles Times,* October 25, 1970, May 15 and 19, 1973; Colorado River Board of California, *California's Stake in the Colorado River* (Los Angeles [1967]), p. 3. The recent decline in southern California's growth rate has caused some state experts to conclude that there will be enough water until the year 2020.

continue to hope for a scientific breakthrough that will produce
a cheap method of desalting sea water. But even if this scheme or
the more grandiose plans to divert water from other basins are
carried to a successful completion, the results, say the experts,
are still years—probably decades—away. In the meantime, California, like the other Colorado River states, must continue to live
with a compact based on water-supply estimates long since
proven false.

VI

The grossly inaccurate stream-flow estimates may be attributed
to faulty gauging equipment and to the unusually wet period
during the early part of the twentieth century, but this explanation is only partially satisfactory. It loses force when one realizes
that the men who negotiated the compact sensed that there was
not enough water to satisfy the demands of everyone. Had they
actually believed otherwise, there would have been no need for
the agreement. But the upper states viewed a pact as the best
way to circumvent legal difficulties and to protect themselves
from faster developing areas downstream. Most Californians saw
it as the means for breaking the congressional logjam holding up
development of the lower river. Nevada, though physically unable to divert much water, saw it as the way to get hydroelectricity and revenue that would bring "progress"—more people,
industry, investment capital—to a poor and underdeveloped state.

Only Arizona balked, and its resistance to the compact seems
altogether understandable. The treaty might have resulted in
some benefits—most notably, flood-control for the Yuma area and
cheap hydroelectricity for the state's mining industry and growing cities—but in 1922 and for decades thereafter most Arizonans
believed the compact would bring far greater disadvantages than
advantages. It provided no protection against California; it offered Arizona no equivalent to the Boulder Canyon Project; it
did not curtail Mexico's development; and it prevented Arizona
from establishing prior rights against the upper basin's share of
water. Other considerations, like Governor George W. P. Hunt's
desire to make political capital out of the compact and George
Maxwell's tirades about the "Asian menace" in Mexico, reinforced
the state's resistance, but they were not decisive. Even Hunt

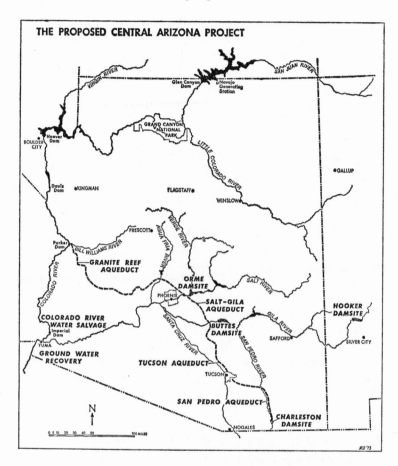

THE PROPOSED CENTRAL ARIZONA PROJECT

seems to have genuinely feared the effects of the compact on
Arizona's future. From the outset he looked upon the Colorado
River as the only resource of importance that could sustain
Arizona's economy once the state's mineral wealth had been
exhausted. A highline canal might be uneconomical in 1922, but
who was to say that it would always be unfeasible? Even those,
like Arthur Powell Davis and George E. P. Smith, who ridiculed
the idea as a pipe dream, conceded that their judgments were
based on contemporary cost estimates. Eventually Arizonans
buckled and ratified the compact; but their earlier stubbornness
received a measure of vindication in 1968, when Congress finally
authorized the Central Arizona Project.

But authorization of the Central Arizona Project did not come easily, and it did not represent in any sense a clear-cut victory for Arizona. To begin with, Arizonans had hoped that the 1963 Supreme Court decision would clear the way for immediate congressional approval of the CAP. That was not the case, however, for it took them five years of hard negotiating to overcome the strong opposition in the House from Californians as well as from some upper-basin representatives, especially Colorado's Wayne Aspinall, powerful chairman of the House Committee on Interior and Insular Affairs, the committee charged with passing on the CAP.

To mollify Aspinall and his upper-state supporters, Arizonans agreed to add a provision to the CAP bill authorizing several reclamation projects within the upper basin. To satisfy Californians, they agreed to a provision specifying that in times of shortage, water for the CAP "shall be so limited as to assure the availability" of 4,400,000 acre-feet for California. In short, California's contracts to the extent of 4,400,000 acre-feet were given a priority over the CAP.

The concession to California proved especially disturbing to Arizonans. Because of declining estimates of stream flow, Indian demands, and differences between the upper and lower basins over the meaning of the compact, Arizonans were forced to recognize that there might someday be insufficient Colorado River water for the CAP. To quiet their fears, they joined with other basin leaders in adding to the bill still another provision that directed the Bureau of Reclamation to study ways of bringing water into the Colorado River Basin from other river systems. The other river systems were not named in the bill, but it was no secret that federal officials considered the Columbia River to be the likely source. Strong protests then came from congressmen in the Pacific Northwest, who forced the inclusion in the bill of yet another provision, which banned interbasin studies for ten years following passage of the measure. Thus amended, the CAP legislation—now formally known as the Colorado River Basin Project bill—finally won congressional approval in September, 1968.[25]

[25] House Committee on Interior and Insular Affairs, *Hearings on Lower Colorado River Basin Project, H.R. 4671 and similar bills,* 89 Cong. (1965–1966), pp. 407–408, 427–429, 434–435, 701–703,

The ban on interbasin studies—even if only temporary—displeased Arizonans, but it seemed a small price to pay for the $1.3 billion Central Arizona Project. Since 1968, many people have begun to question whether any price is worth paying for the CAP. Though Congress authorized the project, it appropriated only a small amount of the total funds needed for construction. Moreover, even those limited funds were not appropriated until 1970 and not released by the administration until 1973. In large part, this lack of enthusiasm reflected a resurgence of the belief that in a time when the nation was accumulating agricultural surpluses, subsidized irrigation was unnecessary and uneconomical. More recently, however, soaring food costs and famine in many parts of the world have prompted some skeptics of the CAP to reassess their views. This turnabout has naturally buoyed the hopes of Arizona's CAP advocates, but it has done little to still the vigorous opposition to the project coming from such quarters as the Sierra Club, Ralph Nader's Center for the Study of Responsible Law, and many preservationist-minded Arizonans. These critics continue to insist that the CAP is uneconomical and will cause ecological calamity by hastening unnecessary growth and destroying much of the state's desert wildlife and virgin flora.

George W. P. Hunt had always considered imported water necessary to promote agriculture and thus sustain the Arizona economy as the mining industry declined. By the 1970s, however, neither mining nor agriculture—which in 1945 had together accounted for 75 percent of the state's income—figured prominently in the economy. Following World War II, the lead was taken by manufacturing firms—Hughes Aircraft, General Electric, Goodyear Aircraft Corporation, Kaiser Aircraft and Electric

---

1099–1105, 1133–1134, passim; see also House Committee on Interior and Insular Affairs, *Hearings on Colorado River Basin Project,* 90 Cong., 1 sess. (1967), passim; House Committee on Interior and Insular Affairs, *Hearings on Colorado River Basin Project, Part II,* 90 Cong., 2 sess. (1968), passim; Richard L. Berkman and W. Kip Viscusi et al., *Damming the West* (New York, 1973), pp. 105–130; Helen M. Ingram, *Patterns of Politics in Water Resource Development: A Case Study of New Mexico's Role in the Colorado River Basin Bill* (Albuquerque, 1969); U.S., *Statutes at Large,* LXXXII: 885.

Corporation, Sperry Gyroscope Company, and scores of similar companies, most of which are light water-users. By 1973, according to critics of the CAP, agriculture was using about 90 percent of Arizona's water and generating only about 10 percent of the state's income. So long as agriculture is declining in economic importance, argue the critics, why bother about bringing in more water? Instead, they contend, state officials should manage more carefully the present water supply and prevent the unchecked growth that has created serious problems for places like southern California. Advocates of the CAP counter that the water is needed to replenish the underground supplies that are fast dwindling because of agricultural expansion and urban use. The state's present development, as well as that of the future, they insist, can be protected only with CAP water.[26] Though construction of the CAP has begun, the opposition from environmentalists, the uncertainty of the future water supply, and the demands of Indians for more water suggest that completion of the project will not come easily.

VII

The years of controversy over the Colorado have persuaded many that an interstate treaty is a poor way of handling water distribution and that Congress should be entrusted with such complicated and politically sensitive questions. Certainly the role of the federal government is clearer now that the Supreme Court has declared unequivocally that Congress has the authority to divide the waters of interstate streams. It is presently possible, claims one legal expert, "to accomplish a fully integrated development-allocation scheme without interference of conflicting state authority. The states will have to negotiate their participation politically, and there is therefore a chance that the result may be a national regional scheme under which no single area of the region can completely frustrate the desire and needs of the region as a whole." [27]

Perhaps so. The federal government can doubtlessly operate

[26] *Los Angeles Times,* January 28, 1973; Berkman and Viscusi, *Damming the West,* pp. 120–130, passim; W. Eugene Hollon, *The Southwest: Old and New* (New York, 1961), pp. 354–355.

[27] David Haber, "Arizona v. California—A Brief Review," *Natural Resources Journal* IV (1964–1965): 26.

more efficiently than states with their conflicting interests; it can, at least theoretically, plan intelligently for the needs of an entire region—indeed, for the needs of the nation—without worrying as much as an interstate commission about the attitudes of state legislatures. This, of course, does not mean that the federal government would or should ignore the states, for state interests and expertise are often essential to the success of a project. In fact, joint federal-state consultation helped produce the recent salinity agreement with Mexico as well as the long-range criteria for operation of Colorado River reservoirs. Moreover, federal-state cooperation has characterized the important so-called Comprehensive Framework Studies aimed at surveying the resources and needs of about half the nation's river basins.

But many informed observers believe that the recent examples of cooperation are largely the result of the federal government's greater authority. It now possesses the leverage to force the states to work with it, as well as with one another. Washington does not necessarily have to exercise its authority to accomplish a particular end; the fact that it can act if it chooses to do so is often leverage enough. Also greatly conducive to cooperation— at least within the Colorado River Basin—is the determination of the basin states to avoid a repetition of the costly Arizona-California controversy. "After [the] Arizona v. California [decision]," recently declared Myron Holburt, chief engineer of the Colorado River Board of California, "there developed a resolve among many basin state representatives to do everything to avoid another major decade-long lawsuit." [28]

Despite these considerations, it is still far from clear whether greater federal authority will bring significant improvement. Much more important than *who* is exercising the authority is the *way* in which it is exercised. The federal government may indeed operate more efficiently and fairly than the states; but to do so, it will have to avoid bureaucratic conflicts like those be-

[28] According to Holburt, the states, not the federal government, have played the leading role during the past decade. "The states," he observes, "by working together and negotiating differences wrote and obtained passage of the 1968 Colorado River Basin Project Act. Since that time the states have negotiated and agreed on many issues and have provided leadership rather than the federal government." Holburt to the author, December 28, 1973.

tween the Army Corps of Engineers and the Reclamation Bureau
that for years held up the development of the Missouri River.[29]
If, on the other hand, greater federal power results, as many expect, in faster development, then the public will have to be especially alert to attempts to construct unnecessary dams and aqueducts that may destroy scenic wonders, promote pollution, and
decrease the water supply through evaporation losses from reservoirs.[30] The federal government is not infallible, a fact that becomes readily apparent when one recalls that it was a federal
official who provided the compact negotiators with the grossly
inaccurate stream-flow data on which they based their water-
allocation formula.

Then, too, it was the federal government that for years paid
little attention to the Indians of the basin. Despite the 1963 decision of the Supreme Court, the position of the Indian is still
far from satisfactory. As Indians learned more than a century
ago during the presidency of Andrew Jackson, the Supreme Court
can make a decision, but it cannot execute it. That situation still
obtains. For example, as late as 1972, nearly a decade after the
1963 decision, the five Indian reservations along the lower river
were irrigating a total of only 66,000 acres, an amount less than
half the available irrigable acreage of about 135,000 acres.[31]

[29] Albert Williams, *The Water and the Power* (New York, 1951),
pp. 204–264. For a recent excellent study that is critical of the federal
government, see W. Turrentine Davis and Donald J. Pisani, *A Case
Study in Interstate Resource Management: The California-Nevada
Water Controversy*, 2 vols. (Davis, Calif., 1973, 1974).

[30] For a sampling of the many accounts critical of the federal gov-
ernment's reclamation and dam-building activities, see Berkman and
Viscusi, *Damming the West;* Boyle, Graves, and Watkins, *The Water
Hustlers;* Arthur E. Morgan, *Dams and Other Disasters* (Boston,
1971); Samuel P. Hays, *Conservation and the Gospel of Efficiency*
(Cambridge, Mass., 1959); Donald Swain, *Federal Conservation
Policy, 1921–1933* (Berkeley, 1963); Arthur Maas, *Muddy Waters:
The Army Engineers and the Nation's Rivers* (Cambridge, Mass.,
1951); Elmo Richardson, *Dams, Parks, & Politics* (Lexington, Ky.,
1973).

[31] At the time of the 1963 decision, some 35,756 acres (using
124,500 acre-feet) were being irrigated. Charles Worthman, assistant
area director, Phoenix Area Office, U.S. Bureau of Reclamation, to
the author, October 25, 1973; Myron B. Holburt, chief engineer,
Colorado Board of California, to the author, March 15, 1973.

Moreover, at two of the reservations—Chemehuevi and Fort Mohave—no land was being cultivated. The explanation given for this situation by Charles Worthman, an official in the Phoenix office of the Bureau of Indian Affairs, is blunt and to the point: "Government funding has been unavailable for irrigation development." Lack of funds, explains Worthman, has forced the tribes to turn to long-term leasing arrangements with non-Indians "as a means of developing their agricultural lands." As of 1972 only 6,500 acres along the lower Colorado were being irrigated by the Indians themselves.[32]

A major reason for the government's slowness in developing Indian lands is found in the declining water supply. Additional water for the reservations will probably mean less water for some non-Indians and possibly no water for many whose rights were established after the reservations were created. Some congressmen are understandably reluctant to anger their non-Indian constituents by voting for funds that would bring water to reservation lands. In 1973 the National Water Commission, an agency created by Congress to study the nation's water resources problems, suggested that the federal government resolve the difficulty by either developing "an alternate source of supply" or by compensating "the non-Indian water users who are injured by later Indian water development." [33] The additional water or compensation would be available to those non-Indians who had initiated their projects before the 1963 Supreme Court decision. Since the development of new water supplies is still years in the future, most attention has focused on compensation. This possibility has attracted supporters, but some political observers, including members of the commission itself, wonder if it will have the desired effect. They fear that legislation to develop the reservations will be even more difficult to achieve when the costs of compensation are added to the expense of reservation water projects. There are

[32] Charles Worthman to the author, October 25, 1973.

[33] National Water Commission, *New Directions in U.S. Water Policy: Summary, Conclusions and Recommendations from the Final Report of the National Water Commission* (Washington, D.C., 1973), p. 66; Monroe E. Price, *Law and the American Indian* (Indianapolis, 1973), p. 323. For the impact of the Central Arizona Project on one Indian community, see William R. Coffeen, "The Effects of the Central Arizona Project on the Fort McDowell Indian Community," *Ethnohistory*, XIX (1972): 345–377.

also some legal experts who seem to question whether the non-Indians are entitled to any compensation. "At least since 1908 when *Winters* was decided," writes Stanford University law professor Charles J. Meyers in reference to the case which established the precedent invoked in *Arizona* v. *California,* "anyone planning a water project could have learned of the Indians' rights, and even before that it would not have taken much imagination to suppose that Indian reservations were entitled to some irrigation water." [34] Though many remain sympathetic to the plight of the non-Indians, the matter of compensation remains unresolved.

Indians and non-Indians on the lower Colorado are also uneasy because of ambiguities in the 1963 *Arizona* v. *California* decision. For example, the Supreme Court failed to anticipate that Indians might wish to use their water for a purpose other than agriculture. Though the Court announced that "the water was intended to satisfy the future as well as the present needs of the Indian Reservations," it measured those needs only in terms of "practicably irrigable acreage." [35] Today, with industrial and municipal uses of water becoming increasingly important, many spokesmen believe that the Indians should be allowed to utilize their water in any way that would best benefit the reservations. Most leaders, both Indian and non-Indian, seem to agree with this position, but they are less agreed on how much water should be made available to the reservations. While some believe that the Indians are entitled to all the water that would have been needed to develop their irrigable acreage, others think that reservation water rights should be determined by the actual use to which the water is put. Though the latter solution appears reasonable, it ignores

[34] Charles J. Meyers, "The Colorado River," *Stanford Law Review* XIX (1966): 72. For a discussion of other major problems involving Indian water rights, see William H. Veeder, "Indian Prior and Paramount Rights to the Use of Water," in Rocky Mountain Mineral Law Institute, *Proceedings of the Sixteenth Annual Institute* (New York, 1971), pp. 631–668; Paul L. Bloom, "Indian 'Paramount' Rights to Water Use," ibid., pp. 669–693; William H. Veeder, "Water Rights: Life or Death for the American Indian," *Indian Historian* V (Summer, 1972): 4–21; Rupert Costo, "Indian Water Rights: A Survival Issue," ibid. (Fall, 1972): 4–6.

[35] *Arizona* v. *California et al.,* 373 U.S. 600 (1963).

the fact that Indian uses could—and doubtlessly would—change over time, thereby creating uncertainty among non-Indians about the extent of their rights. The Indians, for example, might decide to take their fields out of cultivation and to use their water for something like a nuclear power plant, which could require more water than that consumed in growing crops.[36] Until questions like these are satisfactorily resolved, tensions on the lower Colorado can be expected to mount.

Still another problem has emerged because the Supreme Court failed to specify whether the Indians could sell or lease their water rights for use on non-reservation lands. While some spokesmen believe the Indians should be permitted to sever their water rights from the reservations and obtain needed income immediately, others question the wisdom of such a move. "It would not be too much of an exaggeration," warns law professor Monroe E. Price, "to say that the conversion of water rights to money is not altogether different from the transference of communally held land to money in the nineteenth century. The economic use of exploited assets makes sense but the corrosive effect on the future of the reservation may be substantial." According to Price, the leasing of water rights would present as many hazards as selling them. "Vested economic interests will be established based on the Indian water [and] . . . there will be difficulties in effective recapturing, unless alternate supplies of water are developed during the lease period by the non-Indian users." [37] As already noted, the development of alternate supplies is, at best, years in the future. Thus, the direction of development on the Indian and non-Indian lands of the lower Colorado remains fraught with uncertainty.

For Indians elsewhere in the basin, the situation is even less satisfactory, a condition due in no small part to another limitation

[36] Interview with Raymond Simpson, attorney for the Confederation of Indian Tribes of the Colorado River, May 8, 1974; and interview with Vernon E. Valantine, principal hydraulic engineer, Colorado River Board of California, April 24, 1974. See also Confederation of Indian Tribes of the Colorado River, *Blueprint for Action* (Long Beach, Calif., Sept. 5, 1972).

[37] Price, *Law and the American Indian*, pp. 323–324; see also Bill Leaphart, "Sale and Lease of Indian Water Rights," *Montana Law Review* XXXIII (1972): 266–276.

of the 1963 decision. The Court dealt only with the rights of lower-basin Indians along the mainstream; nothing was said about the reservations along the tributaries or in the upper basin. This omission has led to new controversies. In 1969, for example, lawyers for the Navajo Indians, who number more than 130,000 and constitute the largest tribe in the United States, announced plans to bring suit for as much as ten million acre-feet of Colorado River water. The Navajo reservation, located primarily in northeastern Arizona, is a desolate place where, in the 1960s, about 40 percent of the labor force was unemployed and the median income for an average family of five was $2,600.[38] More recent appraisals of the Indian's situation do not indicate improvement. In 1972 the unemployment rate for Navajos was 43 percent.[39]

Despite the controversies surrounding the Colorado River Compact, it remains the fundamental law of the river. It must, of course, be read in light of Supreme Court decisions and supplementary legislation like the Boulder Canyon Act, the California Limitation Act, the upper-basin compact, and other measures which incorporate it by reference. Still, it remains the basic interstate law governing the actions of all federal and state officials. It is, in the opinion of local and national leaders, "very much a live issue," as "alive" as any constitution or treaty that affects the lives of millions of people.

But the larger significance of the Colorado River Compact

[38] When the value of free goods and services is included, the average family income in 1960 was $3,225. U.S. Bureau of Indian Affairs, "The Navajo Yearbook, 1951–1961: A Decade of Progress," *Report No. viii*, comp. by Robert W. Young (Window Rock, Ariz., 1961), p. 228; U.S. Congress, Joint Economic Committee, "Toward Economic Development for Native American Communities," *Joint Committee Print*, 91 Cong., 1 sess. (1969), pp. 112, 228, passim; *Los Angeles Times*, December 15, 1969.

[39] U.S. Bureau of Indian Affairs, Statistics Division, *Estimates of Resident Indian Population and Labor Force Status; By State and Reservation: March 1972*, mimeographed (Washington, D.C., September, 1972), p. 4; see also Heinrich J. Thiele, et al., *Navajo Water Resources, Supplies and Management and the Proposed Navajo Tribal Water Authority (NTWA), A Reservation-Wide Water Study* (Window Rock, Ariz., 1966).

clearly transcends the Colorado River Basin and even the arid western United States. It marked the first time under the Constitution that a group of states apportioned the water of an interstate stream for consumptive use and the first time that more than two or three states negotiated a treaty to settle any sort of problem among themselves. It established a precedent that other states soon imitated, though no subsequent water treaty involved as many states or dealt with an area as large, or a set of problems as complex, as those of the Colorado. It precipitated struggles that threw into sharp relief the interaction between the local and the national levels, between state governments and the federal government, between private interests and public, between the East and the West, between the United States and Mexico. This does not mean that such interaction was always sought or even welcomed, but it was always present.

As indicated at the outset, a major theme in this study has been federalism, the concept embracing the ongoing attempt to accommodate local autonomy to national unity, the rights of the states to the rights of the central government. The Colorado River struggle provides a valuable insight into the federal process and documents a major evolution in national public water policy. That policy has been marked by the emergence of the government in Washington as the most powerful authority over the Colorado River and, by extension, over other interstate and navigable streams as well. Though at first reluctant to do more than encourage the states to settle their differences, Congress has emerged as not only arbiter but also policy maker in areas heretofore thought to be outside its dominion. Indeed, Congress may now even have the power to void interstate compacts and to reallocate the waters of rivers like the Colorado according to some other formula.[40] The situation nearly a century ago, when Colorado River development began, was far different. Today Congress possesses sufficient authority to virtually coerce the states to obey its commands—though, of course, those commands are subject to judicial review. Some might question the wisdom

[40] Legal scholar Frank J. Trelease considers this possibility to be one of the major unanswered questions prompted by the 1963 *Arizona* v. *California* decision. See Trelease, "Arizona v. California: Allocation of Water Resources to People, States, and Nation," in Philip B. Kurland, ed., *The Supreme Court Review, 1963* (Chicago, 1963), pp. 203–204.

of this shift of power to Washington, but none can deny its existence or its significance for the American West and the American federal system.

In those instances where a water-allocation compact has worked reasonably well (as, for example, in the case of the upper-basin compact of 1948), the central government has played a rather unobtrusive role. But where, as in the Arizona-California controversy, the states have failed to resolve differences of far-reaching importance, the national government has indicated clearly that it can and will impose its own solution. Thus, the Colorado River story testifies unmistakably to the growing power of the federal government and provides additional evidence of the remarkable flexibility of the American federal system.[41]

The story unfolded here also suggests that the states themselves are politically and financially incapable of formulating and executing major reclamation programs. On the other hand, despite their sharp differences, the states have demonstrated a capacity—albeit an uneven capacity—for integrating federal and state water policies. The tandem arrangement of the Colorado River Compact and the Boulder Canyon legislation is a major case in point. Other examples could also be cited, most notably the Upper Colorado River Storage Project Act of 1956, which was made possible by the upper-basin compact of 1948. Scholars

[41] Some informed observers have noted the increase in federal authority in other areas and have concluded that cooperative federalism is on its way out. "Resting as it does primarily on the superior fiscal resources of the National Government, Cooperative Federalism," writes Edward S. Corwin, "has been, to date, a short expression for a constantly increasing concentration of power at Washington in the instigation and supervision of local policies." See Corwin, "The Passing of Dual Federalism," *Virginia Law Review* XXXVI (1950): 21. For views that acknowledge the national government's increased power over water resources but still believe that the states have a major role to play, see Joseph L. Sax, "Problems of Federalism in Reclamation Law," *University of Colorado Law Review* XXXVII (1964–1965): 83; and National Water Commission, *Federal-State Relations in Water Law*, by Frank J. Trelease (Washington, D.C., 1971), pp. 87–88, passim. An earlier and perceptive analysis of the roles of the federal government and, especially, the states is Ernest A. Engelbert, "Federalism and Water Resources Development," *Law and Contemporary Problems* XXII (1957), 325–350.

agree that the upper-basin agreement represents a considerably more successful integration of federal and state interests than the compact of 1922.[42] But this success was, of course, largely possible because the negotiators of 1948 were able to profit by the mistakes of the negotiators of 1922.

This record of past mistakes and successes also seems to possess significance for those states and nations elsewhere in the world that have rivers in common. Israel and Jordan, India and Pakistan, Egypt and the Sudan, Turkey and Syria, and many other independent nations, as well as states belonging to federal systems, should note carefully the consequences of ambiguous or shortsighted water treaties. Too often such faulty agreements lead to friction and the need to renew negotiations at a time when larger populations and increased demands for water make settlements extremely difficult to achieve. For federal governments— like those of Argentina, India, and Australia—that have a water-law system similar in many respects to that of the United States, such treaties may also set the stage for major increases in the power of the central government.[43] Because of the complexity and magnitude of interstate river developments, national leaders elsewhere, like those in the United States, may be understandably reluctant to stand by idly while states squabble over their "rights."

Though the implications of the Colorado River Compact are national and international in scope, the compact's major influence has obviously been on the American West, especially the Southwest. It opened the way for not only the Boulder Canyon Project but also for major dams—perhaps too many—at Flaming Gorge,

[42] See, for example, Frederick Zimmermann and Mitchell Wendell, *The Interstate Compact Since 1925* (Chicago, 1951), pp. 14–16, 59–60; Conrad McBride, "Federal-State Relations in the Development of the Water Resources of the Colorado River Basin" (Ph.D. diss., University of California, Los Angeles, 1962), p. 2, passim. Naturally, examples can be cited of federal-state cooperation in water resources development in other parts of the country. See Engelbert, "Federalism and Water Resources Development," 337–340, passim.

[43] For a discussion of water-law systems in more than fifty countries, see United Nations, Dept. of Economic and Social Affairs, *Abstraction and Use of Water: A Comparison of Legal Regimes* (New York, 1972).

Glen Canyon, Davis, Parker, Imperial, and other locations. It cleared the way for aqueducts running hundreds of miles and feeding the growth of such huge metropolitan centers as Denver, Salt Lake City, San Diego, and Los Angeles. It sparked bitter conflicts among public agencies over reclamation plans and the generation of electrical energy. It touched off epic battles between advocates of public and private production of hydroelectricity, and it did so before TVA had become a controversial political issue. The drafters of the compact would be chagrined to learn that the principal beneficiaries of their work are cities and industries rather than the farmers, in whom they were primarily interested. They would doubtlessly be annoyed to learn that the dams they envisaged have contributed to serious pollution problems, and they might be perplexed to discover that many now question their love affair with growth and their overwhelming desire to *use* rivers rather than to preserve them.

Ultimately, however, they need say no more than that they were pioneers. Theirs was the first attempt to divide the waters of an interstate river for consumptive use, and if their actions fell short of perfection, they had nonetheless sought a bold solution to a great regional problem of national and international significance.

APPENDIX

Colorado River Compact*

The States of Arizona, California, Colorado, Nevada, New Mexico, Utah, and Wyoming, having resolved to enter into a compact under the Act of the Congress of the United States of America approved August 19, 1921 (42 Statutes at Large, page 171), and the Acts of the Legislatures of the said States, have through their Governors appointed as their Commissioners:

W. S. Norviel for the State of Arizona.

W. F. McClure of the State of California,

Delph E. Carpenter for the State of Colorado,

J. G. Scrugham for the State of Nevada,

Stephen B. Davis, Jr., for the State of New Mexico,

R. E. Caldwell for the State of Utah,

Frank C. Emerson for the State of Wyoming,

who, after negotiations participated in by Herbert Hoover, appointed by the President as the representative of the United States of America, have agreed upon the following articles:

ARTICLE I

The major purposes of this compact are to provide for the equitable division and apportionment of the use of the waters of

* H. Doc. 605, 67 Cong., 4 sess. (1923), pp. 8–12.

the Colorado River System; to establish the relative importance of different beneficial uses of water; to promote interstate comity; to remove causes of present and future controversies; and to secure the expeditious agricultural and industrial development of the Colorado River Basin, the storage of its waters, and the protection of life and property from floods. To these ends the Colorado River Basin is divided into two Basins, and an apportionment of the use of part of the water of the Colorado River System is made to each of them with the provision that further equitable apportionments may be made.

ARTICLE II

As used in this compact:

(a) The term "Colorado River System" means that portion of the Colorado River and its tributaries within the United States of America.

(b) The term "Colorado River Basin" means all of the drainage area of the Colorado River system and all other territory within the United States of America to which the waters of the Colorado River System shall be beneficially applied.

(c) The term "States of the Upper Division" means the States of Colorado, New Mexico, Utah, and Wyoming.

(d) The term "States of the Lower Division" means the States of Arizona, California, and Nevada.

(e) The term "Lee Ferry" means a point in the main stream of the Colorado River one mile below the mouth of the Paria River.

(f) The term "Upper Basin" means those parts of the States of Arizona, Colorado, New Mexico, Utah, and Wyoming within and from which waters naturally drain into the Colorado River System above Lee Ferry, and also all parts of said States located without the drainage are[a] of the Colorado River System which are now or shall hereafter be beneficially served by waters diverted from the system above Lee Ferry.

(g) The term "Lower Basin" means those parts of the States of Arizona, California, Nevada, New Mexico, and Utah within and from which waters naturally drain into the Colorado River System below Lee Ferry, and also all parts of said States located without the drainage area of the Colorado River System which are now or shall hereafter be beneficially served by waters diverted from the system below Lee Ferry.

(h) The term "domestic use" shall include the use of water for household, stock, municipal, mining, milling, industrial, and other like purposes, but shall exclude the generation of electrical power.

ARTICLE III

(a) There is hereby apportioned from the Colorado River system in perpetuity to the Upper Basin and to the Lower Basin, respectively, the exclusive beneficial consumptive use of 7,500,-000 acre-feet of water per annum, which shall include all water necessary for the supply of any rights which may now exist.

(b) In addition to the apportionment in paragraph (a), the Lower Basin is hereby given the right to increase its beneficial consumptive use of such waters by one million acre-feet per annum.

(c) If, as a matter of international comity, the United States of America shall hereafter recognize in the United States of Mexico any right to the use of any waters of the Colorado River System, such waters shall be supplied first from the waters which are surplus over and above the aggregate of the quantities specified in paragraphs (a) and (b); and if such surplus shall prove insufficient for this purpose, then the burden of such deficiency shall be equally borne by the Upper Basin and the Lower Basin, and whenever necessary the States of the Upper Division shall deliver at Lee Ferry water to supply one-half of the deficiency so recognized in addition to that provided in paragraph (d).

(d) The States of the Upper Division will not cause the flow of the river at Lee Ferry to be depleted below an aggregate of 75,000,000 acre-feet for any period of ten consecutive years reckoned in continuing progressive series beginning with the first day of October next succeeding the ratification of this compact.

(e) The States of the Upper Division shall not withhold water, and the States of the Lower Division shall not require the delivery of water which can not reasonably be applied to domestic and agricultural uses.

(f) Further equitable apportionment of the beneficial uses of the waters of the Colorado River System unapportioned by paragraphs (a), (b), and (c) may be made in the manner provided in paragraph (g) at any time after October first, 1963, if and when either Basin shall have reached its total beneficial consumptive use as set out in paragraphs (a) and (b).

(g) In the event of a desire for a further apportionment, as provided in paragraph (f), any two signatory States, acting through their Governors, may give joint notice of such desire to the Governors of the other signatory States and to the President of the United States of America, and it shall be the duty of the Governors of the signatory States and of the President of the United States of America forthwith to appoint representatives, whose duty it shall be to divide and apportion equitably between the Upper Basin and Lower Basin the beneficial use of the unapportioned water of the Colorado River System, as mentioned in paragraph (f), subject to the legislative ratification of the signatory States and the Congress of the United States of America.

ARTICLE IV

(a) Inasmuch as the Colorado River has ceased to be navigable for commerce and the reservation of its waters for navigation would seriously limit the development of its basin, the use of its waters for purposes of navigation shall be subservient to the uses of such waters for domestic, agricultural, and power purposes. If the Congress shall not consent to this paragraph, the other provisions of this compact shall nevertheless remain binding.

(b) Subject to the provisions of this compact, water of the Colorado River System may be impounded and used for the generation of electrical power, but such impounding and use shall be subservient to the use and consumption of such water for agricultural and domestic purposes and shall not interfere with or prevent use for such dominant purposes.

(c) The provisions of this article shall not apply to or interfere with the regulation and control by any State within its boundaries of the appropriation, use, and distribution of water.

ARTICLE V

The chief official of each signatory State charged with the administration of water rights, together with the Director of the

United States Reclamation Service and the Director of the United States Geological Survey, shall cooperate, ex officio:

(a) To promote the systematic determination and coordination of the facts as to flow, appropriation, consumption and use of water in the Colorado River Basin, and the interchange of available information in such matters.

(b) To secure the ascertainment and publication of the annual flow of the Colorado River at Lee Ferry.

(c) To perform such other duties as may be assigned by mutual consent of the signatories from time to time.

ARTICLE VI

Should any claim or controversy arise between any two or more of the signatory States (a) with respect to the waters of the Colorado River System not covered by the terms of this compact; (b) over the meaning or performance of any of the terms of this compact; (c) as to the allocation of the burdens incident to the performance of any article of this compact or the delivery of waters as herein provided; (d) as to the construction or operation of works within the Colorado River Basin to be situated in two or more States, or to be constructed in one State for the benefit of another State; or (e) as to the diversion of water in one State for the benefit of another State; the Governors of the States affected, upon the request of one of them, shall forthwith appoint Commissioners with power to consider and adjust such claim or controversy, subject to ratification by the Legislatures of the States so affected.

Nothing herein contained shall prevent the adjustment of any such claim or controversy by any present method or by direct future legislative action of the interested States.

ARTICLE VII

Nothing in this compact shall be construed as affecting the obligations of the United States of America to Indian tribes.

ARTICLE VIII

Present perfected rights to the beneficial use of waters of the Colorado River System are unimpaired by this compact. Whenever storage capacity of 5,000,000 acre-feet shall have been provided on the main Colorado River within or for the benefit of the Lower Basin, then claims of such rights, if any, by appropriators or users of water in the Lower Basin against appropriators or users of water in the Upper Basin shall attach to and be satisfied from water that may be stored not in conflict with Article III.

All other rights to beneficial use of waters of the Colorado River System shall be satisfied solely from the water apportioned to that basin in which they are situate.

ARTICLE IX

Nothing in this compact shall be construed to limit or prevent any State from instituting or maintaining any action or proceeding, legal or equitable, for the protection of any right under this compact or the enforcement of any of its provisions.

ARTICLE X

This compact may be terminated at any time by the unanimous agreement of the signatory States. In the event to [of] such termination all rights established under it shall continue unimpaired.

ARTICLE XI

This compact shall become binding and obligatory when it shall have been approved by the Legislatures of each of the signatory States and by the Congress of the United States. Notice of approval by the Legislatures shall be given by the Governor of each signatory State to the Governors of the other signatory States and to the President of the United States, and the President of the United States is requested to give notice to the Governors of the signatory States of approval by the Congress of the United States.

In witness whereof the Commissioners have signed this compact in a single original, which shall be deposited in the archives of the Department of State of the United States of America and of which a duly certified copy shall be forwarded to the Governor of each of the signatory States.

Done at the City of Santa Fe, New Mexico, this twenty-fourth day of November, A.D. one thousand nine hundred and twenty-two.

(Signed)	W. S. Norviel.
(Signed)	W. F. McClure.
(Signed)	Delph E. Carpenter.
(Signed)	J. G. Scrugham.
(Signed)	Stephen B. Davis, Jr.
(Signed)	R. E. Caldwell.
(Signed)	Frank C. Emerson.

Approved:

    (Signed)   Herbert Hoover

Bibliography

Interviews and Solicited Opinions

Armstrong, Ellis L. Commissioner of the U.S. Bureau of Reclamation.

Bishop, Floyd A. Wyoming State Engineer.

Carpenter, Donald. Judge; son of Delph Carpenter. Greeley, Colorado.

Ely, Northcutt. Attorney; and long-time prominent figure in Colorado River matters. Washington, D.C.

Friedkin, Joseph F. Commissioner, United States Section, International Boundary and Water Commission, United States and Mexico.

Holburt, Myron B. Chief Engineer, Colorado River Board of California.

Kelly, William R. Attorney, prominent figure in Colorado River matters. Greeley, Colorado.

Lee, Gilbert W. Deputy City Attorney, Los Angeles Department of Water and Power; former Supervising Hydraulic Engineer, Colorado River Board of California.

Maddock, Thomas. Late Arizona state official. Safford, Arizona.

Mueller, John W. Acting Regional Director, Upper Colorado Regional Office, U.S. Bureau of Reclamation.

Ogilvie, J. L. Manager, Denver Board of Water Commissioners.

Reynolds, S. E. New Mexico State Engineer.

Simpson, Raymond. Attorney for the Confederation of Indian Tribes of the Colorado River.

Smith, J. Hubert. Son of Anson Smith.

Sparks, Felix L. Director, Colorado Water Conservation Board.

Steiner, Wesley. Arizona State Water Engineer.

Valantine, Vernon E. Principal Hydraulic Engineer, Colorado River Board of California.

Williams, Alan J. General Manager, Colorado River Association.

Worthman, Charles. Assistant Area Director, Phoenix Area Office, U.S. Bureau of Indian Affairs.

MANUSCRIPTS

Adams, Frank. Adams Papers. Water Resources Center Archives, University of California, Berkeley.

Allen, Robert A. Allen Papers. University of Nevada, Reno.

Arizona. Papers of the Arizona governors and Arizona state agencies. Arizona State Archives, Phoenix.

Bashore, Harry W. Bashore Papers. Western History Research Center, University of Wyoming, Laramie.

Boyle, Emmet D. Boyle Papers. Nevada State Historical Society, Reno. Other valuable Boyle papers are in the Nevada State Archives, Carson City.

California. Colorado River Board. Board Papers. Los Angeles, California.

———. Department of Water Resources Archives. Sacramento, California.

———. Papers of the California governors and California state agencies. California State Archives, Sacramento.

Carpenter, Delph. Carpenter Papers. When I examined the Delph Carpenter Papers, they were in the possession of his son, Judge Donald A. Carpenter, Greeley, Colorado. Judge Carpenter still possesses many valuable documents, but he has deposited most of his father's papers in the Hoover Presidential Library, West Branch, Iowa. Some materials are also held by Charles A. Dobbel, Santa Cruz, California.

Colorado. Papers of the Colorado governors and Colorado state agencies. Colorado State Archives, Denver.

Colorado River Land Company. Papers. M. H. Sherman Foundation, Corona del Mar, California.

Colter, Frederick T. Colter Papers. Arizona State Archives, Phoenix.

Davis, Arthur Powell. Davis Papers. Western History Research Center, University of Wyoming, Laramie.

Douglas, Lewis. Douglas Papers. University of Arizona, Tucson.

Ely, Northcutt. Ely Papers. Stanford University, Stanford, California.

Grunsky, Carl E. Grunsky Papers. California State Archives, Sacramento.

Harper, Sinclair O. Harper Papers. Western History Research Center, University of Wyoming, Laramie.

Haynes, John R. Haynes Papers. University of California, Los Angeles.

Hichborn, Franklin. Hichborn Papers. University of California, Los Angeles.

Hoover, Herbert. Hoover Papers. Hoover Presidential Library, West Branch Iowa; Hoover Institution, Stanford University, Stanford, California.

Hunt, George W. P. "Autobiography." Arizona State Archives, Phoenix.

————. Hunt Papers. Arizona State Archives, Phoenix; Arizona State University, Tempe.

————. Hunt Scrapbooks, 1910–1932. University of Arizona, Tucson.

Imperial Irrigation District. Papers. El Centro and Imperial, California.

Imperial Water Company. Papers. Honnold Library, Claremont Colleges, Claremont, California.

Johnson, Hiram. Johnson Papers. Bancroft Library, University of California, Berkeley.

Jones, Herbert C. Jones Papers. Stanford University, Stanford, California.

Kendrick, John B. Kendrick Papers. Western History Research Center, University of Wyoming, Laramie.

Lippincott, Joseph B. Lippincott Papers. Water Resources Center Archives, University of California, Berkeley.

Los Angeles Department of Water and Power. Papers. Los Angeles, California.

McCluskey, Henry S. McCluskey Papers. Arizona State University, Tempe.

Maddock, Thomas. Maddock Papers. Arizona Historical Society, Tucson; Arizona State University, Tempe.

Maxwell, George H. Maxwell Papers. Western History Research Center, University of Wyoming, Laramie.

México. Secretaría de Relaciones Exteriones. Papers of the Comisión Internacional de Límites entre México y los Estados Unidos, México, D. F.

Nevada. Papers of the Nevada governors and Nevada state agencies. Nevada State Archives, Carson City.

New Mexico. Papers of the New Mexico governors and New Mexico state agencies. New Mexico State Archives, Santa Fe.

Oddie, Tasker L. Oddie Papers. Huntington Library, San Marino, California; Nevada State Historical Society, Reno.

Perry, C. H. Perry Papers. Honnold Library, Claremont Colleges, Claremont, California.

Peterson, J. T. Peterson Papers. Western History Research Center, University of Wyoming, Laramie.

Pittman, Key. Pittman Papers. Library of Congress, Washington, D.C.; Nevada State Historical Society, Reno.

Rockwood, Charles Robinson. Rockwood Papers. Honnold Library, Claremont Colleges, Claremont, California.

Scrugham, James G. Scrugham Papers. Nevada State Historical Society, Reno. Other valuable Scrugham Papers are in the Nevada State Archives, Carson City.

Smith, Alfred Merritt. Smith Papers. University of Nevada, Reno.

Smith, George E. P. Smith Papers. Arizona Historical Society, Tucson.

Smoot, Reed. Smoot Papers. Brigham Young University, Provo, Utah.

Squires, Charles P. Squires Papers. University of Nevada, Las Vegas.

Swing, Phil D. Swing Papers. Department of Special Collections, University of California, Los Angeles. The Swing Papers formerly in the offices of the Colorado River Board of California are also now at UCLA. Other Swing materials are in the Imperial County Pioneers' Museum, Imperial, California, and the San Diego County Law Library, San Diego, California.

United States Department of the Interior. Bureau of Reclamation Papers. National Archives, Washington, D.C.

United States Department of Justice. Department of Justice Papers. National Archives, Washington, D.C.

United States Department of State. Department of State Papers. National Archives, Washington, D.C.

United States Secretary of the Interior Papers. National Archives, Washington, D.C.

Utah. Papers of the Utah governors and Utah state agencies. Utah State Archives, Salt Lake City.

Warren, Francis. Warren Papers. Western History Research Center, University of Wyoming, Laramie.

Wilbur, Ray Lyman. Wilbur Papers. Stanford University, Stanford, California.

Winsor, Mulford. Winsor Papers. Arizona State Archives, Phoenix.

Wyoming. Papers of the Wyoming governors and Wyoming state agencies. Wyoming State Archives, Cheyenne.

GOVERNMENT PUBLICATIONS

Arizona. Colorado River Commission (name varies). *Annual Reports.*
——. ——. *The Arizona Question.* Phoenix, 1928.
——. ——. *Arizona's Rights in the Colorado River.* Phoenix, 1929.
——. ——. *Partial Proceedings of Conference of Governors . . . on the Colorado River, Held at Denver, Colorado, Aug. 22 to Sept. 1, 1927.* Phoenix, September 24, 1927.

————. ————. *Partial Proceedings of Conference of Governors . . . on the Colorado River Held at Denver, Colorado, Aug. 22 to Sept. 1, 1927.* [Phoenix], 1927.

————. ————. *Partial Proceedings of Conference of Governors . . . on the Colorado River (Second Session), Held at Denver, Colorado, Sept. 19 to Oct. 4, 1927.* Phoenix, October 15, 1927.

————. Colorado River Committee. *Report of the Arizona Colorado River Committee Appointed by Gov. Geo. W. P. Hunt.* Phoenix, January 1, 1927.

————. ————. *Statement before the Federal Power Commission. . . .* N.p., September 24, 1923.

Arizona Engineering Commission. *Report Based on Reconnaissance Investigation of Arizona Land Irrigable from the Colorado River.* N.p., July 5, 1923.

Arizona. *Journal of the Arizona House.*

————. *Journal of the Arizona Senate.*

————. *Official Report of the Proceedings of the Colorado River Conference.* Phoenix, August 17, 1925.

————. *Plan of Development of the Colorado River Submitted by [the] Arizona Delegations to [the] California and Nevada Delegations, Dec. 14, 1925.* Miami, Arizona, 1925.

California. Colorado River Board (name varies). *Annual Reports.*

————. ————. *California's Stake in the Colorado River.* See various editions.

————. ————. *Need for Controlling Salinity of the Colorado River.* N.p., August, 1970.

————. ————. *Salinity Problems in the Lower Colorado River Area.* Sacramento, September, 1962.

————. ————. *Analysis of Boulder Canyon Project Act.* Sacramento, 1930.

————. ————. *Answer by California Colorado River Commission to Proposed Basis of Division of Water between the Lower Division of the Colorado River Basin, as Submitted by the Governors of the Upper Division on September 20, 1927.* N.p. [1927].

————. ————. *Colorado River and the Boulder Canyon Project.* Sacramento, 1931.

————. Department of Engineering. "Irrigation Districts in California, 1887–1915." By Frank Adams. *Department of Engineering Bulletin No. 2.* Sacramento, 1917.

————. Department of Public Works. "Irrigation Districts of California." By Frank Adams. *Department of Public Works Bulletin No. 21.* Sacramento, 1921.

————. *Journal of the California Assembly.*

————. *Journal of the California Senate.*

Colorado. *Journal of the Colorado House.*
―――. *Journal of the Colorado Senate.*
Colorado River Conference. *Official Report of the Colorado River Conference Between Delegates Representing California, Nevada, and Arizona* [Aug. 17, 1925]. Phoenix [1925].
Metropolitan Water District of Southern California. *Annual Reports.*
―――. *Colorado River Aqueduct.* See various editions.
―――. *Colorado River Aqueduct, an Estimate of the Distribution of Benefits Which Will Accrue to Other States than California from the Use of Public Works Administration Funds in the Construction of the Colorado River Aqueduct.* Los Angeles, 1933.
―――. *The Great Aqueduct: The Story of the Planning and Building of the Colorado River Aqueduct.* Los Angeles, 1941.
México. Comisión Nacional de Irrigación. *Irrigación en México.*
―――. ―――. *Irrigation in Mexico.* México, D. F., 1936.
―――. ―――. *La Obra de la Comisión, Nacional de Irrigación Durante el Regimen del Sr. Gral. de División, Lazaro Cárdenas, 1934–1940.* México, D. F., 1940.
―――. ―――. *Obra Realizada de 1926 a 1940 y Programa para el Sexenio 1941–1946.* By Adolfo Orive Alba. México, D. F., 1942.
―――. Secretaría de Fomento. Colonización e Industria. *Memoria de la Comisión del Instituto Geológico de México que Exploró la Región Norte de la Baja California.* México, D. F., 1913.
―――. ―――. *Dictámenes Sobre el Abuso de las Aguas de los Rios Bravo, Colorado y Sus Afluentes.* México, D. F., 1892.
―――. Secretaría de Relaciones Exteriones. *Memoria.*
―――. ―――. Oficina de Límites y Aguas. *El Problema de los Aguas Internacionales entre México y los Estados Unidos, Su Origin, Desarrollo y Resolución: El Tratado Internacional de Aguas de 3 de Febrero de 1944.* México, D. F., September., 1945.
―――. ―――. "Las Relaciones Internacionales de México, 1935–1956 (a Traves de los Mensajes Presidenciales)," *Archivo Histórico Diplomático Mexicano,* Segunda Serie, Numero 9. México, D. F., 1957.
―――. ―――. Oficina de Límites y Aguas Internacionales. *El Tratado de Aguas Internacionales Celebrado entre México y los Estados Unidos el 3 de Febrero de 1944. Antecedentes, Consideraciones y Resoluciones del Problema de las Aguas Internacionales.* México, D. F., 1947.
―――. ―――. *Tratado sobre Aguas Internacionales Celebrado entre México y los Estados Unidos con Fecha 3 de Febrero de 1944.* México, D. F. [1945].
Nevada. *Journal of the Nevada Assembly.*
―――. *Journal of the Nevada Senate.*

New Mexico. *Journal of the New Mexico House.*
――――. *Journal of the New Mexico Senate.*
――――. Office of the State Engineer. "Hydrologic Summary: New Mexico Streamflow and Reservoir Content, 1888–1954," *Technical Report No. 7.* Santa Fe, 1959.
United Nations. Department of Economic and Social Affairs. *Abstraction and Use of Water: A Comparison of Legal Regimes.* New York, 1972.
United States. Attorneys General. *Official Opinions.*
――――. Congress. *Congressional Globe.*
――――. ――――. *Congressional Record.*
――――. ――――. *Official Congressional Directories.*
――――. ――――. House and Senate Joint Economic Committee. "Toward Economic Development for Native American Communities." *Joint Committee Print.* 91 Cong., 1 sess. 1969.
United States. Congress. House of Representatives. Documents and Reports:
43 Cong., 1 sess. "Geographic and Geological Surveys West of the Mississippi," *H. Rept. 612.* 1874. Serial No. 1626.
44 Cong., 2 sess. "Report of the Secretary of War," *H. Ex. Doc. 1.* 1876. Serial No. 1742.
45 Cong., 2 sess. "Report on the Lands of the Arid Region of the United States," *H. Ex. Doc. 73.* By J. W. Powell. 1878. Serial No. 1805.
51 Cong., 1 sess. "Irrigation of Arid Lands—International Boundary—Mexican Relations," *H. Rept. 490.* 1890. Serial No. 2808.
55 Cong., 2 sess. "Preliminary Examination of Reservoir Sites in Wyoming and Colorado," *H. Doc. 141.* 1897. Serial No. 3666.
58 Cong., 2 sess. "Colorado River, Arizona and California," *H. Doc. 204.* 1903. Serial No. 4672.
58 Cong., 3 sess. "Use of Waters of the Lower Colorado River for Irrigation," *H. Doc. 204.* 1905. Serial No. 4830.
61 Cong., 2 sess. "Lower Colorado River," *H. Doc. 972.* 1910. Serial No. 5836.
61 Cong., 3 sess. "Southern Pacific Imperial Valley Claim," *H. Rept. 1936.* 1911. Serial No. 5851.
62 Cong., 2 sess. "Work of the Interior Department," *H. Doc. 504.* 1912. Serial No. 6321.
63 Cong., 2 sess. "Colorado River, California, and Arizona," *H. Doc. 1141.* 1914. Serial No. 6622.
63 Cong., 3 sess. "Protection of Lands and Property in the Imperial Valley, California," *H. Doc. 1476.* 1915. Serial No. 6888.
64 Cong., 1 sess. "Plan for Protection of Imperial Valley, California," *H. Doc. 586.* 1916. Serial No. 7098.

67 Cong., 1 sess. "Division and Apportionment, Waters of the Colorado," *H. Rept. 191.* 1921. Serial No. 7920.

67 Cong., 4 sess. "Colorado River Compact," *H. Doc. 605.* 1923. Serial No. 8215.

69 Cong. 2 sess. "Boulder Canyon Reclamation Project," *H. Rept. 1657.* 1926. Serial No. 8688.

69 Cong., 2 sess. "Federal Power Commission Licenses Affecting the Colorado River," *H. Rept. 2285.* 1927. Serial No. 8689.

70 Cong., 1 sess. "Boulder Canyon Project," *H. Rept. 918.* 1928. Serial No. 8836.

70 Cong., 2 sess. "Report of the Colorado River Board on the Boulder Dam Project," *H. Doc. 446.* 1928. Serial No. 9035.

70 Cong., 2 sess. "Restricting Federal Power Commission Licenses Affecting the Colorado River," *H. Rept. 2621.* 1929. Serial No. 8980.

71 Cong., 2 sess. "Report of American Section, International Water Commission, United States and Mexico," *H. Doc. 359.* 1930. Serial No. 9233.

73 Cong., 2 sess. "Development of the Rivers of the United States," *H. Doc. 395.* 1934. Serial No. 9815.

77 Cong., 1 sess. "Bullshead (Davis) Dam Project," *H. Doc. 186.* 1941. Serial No. 10598.

80 Cong., 1 sess. "The Colorado River," *H. Doc. 419.* 1947. Serial No. 11147.

80 Cong., 2 sess. "The Hoover Dam Documents," *H. Doc. 717.* 1948. Serial No. 11229.

81 Cong., 1 sess. "Central Arizona Project," *H. Doc. 136.* 1949. Serial No. 11320.

————. ————. ————. Hearings:

Committee on Claims. "Southern Pacific Imperial Valley Claim." *Hearings on H. J. Res. 259.* 64 Cong., 2 sess., 1917.

Committee on Flood Control. "Colorado River in Arizona." *Hearings.* 65 Cong., 3 sess., 1919.

————. "Colorado River Survey, Imperial Valley Project." *Hearings on H.R. 3475.* 66 Cong., 1 sess., 1919.

Committee on Interior and Insular Affairs. "Central Arizona Project." *Hearings on H.R. 1500 and H.R. 1501.* 82 Cong., 1 sess., 1951.

————. "Colorado River Basin Project." *Hearings.* 90 Cong., 1 sess., 1967.

————. "Colorado River Basin Project, Part II." *Hearings.* 90 Cong., 2 sess., 1968.

————. "Lower Colorado River Basin Project." *Hearings on H.R. 4671 and similar bills.* 89 Cong., 1965–1966.

Committee on Interstate and Foreign Commerce. "Renaming of the Grand River, Colorado." *Hearings.* 66 Cong., 3 sess., 1921.

Committee on Irrigation and Reclamation. "Colorado River Basin." *Hearings on H.R. 6251 and H.R. 9826.* 69 Cong., 1 sess., 1926.

———. "Protection and Development of Lower Colorado River Basin." *Hearings on H.R. 2903.* 68 Cong., 1 sess., 1924.

———. "Protection and Development of Lower Colorado River Basin." *Hearings on H.R. 5773.* 70 Cong., 1 sess., 1928.

———. "Regulating the Colorado River." *Hearings on H.R. 5770.* 70 Cong., 1 sess., 1928.

Committee on Irrigation of Arid Lands. "All-American Canal in Imperial and Coachella Valleys, California." *Hearings on H.R. 6044.* 66 Cong., 1919.

———. "All-American Canal in Imperial County, California." *Hearings on H.R. 6044.* 66 Cong., 1 sess., 1919.

———. "Protection and Development of the Lower Colorado River Basin." *Hearings on H.R. 11449.* 67 Cong., 2 sess., 1922 and 1923.

Committee on the Judiciary. "Granting the Consent of Congress to Certain Compacts." *Hearings on H.R. 6821.* 77 Cong., 1 sess., 1921.

Committee on Public Lands. "Salton Sea, California, Imperial Valley, and Lower Colorado River." *Hearings.* 59 Cong., 2 sess., 1907.

———. Subcommittee on Irrigation and Reclamation. "The Upper Colorado River Basin Compact." *Hearings.* 81 Cong., 1 sess., 1949.

Committee on Rules. "Boulder Dam." *Hearings on H.R. 9826.* 69 Cong., 2 sess., 1927.

———. ———. Senate. Documents and Reports:

33 Cong., 2 sess. "Reports of the Explorations and Surveys, to Ascertain the Most Practicable and Economical Route for a Railroad from the Mississippi River to the Pacific Ocean," *S. Ex. Doc. 78.* 1856. Serial No. 758.

50 Cong., 1 sess. "Reservoirs in Arid Regions of the United States," *S. Ex. Doc. 163.* 1888. Serial No. 2513.

59 Cong., 2 sess. "Imperial Valley or Salton Sink Region," *S. Doc. 212.* 1907. Serial No. 5071.

60 Cong., 1 sess. "Irrigation in Imperial Valley, California: Its Problems and Possibilities," *S. Doc. 246.* 1908. Serial No. 5291.

61 Cong., 2 sess. "Brief and Memorandum Relating to Riparian and Water Rights of the Federal Government and of the Various States," *S. Doc. 351.* 1910. Serial No. 5657.

354   *Bibliography*

62 Cong., 2 sess. "Colorado River," *S. Doc. 867.* 1912. Serial No. 6178.

62 Cong., 2 sess. "Flood Waters of the Colorado River," *S. Doc. 846.* 1912. Serial No. 6178.

64 Cong., 1 sess. "Imperial Valley, California," *S. Doc. 232.* 1916. Serial No. 6951.

64 Cong., 1 sess. "River Regulation, Flood Control, and Water Conservation and Utilization," *S. Doc. 550.* 1916. Serial No. 6953.

65 Cong., 1 sess. "The Colorado River in Its Relation to the Imperial Valley, California," *S. Doc. 103.* 1917. Serial No. 7265.

67 Cong., 1 sess. "Disposition of Waters of Colorado River," *S. Rept. 180.* 1921. Serial No. 7918.

67 Cong., 2 sess. "Problems of Imperial Valley and Vicinity," *S. Doc. 142.* 1922. Serial No. 7977.

67 Cong., 4 sess. "Southern Pacific Co.," *S. Rept. 1066.* 1923. Serial No. 8156.

69 Cong., 1 sess. "Boulder Canyon Reclamation Project," *S. Rept. 654.* 1926. Serial No. 8525.

69 Cong., 1 sess. "Glen Canyon, Bridge Canyon, and Arizona High Line Canal," *S. Doc. 113.* 1926. Serial No. 8558.

69 Cong., 2 sess. "Control of Power Companies," *S. Doc. 213.* 1927. Serial No. 8703.

69 Cong., 2 sess. "Lower Rio Grande and Lower Colorado Rivers," *S. Rept. 1455.* 1927. Serial No. 8685.

70 Cong., 1 sess. "Utility Corporations," *S. Doc. 92.* 1930. Serial Nos. 8855–58.

70 Cong., 1 sess. "Equitable Use of Waters of Lower Colorado River and Rio Grande," *S. Doc. 163.* 1928. Serial No. 8871.

70 Cong., 1 sess. "Boulder Canyon Project," *S. Rept. 592.* 1928. Serial No. 8830.

70 Cong., 2 sess. "Colorado River Development," *S. Doc. 186.* 1929. Serial No. 8989.

79 Cong., 1 sess. "Water Supply Below Boulder Dam," *S. Doc. 39.* 1945. Serial No. 10951.

———. ———. ———. Hearings:

Committee on Appropriations. "Second Deficiency Appropriation Bill, 1930." *Hearings.* 71 Cong., 2 sess., 1930.

Committee on Foreign Relations. "Water Treaty with Mexico." *Hearings.* 79 Cong., 1 sess., 1945.

Committee on Interior and Insular Affairs. "Central Arizona Project." *Hearings on S. 1685.* 88 Cong., 2 sess., 1964.

———. "Central Arizona Project and Colorado River Water Rights." *Hearings on S. 75 and S. J. Res. 4.* 81 Cong., 1 sess., 1949.

————. "Colorado River Storage Project." *Hearings on S. 1555.* 83 Cong., 2 sess., 1954.

————. "Colorado River Water Rights." *Hearings on S. J. Res. 145.* 80 Cong., 2 sess., 1948.

————. "Release of Colorado River Water." *Hearings.* 87 Cong., 2 sess., 1962.

Committee on Irrigation and Reclamation. "Arizona Water Resources." *Hearings on S. Res. 306.* 78 Cong., 2 sess., 1944.

————. "Colorado River Basin." *Hearings on S. 727.* 68 Cong., 2 sess., 1924 and 1925.

————. "Colorado River Basin." *Hearings on S. 728 and S. 1274.* 70 Cong., 1 sess., 1928.

————. "Colorado River Basin." *Hearings on S. Res. 320.* 69 Cong., 1 sess., 1925.

————. Department of Agriculture. "Irrigation Agriculture in the West." *Miscellaneous Publication No. 670.* Washington, D.C., November, 1948.

————. ————. "The Quality of Water for Irrigation Use." By W. V. Wilcox. *Technical Bulletin No. 962.* Washington, D.C., 1948.

————. ————. "Selected Problems in the Law of Water Rights in the West." By Wells A. Hutchins. *Miscellaneous Publications No. 418.* Washington, D.C., 1942.

————. ————. "Silt in the Colorado River and Its Relation to Irrigation." By Samuel Fortier and Harry F. Blaney. *Technical Bulletin No. 67.* Washington, D.C., 1928.

————. Department of Commerce. Bureau of the Census. *Censuses of the United States.*

————. ————. ————. *Irrigation: California.* Washington, D.C., 1920.

————. ————. ————. *Irrigation of Agricultural Lands, 1930.* Washington, D.C., 1932.

————. ————. ————. *Irrigation of Agricultural Lands, 1940: Tabular and Graphic Presentation.* Washington, D.C., 1943.

————. ————. ————. *Statistical Abstracts of the United States.*

————. ————. ————. *United States Census of Agriculture: 1945.* 2 vols. Washington, D.C., 1946–1947.

————. ————. Bureau of Foreign and Domestic Commerce. "Mexican West Coast and Lower California: A Commercial and Industrial Survey." *Special Agents Series No. 220.* By P. L. Bell and H. Bentley MacKenzie. Washington, D.C., 1923.

————. Department of the Interior. All-American Canal Board. *The All-American Canal: Report of the All-American Canal Board.* Washington, D.C., 1920.

——. ——. Bureau of Indian Affairs. "The Navajo Yearbook, 1951–1961: A Decade of Progress," *Report No. viii,* comp. by Robert W. Young. Window Rock, Arizona, 1961.

——. ——. ——. Statistics Division. *Estimates of Resident Indian Population and Labor Force Status; By State and Reservation: March 1972.* Mimeographed. Washington, D.C., September, 1972.

——. ——. Bureau of Reclamation. *Annual Reports.*

——. ——. ——. *The Colorado River.* Washington, D.C., March, 1946.

——. ——. ——. *Colorado River Water Quality Improvement Program.* Washington, D.C., February, 1972.

——. ——. ——. *Development of the Lower Colorado River.* Washington, D.C., 1928.

——. ——. ——. *Federal Reclamation Laws.* 2 vols. Washington, D.C., 1958–1959.

——. ——. ——. "General History and Description of Project." *Boulder Canyon Project, Final Reports,* Part 1, Bulletin 1. Boulder City, Nevada, December 1, 1948.

——. ——. ——. *Pacific Southwest Water Plan.* Washington, D.C., January 1964.

——. ——. ——. *Reclamation Era* (title varies).

——. ——. ——. *Report on Central Arizona Project.* Washington, D.C., 1947.

——. ——. ——. "Report on the Problems of the Colorado River Basin." By Frank E. Weymouth. Typescript. 9 vols. Washington, D.C., February, 1924.

——. ——. ——. *Second Supplement to "Report on Water Supply of the Lower Colorado River Basin Project Planning Report, November 1952."* Boulder City, Nevada, October, 1963.

——. ——. ——. "The Story of Boulder Dam." *Conservation Bulletin No. 9.* Washington, D.C., 1941.

——. ——. ——. "The Story of Hoover Dam." *Conservation Bulletin No. 9.* Washington, D.C., 1961.

——. ——. *Documents on the Use and Control of the Waters of Interstate and International Streams.* Washington, D.C., 1956.

——. ——. Federal Water Pollution Control Administration. Colorado River Basin Water Quality Control Project. *The Mineral Quality Problem in the Colorado River Basin.* Denver, Colo., 1970.

——. ——. Geological Survey. "Quality of Water of Colorado River in 1925–1926." By W. D. Collins and C. S. Howard. *Water-Supply Paper 596.* Washington, D.C., 1928.

——. ——. Geological Survey. *Water Supply Papers.*

——. ——. *The Hoover Dam Power and Water Contracts and*

Related Data. By Ray Lyman Wilbur and Northcutt Ely. Washington, D.C., 1933.

————. Department of State. International Boundary and Water Commission, United States and Mexico. *Water Bulletin.*

————. Environmental Protection Agency. *The Mineral Quality Problem in the Colorado River Basin.* Washington, D.C., 1971.

————. Federal Power Commission. *Annual Reports.*

————. *Arizona Power Survey.* Washington, D.C., March, 1942.

————. "National Power Survey: Principal Electric Utility Systems in the United States, 1935." *Power Series No. 2.* Washington, D.C., 1936.

————. Library of Congress. Division of Bibliography. *The Colorado River, with Special Reference to the Boulder Dam.* Mimeographed. Washington, D.C., 1935.

————. ————. *List of References on the Colorado River and Its Tributaries. Supplementive Bibliography Compiled in 1922 by Bertha L. Walsworth.* Mimeographed. Washington, D.C., 1926.

————. National Resources Committee. *Regional Factors in National Planning and Development.* Washington, D.C., 1935.

————. National Resources Planning Board. "Interstate Water Compacts, 1785 to 1941." *Technical Paper No. 5.* Washington, D.C., 1942.

————. National Water Commission. *Courts and Water* [PB 211 974]. By Grant P. Thompson. Washington, D.C., 1972.

————. ————. *The Federal-State Regional Corporation* [PB 202 997]. By Richard A. Solomon. Washington, D.C., 1971.

————. ————. *Federal-State Relations in Water Law* [PB 203 600]. By Frank J. Trelease. Washington, D.C., 1971.

————. ————. *Institutional Arrangements for Water Resource Development* [PB 207 314]. By Vincent Ostrom. Washington, D.C., 1971.

————. ————. *Intergovernmental Relations in Water Resources Activities* [PB 210 358]. Washington, D.C., n.d.

————. ————. *Interstate Water Compacts* [PB 202 998]. By Jerome C. Muys. Washington, D.C., 1971.

————. ————. *New Directions in U.S. Water Policy: Summary, Conclusions and Recommendations from the Final Report of the National Water Commission.* Washington, D.C., 1973.

————. President's Water Resources Policy Commission. *Report.* 3 vols. Washington, D.C., 1950.

————. *Statutes at Large.*

Upper Colorado River Commission (name varies). *Annual Reports.*

Utah. *Journal of the Utah House.*

————. *Journal of the Utah Senate.*

Wyoming. *Documents on the Use and Control of Wyoming's Interstate Streams: Compacts, Treaties, and Court Decrees.* Cheyenne, 1957.

————. *Journal of the Wyoming House.*

————. *Journal of the Wyoming Senate.*

COURT CASES

Arizona v. *California,* 283 U.S. 423 (1931).

Arizona v. *California,* 292 U.S. 341 (1934).

Arizona v. *California et al.,* 298 U.S. 558 (1936).

Arizona v. *California et al.,* 373 U.S. 546 (1963).

Arizona v. *California et al.,* 376 U.S. 340 (1964).

Coffin v. *Left Hand Ditch Co.,* 6 Colo. 443 (1882).

Crisman v. *Heiderer,* 5 Colo. 589 (1881).

Donnelly v. *United States,* 228 U.S. 243 (1913).

Fuller v. *Swan River,* 12 Colo. 12 (1888).

Hill v. *King,* 8 Calif. 336 (1857).

Kansas v. *Colorado,* 185 U.S. 143 (1902).

Kansas v. *Colorado,* 206 U.S. 46 (1907).

Lux v. *Haggin,* 69 Calif. 255 (1886); 4 Pac. 919 (1884); 10 Pac. 674 (1886).

Pollard's Lessee v. *Hagan et al.,* 3 Howard 212 (1845).

Schilling v. *Rominger,* 4 Colo. 100 (1878).

Shiveley v. *Bowlby,* 152 U.S. 1 (1894).

Sieber v. *Frink,* 7 Colo. 148 (1883).

United States v. *Arizona,* 295 U.S. 174 (1935).

Winters v. *United States,* 207 U.S. 564 (1908).

Wyoming v. *Colorado,* 259 U.S. 419 (1922).

Wyoming v. *Colorado,* 286 U.S. 494 (1932).

Yunker v. *Nichols,* 1 Colo. 551 (1872).

NEWSPAPERS AND PERIODICALS

American Society of Civil Engineers Transactions

Arizona Mining Journal

Boulder Dam Association Bulletin

Brawley News

Calexico Chronicle

Cheyenne *Wyoming State Tribune*

Colorado River Association Newsletter

Denver Post

Denver *Rocky Mountain News*

El Centro Press
El Centro Progress
Engineering News-Record
Fresno Bee
Grand Junction *Daily News*
Grand Junction *Daily Sentinel*
Imperial Enterprise
Imperial Valley Press
Intake
Kingman *Mohave County Miner*
Laramie *Republican-Boomerang*
Las Vegas Age
Los Angeles Examiner
Los Angeles Express
Los Angeles Herald
Los Angeles Herald-Examiner
Los Angeles Times
Maxwell's Talisman
Metropolitan Water District of Southern California *Colorado River Aqueduct News*
New York Herald Tribune
New York Times
Pacific Builder and Engineer
Phoenix *Arizona Republic*
Phoenix *Arizona Republican*
Phoenix Gazette
Prescott *Weekly Arizona Miner*
Riverside Daily Press
Riverside Enterprise
Sacramento Bee
Salt Lake City *Deseret News*
Salt Lake Tribune
San Diego Sun
San Diego Tribune
San Diego Union
Santa Fe New Mexican
Southwest
Time
Tucson *Arizona Daily Star*
Tucson *Arizona Citizen*
Tucson *Citizen*
Washington Herald
Western Construction News

ARTICLES

Adams, Thomas C. "Development of the Colorado River in the Upper Basin." *American Society of Civil Engineers Transactions* CV (1940): 1345–1375.

Alexander, Thomas G. "John Wesley Powell, the Irrigation Survey, and the Inauguration of the Second Phase of Irrigation Development in Utah." *Utah Historical Quarterly* XXXVII (1969): 190–206.

————. "The Powell Irrigation Survey and the People of the Mountain West." *Journal of the West* VII (1968): 48–53.

"Arthur Powell Davis." *Reclamation Era* XXXVI (February, 1950): 34–36.

Atwood, Albert W. "The Struggle for Future Greatness." *Saturday Evening Post*, October 9, 1926, p. 22.

Bakken, Gordon M. "The English Common Law in the Rocky Mountain West." *Arizona and the West* XI (1969): 109–128.

Ballard, R. H. "Electrical Industry Objects Only to Power Feature of Boulder Dam Bill." *Electrical World*, April 28, 1928, p. 870.

Balzar, F. B. "Nevada—and the Colorado." *Community Builder* I (March, 1928): 37–40.

Bancroft, George J. "Diversion of Water from the Western Slope." *Colorado Magazine* XXI (1944): 178–181.

Bannister, L. Ward. "Interstate Rights in Interstate Streams in the Arid West." *Harvard Law Review* XXXVI (1923): 960–986.

Bennett, N. B., Jr. "The Upper Colorado River Basin Compact is Signed." *Reclamation Era* XXXIV (December, 1948): 221.

Bingham, Jay R. "Reclamation and the Colorado." *Utah Historical Quarterly* XXVIII (1960): 233–249.

Bissell, Charles A., and Weymouth, Frank E. "Arthur Powell Davis." *Transactions of the American Society of Civil Engineers* C (1935): 1582–1591.

Bitner, M. S. "The Colorado–Big Thompson Project." *Reclamation Era* XXX (September, 1940): 267–269.

Bloom, Paul L. "Indian 'Paramount' Rights to Water Use." In Rocky Mountain Mineral Law Institute. *Proceedings of the Sixteenth Annual Institute*, pp. 669–693. New York, 1971.

Breitenstein, Jean S. "Some Elements of Colorado Water Law." *Rocky Mountain Law Review* XX (1950): 343–356.

————. "The Upper Colorado River Basin Compact." *State Government* XXII (1949): 214.

"Building of Boulder Canyon Project Recommended." *New Reclamation Era* XVII (February, 1926): 20–22.

Caldwell, Fred S. "Legal Rights of Arizona and California in the Colorado River." *Rocky Mountain Law Review* XI (1938): 1–11.

Caldwell, L. K. "Interstate Cooperation in River Basin Development." *Iowa Law Review* XXXII (1947): 232–243.

Carman, E. C. "Sovereign Rights and Relations in the Control and Use of American Waters." *Southern California Law Review* III (1929–1930): 84–100, 152–172, 266–319.

Carpenter, Delph. "Application of the Reserve Treaty Powers of the States to Interstate Water Controversies." *Colorado Bar Association Report* XXIV (1921): 45–101.

———. "Conflict of Jurisdiction Respecting Control of Waters in Western States." *Rocky Mountain Law Review* II (1930): 162–172.

———. "Interstate River Compacts and Their Place in Water Utilization." *Journal of the American Water Works Association* XX (1928): 756–773.

Carr, Ralph. "Delph Carpenter and River Compacts between Western States." *Colorado Magazine* XXI (January, 1944): 4–14.

Carson, Charles A. "Arizona's Interest in the Colorado River." *Rocky Mountain Law Review* XIX (1947): 352–358.

Caughey, John. "The Insignificance of the Frontier in American History." *Western Historical Quarterly* V (1974): 5–16.

Chamberlin, Eugene K. "Mexican Colonization versus American Interests in Lower California." *Pacific Historical Review* XX (1951): 43–55.

Chatfield, C. H. "Denver's Future Water Supply." *Official Bulletin of the Colorado Society of Civil Engineers*, June-July, 1922, pp. 1–2.

Clements, George P. "Parceling Out the Colorado River." *Southern California Business*, January, 1923, pp. 13–15.

Clyde, Edward W. "The Colorado River Decision—1963." *Utah Law Review* VIII (1962–1964): 299–312.

———. "Present Conflicts on the Colorado River." *Rocky Mountain Law Review* XXII (1960): 534–565.

Clyde, George D. "History of Irrigation in Utah." *Utah Historical Quarterly* XXVII (1959): 27–36.

Coffeen, William R. "The Effects of the Central Arizona Project on the Fort McDowell Indian Community." *Ethnohistory* XIX (1972): 345–377.

Colby, William E. "The Freedom of the Miner and Its Influence on Water Law." In *Legal Essays in Tribute to Orrin Kip McMurray*, edited by Max Radin, pp. 67–84. Berkeley, 1935.

Cole, Donald B. "Transmountain Water Diversion in Colorado." *Colorado Magazine* XXV (1948): 49–65, 118–133.

"Colorado–Big Thompson Project." *Reclamation Era* XXXIII (April, 1947): 83–86.

Conkin, Paul K. "The Vision of Elwood Mead." *Agricultural History* XXXIV (1960): 88–97.

Corker, Charles E. "Federal-State Relations in Water Rights Adjudication and Administration." In Rocky Mountain Mineral Law Institute, *Proceedings of the Seventeenth Annual Institute*, pp. 579–611. New York, 1972.

———. "Water Rights and Federalism—The Water Rights Settlement Bill of 1957." *California Law Review* XLV (1957): 604–637.

Corwin, Edward S. "The Passing of Dual Federalism." *Virginia Law Review* XXXVI (1950): 1–24.

Costo, Rupert. "Indian Water Rights: A Survival Issue." *Indian Historian* V (Fall, 1972): 4–6.

Dana, Marshall N. "Reclamation, Its Influence and Impact on the History of the West." *Utah Historical Quarterly* XXVII (1959): 39–49.

Darrah, William Culp. "Powell of the Colorado." *Utah Historical Quarterly* XXVIII (1960): 223–231.

Davis, Arthur Powell. "The Colorado River Surveys." *Community Builder* I (March, 1928): 13–19.

———. "Development of the Colorado River: The Justification of Boulder Dam." *Atlantic Monthly*, February, 1929, pp. 254–263.

Dellwo, Robert D. "Indian Water Rights—The Winters Doctrine Updated." *Gonzaga Law Review* VI (1970–1971): 215–240.

Dern, George H. "Utah's Position on the Colorado." *Community Builder* I (March, 1928): 41–44.

Dodd, Alice Mary. "Interstate Compacts." *U.S. Law Review* LXX (1936): 557–578.

Dowd, M. J. "Silt Problems of Imperial Irrigation District as Affected by Completion of Boulder Dam." *Civil Engineering* IX (1939): 609–611.

Dunbar, Robert G. "History of Agriculture." In *Colorado and Its People*, edited by LeRoy Hafen, vol. 2, pp. 120–157. New York, 1948.

———. "The Origins of the Colorado System of Water-Right Control." *Colorado Magazine* XXVII (1950): 241–262.

———. "Water Conflicts and Controls in Colorado." *Agriculture History* XXII (1948): 180–186.

Dykstra, Clarence A., ed. "Colorado River Development and Related Problems," *American Academy of Political and Social Science Annals* CSLVIII (March, 1930), pt. II.

"Ending the Battle for the Colorado." *Stanford Law Review* II (1950): 334–344.

Engelbert, Ernest A. "Federalism and Water Resources Development." *Law and Contemporary Problems* XXII(1957):325–350.
———. "The Origins of the Pacific Southwest Water Plan." in *New Horizons for Resources Research,* pp. 125–204. Boulder, Colo., 1965.
Forbes, Jack D. "Indian Horticulture West and Northwest of the Colorado River." *Journal of the West* II (1963): 1–14.
Forbes, R. H. "History of Irrigation Development in Arizona." *Reclamation Era* XXVI (October, 1936): 226–227.
Forester, D. M. "The Imperial Dam, All-American Canal System, Boulder Canyon Project." *Reclamation Era* XXIX (February, 1939): 28–36.
Fox, Irving K. "Water: Supply, Demand and the Law." *Rocky Mountain Law Review* XXXII (1960): 452–463.
Frankfurter, Felix and Landis, James M. "The Compact Clause of the Constitution—A Study in Interstate Adjustments." *Yale Law Journal* XXXIV (1925): 685–758.
Frantz, Albert T. "The Law Mirrors History." In *Essays in Legal History in Honor of Felix Frankfurter,* edited by Morris D. Forkosch, pp. 77–85. New York, 1966.
Galbraith, W. J. "The Reason for an Interstate Colorado River Pact." *Arizona Mining Journal* VI (January 15, 1923): 17–18.
Ganoe, John T. "The Origin of a National Reclamation Policy." *Mississippi Valley Historical Review* XVIII (1931): 34–52.
Gookin, W. S. "Central Arizona Project." *Reclamation Era* XXXV (January, 1949): 5–8; (February, 1949): 28.
Gopalakrishnan, Chennat. "The Doctrine of Prior Appropriation and Its Impact on Water Development: A Critical Survey." *American Journal of Economics and Sociology* XXXII (1973): 61–72.
Gressley, Gene M. "Arthur Powell Davis, Reclamation and the West." *Agriculture History* XLII (1968): 241–257.
Grunsky, C. E. "International and Interstate Aspects of the Colorado River Problem." *Science* LVI (November 10, 1922): 521–527.
Haber, David. "Arizona v. California—A Brief Review." *Natural Resources Journal* IV (1964–1965): 17–28.
Hadley, Howard D. "Progress in Colorado River Project." *Saturday Night,* April 8, 1922, p. 5.
Halseth, Odd A. "Arizona's 1500 Years of Irrigation History." *Reclamation Era* XXXIII (December, 1947): 251–254.
Hamele, Ottamar. "Federal Water Rights in the Colorado River." *Annals of the American Academy of Political and Social Science* CXXXV (January, 1928): 143–149.
———. "The Colorado River Compact." *Reclamation Record* XIII (December, 1922): 302–305.

Hampton, E. L. "The Battle with the Colorado." *Review of Reviews* LXVI (November, 1922): 525–531.

Harding, S. T. "Background of California Water and Power Problems." *California Law Review* XXXVIII (1950): 547–571.

Heard, Dwight B. "The Colorado River Controversy." *Review of Reviews* LXXVI (December, 1927): 624–628.

Hendricks, William O. "Developing San Diego's Desert Empire." *Journal of San Diego History* XVII (Summer, 1971): 1–11.

Hill, Raymond A. "Development of the Rio Grande Compact of 1938," *Natural Resources Journal* XIV (1974): 163–199.

Holsinger, M. Paul. "Wyoming v. Colorado Revisited: The United States Supreme Court and the Laramie River Controversy, 1911–1922." *Annals of Wyoming* XLII (1970): 47–56.

Hoover, Herbert. "Address by Secretary Hoover [before the Commonwealth Club of California]. *Transactions of the Commonwealth Club of California* XVII (1922): 449–458.

———. "Colorado River Development." *Industrial Management* LXIII (May, 1922): 291.

———. "The Colorado River Problem." *Community Builder* I (March, 1928): 9–12.

———. "Harness the Colorado." *Southern California Business*, October, 1926, p. 45.

Hosmer, Helen. "Imperial Valley." *American West* III (Winter, 1966): 34–49.

Houghton, N. D. "Problems in Public Power Administration in the Southwest—Some Arizona Applications." *Western Political Quarterly* IV (1951): 116–129.

———. "Problems of the Colorado River as Reflected in Arizona Politics." *Western Political Quarterly* IV (1951): 634–643.

Howard, C. S. "Irrigation and Water Quality." *Reclamation Era* XXXIX (January, 1953): 1; (February, 1953): 39–40.

Hudson, James J. "California National Guard and the Mexican Border, 1914–1916." *California Historical Society Quarterly* XXXIV (1955): 157–171.

Hundley, Norris, jr. "Clio Nods: *Arizona v. California* and the Boulder Canyon Act: A Reassessment." *Western Historical Quarterly* III (1972): 17–51.

———. "The Colorado Waters Dispute." *Foreign Affairs* XLII (1963–1964): 495–500.

———. "The Politics of Reclamation: California, the Federal Government, and the Origins of the Boulder Canyon Act: A Second Look." *California Historical Quarterly* LII (1973): 292–325.

———. "The Politics of Water and Geography: California and the

Mexican-American Treaty of 1944." *Pacific Historical Review* XXXVI (1967): 209–226.

Hunt, George W. P. "The Arizona Position." *Community Builder* I (March, 1928): 20–22.

Hutchins, Wells A., and Steele, Harry A. "Basic Water Rights Doctrines and Their Implications for River Basin Development." *Law and Contemporary Problems* XXII (1957): 276–300.

Johnson, Hiram. "The Boulder Canyon Project." *Annals of the American Academy of Political Science* CXXXV (1928): 150–156.

————. "The Boulder Canyon Project." *Community Builder* I (March, 1928): 45–51.

Jones, Paul. "Reclamation and the Indian." *Utah Historical Quarterly* XXVII (1959): 51–56.

Kelly, Desmond G. "California and the Colorado River." *California Law Review* XXXVIII (1950): 696–717.

Kelly, William. "Colorado–Big Thompson Initiation, 1933–1938." *Colorado Magazine* XXXIV (1957): 66–74.

————. "The Colorado River Problem." *American Society of Civil Engineers: Tranactions* LXXXVIII (1925): 306–437.

————. "Rationing the Rivers: A Decade of Interstate Waters and Interstate Commerce in the Supreme Court." *Rocky Mountain Law Review* XIV (1941): 12–20.

Knight, Oliver. "Correcting Nature's Error: The Colorado–Big Thompson Project." *Agricultural History* XXX (1956): 157–169.

Kruckman, Arnold. "Inside Story of River Conference." *Saturday Night*, November 18, 1922, p. 5.

Laird, A. D. K. "Desalting Technology." In *California Water: A Study in Resource Management*, edited by David Seckler, pp. 127–160. Berkeley and Los Angeles, 1971.

Lamar, Howard. "Persistent Frontier: The West in the Twentieth Century." *Western Historical Quarterly* IV (1973): 5–25.

Lasky, Moses. "From Prior Appropriation to Economic Distribution of Water by the State—Via Irrigation Administration." *Rocky Mountain Law Review* I (1929): 161–216, 248–270; II: 35–58.

Leach, Richard H. "The Interstate Compact, Water, and the Southwest: A Case Study in Compact Utility." *Southwestern Social Science Quarterly* XXXVIII (1957): 236–247.

————. "The Status of Interstate Compacts Today." *State Government* XXXII (1959): 134–139.

Leaphart, Bill. "Sale and Lease of Indian Water Rights." *Montana Law Review* XXXIII (1972): 266–276.

Leatherwood, Elmer. "My Objections to the Boulder Dam Project." *Annals of the American Academy of Political and Social Science* CXXXV (1928): 133–140.

Lee, Lawrence B. "William Ellsworth Smythe and the Irrigation Movement: A Reconsideration." *Pacific Historical Review* XLI (1972): 289–311.

Lilley, William, III, and Gould, Lewis L. "The Western Irrigation Movement, 1878–1902: A Reappraisal." In *The American West: A Reorientation,* edited by Gene M. Gressley, pp. 57–75. Laramie, Wyo., 1966.

Lippincott, J. G. "Mulholland's Memory." *Civil Engineering* IX (1939): 199.

McClellan, L. N. "Utilization of Colorado River Power." *Reclamation Era* XXXI (January, 1944): 8–10.

McGregor, A. G. "Some Reasons Why Arizona Should Not Ratify the Pact." *Arizona Mining Journal* VI (January 15, 1923): 24.

McKinley, Charles. "The Management of Water Resources under the American Federal System." In *Federalism: Nature and Emergent,* edited by Arthur W. Macmahon, pp. 328–351. New York, 1955.

Maxwell, George H. "Shall America be Developed? The Truth About the Compact." *Arizona Mining Journal* VI (January 15, 1923): 33.

———. "The Truth About the Colorado River." *The Signal* (May 4, 1923), p. 3.

Mead, Elwood. "Hoover Dam." *Civil Engineering* I (1930): 3–8.

———. "The Utilization of the Colorado River." *New Reclamation Era* XVII (March, 1926): 38–42.

Meyers, Charles J. "The Colorado River." *Stanford Law Review* XIX (1966): 1–75.

——— and Noble, Richard L. "The Colorado River: The Treaty with Mexico." *Stanford Law Review* XIX (1967): 367–419.

Miller, Gerald R. "Indians, Water, and the Arid Western States—A Prelude to the Pelton Decision." *Utah Law Review* V (1957): 495–510.

Miller, Gordon R. "Shaping California Water Law, 1781 to 1928." *Southern California Quarterly* LV (1973): 9–42.

Morrison, Margaret D. "Charles Robinson Rockwood: Developer of the Imperial Valley." *Southern California Quarterly* XLIV (1962): 307–330.

Mulholland, William. "Water from the Colorado River," *Community Builder* I (March, 1928): 23–27.

Murphy, Ralph. "Arizona's Side of the Question." *Sunset Magazine,* April, 1926, pp. 34–37.

Nelson, Wesley R. "The Boulder Canyon Project." In *Annual Report of the Board of Regents of the Smithsonian Institution, 1935,* pp. 429–452. Washington, D.C., 1936.

Niles, Russell D. "Arizona v. California." *New York University Law Quarterly Review* X (1932): 188–212.

———. "Legal Background of the Colorado River Controversy." *Rocky Mountain Law Review* I (1929): 73–101.

———. "The Swing-Johnson Bill and the Supreme Court." *Rocky Mountain Law Review* III (1930): 1–24.

Norcross, Fred N. "Genesis of the Colorado–Big Thompson Project." *Colorado Magazine* XXX (1953): 29–37.

Norviel, W. S. "The Colorado River Compact Means Much to Southwest." *Arizona Mining Journal* VI (January 15, 1923): 34.

Null, James A. "Water Use as a Property Right," *Colorado Magazine* XXII (1974): 317–327.

Olson, Reuel L. "Legal Problems in Colorado River Development." *American Academy of Political and Social Science Annals* CXXXV (1928): 108–114.

———. "Relationship of *Wyoming* v. *Colorado* to Colorado River." *Los Angeles Bar Association Bulletin* II (November 4 and 18, 1926).

Parsons, Malcolm B. "Limitations on Continued Colorado River Development in Arizona." *Rocky Mountain Law Review* XX (1948): 280–287.

———. "Origins of the Colorado River Controversy in Arizona Politics, 1922–1923." *Arizona and the West* IV (1962): 27–44.

———. "Party and Pressure Politics in Arizona's Opposition to Colorado River Development." *Pacific Historical Review* XIX (1950): 47–58.

"Pollution and Political Boundaries: U.S.–Mexican Environmental Problems." *National Resources Journal* XII (October, 1972).

Pomeroy, Earl. "Toward a Reorientation of Western History: Continuity and Environment." *Mississippi Valley Historical Review* XLI (1955): 579–599.

Pinchot, Gifford. "Who Owns Our Rivers?" *Nation*, January 18, 1928, pp. 64–66.

Ranquist, Harold. "Effect of Changes in Place and Nature of Use of Indian Rights to Water Reserved under the 'Winters Doctrine.'" *National Resources Lawyer* V (1972), 34–41.

Reid, Bill G. "Franklin K. Lane's Idea for Veteran's Colonization, 1918–1921." *Pacific Historical Review* XXXIII (1964): 447–461.

Rex, Robert W. "Geothermal Resources in the Imperial Valley." In *California Water: A Study in Resource Management*, edited by David Seckler, pp. 190–205. Berkeley and Los Angeles, 1971.

"River Basin Development." *Law and Contemporary Problems* XXII (1957): 155–322.

Sax, Joseph L. "Problems of Federalism in Reclamation Law." *University of Colorado Law Review* XXXVII (1964–1965): 49–84.

Schonfeld, Robert G. "The Early Development of California's Imperial Valley." *Southern California Quarterly* L (1968): 279–309, 395–426.

Scofield, Carl S. "The Salinity of Irrigation Water." In *Annual Report of the Board of Regents of the Smithsonian Institution, 1935*, pp. 275–288. Washington, D.C., 1936.

Scott, Robert D. "Kansas v. Colorado Revisited." *American Journal of International Law* LII (1958): 432–454.

Shaw, Lucien. "The Development of the Law of Waters in the West." *California Law Review* X (1922): 443–460.

Sloan, Richard E. "Pact Criticism Is Largely on What It Does Not Say." *Arizona Mining Journal* VI (January 15, 1923): 29.

Smedley, Chester E. "Letter on the Transmountain Water Diversion Article [by Donald B. Cole]." *Colorado Magazine* XXV (1948): 232–235.

Smith, G. E. P. "An Equitable Basis for Solution of the Colorado River Controversy." *Progressive Arizona and the Great Southwest* IX (October, 1929): 12; (November, 1929): 22; (December, 1929): 26.

———. "Arizona Reclamation Limits." *Western Construction News* XX (August, 1945): 104–107.

———. "The Colorado River and Arizona's Interest in Its Development." *University of Arizona Agricultural Experiment Station Bulletin No. 95* (February 25, 1922), pp. 529–546.

———. "A Discussion of Certain Colorado River Problems." *University of Arizona Agricultural Experiment Station Bulletin No. 100* (February 10, 1925), pp. 143–175.

Sondheim, Harry B. and Alexander, John R. "Federal Indian Water Rights: A Retrogression to Quasi-Riparianism?" *Southern California Law Review* XXXIV (1960): 1–61.

Spear, William. "Most Objections Have Nothing to Do with Pact." *Arizona Mining Journal* VI (January 15, 1923): 18.

Stephenson, W. A. "Appropriation of Water in Arid Regions." *Southwestern Social Science Quarterly* XVIII (1937): 215–226.

Sterling, Everett W. "The Powell Irrigation Survey, 1888–1893." *Mississippi Valley Historical Review* XXVII (1940): 421–434.

Stetson, Clarence C. "Making an Empire to Order." *World's Work* XLV (November, 1922): 92–102.

Stinson, Howard R. "Western Interstate Water Compacts." *California Law Review* XLV (1957): 655–664.

Stone, Clifford H. "Colorado's 100 Years of Irrigation." *Reclamation Era* XXXVIII (June, 1952): 137.

————. "Federal *versus* State Control of Water." *Rocky Mountain Law Review* XII (1940): 69–76.

Sykes, Godfrey. "The Delta and Estuary of the Colorado River." *Geographical Review* XVI (1926): 232–255.

Teilman, Hendrick. "The Role of Irrigation Districts in California's Water Development." *American Journal of Economics and Sociology* XXII (1963): 409–415.

Tuttle, Edward D. "The River Colorado." *Arizona Historical Review* I (1928): 50–68.

Trelease, Frank J. "Arizona v. California: Allocation of Water to People, States, and Nation." In *The Supreme Court Review, 1963,* edited by Philip B. Kurland, pp. 158–205. Chicago, 1963.

Van Petten, Donald R. "Arizona's Stand on the Santa Fe Compact and the Boulder Dam Project Act." *New Mexico Historical Review* XVII (1942): 1–20.

Veeder, William H. "Indian Prior and Paramount Rights to the Use of Water." In Rocky Mountain Mineral Law Institute, *Proceedings of the Sixteenth Annual Institute,* pp. 631–668. New York, 1971.

————. "Water Rights: Life or Death for the American Indian." *Indian Historian* V (Summer 1972): 4–21.

————. "Winters Doctrine Rights: Keystone of National Programs for Western Land and Water Conservation and Utilization." *Montana Law Review* XXVI (1965): 149–172.

Vetter, C. P. "Technical Aspects of the Silt Problem on the Colorado River." *Civil Engineering* X (1940): 698–701.

Von KleinSmid, Rufus B. "League of the Southwest: What It Is and Why." *Arizona, the State Magazine* XI (May, 1920): 5.

Waite, G. Graham. "International Treaties Affecting Western Water Rights." *Land and Water Review* IV (1969): 67–96.

"Water Resources." *Law and Contemporary Development* XXII (1957): 323–537.

Wiel, Samuel C. "Fifty Years of Water Law." *Harvard Law Review* L (1936–1937): 252–304.

————. "One Aspect of the Colorado River Interstate Agreement." *California Law Review* XI (1922–1923): 145–155.

————. "Public Policy in Western Water Decisions." *California Law Review* I (1912): 11–31.

Williams, Wayne. "The Colorado River and the Constitution." *American Bar Association Journal* XII (1926): 839–841.

————. "Irrigation Law in Colorado." *Rocky Mountain Law Review* X (1938): 87–104, 178–192.

————. "A Treaty Among States: How the Southwest Will Regulate and Utilize the Flood Waters of the Colorado River." *Review of Reviews* LXV (June, 1922): 619–622.

Bibliography

Wilmer, Mark. "*Arizona* v. *California*: A Statutory Construction Case." *Arizona Law Review* VI (1964–1965): 40–64.

Woodward, Sherman M. "Arthur Powell Davis." In *Dictionary of American Biography* XI, supplement one, pp. 224–225. New York, 1944.

Young, C. C. "The California Position." *Community Builder* I (March, 1928): 33–36.

PAMPHLETS

Arizona Highline Reclamation Association. *Arizona Highline Canal.* Phoenix, 1923, 1934.

Bannister, L. Ward. *Colorado River and the Swing-Johnson Bill: Address by L. Ward Bannister to the United States Chamber of Commerce (Western Division), Colorado Springs, December 7, 1926,* N.p., 1926.

———. *The Swing-Johnson Bill and Other Water Legislation—A Reply to Senator Phipps.* N.p., Jan. 1927.

Bohn, Frank, ed. *Boulder Dam.* New York, 1927.

Boulder Dam Association. *Boulder Dam Project Should Not be Delayed by Arizona.* Los Angeles, 1926.

———. *The Federal Government's Colorado River Project.* Los Angeles, 1927.

———. *The Story of a Great Government Project for the Conquest of the Colorado River.* Los Angeles, 1928.

Brook, Harold H. *The International Aspects of the Rio Grande Project, Texas and New Mexico.* Las Cruces, New Mexico, 1922, 1923.

Carpenter, Delph. *Colorado River—Boulder Canyon Dam Bill.* Denver, 1926.

———. *Conflict of Jurisdiction Respecting Control of Waters in Western States.* N.p., 1929.

Chandler, Harry. *Imperial Valley's Most Essential Need is a Flood Control and Storage Dam in the Colorado River.* N.p., n.d.

———. *The Other Side of the Question.* N.p. [July, 1924].

Clark, Walter Gordon. *The Colorado River: History [of] Seven-States Compact and Future Development.* [Los Angeles, 1924].

———. *Colorado River Problems: Views of General Goethals and Walter G. Clark, Consulting Engineers on Arizona's Rights to Tributary Streams in the Lower Colorado Basin.* Phoenix [1924].

Colter, Fred T. *Speech and Replies of Hon. Fred T. Colter . . . on the Colorado River Compact.* Phoenix, February 27, 1923.

D'Autremont, H. H. *More Data on the Colorado River Question.* Tucson, 1943.

Davis, Arthur P. *The Single Tax from the Farmer's Standpoint.* Minneapolis, 1897.

Dern, George H. *The Colorado River.* Colorado Springs, December 7, 1926.

Dimock, Marshall E., and Benson, George C. S. "Can Interstate Compacts Succeed: The Uses and Limitations of Interstate Agreements," *Public Policy Pamphlet No. 22.* Chicago, 1937.

Dowd, M. J. *The Colorado River Flood-Protection Works of Imperial Irrigation District: History and Cost.* El Centro, California, July, 1951.

————. *Historic Salton Sea.* 4th Printing. N.p., April, 1965.

Favour, A. H. *Arizona's Rights in the Colorado River.* N.p., August 16, 1929.

Greer, F. W. *Boulder Dam and Cotton.* Columbia, S.C., 1927.

Grimes, Oliver J. *The Colorado River Problem.* Salt Lake City [1927].

Heard, Dwight B. *The Heard Plan for Co-operative Action Provides for Immediate Development of Resources of the Colorado River.* N.p., 1924.

————. *Some of the Views of Hon. Dwight B. Heard on the Colorado River Compact.* Phoenix, 1924.

Heber, A. H. *Address . . . to the Settlers of Imperial Valley.* Los Angeles [1904].

Holt, Luther M., comp. *The Unfriendly Attitude of the United States Government Towards the Imperial Valley . . . .* Imperial, Calif., 1907.

Hoover, Herbert. *The Colorado River Pact.* N.p. [1922].

Hunt, George W. P. *The Arizona Position.* N.p. [1923].

————. *Arizona's Viewpoint on the Colorado River.* Phoenix, August 17, 1925.

————. *The Colorado River and the Swing-Johnson Boulder Canyon Dam Bill.* Phoenix, January 31, 1928.

————. *Letter of Geo. W. P. Hunt, Governor of Arizona to Senator Henry F. Ashurst.* Phoenix, February 3, 1926.

————. *Memorandum of Speech Delivered by Governor George W. P. Hunt of Arizona at Miami, Arizona, Labor Day, Sept. 7, 1925.* Mimeographed. Phoenix, 1925.

————. *Why I Oppose the Approval of the Colorado River Compact.* Tombstone, Ariz., [1923].

Imperial County Board of Supervisors. *Imperial Valley, 1901–1915.* Los Angeles, 1915.

Imperial Irrigation District. *The Boulder Dam All-American Canal Project.* El Centro, California, 1924.

————. *Boulder Dam, All American Canal Project and Imperial Valley Pictorially.* Los Angeles, 1926.

————. *The Boulder Dam, All-American Canal Project—Facts.* Imperial, Calif., 1924.

Imperial Land Company. *Imperial Catechism: Questions and Answers Regarding the Imperial Valley, August, 1903.* 12th ed., rev., Los Angeles, March, 1904.

Knapp, Cleon T. *History and Status of the Colorado River Controversy.* Phoenix, 1948.

Kruckman, Arnold. *The Colorado River Riddle.* Los Angeles [1922?].

League of the Southwest. *League of the Southwest: What It Is and Why.* [Los Angeles, 1920].

Leatherwood, Elmer. *Forcing the Government into Business.* N.p., n.d.

Los Angeles Colorado River Association. *California and the Colorado River.* Los Angeles, 1952.

Los Angeles Department of Water and Power. *Data on Available Water Supply and Future Requirements of Los Angeles and the Metropolitan Area.* Los Angeles, 1928.

————. *That Two Million People Might Live.* Los Angeles, August, 1928.

McClure, W. F. *Statement by W. F. McClure, State Engineer, to Governor Friend W. Richardson.* Sacramento, 1925.

McCreery, James W. *Interstate Waters and the Colorado River Commission.* N.p., 1922.

McPherrin, R. D. *Imperial Valley and Its Relation to Colorado River Problems.* N.p. [1921].

Maddock, Thomas. *An Arizona Argument.* Phoenix, 1925.

————. *Reasons for Arizona's Opposition to the Swing-Johnson Bill and Santa Fe Compact.* Phoenix [1927].

Malone, George W. *Boulder Canyon Lower Colorado River Power and Water Set-up.* Carson City, Nev., 1928.

Metropolitan Water District of Southern California. . . . *Colorado River Aqueduct: the Need, Growth, Engineering Features, Financial Status, and Progress.* . . . Los Angeles, 1935.

Moody, Burdett. *The Colorado River Boulder Canyon Project and the All-American Canal.* Los Angeles, 1925.

Pinchot, Gifford. *Giant Power.* Philadelphia, June 17, 1923.

————. *The Power Monopoly, Its Makeup and Its Menace.* N.p., n.d.

Seiberling, Frank A. *The Colorado River and Its Utilization.* Phoenix [1920].

Shadegg, Stephen C. *Arizona: An Adventure in Irrigation.* Phoenix, 1949.

Smith, G. E. P. *The Colorado River and Arizona's Interest in Its Development.* Tucson, 1922.

————. *An Equitable Basis for Solution of the Colorado River Controversy.* Tucson, Ariz., 1925.

Ward, Charles. *Explanation of Terms in the Colorado River Controversy between Arizona and California.* Prescott, Ariz., August 1, 1929.

West Side Imperial Irrigation Company. *An All-American Canal for Imperial Valley: Why It Should Be Built.* Los Angeles, n.d.

Weymouth, Frank E. *Water Needs and Financial Aspects of the Metropolitan Water District Project.* Los Angeles, 1931.

White, Samuel. *Memorandum of Law Points and Authorities Respecting the Rights of Arizona in the Colorado River Prepared and Submitted to Hon. George W. P. Hunt, Governor of Arizona.* Phoenix, September 8, 1925.

Winsor, Mulford. *Mulford Winsor Exposes Governor Hunt's Stand on the Colorado River Pact.* N.p. [1926?].

OTHER PUBLISHED MATERIALS

Ackerman, Edward A., and Löf, George O. G. *Technology in American Water Development.* Baltimore, 1959.

Alexander, J. A. *The Life of George Chaffey.* Melbourne, 1928.

Bailey, G. *Water Resources of California.* Sacramento, 1927.

Baker, D. M. and Conkling, Harold. *Water Supply and Utilization: An Outline of Hydrology from the Viewpoint of the Arid Section of the United States together with an Outline of Water Law and Its Administration as It Has Developed in the Arid States.* New York, 1930.

Baker, James H., and Hafen, LeRoy R., eds. *History of Colorado.* 5 vols. Denver, 1927.

Baker, T. Lindsay, et al. *Water for the Southwest.* New York, 1973.

Barton, Weldon V. *Interstate Compacts in the Political Process.* Chapel Hill, 1967.

Baumhoff, Richard G. *The Dammed Missouri Valley.* New York, 1951.

Berkman, Richard L. and Viscusi, W. Kip, et al. *Damming the West: Ralph Nader's Study Group Report on the Bureau of Reclamation.* New York, 1973.

Black, Robert. *Island in the Rockies: The History of Grand County, Colorado, to 1930.* Boulder, 1969.

Blake, Nelson. *Water for the Cities.* Syracuse, New York, 1956.

Bogart, Ernest L. *The Water Problem of Southern California.* Urbana, 1934.

Boyle, Robert H., et al. *The Water Hustlers.* San Francisco, 1971.

Brandes, Joseph. *Herbert Hoover and Economic Diplomacy: Department of Commerce Policy, 1921–28.* Pittsburgh, 1962.

Carr, Donald. *Death of the Sweet Waters.* New York, 1966; rev. ed., 1971.

Castetter, Edward F. and Bell, Willis H. *Yuman Indian Agriculture.* Albuquerque, 1951.

Chan, Loren B. *Sagebrush Statesman: Tasker L. Oddie of Nevada.* Reno, 1973.

Clark, Robert. *New Mexico Water Resource Law.* Albuquerque, 1964.

Clark, Robert E., ed. *Waters and Water Rights.* 7 vols., Indianapolis, 1967.

Colorado Water Conversation Board. *A Hundred Years of Irrigation in Colorado . . . , 1852–1952.* Denver and Fort Collins, 1952.

——. *Inter-State Compacts.* 4 vols. Denver, n.d.

Compañía Mexicana de Terrenos del Río Colorado, S. A. *Colonización del Valle de Mexicali, B. C.* México, D. F., 1958.

Confederation of Indian Tribes of the Colorado River. *Blueprint for Action.* Long Beach, Calif., 1972.

Cooper, Erwin. *Aqueduct Empire.* Glendale, Calif., 1968.

Corle, Edwin. *The Gila, River of the Southwest.* New York, 1951.

Cory, H. T. *The Imperial Valley and the Salton Sink.* San Francisco, 1915.

Coulson, H. J. W. *Coulson and Forbes on the Law of Waters, Sea, Tidal and Inland, and Lake Drainage.* 6th ed. London, 1952.

Council of State Governments. *Interstate Compacts, 1783–1956.* Chicago, July, 1956.

Cross, Jack Lee, ed. *Arizona: Its People and Resources.* Tucson, 1960.

Darrah, William Culp. *Powell of the Colorado.* Princeton, 1951.

Davis, Arthur Powell. *Irrigation Works Constructed by the United States.* New York, 1917.

Dunbier, Roger. *The Sonoran Desert.* Tucson, 1968.

Elliott, Russell R. *History of Nevada.* Lincoln, 1973.

Farnham, Henry P. *Law of Waters and Water Rights.* 3 vols. Rochester, 1909.

Farr, Finis C., ed. *The History of Imperial County, California.* Berkeley, 1918.

Faulk, Odie B. *Arizona: A Short History.* Norman, 1970.

Fogelson, Robert. *The Fragmented Metropolis: Los Angeles, 1850–1930.* Cambridge, Mass., 1967.

Fritz, Percy Stanley. *Colorado: The Centennial State.* New York, 1941.

Garnsey, Morris. *America's New Frontier: The Mountain West.* New York, 1950.

Gates, Paul W. *History of Public Land Law Development.* Washington, D.C., 1968.

Gates, William H., comp. *Hoover Dam, Including the Story of the Turbulent Colorado River.* Los Angeles [1938].

Glass, Mary Ellen. *Water for Nevada: The Reclamation Controversy, 1885–1902.* Carson City, Nev., 1964.

Goff, John S. *George W. P. Hunt and His Arizona.* Pasadena, Calif., 1973.

Gordon, Suzanne. *Black Mesa: The Angel of Death.* New York, 1973.

Graham, Frank, Jr. *Disaster by Default: Politics and Water Pollution.* New York, 1966.

Graves, W. Brooke. *American Intergovernmental Relations: Their Origins, Historical Development and Current Status.* New York, 1964.

Hafen, LeRoy R., ed. *Colorado and Its People.* 4 vols. New York, 1948.

Harding, Sidney T. *Water in California.* Palo Alto, 1960.

Hays, Samuel P. *Conservation and the Gospel of Efficiency: The Progressive Conservative Movement, 1890–1920.* Cambridge, Mass., 1959.

Heffernan, W. T. *Personal Recollections,* and C. R. Rockwood, *Born of the Desert.* 2 vols. in 1. Calexico, Calif., 1930.

Hicks, John D. *Republican Ascendancy, 1921–1933.* New York, 1963.

Hinton, Richard J. *The Hand-Book to Arizona.* San Francisco, 1878.

Hollon, W. Eugene. *The Great American Desert.* New York, 1966.

———. *The Southwest: Old and New.* New York, 1961.

Hoover, Herbert. *The Memoirs of Herbert Hoover.* 3 vols. New York, 1952.

Howe, Edgar F. and Wilbur J. Hall. *The Story of the First Decade.* Imperial, Calif., 1910.

Hubbard, Preston J. *Origins of the TVA: The Muscle Shoals Controversy, 1920–1932.* Nashville, 1961.

Hudson, James. *Irrigation Water Use in the Utah Valley, Utah.* Chicago, 1962.

Huffman, Roy E. *Irrigation Development and Public Water Policy.* New York, 1953.

Humlum, J. *Water Development and Water Planning in the Southwestern United States.* Aarhus, Denmark, 1969.

Hundley, Norris, jr. *Dividing the Waters: A Century of Controversy between the United States and Mexico.* Berkeley and Los Angeles, 1966.

Hutchins, Wells A. *The California Law of Water Rights.* Sacramento, 1956.

Imperial Valley Pioneers Society. *The Imperial Valley.* 2 vols. El Centro, Calif., 1956, 1958.

Ingram, Helen M. *Patterns of Politics in Water Resource Development: A Case Study of New Mexico's Role in the Colorado River Basin Bill.* Albuquerque, 1969.

Jackson, W. Turrentine, and Pisani, Donald J. *A Case Study in Interstate Resource Management: The California-Nevada Water Controversy.* 2 vols. Davis, Calif., 1973, 1974.

Kennan, George. *The Salton Sea: An Account of Harriman's Fight with the Colorado River.* New York, 1917.

Kerwin, Jerome G. *Federal Water-Power Legislation.* New York, 1926.

King, Judson. *The Conservation Fight: From Theodore Roosevelt to the Tennessee Valley Authority.* Washington, D.C., 1959.

Khalaf, Jassim. *The Water Resources of the Lower Colorado River Basin.* Chicago, 1951.

Kinney, Clesson S. *A Treatise on the Law of Irrigation and Water Rights.* 2nd ed. 4 vols. San Francisco, 1912.

Kinsey, Don J. *The River of Destiny: The Story of the Colorado River.* Los Angeles, 1928.

Kleinsorge, Paul N. *The Boulder Canyon Project.* Palo Alto, 1941.

Kniffen, Fred B. *The Natural Landscape of the Colorado Delta.* Berkeley, 1932.

———. *The Primitive Cultural Landscape of the Colorado Delta.* Berkeley, 1931.

Knowlton, Clark S., ed. *International Water Law Along the Mexican-American Border.* El Paso, 1968.

Larson, T. A. *History of Wyoming.* Lincoln, 1965.

Leach, Richard, and Sugg, Redding S., Jr. *The Administration of Interstate Compacts.* Baton Rouge, 1959.

League of the Southwest. *Proceedings of the Third Convention of the League of the Southwest at the Trinity Auditorium in Los Angeles, California, April 1, 2, 3, 1920.* [Los Angeles, 1920].

Lillard, Richard G. *Desert Challenge: An Interpretation of Nevada.* New York, 1942.

Lloyd, Craig. *Aggressive Introvert: Herbert Hoover and Public Relations Management, 1912–1932.* Columbus, Ohio, 1972.

Lloyd, Earl, and Paul A. Rechard. *Documents on the Use and Control of Wyoming Interstate Streams.* Cheyenne, 1957.

Long, Joseph R. *A Treatise of the Law of Irrigation.* 2nd ed. Denver, 1916.

Lowitt, Richard. *George W. Norris: The Persistence of a Progressive, 1913–1933.* Urbana, 1971.

Maas, Arthur. *Muddy Waters: The Army Engineers and the Nation's Rivers.* Cambridge, Mass., 1951.

McCluskey, H. S., comp. *Compiled Messages of Geo. W. P. Hunt and*

Thos. E. Campbell, Governors of Arizona from 1912–1928 Inclusive. 2 vols. N.p., n.d.

McConnell, Grant. *Private Power & American Democracy.* New York, 1966.

MacDougal, D. M., et al. *The Salton Sea.* Washington, D.C., 1914.

McMechen, Edgar C. *The Moffat Tunnel of Colorado: An Epic of Empire.* 2 vols. Denver, 1927.

McWilliams, Carey. *Southern California Country.* New York, 1946.

Mann, Dean E. *The Politics of Water in Arizona.* Tucson, 1963.

Martin, Roscoe C. *Water for New York: A Study in State Administration of Water Resources.* Syracuse, N.Y., 1960.

Martin, Roscoe C., et al. *River Basin Administration and the Delaware.* Syracuse, N.Y., 1960.

Martinez, Pablo L. *A History of Lower California.* México, D. F., 1960.

Mead, Elwood. *Irrigation Institutions.* New York, 1910.

Michael, W. H. *Michael and Will on the Law Relating to Water.* London, 1950.

Moeller, Beverly B. *Phil Swing and Boulder Dam.* Berkeley and Los Angeles, 1971.

Morgan, Arthur E. *Dams and Other Disasters.* Boston, 1971.

Moss, Frank. *The Water Crisis.* New York, 1967.

Nadeau, Remi. *The Water Seekers.* New York, 1950; rev. ed., 1974.

Nash, Gerald. *The American West in the Twentieth Century: A Short History of an Urban Oasis.* Englewood Cliffs, N.J., 1973.

Newell, Frederick H. *Irrigation in the United States.* New York, 1902.

Norris, George. *Fighting Liberal.* New York, 1945.

Olson, Reuel L. *The Colorado River Compact.* Los Angeles, 1926.

Ostrander, Gilman. *Nevada: The Great Rotten Borough, 1859–1964.* New York, 1966.

Ostrom, Vincent. *Metropolitan Los Angeles.* Los Angeles, 1953.

——. *Water and Politics.* Los Angeles, 1953.

Paré, Madeline F., and Fireman, Bert M. *Arizona Pageant.* Phoenix, 1965.

Pinchot, Gifford. *The Power Monopoly.* N.p., 1928.

Pourade, Richard. *The Rising Tide.* San Diego, 1967.

Richardson, Elmo. *Dams, Parks & Politics: Resource Development & Preservation in the Truman-Eisenhower Era.* Lexington, Ky., 1973.

——. *The Politics of Conservation, 1897–1913.* Berkeley and Los Angeles, 1962.

Ridgeway, Marian E. *Interstate Compacts: A Question of Federalism.* Carbondale, Ill., 1971.

Rifkind, Simon H. *Report of the Special Master on Arizona v. California.* N.p., December 5, 1960.

Robinson, Edgar Eugene, and Edwards, Paul C., eds. *The Memoirs of Ray Layman Wilbur, 1875–1949*. Stanford, Calif., 1960.

Rockwood, C. R., *Born of the Desert*, and Heffernan, W. T., *Personal Recollections*. 2 vols. in 1. Calexico, Calif., 1930.

Saunderson, Mont H. *Western Land and Water Use*. Norman, 1950.

Scrugham, James G., ed. *Nevada: A Narrative of the Conquest of a Frontier Land*. 3 vols. Chicago and New York, 1935.

Schulman, Edmund. "Tree-Ring Hydrology of the Colorado River Basin." *University of Arizona Laboratory of Tree-Ring Research Bulletin No. 2*. Tucson, 1946.

Seckler, David, ed. *California Water*. Berkeley, 1971.

Simmons, Ralph B., comp. *Boulder Dam and the Great Southwest*. Los Angeles, 1936.

Sloan, Richard E. and Adams, Ward R. *History of Arizona*. 4 vols. Phoenix, 1930.

Slosson, Preston W. *The Great Crusade and After, 1914–1928*. New York, 1930.

Smith, Courtland. *The Salt River Project*. Tucson, 1972.

Smith, Stephen C., and Castle, Emery, eds. *Economics and Public Policy in Water Resource Development*. Ames, Iowa, n.d.

Smythe, William E. *The Conquest of Arid America*. New York, 1900, rev. ed. 1905.

Stegner, Wallace. *Beyond the Hundredth Meridian*. Boston, 1954.

Steinel, Alvin T. *History of Agriculture in Colorado, 1858–1926*. Ft. Collins, Colo., 1926.

Stone, Clifford, ed. *Interstate Cooperation*. Denver, 1946.

Stone, Wilbur F. *History of Colorado*. 3 vols. Chicago, 1918.

Swain, Donald. *Federal Conservation Policy, 1921–1933*. Berkeley and Los Angeles, 1963.

Sykes, Godfrey G. *The Colorado Delta*. Washington, D.C., 1937.

Teele, Ray P. *Irrigation in the United States*. New York, 1915.

Terrell, John Upton. *The Man Who Rediscovered America: A Biography of John Wesley Powell*. New York, 1969.

———. *War for the Colorado River*. 2 vols. Glendale, Calif., 1965.

Thiele, Heinrich, et al. *Navajo Water Resources, Supplies and Management and the Proposed Navajo Tribal Water Authority (NTWA), A Reservation-Wide Water Study*. Window Rock, Ariz., 1966.

Thompson, Carl D. *Confessions of the Power Trust*. New York, 1932.

Thursby, Vincent V. *Interstate Cooperation: A Study of the Interstate Compact*. Washington, D.C., 1953.

Tompkins, Dorothy Campbell. *Water Plans for California*. Berkeley, 1961.

Tout, Otis. *The First Thirty Years, 1901–1931*. San Diego [1931].

Trouver, Ellen Lloyd, ed. *Chronology and Documentary Handbook of the State of Arizona.* New York, 1972.

Twentieth Century Fund. *Electric Power and Government Policy.* New York, 1948.

Ubbelohde, Carl, Benson, Maxine, and Smith, Duane A. *A Colorado History.* 3rd ed. Boulder, 1972.

Vennard, Edwin. *Government in the Power Business.* New York, 1968.

Vivanco, Aurelio de. *Baja California al Día: Lower California Up-to-Date.* [Los Angeles], 1924.

Walsworth, Bertha L. *The Colorado River and Its Tributaries: A Bibliography.* Mimeographed. Riverside, Calif., 1922.

Waters, Frank. *The Colorado.* New York, 1946.

Webb, Walter P. *The Great Plains.* Boston, 1931.

Weidner, Charles H. *Water for a City: A History of New York City's Problem from the Beginning to the Delaware River System.* New Brunswick, N.J., 1974.

White, Gilbert F. *The Future of Arid Lands.* Washington, D.C., 1956.

Wibberly, Leonard. *Wes Powell: Conqueror of the Grand Canyon.* New York, 1958.

Widstoe, John A. *In A Sunlit Land.* Salt Lake City, 1952.

Wiel, Samuel C. *Water Rights in the Western States.* 3rd ed. 2 vols. San Francisco, 1911.

Williams, Albert N. *The Water and the Power.* New York, 1951.

Wollman, Nathaniel and Bonem, Gilbert W. *The Outlook for Water: Quality, Quantity, and National Growth.* Baltimore, 1971.

Woodbury, D. O. *The Colorado Conquest.* New York, 1941.

Wright, Jim [James]. *The Coming Water Famine.* New York, 1966.

Wyllys, Rufus K. *Arizona: History of a Frontier State.* Phoenix, 1950.

Yates, Richard, and Marshall, Mary. *The Lower Colorado River: A Bibliography.* Yuma, 1974.

Zimmermann, Frederick L. and Wendell, Mitchell, *The Interstate Compact Since 1925.* Chicago, 1951.

————. *The Law and Use of Interstate Compacts.* Chicago, 1961.

OTHER UNPUBLISHED MATERIALS

Adams, Frank. "Frank Adams, University of California, on Irrigation, Reclamation, and Water Administration." Regional Cultural History Project, University of California, Berkeley, 1959.

Alexander, Thomas G. "The Federal Frontier: Interior Departmental Financial Policy in Idaho, Utah, and Arizona, 1863–1896." Ph.D. dissertation, University of California, Berkeley, 1965.

Allen, Richard C. "Governor George H. Dern and Utah's Participation in the Colorado River Compact, 1922–1933." M.A. thesis, University of Utah, 1958.

Andrew, Bunyan. "Rivers as Interstate Boundaries in the United States." Ph.D. dissertation, University of California, Berkeley, 1946.

Aston, Rollah E. "Boulder Dam and the Public Utilities." M.A. thesis, University of Arizona, 1936.

August, Stephen M. "Resolution of Water Regulation Conflict in the Colorado River Basin: The Interstate Compact." M.A. thesis, University of Colorado, 1972.

Barney, David R. "Arizona and Public Utility Control: A Problem in Constitutional Law and Politics." M.A. thesis, Arizona State University, 1962.

Benson, George C. S. "Public Opinion and the Development of the Colorado River." Senior Honor's Thesis, Pomona College, Claremont, Calif., 1928.

Borek, Theodore. "Some Significant Factors Affecting the Growth and Development of the Arid Region of the Southwestern United States to 1950." Ph.D. dissertation, University of Pittsburgh, 1960.

Burch, Vance L. "Hoover Dam." M.S. thesis, Kansas State University, 1933.

Carr, William J. "Memoirs." Oral History Project, University of California, Los Angeles, 1959.

Chamberlin, Eugene K. "United States Interests in Lower California." Ph.D. dissertation, University of California, Berkeley, 1950.

Cognac, Robert E. "The Senatorial Career of Henry Fountain Ashurst." M.A. thesis, Arizona State University, 1953.

Collins, Kay. "The Transmountain Diversion of Water from the Colorado River: A Legal-Historical Study." M.A. thesis, University of New Mexico, 1965.

Coolidge, Richard N. "History of the Colorado River during the Steamboat Era." M.A. thesis, San Diego State College, 1963.

Cordova, Alfred G. "Octaviano Ambrosio Larrazolo, The Prophet of Transition in New Mexico: An Analysis of His Political Life." M.A. thesis, University of New Mexico, 1950.

Coty, Helen K. "Bibliography of the Colorado River Basin." Typescript. Phoenix, March, 1958. Arizona State Archives, Phoenix.

Cox, James Lee. "The Development and Administration of Water Supply Programs in the Denver Metropolitan Area." Ph.D. dissertation, University of Colorado, 1966.

Cummings, Larry G. "Arizona's Stand in the Colorado River Controversy." M.A. thesis, University of Southern California, 1963.

Darnell, William I. "The Imperial Valley, Its Physical and Cultural Geography." M.A. thesis, San Diego State College, 1959.

Davison, Stanley R. "The Leadership of the Reclamation Movement, 1875–1902." Ph.D. dissertation, University of California, Berkeley, 1951.

Deuel, Philip. "The Diversion of Waters from Interstate Streams as a Quasi International Question, Including Particular Reference to the Colorado." Ph.D. dissertation, University of California, Berkeley, 1925.

D'Evelyn, Richard D. "Colorado River Development in Relation to the State of California." Undergraduate paper, Claremont Men's College, Claremont, Calif., 1953.

Diemer, Robert B. "Thirty Years with the Metropolitan Water District." Oral History Program, University of California, Los Angeles, 1971.

Dowd, M. J. "History of Imperial Irrigation District and the Development of Imperial Valley." Typescript. El Centro, Calif., 1956. Library of the Imperial Irrigation District, El Centro, Calif.

Elder, Clayburn C. "Clayburn C. Elder: Hydrographic Engineer." Oral History Program, University of California, Los Angeles, 1969.

Fleming, Frances. "The History of Steam Transportation on the Colorado River." M.A. thesis, Arizona State University, 1950.

Force, Edwin T. "The Use of the Colorado River in the United States, 1850–1933." Ph.D. dissertation, University of California, Berkeley, 1936.

Fox, Charles K. "The Alkali and Salt Problem in the Pacific Southwest, with Special Reference to the Use of the Colorado River Waters in Southern California." Typescript. Los Angeles, [1937?]. Honnold Library, Claremont Colleges, Claremont, Calif.

———. "The Colorado Delta." Mimeographed. Los Angeles, 1936. University of California, Los Angeles.

Goodman, Edward. "Boulder Dam Project before Congress." M.A. thesis, Stanford University, 1931.

Gordon, Alexander. "Irrigation in the Arid Section of the United States." Ph.D. dissertation, Cornell University, 1927.

Gould, Alan Brant. "Secretary of the Interior Walter L. Fisher and the Return to Constructive Conservation: Problems and Policies of the Conservation Movement, 1900–1913." Ph.D. dissertation, West Virginia University, 1969.

Gramlich, Samuel V. "Salinity: Mexico versus the United States on Colorado River Water." M.A. thesis, Pacific Union College, 1964.

Gruber, Nancy A. "The Development of Two-Party Competition in Arizona." M.A. thesis, University of Illinois, 1961.

Hatter, Menzo E. "The Major Issues in Arizona's Gubernatorial Campaigns." M.A. thesis, Arizona State University, 1951.

Henderson, David A. "Agriculture and Livestock Raising in the Evo-

382   *Bibliography*

1964.
Hendricks, W. O. "Guillermo Andrade and Land Development on the Mexican Colorado River Delta, 1874–1905." Ph.D. dissertation, University of Southern California, 1967.
Hinds, Julian. "Western Dam Engineer." Oral History Program, University of California, Los Angeles, 1971.
Horning, E. C. "Reclamation of Arizona's Arid Lands." M.A. thesis, University of Oklahoma, 1942.
Jennings, William H. "William H. Jennings: Water Lawyer." Oral History Program, University of California, Los Angeles, 1967.
Johnson, Alan V. "Governor G. W. P. Hunt and Organized Labor." M.A. thesis, University of Arizona, 1964.
Jones, Margaret Jean. "The Opening of the Colorado Desert Basin." M.A. thesis, University of California, Berkeley, 1942.
Kight, Grace A. "History of the Santa Fe Compact." M.A. thesis, University of Arizona, 1927.
Killoran, Philip S. "Interstate and International Problems on the Colorado River and the Rio Grande. M.A. thesis, University of Vermont, 1952.
Kluger, James R. "Elwood Mead: Irrigation Engineer and Social Planner." Ph.D. dissertation, University of Arizona, 1970.
McBride, Conrad L. "Federal-State Relations in the Development of the Water Resources of the Colorado River Basin." Ph.D. dissertation, University of California, Los Angeles, 1962.
McKinney, Alice. "Arizona's Congressional Delegation, 1912–1921." Ph.D. dissertation, Stanford University, 1955.
Mayo, Dwight E. "Arizona and the Colorado River Compact." M.A. thesis, Arizona State University, 1964.
Metcalf, Barbara Ann. "Oliver M. Wozencraft in California, 1849–1887." M.A. thesis, University of Southern California, 1963.
Milliman, Jerome W. "The History, Organization and Economic Problems of the Metropolitan Water District of Southern California." Ph.D. dissertation, University of California, Los Angeles, 1956.
Mott, Orra Anna Nathalie. "The History of Imperial Valley." M.A. thesis, University of California, Berkeley, 1922.
Olsen, Benjamin L. "The Administration of Water Resource Programs in California." Ph.D. dissertation, Stanford University, 1955.
Parsons, Malcolm B. "The Colorado River in Arizona Politics." M.A. thesis, University of Arizona, 1947.
Praisner, Edward M. "A Political Study of James F. Hinkle and His Governorship, 1923–1925." M.A. thesis, University of New Mexico, 1950.

Rait, Mary. "Development of Grand Junction and the Colorado Valley to Palisade from 1881 to 1931." M.A. thesis, University of Colorado, 1931.

Ready, Lester S. "Report of L. S. Ready on Meeting of League of the Southwest, Riverside, December 8th, 9th, and 10th, 1921: and Hearing by Secretary of the Interior, A. B. Fall, on Colorado River Development, San Diego, December 12th, 1921." Typescript. Engineering Library, Stanford University, Stanford, Calif.

Reed, Harold J. "Colorado River Water for the Los Angeles Metropolitan Area, 1922–1928: With Special Reference to the Legislative Enactments." M.A. thesis, Claremont Colleges, 1939.

Rexroad, Vorley M. "The Two Administrations of Governor Richard C. Dillon." M.A. thesis, University of New Mexico, 1948.

Richard, John Bertram. "State Administration and Water Resources in Wyoming." Ph.D. dissertation, University of Illinois, 1965.

Rizvi, Syed Saghir Ahmed. "Investigation of Water Supply Depletion in the Upper Colorado River Basin." Ph.D. dissertation, University of Colorado, 1967.

Romer, Margaret. "History of the City of Calexico." M.A. thesis, University of Southern California, 1923.

Sewell, William M. "Studies in the Development of Irrigation and Hydroelectric Power in California." M.A. thesis, Occidental College, 1928.

Shamberger, Hugh. "Memoirs of a Nevada Engineer and Conservationist." Oral History Project, University of Nevada, Reno, 1967.

Skinner, Robert A. "Progress of the Metropolitan Water District: Recollections." Oral History Program, University of California, Los Angeles, 1970.

Smith, Courtland L. "The Salt River Project in Arizona: Its Organization and Integration with the Community." Ph.D. dissertation, University of Arizona, 1968.

Smith, Jack H. "The Economic Impact of the Development of the Upper Colorado River Basin in Colorado." M.A. thesis, University of Colorado, 1949.

Smith, Melvin T., "The Colorado River: Its History in the Lower Canyon Area." Ph.D. dissertation, Brigham Young University, 1972.

Smith, Winifred. "The Controversy between Arizona and California over the Boulder Dam Project Act." M.A. thesis, University of Southern California, 1931.

Strebel, George Lofstrom. "Irrigation as a Factor in Western History, 1847–1890." Ph.D. dissertation, University of California, Berkeley, 1966.

Thompson, Robert G. "The Administration of Governor Arthur T. Hannett: A Study of New Mexico Politics, 1925–1927." M.A. thesis, University of New Mexico, 1950.

Van Valen, Nelson S. "Power Politics: The Struggle for Municipal Ownership of Electric Utilities in Los Angeles, 1905–1937." Ph.D. dissertation, Claremont Graduate School, 1963.

Wilson, Richard E. "Legal and Institutional Barriers in Water Allocation—A Nevada Case Study." Ph.D. dissertation, Stanford University, 1969.

Index

Alamo Channel, 20, 21, 22, 28, 46, 205

All-American Canal, 52, 86, 94, 95, 100, 113, 114, 118, 171, 206, 208, 209, 226, 230, 231, 256, 268, 271, 284, 285, 296; Imperial Valley desire for, 17–52 and passim; origin of idea for, 36 ff.; and Imperial Irrigation District, 36–52 and passim; and Mark Rose, 37–39, 42–43, 45–51 and passim; and Harry Chandler, 40, 230; and Phil Swing, 41–51 and passim; and Fall-Davis Report, 169–170

All-American Canal Association of Los Angeles, 41

All-American Canal Board: appointed, 39; reports of, 40, 47

Allison, J. Chester, 37n

American Legion, 226, 238

Anderson, George, 100

Andrade, Guillermo, 26; negotiates agreement with Rockwood, 22–23

Arentz, Samuel, 172

Arizona, 5, 39, 43n, 53, 56, 110, 117, 123, 124, 134, 136, 142–143, 144, 147, 149, 155, 159–166, 178, 181, 183, 186, 189, 190–191, 202, 203, 212, 225, 227, 228, 254, 261, 262, 264, 267, 268, 269, 276, 277, 278, 280, 286, 291, 307, 322, 327, 332; and hydroelectric power, 121, 122 and passim; irrigable acreage in, 147, 148; and Swing-Johnson Bill, 171–172; and Carpenter's compact proposal, 186; ratification struggle in, over compact, 215, 232–253, 258

and passim; and Mexico, 240; and Federal Power Commission, 248–249; approves compact with reservations, 258; and attempts to negotiate lower-basin compact, 258–260, 264–266, 282–285, 286–287, 290–291; opposes Boulder Canyon Project Bill, 271–272 and passim; and *Arizona* v. *California* (1931), 288–290; and *Arizona* v. *California* (1934), 291–293, 307; and *U.S.* v. *Arizona*, 294; and *Arizona* v. *California* (1936), 294–295; negotiates water contract, 295; ratifies Colorado River Compact, 295–299; and Central Arizona Project, 299–302, 323–326, 329n; and upper-basin compact, 301; and *Arizona* v. *California* (1963), 302–306, 309–310, 313, 324; and definition of surplus water, 309–311; and meaning of "beneficial consumptive use," 313–314

Arizona Colorado River Commission, 201n

Arizona Highline Canal, 159–164, 190, 233, 241, 247; map of, 160

Arizona Highline Reclamation Association, 160, 247–248, 299

Arizona Mining Journal, 238–239

Arizona Republican, 234, 239, 252

Arizona v. *California* (1931), 279n, 288–290

Arizona v. *California* (1934), 291–293, 307

Arizona v. *California* (1936), 294–295